SHADOW AND SUBSTANCE

Previous books by JOHN P. ROCHE

The Quest for the Dream

The Dynamics of Democratic Government (in collaboration with
    Murray S. Stedman, Jr.)

Courts and Rights

The American Image: The Political Process (in collaboration with
    Leonard W. Levy)

Essays on the
Theory and Structure
of Politics

SHADOW
AND
SUBSTANCE

John P. Roche

Collier Books
Collier-Macmillan Ltd.   London

Library of Congress Catalog Card Number: 64-12174

FIRST COLLIER BOOKS EDITION 1969

Shadow and Substance has been published in a hardcover edition by The Macmillan Company

The Macmillan Company
Collier-Macmillan Canada Ltd., Toronto, Ontario

Printed in the United States of America

TO
Robert E. Cushman
Mario Einaudi
Clinton Rossiter
and
The Memory of Elias Huzar

Preface

One who like myself enjoys writing essays and short commentaries often suspects he was born on the wrong side of the Atlantic. In the United States, particularly in scholarly circles, the essay seems to be a dying art form and I feel most at home in this anachronistic genre. Thus I welcome with narcissistic pleasure the opportunity to bring together this collection of articles, reviews, and feuilletons, which have appeared in a variety of journals over the past decade. Admittedly they are the cream of the crop; I have felt under no obligation to republish the whole corpus and have excluded both highly technical legal studies and some pretentious efforts at conspicuous erudition. I have made only minor alterations, notably to eliminate overlap (in preparing this book I have discovered how fond I am of certain words and formulations, and have vowed repentence: I shall not use *Kafkaesque* or *existential* again for at least six months). Some trivial factual errors have been corrected, some footnotes trimmed, and some delphic comments omitted. A certain amount of overlap remains and I offer no apology for it. The fact is that over the years I returned to certain subjects several times attempting to refine my views, often to different audiences, and the reader can discover how my emphasis has changed. I have, for example, been struggling with the proper role of the courts in the American system, and in democratic political theory, and I confess that I have yet to devise a formulation which satisfies me. I doubt if I ever will.

As the reader will discover, I have changed my mind about a number of things as the years have gone by. If anything, I suspect

I have become more nominalistic, more leery of ideological explanations of behavior that can be explained on a simpler basis. My indebtedness to the work of Frederic Maitland, Gaetano Mosca, and Sir Lewis Namier is apparent throughout. My specific gratitude to my teachers—who were simultaneously mentors, inquisitors, critics, and friends—is acknowledged in the dedication.

There would be no particular point to elaborating here the notions about politics, history, and political theory that underpin the essays in this volume. There is, however, one point that should be made. Because I describe what seems to me to be true, rather than what I would like to be true, I have been accused of all sorts of odd heresies ranging from "conservatism" (of all things!) to intellectual schizophrenia. Let me state here and now what I take to be the obligation of the historian. He must under no circumstances adjust his view of reality, past or present, to fit his *a prioris*. While I am a liberal, and proud of it, I am not a public-relations man for the liberal view of American history. It is not my function to manipulate American history in order to buttress contemporarily useful liberal myths. Thus, while I should like to see the Supreme Court follow the *decisional pattern* of Justice Hugo Black as it has developed over the past fifteen years, I have no patience with the attempt by liberal scholars to provide a historical base for the Black concept of First Amendment "absolutes." In short, I think it is a mortal sin in a scholar to force history into the mold of his aspirations. If this is schizophrenia or conservatism, critics must make the most of it.

Finally, I should like to thank my friend Leonard W. Levy for his constant barrage of criticism, encouragement, and useful data, and Peter V. Ritner of The Macmillan Company who provided the institutional framework and support for this volume. And I also appreciate the generosity of the Social Science Research Fund of the University of Chicago which supported the preparation of the manuscript.

J. P. R.

WALTHAM, MASSACHUSETTS
February 11, 1964

Contents

Preface   vii

I. The Sources of American Liberty

American Liberty: An Examination of the Tradition of
    Freedom   3
We've Never Had More Freedom   39
New-Fashioned American Radicals   48
A Sane View of Nonconformity   57
The Curbing of the Militant Majority   65
A Review of *Freedom's Fetters*   78
A Review of *The Lean Years*   85

II. The Theory and Practice of American Constitutionalism

The Founding Fathers: A Reform Caucus in Action   91
Executive Power and Domestic Emergency: The Quest
    for Prerogative   127
The Utopian Pilgrimage of Mr. Justice Murphy   162
Judicial Self-Restraint   194
Political Science and Science Fiction   209
A Review of *Nine Men* and of *The Supreme Court
    in the American System of Government*   215
A Review of *Prejudice, War, and the Constitution*   222
A Review of *Render unto Caesar*   227
McCloskey v. *Diamond*: A Comment   240
A Review of *Banks and Politics in America*   247
A Review of *The Antifederalists*   252

ix

III. The Socialist Impulse

The Crisis in British Socialism   257
The Triumph of Primitivism   269
The Case of Victor Serge   280
The Bureaucrat and the Enthusiast [with Stephen Sachs]   302
A Review of *Labour and Politics*   320

IV. Liberal Salvos

The McCarthy Issue [with Constance L. Roche]   327
Explaining Away McCarthy: A Review of *McCarthy
   and His Enemies*   340
Memoirs of a "Subversive"   344
Can Morality Be Legislated? [with Milton M. Gordon]   351
Security and the Press   359
Sergeant McKeon and the Cult of Violence   370
Semper Precocious: A Review of *The Last Parallel*   374
The Pasternak Award   377
Can Kennedy Set Them Afire?   380
The Image of Freedom   383
Confessions of an Interventionist   390
Further Thoughts on Intervention   394
The Abolitionist Centennial   400
The Illusion of Invincibility   405
Do-It-Yourself Survival   411
"Menace" from the Right   416
The Limits of Kennedy's Liberalism   423
Memo to Today's "Young Radicals"   432
A Review of *The Ordeal of Power*   442
Index   447

I. The Sources of American Liberty

American Liberty:
An Examination of the
Tradition of Freedom

Resolved, *That any person who shall, by speaking or writing, assert or maintain that any person or persons other than the General Assembly of this Colony, have any right or power to impose or lay any taxation on the people here, shall be deemed an enemy to His Majesty's Colony.*—PATRICK HENRY, Proposed *Resolve* on Stamp Act, May 30, 1765.

Give me liberty or give me death.—PATRICK HENRY, *Remarks* to Virginia Convention, March 23, 1775.

There has been no shortage of analyses, to say nothing of tracts, dealing with the general question of American liberty; but viewed *sub specie aeternitatis*, they all seem to suffer from a congenital weakness: whether hortatory, monitory, or deprecatory, they deal with abstract Americans acting in accordance with deductively formulated principles. From the Marxists at one end of the spectrum we have learned that American freedom is a fake, a deceptive myth perpetuated by the cunning bourgeoisie for its class ends. From the professional patriots at the other pole, we hear that American civilization is and always has been the natural habitat of freedom. One school waves Old Glory, while the other mobilizes data to prove that American dedication to liberty is rank hypocrisy. Useful catalogues of rhetoric—for Independence Day or May Day, depending on one's viewpoint—have thus been compiled, but all hands have engaged in a conspiracy against defining the crucial term *liberty*.

Thus, when all is said and done, we have discovered little of

Reprinted, with permission, from Milton Konvitz and Clinton Rossiter, Eds., *Aspects of Liberty* (Cornell University Press, 1958), pages 129–162.

what liberty has meant in precise institutional terms to individual Americans or groups of Americans. Instead we have been supplied with primer syllogisms that might be set forth as follows:

The flag shakers

Radical denounces capitalism = subversion of American liberty;
Patriots lynch radical = righteous vengeance of a free people.

The denigrators

Mineowner murders Wobbly = act of capitalist oppression;
Wobblies dynamite mine and owner = workingclass blow for liberty.

While I would never assert that any student could approach his subject matter in a spirit of complete objectivity, I have attempted in the pages that follow to appraise the nature of American liberty without ideological bias. In other words, while my angle of vision may have its defects, I have not gone tramping through American history to document a Socialist or a patriotic sermon. It is my fundamental contention that only by discovering precisely how liberty was defined by discrete American groups or subcultures can we evaluate the actual meaning of the concept at any given point in our history. Indeed, only in this fashion can we ascertain whether there has in fact been an American "tradition" of liberty.

This matter of traditions deserves some discussion. Frederic W. Maitland was fond of observing that Sir Henry Spelman—the great seventeenth century historian of British institutions—not William the Conqueror, introduced feudalism into England. In a similar sense, one may suspect that a good many traditions that we encounter from time to time are in essence the creations of scholars with talent for retrospective symmetry. Clinton Rossiter's *Conservatism in America* comes to mind here, as, for that matter, does Louis Hartz's *The Liberal Tradition in America*. To those who feel that the phrase "retrospective symmetry" is too severe, I submit in evidence a statement from the latter work.

"When asked concerning his social philosophy," Mr. Hartz states, "President Franklin D. Roosevelt once said that he was a Democrat and a Christian, which meant, needless to say, that he was as good an irrational Lockian as Grover Cleveland." [1] Though, needless to say, this is a private fight among irrational Lockians, I suggest that a tradition cannot be built on such Delphic pronouncements.

Indeed, it is my contention that, if we are to understand the meaning of such conceptions as liberty, responsibility, equality, due process, we must look to institutional forms for the ultimate, or at least penultimate, answers. We must investigate actions as well as rhetoric, and base our judgments on the degree to which the former match the latter, the degree to which practice conforms to precept. Moreover, if we are to talk meaningfully of a "tradition," we must demonstrate that there is some *institutional* connection between the discrete historical episodes adduced in evidence—not merely rhetorical plagiarism.

To avoid misunderstanding, let me take a historical instance of spurious tradition-making. The French Huguenots of the sixteenth and seventeenth centuries, one may learn, belonged to the "constitutional tradition." At this point there appears a footnote citing the *Vindiciae contra tyrannos*. Now the *Vindiciae* was an assertion of constitutionalism, and was in the view of experts the outstanding political essay produced by the Huguenots in their polemical exchange with the Jesuits. But before we tuck the Huguenots in the drawer marked "constitutionalism," and take passage to England to the next stage of the tradition—the "common lawyers," or perhaps the "independents"—it would be in order to take a closer look at the other tracts produced by the French Protestants, those tracts that have neither the force nor the timelessness of the *Vindiciae*. And these reveal a peculiar twist indeed, for the Jesuits, who at the time of the *Vindiciae* (1577) were chanting *Quod principi placuit legis vigorem habet* [the prince's will has the force of law] from the housetops, subsequently developed a real affection for popular sovereignty, while the Huguenots later became strong supporters of the royal prerogative. As Gooch put it, in midbattle the antagonists "exchanged rapiers"; [2] and the rationale was not hard to discover.

Onto the stage strode Henry IV, a Catholic from real-estate rather than from real spiritual convictions, from whom the Huguenots expected great things and against whom the Jesuits were prepared to appeal to the overwhelmingly Catholic populace.[3]

This emphasis is perhaps unnecessary, but the uncomplaining past has traditionally been the victim of scholars who trespass *vi et armis* upon the affairs of their ancestors and have a congenital weakness for System that leads them to manufacture traditions and discover "deep policy in some clerk's flourish." [4] This trespass is essential unless we are willing to learn mathematics and become "behavioral scientists," but it must be undertaken with great caution and with vigorous reliance on Ockham's razor to prevent us from assigning superfluous *teles* to the mute deceased. This suggests a somewhat more haphazard view of life than is common among political theorists (who have, after all, a vested interest in systems and traditions), and may seem like an undue depreciation of the role of ideas in history. Yet it is my contention that ideas are no stronger than the institutions that give them meaning, and are frequently subservient to powerful institutional patterns. It was Maitland who pointed out in a luminous essay that the victory of English common law over the Roman-law invasion of the fifteenth and sixteenth centuries was due more to the system of legal education in the Inns of Court than to the merits of the common law itself.[5] This may be a depressing conclusion for the man of ideas to accept, but it is nonetheless vitally significant for the history of ideas.

So much for the analysis of traditions. Now we must turn to the question of individual placement. It is my view that in examining the attitudes of an individual, it is essential to penetrate the rhetorical surface to the subterranean level of definitions. To take another example from the past, John Milton is often considered on the basis of his *Aeropagitica* as a firm believer in freedom of opinion. But to understand the precise meaning of freedom of opinion in Milton's framework, one must carefully size up his exceptions, the opinions that do not merit freedom or do not qualify as "opinion" in the first place. And his list of exceptions, though short, is qualitatively formidable: Catholics, believers in "open superstition," and any who express views that are "impious or evil absolutely, either against faith or manners." [6] By my reckoning, this would include at the very least Catholics, atheists, Unitarians, and Antinomians. Once the field is thus narrowed by definition, it becomes apparent that Milton believed in freedom of opinion for basically "right-thinking" people. As he put it quite clearly, it was "*neighboring* differences, or rather indifferences," that deserved toleration. [7]

To say this is not to accuse Milton of dishonesty or intellectual chicanery; it is merely to assert that by my standards Milton did not believe in freedom of opinion. Had one confronted him with this statement, I suspect he would have replied, in anticipation of the Smith Act, that to be a papist, atheist, or blasphemer was not to hold an opinion, but to engage in subversive activity. This definitional gambit is at the center of all controversies over the extent of liberty, and makes it quite possible for freedom and oppression to walk arm in arm by simply defining detested opinions as subversive actions, *ipso facto* beyond the protection of libertarian principles. There is no necessary insincerity involved in this definitional maneuver; Milton believed firmly in liberty as he defined it. Yet on a wholly impersonal basis I insist that freedom of opinion, *to have any analytical significance*, must involve freedom for those opinions held to be basically wrong, or in the language of Milton's day, heretical and impious. The reader may disagree with this definition if he so chooses, but he must keep it in mind if he is to understand the framework of the analysis to follow.

With these procedural considerations in mind, let us turn to American political thought and specifically to the nature of American liberty. The remarks that follow are a prelude to a broader study to be based on far more intensive research than has yet been possible, and must therefore be considered tentative and preliminary. But on the basis of present data certain general considerations seem to hold up under close scrutiny. In the first place, it appears that freedom today rests on a radically different institutional base from freedom in preindustrial America. This I have formulated in two hypotheses:

First, the individual liberty that was characteristic of early American society was a function of the openness and pluralism that was characteristic of the times rather than of any centralized libertarian ideology.

Second, the individual freedom of contemporary American society is largely a function of the impersonalization and bureaucratization of social relationships, and of the formalization of these interactions in a meaningful, national legal conception: due process of law.

The remainder of this essay will be devoted to an examination of these two hypotheses. Since the major line of division between the two epochs described is that which separates a predominantly rural society from one essentially urban, the discussion will be broken into two sections, one dealing with "Freedom in Rural America," and the other with "Freedom in Urban America."

Freedom in Rural America

When the historian looks back at the intellectual and social history of the early United States, he notes an enormous diversity of opinion. From this it is an easy step to conclude that there was toleration of divergent views among the population at large. However, from a different vantage point, tolerance as the precondition for diversity seems to be a *non sequitur:* what has been overlooked is the fact that until at least the turn of the twentieth century, and in extensive areas of the nation later, the United States was an extremely heterogeneous country, dotted with subcultures. It is my contention that the diversity of opinion was a consequence not of tolerance and mutual respect—an overall ideology of freedom—but of the existence of many communities within the society each with its own canons of orthodoxy. In other words, if one looked hard enough, it was probably that he could find somewhere in the United States a community that shared his own peculiar views—whether religious, vegetarian, polygamous, Socialist, or whatever—and joining it, he could help imposing group beliefs on all within reach.

In short, one could find a microcosm to be intolerant *with,* and the United States was notoriously the happy hunting ground of what Riesman has acutely termed "vested heresies." True, there was no centralized authoritarian state on the European model; for obvious geographical and social reasons, Tudor principles of centralization, like the feudalism they were designed to destroy, did not survive the sea passage.[8] But, as liberal commentators sometimes forget, the centralized state is not the only institution capable of oppression; the parish can be as coercive as the state, and decentralized authoritarianism can be as severe in its impact on the individual as the centralized variety. One finds few earmarks of libertarianism—of respect for views considered fundamentally wrong—in early American society.

The archetype for many diverse communities later established on the twin principles of freedom for truth and suppression for error was "Zion in the Wilderness," the Massachusetts Bay Colony. Unlike the Brownist settlers of Plymouth, who were separatists and refugees from the wrath of the Establishment, the men who built the Bay Colony came to this country to establish the theocracy that the laws of England would not permit, the religious absolutism that was denied them by a latitudinarian spirit in Church and Crown.[9] Indeed, properly speaking, they were not separatists at all; even such a conspicuous theological eccentric as Roger Williams was on his arrival in 1631 technically a priest of the Church of England.[10] The Puritan approach to toleration was summarized with vigor and clarity by Nathaniel Ward, in *The Simple Cobler of Aggawam in America*, when he stated: "He that is willing to tolerate any unsound opinion that his own may also be tolerated hangs God's Bible at the Devil's Girdle."

While there was little toleration in the colonies, no one could assert that the countryside seethed with oppression. There was little need for it. Wise Unitarians avoided the Anglican or Puritan establishments; Puritans, unless they were seeking expulsion, steered clear of the Anglican colonies, and devout Anglicans reciprocated; Anabaptists, Quakers, and other sectarians were well advised to confine their proselytizing to Pennsylvania and Rhode Island. Catholics, who were associated in the public mind with the international French conspiracy, had the most difficult time of all. Only in Pennsylvania, where William Penn had established such minimal religious standards as belief in one God and Jesus Christ, was the door consistently open, or perhaps ajar, to those of the Roman faith. Indeed, at the close of the colonial period, the only place where the public exercise of Catholic rites was permitted was Pennsylvania, and this was over the protest of the last governor.[11]

These religious restrictions were not considered, I suspect, as limitations on opinion at all. Theology and politics were so woven together in the minds of men like Milton, Winthrop, and Ward that heretical views were by definition acts of treason. With Catholics the foundation for this charge was obvious and not merely theological: the French, the enemy to the north, were often supporters of the cause of British Catholicism, and subventors of several rebellions in Scotland and Ireland in behalf of the Stuart pretenders. The atheist was not considered merely an eccentric with a grudge against God, but was an agent of Lucifer, determined to destroy religion, the basic pillar of legitimacy and stability. The Quaker and the Anabaptist, with their disruptive religious subjectivism that had led in England to James Naylor and on the Continent to the chiliastic nightmare at Münster, were viewed as threats to public order. Even the long-suffering Roger Williams finally slapped a treason indictment against one such "for his open defiance against our charter . . . and for saying that it was against his conscience to yield obedience to any human order amongst men." [12] Religious conviction and political action converge in a sentiment like this, and it is not surprising that a definition of opinion was so drawn as to exclude these, and other, nonconformists from any dispensations to freedom of religion. A later secular age would scoff at the draftsmen for their bigotry and be prepared to tolerate any nonsense from a pulpit, neglecting to note that they applied the same technique of definitional exclusion in areas they believed important—only religion was not within the significant ambit.

In the interest of fairness, this point requires further emphasis and exemplification. Thomas Jefferson observed in his *Notes on Virginia,* "It does me no injury for my neighbor to say there are twenty gods, or no God. It neither picks my pocket nor breaks my leg." [13] But to his indifferentism in this area, we should compare his agitated insistence that the Board of Visitors of the University of Virginia should have the power to select the textbooks in government used at that institution. In this connection, he wrote to Joseph Cabell:

There is one branch [of learning] in which we are the best judges, in which heresies may be taught of so interesting a character to our own State, and to the United States, as to make it a duty to lay down the principles which shall be taught. It is that of government. . . . It is our duty to guard against the dissemination of [Federalist-Nationalist] principles among our youth, and the diffusion of that poison, by a previous prescription of the texts to be followed in their discourses.[14]

In other words, while matters of religion seemed to Jefferson to be wholly without the area of important social functions, political opinions did pick his pocket and break his leg, and the state could quite legitimately act to prevent ideological poison from spreading through the body politic. Jefferson used the same loaded dice as the Puritans, logically speaking, but he threw them from a different cup.

Though few people, and fewer public institutions, in the colonial period were dedicated to religious toleration, the important fact was that no one corpus of religious belief attained monopoly status. Colonial America was an open society dotted with closed enclaves, and one could generally settle in with his cobelievers in safety and comfort, and exercise the right of oppression. Generally speaking, there was open season on Catholics and atheists; where they had the power, the Puritans harassed the Anglicans, and the favor was returned in those colonies with an Anglican establishment; and probably a record of some sort was established in South Carolina where the English Protestants at one time ganged up on the French Huguenots.[15] But no one establishment achieved hegemony, and there was a perpetual clamor for toleration from the various persecuted minorities, a clamor that had vast political implications, since freedom of speech was originally thought of as part of freedom of religion. As Figgis observed, "Political liberty is the residuary legatee of ecclesiastical animosities."[16] The demands for freedom were usually in essence demands for the right to establish true doctrine, but they were demands for freedom nonetheless, and contributed to an atmosphere of liberty and toleration.

The striking outcome was that there developed in the United States a political elite prepared to institutionalize this short-run interest in freedom in a Constitution that would make centralized tyranny impossible. In fact, it is my contention that Figgis's quasi-mechanical theory of the origin of political liberty was consciously held by those key figures Thomas Jefferson, James Madison, and John Adams, and implicitly held by the bulk of the political leaders of the time, including many of the anticonstitutional group. Alexander Hamilton, that lonely prophet of centralization, was the outstanding exception.

The road to freedom in this view lay through diffusion of power. Recognizing that the spirit of liberty may be willing, but the flesh may, and probably will, be weak, the key formulators of American constitutionalism did not expect that freedom could be guaranteed by rhetorical exhortations or bills of rights inscribed on parchment. They were too intimately acquainted with the political life of their time to trust abstract guarantees; the Liberty Boys had, after all, dealt extensively and sometimes condignly with un-American activities, broadly defined, as a reading of the statutes passed by the states during the American Revolution will readily demonstrate. This was the heyday of direct democracy, and those who extoll the grass-roots freedom of the town meeting and the frontier, and bewail the fact that the growth of the industrial state has created an impersonal civilization, too often forget that the other side of the direct democracy of the town meeting was the spontaneous democracy of the lynching, that ultimate symbol of the sovereignty of numbers.

Clearly, all loyal Americans believed in freedom. Was this not the very point at issue with the British? Yet freedom did not involve the right to be pro-British, and one of the classic definitions of freedom of the press can be found in the demand of the Newport, Rhode Island, Committee of Inspection in March, 1775—a year before the Independence—that James Rivington's *New York Gazetteer* be boycotted. This committee, urging that the paper be shunned, justified its stand in terms of freedom of the press, which it defined as "the diffusion of liberal sentiments on the administration of Government." [17] The sentiments of Patrick Henry used as a headnote to this essay are also opposite here, and even

more in point were the activities of the Sons of Liberty in dealing with "disloyal," that is, loyal, merchants who refused to cooperate in the nonimportation movement of the early 1770's.[18]

The wartime Sedition Acts passed by the states were very
severe, and in no sense limited in scope to overt acts against the
American cause. Opinions were treated as overt acts and punished as such. To take but two examples, the Virginia treason
statute of October, 1776, provided that any resident of the state
who

by any word, open deed, or act [defended] the authority, jurisdiction, or power, of the king or parliament [or attributed] any such
authority, jurisdiction, or power, to the king or parliament of Great
Britain [could be fined not more than £20,00 and imprisoned for
not more than five years].[19]

A New York statute of 1781 contained similar provisions, holding it to be a felony—and an unclergyable one at that—to know-
ingly preach, teach, write, print, declare, or maintain "that the
King of Great Britain hath, or of Right ought to have, any Authority, or Dominion, in or over this State, or the Inhabitants
thereof." [20]

These statutes were the work of a militant majority determined
to stamp out Toryism root and branch, and a further study of
the punitive legislation of this period suggests that many of the
detailed harassments devised were not generally operative, but
were held in reserve for use should an opportunity present itself.
Thus if the loyal citizens of Kingston, New York, encountered
a particularly sullen Tory who did nothing overtly disloyal, there
was a web of repressive measures that could be dropped over his
head by the local citizenry. Tories presumably knew the facts of
life, and either got out or dissimulated patriotism. Indeed, Walter
Millis has suggested that the real function of the militia in the
American Revolution was not so much military as paramilitary:
it kept anti-British opinion dominant in the countryside by quasi-
vigilante activities.[21]

This direct democracy clearly made its impact on the founders
of the Republic. Hamilton, as one would expect in view of his
aristocratic bias, took a very dim view of *vox populi;* Jefferson,
who was always far more antimajoritarian in his actions and

speculative writings than in his speeches, inveighed against legislative supremacy and by implication against direct democracy in his *Notes on Virginia;* James Wilson was devoting his time and superb organizational talent to revising the radical Pennsylvania Constitution of 1776; John Adams was drafting for Massachusetts a constitution that was a paradigm of the principle of equilibrium; and James Madison was meditating long and hard on the social and political virtues of conflict, of what might almost be termed institutionalized anomie.

The key question confronting these men and their peers at the close of the war and during the Articles of Confederation was how could liberty be preserved from the twin disasters of tyranny and anarchy? In their efforts to find an answer, they ransacked the history of the past and collated it with their own experience in a fashion most remarkable. One minute John Adams would be taking note of the activities of fourteenth century Florentines, and the next, remarking that this reminded him of the situation in Congress in 1776. There is, indeed, a peculiarly disembodied quality about their thinking on government; it is almost as though they were prepared to admit that they too would become tyrants if an opportunity presented itself but that a government should be devised that would make this impossible. In the Constitution this theorizing came to grips with reality, and the solution evolved for avoiding both the peril of anarchy and that of tyranny was the creation of a mechanical wonder—a dynamic equilibrium. Liberty was to be a by-product of conflict and balance, not a positive creation of public policy.

This view—and the air of disembodiment I mentioned above—appears most clearly in a remarkable issue of *The Federalist.* In Number 51, dealing with the fragmentation of power (which should, incidentally, be read in conjunction with Number 10 to get the full impact of Madison's social theory), Madison employs the mechanical analogue with brilliance and precision. After examining the principle of checks and balances within the proposed government (a section recommended to those who talk glibly about the "separation of powers"), the author moves on to the problem of group relations in a republic. "It is of great importance in a republic," he begins, "not only to guard the society against the oppression of its rulers, but to guard one part of the society against the injustice of the other part." [22] The section that follows must be quoted at some length, for it is crucial to my argument:

If a majority be united by a common interest, the rights of the minority will be insecure. There are but two methods of providing against this evil: the one by creating a will in the community independent of the majority—that is, of the society itself; the other, by comprehending in the society so many separate descriptions of citizens as will render an unjust combination of a majority of the whole very improbable, if not impracticable. . . .

The second method will be exemplified in the federal republic of the United States. Whilst all authority in it will be derived from and dependent on the society, the society itself will be broken into so many parts, interests, and classes of citizens, that the rights of individuals, or of the minority, will be in little danger from interested combinations of the majority. *In a free government the security for civil rights must be the same as that for religious rights.* It consists in the one case in the multiplicity of interests, and in the other in the multiplicity of sects. The degree of security *in both cases will depend on the number of interests and sects.*[23]

Now, this is singularly cold-blooded political theory, worthy of the great political geometer Hobbes himself, for it assumes original sin in all hands and predicates the survival of liberty on the successful operation of a mechanical principle of conflict and diffusion. Nowhere does Madison say that power in the hands of an enlightened majority needs no checkrein; indeed, he explicitly denies the conception of the enlightened majority or, in a different formulation, of a virtuous general will. The survival of freedom thus depends on institutions that guarantee conflict— he conceived of the Republic as armed pluralism.

Viewed from another angle, Madison is defining freedom as the absence of *centralized* oppressive power, not as a positive condition of enlightenment. In the same way that religious sects fought one another for the right to coerce, so the many political interests in the Republic will pursue their selfish ends and come in conflict with the ambition of their neighbors. Freedom occurs when no individual interest can institutionalize its truth as *the* public interest. In short, we have a political formulation of Adam

Smith's economic proposition that the pursuit of individual self-interest results in a public good. To quote the Fifty-first *Federalist* again, "In the extended republic of the United States, and among the great variety of interests, parties, and sects which it embraces, a coalition of a majority of the whole society could seldom take place on any other principles than those of justice and the general good." [24] The protection of liberty thus rests on diffusion of the power to oppress rather than on exorcism, or pretended exorcism, of oppression by libertarian formulas. As Madison told the Virginia Convention in reference to freedom of religion, "If there were a majority of one sect, a bill of rights would be a poor protection for liberty." [25]

Although he emphasized governmental more than social structure, John Adams fully shared Madison's conviction that a good mechanism could do far more to preserve liberty than would pious rhetoric. "None but an idiot or a madman ever built a government upon a disinterested principle," [26] observed the dour sage of Braintree, and he set forth his own credo: "Men must search their own hearts and confess the emulation [ambition] that is there: and provide checks to it." [27] His views on the need for equilibrium were set forth endlessly in his various works, notably in the three volumes of *A Defence of the Constitutions of Government of the United States of America* (1787–1788), but were neatly summarized in the margin of his copy of Mary Wollstonecrafts's *Historical and Moral View of the Origin and Progress of the French Revolution:*

Nothing short of an independent power above the [factious people] able to check their majorities ever can keep them within bounds. It is the interest and the policy of the people for their own safety *always to erect and maintain such a power.* . . . Power must be opposed to power, force to force, strength to strength, interest to interest, as well as reason to reason, eloquence to eloquence, and passion to passion.[28]

Or, as he summarized the function of government in an incisive phrase, "When cunning and force united are balanced against cunning and force united, reason must be armed to mediate between them. There must be an armed neutrality." [29]

The views of Madison and Adams are complementary: by

combining them we get, I believe, a clear insight into the nature of the Republic, the Republic that had as its *telos* the establishment and maintenance of ordered liberty. An armed pluralism—society—confronted an "armed neutrality"—government, and the Constitution supplied the ground rules for the conflict that ensued. Out of this conflict in which the participants had both an antagonistic and a symbiotic function there would emerge a public policy free from passion, a commonwealth in which it would be impossible for any part to establish dominion over the whole. The great enemy of good government and liberty was "enthusiasm," which these Deists rejected in both its religious and political manifestations, and under this heading they included the passions of both the just and the unjust.

As political theory this is both quite sophisticated and singularly naïve. It is sophisticated in that it essays to put the operation of government and the protection of liberty beyond the reach of even the most dedicated enthusiast, and does this not by establishing a Platonic republic in which harmony will be imposed by the wise, but by fragmenting sovereignty and setting the wolves to guard each other. Some have seen in this approach an underpinning of Calvinism, of the conviction that man is a wicked and perverse creature, but this seems to me an error. In my view, they viewed man as a mixture of good and evil, and were certain that given the proper institutions, those which would inhibit his evil tendencies and force reason to the fore, the good in men would triumph. In a sense, they stood Hobbes on his head by insisting that only a government founded on freedom and equilibrium could establish real security and that this involved not suppression of the *bellum omnium in omnes*, but its socialization.

Yet, as events were to demonstrate, Madison's conception was also profoundly naïve, for it rested on two fundamental but unrecognized principles about the nature of society. First, like Smith's economic theory, there is the assumption of natural harmony, the proposition that when all the fighting is over and all the pluralities have had their licks, a public policy that incorporates "justice and the general good" will emerge. Taken for granted here is a willingness on the part of all participants to

play by the rules. A faction may disagree about substantive matters—about the content of particular items of policy—but it will
not overturn the cardtable and shoot the other players. In short,
there will be *procedural consensus*. The Deists, like their Stoic
ancestors, assumed the ultimate sovereignty of *recta ratio*, with
the consequence that they found it difficult, if not impossible, to
conceive of differences that could not be reconciled if reason
were given adequate play.

Second, the Madisonian view assumes multipolarism, the continuing existence of many power centers competing with one
another, forming temporary coalitions, then wandering off to
join other allies in eternally new configurations. This social
fluidity was the clandestine premise of American constitutionalism; monolithic majorities, social stases were simply defined out
of the American future as a medieval priest would exorcise devils
from a newly built castle. But what if a national faction arises
capable of capturing a majority of the state legislatures, the Presidency, and the House of Representatives? Are not all the delicate balances and ingenious counterweights of the Constitution
rendered impotent to protect the minority? This was no academic
question, for within a decade the anti-Federalists were looking
down the barrels of a triple-barreled shotgun in the hands of the
Federalists—the combination of Presidency, Congress, and courts
that passed and enforced the Alien and Sedition Acts [30]—and
Madison and Jefferson were desperately engaged in devising a
new set of rules to protect a minority when the Constitution
went off its tracks. John C. Calhoun's *Disquisition on Government* is a tedious and convoluted effort to achieve the same goal
in a later bipolar situation.

I have gone into this in some detail because it seems to me important to realize that the generally accepted view at the time
the nation was founded was that individual freedom, far from
being protected by transcendent legal principles, depended on
two essentially mechanical propositions: *first*, the strength of
one's group, its ability to fight off attempts at domination; and,
second, the fragmentation of power among many groups, the absence of monolithic configurations. The freedom the Constitution
was intended to guarantee was corporate rather than individual;

constitutional government in the United States was to be incapable of destroying the liberty of its constituent bodies and establishing *centralized* authoritarianism. What went on within the constituent bodies was none of the general government's business, with only limited and ambiguous exceptions, that is, limitations on *ex post facto* laws, bills of attainder, laws violating the obligation of contract, state intrusions into foreign relations, or the establishment of monarchial state governments. The inner life of the states, or of private organizations within the states, was thus beyond constitutional jurisdiction, and a Bill of Rights was added to buttress this exclusion.

It is hard for us today to realize the scope of state power at that time, for we live in the shadow of the Fourteenth Amendment and the nationalizing of freedom that has taken place under its auspices. Recall, however, that except as limitations were provided by state constitutions or state laws, state governments had enormous powers over their inhabitants. Two states, Massachusetts and Connecticut, continued their establishments of religion on into the nineteenth century; and had any state, say, chosen to make Catholicism the state religion and execute heretics, or to establish Presbyterianism and hang Catholics, there was no external check that could be constitutionally invoked. The minority could get out or engage in what amounted to civil wars *in petito*.

Formal religious establishments were going out of fashion in the early nineteenth century (Connecticut abolished hers in 1818, and Massachusetts followed suit in 1833), but this did not mean that there was full religious toleration in the states. The somber saga of Mormonism, to say nothing of the desperate street fighting between Know-Nothing gangs and Irish Catholic home guards that occurred in most of the large cities of the Northeast as the "True Americans" went forth to burn down Catholic churches, is adequate evidence to the contrary.[31] Even the Masons found themselves momentarily featured as sinister, un-American conspirators, and were subjected to various official and unofficial harassments.[32] Without attempting a retread of Gustavus Myers's *History of Bigotry in the United States*,[33] suffice it here to say that the extent to which one enjoyed freedom of religion depended on the degree to which his religious sentiments offended his neighbors.

Again it must be emphasized that to say this is not to claim that persecution was rife: the average white Protestant American went through life with complete freedom, and reciprocated by bestowing on other white Protestant Americans the blessings of liberty. Moreover, if things got too rough for a minority, it could probably emulate the Latter-day Saints by finding an isolated spot beyond the long arm of the vicinage and the direct democracy of irate neighbors. And before one weeps too vigorously for the poor, persecuted victims, it should also be recalled that persecution was a two-way proposition: the Presbyterian who attempted to explain the evils of Romish dominations to an Irish Catholic community, or the Baptist who tried to explain to the Mormons of Nauvoo or Salt Lake City that Joseph Smith was a blasphemer and forger, were seldom greeted in the spirit of Christian love.

The same principle applied in political matters. If a state, or a section of a state for that matter, chose to persecute political nonconformists, there was seldom any legal or constitutional remedy, and then only those supplied by state law. The classic instance of moral laissez faire was, of course, the constitutional arrangement that permitted the existence of human slavery in any state that chose to permit the practice. In defense of the slave system, Southerners created a body of extreme legislation on the principle that an abolitionist was an agent of a foreign power, and this was reinforced by both "due process of law" and vigorous vigilantism.[34] From *Fettered Freedom*,[35] Russell Nye's fine study of the impact of the slavery controversy on civil liberties, one learns in graphic fashion the meaning of direct democracy, the total absence of protection for the liberty of the nonconformist from the hostility of an aroused countryside. The American legal system has always been vulnerable to community collectivism,[36] and the abolitionists learned the hard way the nature of a law and order founded on the actions of a locally elected sheriff, a locally elected judge, and locally chosen jurors.

Many more examples could be adduced in evidence, but I

think these establish the point that individual freedom in early, rural America depended not on a national principle of fair play, but rather on the ability of an individual to find a community where his views would not engender wrath and its inevitable fellows: the tarpot, lash, and noose. Maitland observed that British liberty was founded on "writs, not rights," and the important thing we must remember is that the centralized national government of our day is a post–Civil War phenomenon. To the extent that the writ of the national government runs to protect individual freedom, it does so on the basis of the Fourteenth Amendment. Before the Civil War the general government was virtually excluded from questions of interpersonal relationships, the federal judiciary—after the collapse of the abortive Federalist effort to establish a common criminal law—rarely became involved in civil rights matters,[37] and local authorities knew who had elected them and for what ends. For a brilliant portrayal of the result, one need only turn to that section of Alexis de Tocqueville's *Democracy in America* entitled "The Unlimited Power of the Majority and Its Consequences." [38]

This is not to say that there were not efforts made to nationalize individual liberty, usually by asserting that the Constitution was really meant to achieve this purpose. The clarion call "It's unconstitutional!" was perpetually emerging from one constituency or another, but the problem was to find a section of the Constitution that could justify such an interpretation. The section most relied upon was the portion of the Fifth Amendment that states flatly that "No person shall be deprived of life, liberty, or property without due process of law." A close student of the due-process clause will object immediately that there are two barriers to using the Fifth Amendment in this fashion. First, while the wording was ambiguous, it was clearly intended to limit only the federal government, and was eventually so explicated by Chief Justice Marshall in *Barron* v. *Baltimore*.[39] Second, the current meaning of due process of law was procedural rather than substantive; that is, to oversimplify, the limitation was not directed toward legislation duly passed, irrespective of its content, but toward arbitrary, capricious official action. Thus, the due-process clause, properly interpreted, could limit only the capricious, arbitrary actions of a judge or an executive officer, and a federal judge or officer at that.

On the first point, I am in full agreement, but with respect to the second, I have my doubts. The distinction between procedural and substantive due process is essentially a law professor's "conceit," [40] invented somewhere in the latter part of the nineteenth century. To our ancestors due process of law was undifferentiated (they had taken no courses in constitutional law from Robert E. Cushman or Edward S. Corwin), and I suspect that there were more substantive, higher-law, overtones than have ever been appreciated. For example, we can find Albert Gallatin rising in the House of Representatives on May 22, 1798, to denounce the proposed Alien Enemies Act as a violation of the Fifth Amendment.[41] Had one queried him on his startling employment of a substantive concept of due process of law, he would probably have been taken aback and replied to the effect that, with all due respect to professors of constitutional law, he just wanted to make it clear that the law was unconstitutional. The superb research of Howard Jay Graham has shown how both the abolitionists and their opponents, who were justifying slavery, similarly employed a substantive concept of the due-process clause.[42] But the important thing is that with the exception of a few state decisions [43] and Chief Justice Taney's holding in the *Dred Scott* case [44] that the Missouri Compromise had been unconstitutional as a violation of the Fifth Amendment, the substantive interpretation of due process of law was not incorporated in American public law prior to the Civil War. In precise terms, this meant that there was no higher law of personal freedom that a persecuted nonconformist could invoke in defense of his liberty. Legally he was on his own unless he could persuade a state court to implement a state bill of rights on his behalf.

Although I have referred to the Civil War as though it were the turning point in the nationalization of liberty, this was true only on the symbolic level. The great War Amendments to the Constitution were designed to nationalize liberty—and not just for the Negroes: the abolitionists had suffered under the lash of parochial justice too often not to intend protection for whites as well.[45] Acting under the seemingly clear authority of Section 5 of the Fourteenth Amendment, Congress passed a series of civil rights bills [46] to put teeth in the principle of national protection. However, the Supreme Court proceeded to draw the fangs from both the Fourteenth Amendment and the civil rights measures,[47] leaving the great abolitionist dream of nationally guaranteed individual freedom a wreck on the reef of legal sophistry. The development of the due-process clause of the Fourteenth Amendment as an instrument for the protection of individual civil liberty had to await its appearance as a shield for individual economic freedom. In a way curiously reminiscent of the growth of British liberty, rights of property, once established, were expanded to protect civil and political freedom.[48] This, however, is to get ahead of the story.

The Civil War, then, was not decisive in the immediate sense, but in long-range terms the Union triumph was vitally important. Not only did northern victory destroy once for all the effective power of sectionalism and put the federal government firmly in the sovereign's saddle, it also led indirectly to an enormous growth of industrialism in the North and eliminated the halter to industrial expansion that southern, agrarian political power had previously supplied—the check that had, for example, prevented the passage of a high protective tariff and national subsidization of railroads.[49] The bells that tolled victory for Lincoln's armies simultaneously sounded a requiem for rural, decentralized America. The transformation of the United States into an urban, industrial nation, which had of course begun earlier, proceeded at a tremendous and constantly accelerating rate in the era after the Civil War: the war was, as Charles A. Beard said, "the Second American Revolution."

Freedom in Urban America

Space will not permit either a detailed examination of the history of due process of law since the passage of the Fourteenth Amendment, or an elaborate discussion of the development of an urban, industrial society in the United States. It is my contention that these two parallel institutional patterns have resulted in a kind of freedom for the nonconforming individual that was unknown in rural America. To put it a little too neatly, in rural America freedom was a function of openness, of the individual's ability to get out of an oppressive environment; in urban America, freedom is a function of impersonalization, of the growth of legal and political institutions that muffle interpersonal and intergroup conflicts. Paradoxically, the collapse of that sense of community so esteemed by sociological commentators seems to have created a new atmosphere of liberty for the nonconformist, who no longer finds himself in face-to-face relationships with his neighbors or subjected to the coercive power of that superb rural police agency, the parish church.

The proposition that underlies this section is that, for better or for worse, the anomie of our urban civilization has, except in the rural areas of the nation and notably the South, vitiated the force of direct democracy, of that tyranny of the majority which de Tocqueville limned so brilliantly. I am not denouncing the bucolic virtues of our ancestors, nor am I denigrating the Jeffersonian dream of the agrarian commonwealth; I am simply suggesting that *from the viewpoint of the dissenter*, individual freedom is today a far more meaningful concept than it was a century or even a half-century ago. A nonconformist in our day is not merely protected when he is in his own ideological hive; he is guaranteed—*de jure* if not always *de facto*—certain minimum protection at the contact points, that is, at the points where he actually carries his gospel into enemy territory. The Jehovah's Witnesses are a walking (and litigating) testimony to the validity of this assertion, and even the Communists today exercise rights that lead the old Wobbly, Socialist, or trade-union organizer to smile condescendingly when the *Daily Worker* proclaims the existence of a "reign of terror" in the United States.

To say this is not, however, to engage in jejeune optimism about the future of American liberty. Ironically, the very factors that have brought about this new freedom for the dissenter have also made possible for the first time in American history the creation of centralized oppression. The locally entrenched nuclei of power, the "armed pluralism," which was the foundation of the

Madisonian construct of liberty could and did oppress the non-conformist, but they also served as a potential counterforce against centralized authoritarianism. The "security risk" in the North during the time of troubles could always go South to a warm and hospitable welcome; the economics professor fired for criticizing the gold standard could replace an economics professor at a western state university fired for advocating mono-metallism. Given the fragmentation of power and opinion that existed, there was no real possibility of a centralized reign of terror.[50] Conversely, the contemporary breakdown of these bastions of parochialism has eliminated from our political mechanism a veto on the activities of the center that could be exercised for good as well as evil ends. The current struggle over desegregation in the Deep South represents an outcropping of Madisonian theory on a Hamiltonian plain, and southern spokesmen are not wholly without theoretical justification in pointing out that troops employed to desegregate schools could also be employed to destroy unions.

If I had to summarize my contention in a sentence, I would say that American society today is characterized by what the great Italian political sociologist Gaetano Mosca called a "high level of juridical defense." [51] While in specific terms this is a legal phenomenon—individuals can go to court, even in the Deep South, and get judges to affirm their constitutional rights—in the broad sense, the legal manifestations rest upon basic political, economic, and social foundations. The most significant factor seems to me to be the increasing power and jurisdiction of the national government that took place as a concomitant, if not as a consequence, of the increasing urbanization and industrialization of the nation. With the bankruptcy of federalism as an operational concept, decision-making on significant matters of American policy became increasingly the monopoly of the national government; and the national government, unlike state governments, was thoroughly insulated against direct democracy.

The Framers of the Constitution have often been accused of profoundly conservative leanings, and the charge is not without substance. But their conservatism lay not·in their fear of change —they were, after all, superb "social engineers"—but in their dread of sudden, passionate alterations in the political structure. As was suggested earlier, the frame of government they created was contrived above all else to frustrate the sudden seizure of power by any faction, however well motivated. True, this does amount to buttressing the *status quo*, but there is no prescription of the substance of the *status quo:* the system will protect a liberal, internationalist public policy from frenzied assaults as effectively as it will sustain a conservative, isolationist one. State governments, even Congress on occasion, have fallen before sudden political tempests, but the winds have generally died before they could overwash the seawall of strategic delay built into the Constitution. To change the metaphor, reformers, both sound and unsound from the democratic viewpoint, have had to bide their time at the gates of the constitutional fortress.

The federal government is insulated against political passion in a way that is not characteristic of state and local governments, and this insulation has contributed to a difference in attitude and action towards nonconformists. To take a concrete instance, the states and their subdivisions have long been engaged in pursuing those members of the populace designed subversive and un-American. This they do under statutes that would probably horrify by their ambiguity and severity even that stern hunter of seditions Justice Samuel Chase. A few of the resulting convictions have been invalidated by the Supreme Court over the years,[52] but in general the states have exercised plenary jurisdiction over their subversives, even when the substantive case was as flimsy as it was in *Gilbert* v. *Minnesota*,[53] *Gitlow* v. *New York*,[54] or, *a fortiori*, *Whitney* v. *California*.[55] On the other hand, the antisubversive activities of the national government, whatever one may think of their constitutionality or expediency, have been conducted with an increasing respect for due process of law. Compare the "Red Raids" of Attorney General Palmer with the actions of Biddle, Clark, and Brownell in the same area, and the development becomes strikingly apparent.

This respect for due process has certainly been less true of the administrative "security programs" than of the judicial indictments and trials; but even on this level the national government's activities have been suffused with a minimal respect for the principles of natural justice,[56] while state programs have generally been little more than quasi-judicial lynchings.[57] Indeed, we have recently seen the Supreme Court intervene in the internal affairs of the New Mexico and California state bars to impose certain standards of fairness on the legal profession,[58] a profession one might expect to find in the vanguard in the struggle for liberty. In another case, the Court frustrated the efforts of the state of New Hampshire to impose its high standards of patriotism and internal security on an occasional lecturer at the state university.[59] This sort of intervention is seldom undertaken by state judges, and was not until recent years undertaken except on rare occasions by the federal courts.

The growth of the due-process clause of the Fourteenth Amendment to the point where it provided legal, if not always practical, protection for the rights of nonconformists should be briefly recapitulated. After initially holding that this clause was purely procedural in content,[60] the Supreme Court, under the vigorous prodding of Justice Stephen J. Field,[61] moved to a view that due process protected certain economic rights even against legislation.[62] This was the basis for Justice Holmes's famous wisecrack, in a dissent otherwise barren of constructive content,[63] that the Fourteenth Amendment was not intended to enact Mr. Herbert Spencer's *Social Statics*. In short, certain natural rights of an economic character were put beyond the profane reach of government; but with respect to civil or political rights, the Court retained its procedural approach until 1923, or 1925, depending on how one interprets Justice McReynolds's holding in *Meyer* v. *Nebraska*.[64] In any event, in 1925 in *Gitlow* v. *New York*,[65] the Court (while affirming Gitlow's conviction for threatening the foundations of the state with his tiresome tracts) ruled that the freedoms protected from national infringement by the First Amendment were also protected from state invasion by the Fourteenth.

To make a long story short,[66] this was later expanded by Justice Cardozo in *Palko* v. *Connecticut* to include within the protection of the due-process clause of the Fourteenth Amendment not only First Amendment freedoms but also those other features of the Bill of Rights that are "of the very essence of a

scheme of ordered liberty." [67] While this may strike the reader
as a masterpiece of studied ambiguity, it has yet supplied the Supreme Court with a rationale for overruling outrageous state decisions, and has served as a gun behind the door that may have
cooled the passions of state judiciaries from time to time. The
great gap in protection of individual liberty occurs in those cases
where the state does nothing to prevent coercion; in American
municipal law, unlike international law, a state is not actionable
for negligence, but current developments in national equity jurisdiction—notably the desegregation process—suggest that perhaps
judicial ingenuity may eventually fill this gap.

The enlargement of the federal jurisdiction by virtue of the
due-process clause is one of the two prongs of the contemporary
attack on the legal powers of the states and their subdivisions. The
other is the doctrine of pre-emption which holds that the exercise
of federal authority over certain areas automatically excludes and
terminates state jurisdiction. Originating as an interpretation of
the commerce power,[68] this rule was applied to the regulation of
aliens in 1941,[69] and in 1956, in a very important act of judicial
legislation, to laws governing sedition.[70] At one stroke, the Court
nullified the sedition laws of forty-eight states and terminated all
prosecutions currently proceeding under their authority. Congress could, if it chose, restore this authority, as it did earlier
when the Court similarly destroyed all state regulation of the
insurance business,[71] but to date all proposals to this end have
failed of enactment.

To sum up the argument thus far, it is submitted that a major
factor in the development of freedom in the United States beyond the "armed pluralism" concept of Madison has been the
growth in power of the national government that has accompanied our emergence as an urban industrial commonwealth. Specifically, the growth of federal power has led to the implementation of a principle of national protection of individual liberty
against the actions of states or municipalities by the judiciary and
to judicial decisions excluding the states from areas of jurisdiction
of vital significance in civil liberty. Moreover, with a full recognition of the dangerous potentialities of unchecked national
power, it is yet contended that the national institutions have

provided a far higher level of juridical defense than the state, have shown a far greater sensitivity to the rights of the individual than has been the case in other jurisdictions.

Now, urbanization and industrialization are quasi-automatic processes of a quite unteleological character. While the growth of industry and of cities has taken place in roughly parallel fashion in various nations, the political institutions that have emerged have differed radically in character from country to country.[72] One need only compare the modern histories of Britain, Germany, Japan, and the U.S.S.R. to see that industrialization can exist under and contribute to a variety of political forms—that is, unless one engages in the Marxist autohypnosis of asserting that Imperial Japan, Nazi Germany, Fascist Italy, Britain, and the United States were all basically similar state forms, resting allegedly on an undifferentiated concept of "capitalism." One can therefore suggest that while industrialization and urbanization were necessary preconditions for the development of the type of liberty we enjoy, they are not sufficient explanations of cause. We must look for other, more subjective factors that have also been important and that indeed may supply us with more insight into proximate cause than do these other long-range impersonal conditions.

On this level of analysis, the level of human action and volition, the most important development of the past half-century seems to me to be the growth of civil liberty elites, that is, leadership groups in the population who are committed to civil rights and publically endorse libertarian principles. Outstanding in this category have been lawyers, closely followed by ministers, teachers, and newspaper editors. Perhaps most important of all have been the professors of law, for as the law has become more and more an educated profession (as distinct from the old system of informal "reading" in a lawyer's office), the rigorous emphasis on procedural regularity and due process that is the mark of the great teacher has permeated the consciousness of generations of students. Moreover, because law today is the access-way to careers in business, labor, and politics even more than it was fifty years ago, business, labor, and political strata have been influenced by this climate of opinion.

More important in specific institutional terms has been the infiltration of national government decision-making groups by the
legal elite. The great legal migration that took place in the 1930's
as a consequence of the mushroom-like growth of the national
administration, particularly the rise of regulatory agencies, resulted in thousands of key jobs being held by strong advocates
of due process of law and civil rights. There was some truth in
the reactionary gibe that the way to power in Washington was
to go to Harvard Law School and then "turn left." There was
a new atmosphere abroad in the government, a rejection of the
laissez-faire tradition of the Republicans; and able young enthusiasts, who a generation ago would probably have gone unthinkingly into private practice or business, flocked to Washington to build the New Jerusalem, the good society of which
F.D.R. appeared to be the Lycurgus.

The full impact of this legal colonization on the civil rights
climate of the national government can be only intuitively ap-
praised, for we are here in an area that defies empirical analysis.
In practice it meant that the thousands of basic, mundane decisions involving human rights—immigration, naturalization, National Labor Relations Board, Farm Security Administration, and
Department of Justice are jurisdictions that come to mind—were
suffused with a new *telos*, a new direction. Felix Frankfurter,
Robert H. Jackson, Wiley Rutledge, William O. Douglas, Hugo
Black, and that paradigm of vigilant libertarianism Frank
Murphy [73] took their places on the Supreme Court, and shortly
a new note began to echo through the musty pages of the *Reports*. In addition, to throw in a really intangible consideration,
the ablest graduates of the best law schools became clerks to
members of the judiciary, with all the potential influence that
this anonymous function can imply.[74] As de Tocqueville saw the
lawyers of his day as a real check on the excesses of local democracy,[75] so we can see the Washington lawyer of the New
Deal period as a force for regularized, impartial procedures that
incorporated a new attitude toward civil liberty.

In a phrase, the United States for the first time in its history
became civil-liberty conscious. This is not to say that no lawyers
formerly believed in civil rights or held government jobs, nor

is it to assert that all lawyers today are enthusiastic about civil liberties—see *Schware* v. *Board of Bar Examiners of the State of New Mexico*.[76] It is rather to suggest that more lawyers today accept the basic principles of civil liberties and that more of these lawyers, partially as an outcome of conscious recruitment by agency heads, occupy decision-making positions in government. To take one key agency, the Department of Justice, as an example may be to indulge in biased selectivity, but it does seem immensely significant that this powerful institution was over such an important span of years directed by such civil-liberties-oriented Attorneys General as Cummings, Murphy, Jackson, and Biddle. The role of Biddle as a defender of civil rights deserves particular mention: as Attorney General throughout World War II he consistently threw the influence of his office against chauvinistic pseudopatriotism and even refused to conduct the President's program for the exclusion and incarceration of the West Coast Japanese and Japanese-Americans.[77] From the viewpoint of civil liberties, World War II was a "good war," and to Biddle —and, of course, the President who appointed and retained him —should go much of the credit. A. Mitchell Palmer could have had a field day.

The improvement of the civil-liberties climate has also been due to the dedicated efforts of crusading individuals and groups *outside* government. It is almost true to say that the American Civil Liberties Union invented civil liberties, for before this organization appeared on the scene shortly after World War I, there was little articulated interest in or concern for liberty except among the various congeries of oppressed minorities. Much the ACLU did directly with its lawyers, but above all it supplied a formula—a public-relations "package"—a body of civil rights doctrine around which could be mobilized the teachers, trade unionists, ministers, editors, and others who had previously lived in atomized impotence. For every dues-paying member there were possibly a hundred nonmembers of the union who looked to it for leadership, for the appropriate formulation, and passed this view on to their communities. Roger Baldwin has commented on the fact that in his visits around the country, ministers in small communities frequently told him how valuable the ACLU's work had been to them and how they tried to pass the civil-liberties message on to their constituents.[78]

There are other considerations that a longer analysis would have to take under examination, for example, the growth of "liberal" political organizations in the big cities and the big-city states, and the impact of World War II and the Cold War on the American self-image; but the evidence adduced above seems to support the contention that civil liberty, individual political freedom, has achieved significant institutionalization in contemporary American society. The conditions of life for the majority of our population are impersonal; that is, the growth of the city saw the disintegration of the rural system of social control based on direct democracy, and slowly a new system of sanctions has emerged, a system founded on the bureaucratization of interpersonal and intergroup conflict. The security dismissal has replaced tar and feathers; the Smith Act has replaced the lynching posse. In a real sense, the very impersonalization of urban life is a condition of freedom: it is quite possible to live differently and believe differently from one's neighbors without their knowing, much less caring, about the deviation. Particularly with the virtual disappearance of the first-generation immigrant, who tended to stick to his ethnic ghetto, there has occurred a breakdown of integrated subcommunities in which direct coercion could be applied, say, to the Jew who sponsored a Yom Kippur Ball, or the Irishman who denounced the Church. The second- and third-generation Americans have typically broken their ties to old sections and scattered out through the city and increasingly the suburbs.

In short, there are in the city no ready-made instruments of social control, of direct democracy. An aggrieved citizen does not organize a lynching bee; he calls the cops or the Health Department: he is government-minded, and is inclined to leave the protection of his lares and penates, as well as his personalty, to organs of the state. Typically, he will have no arms in his home, and no inclination toward bellicosity; even organizations such as the American Legion, which attempt to impose sanctions on various forms of unorthodox behavior, seldom make a significant dent in the great wall of indifference. Nonconformity, a psychological manifestation of strong individualism, is paradoxically sheltered by a blanket of urban, perhaps even urbane, anonymity and indifference. The ring of New York policemen who used to stand around Joe McWilliams, the pro-Nazi agitator, before World War II as he poured out his venom against "the Eskimos" was symbolic of this new development. A century ago they would either have been leading the mob in lynching McWilliams or beating up his hecklers, but in the New York of 1940 they simply stood like statues, and a police stenographer took down McWilliams's every word in the event that a legal action might ensue. The words of one of these policemen might serve as the epitaph of direct democracy: pushing off an angry young Jew who rushed at McWilliams with blood in his eye, the statue observed, "If you want a fight, son, join the Marines." [79] Even antisocial behavior has been institutionalized! [80]

Conclusion

While this essay may have wandered through some seemingly unrelated fields, there is a thread that provides consistency and relevance. It is my contention that there is no "tradition of liberty" in the United States, but two traditions. Each of these traditions is founded on its own set of premises and rooted in its own historic and social context. A homogeneous rural society visualized liberty as a by-product of social conflict and defined it as the absence of centralized oppressive power. An increasingly homogeneous urban society defines liberty quite differently—as a function of social cohesion institutionalized as due process of law. The Madisonian theory of liberty was not at root concerned with interpersonal relationships; it was aimed at achieving group equilibriums. The modern theory of liberty, in contrast, is vitally concerned with the status of the individual, the individual who is permanently part of a great society and cannot take refuge from his enemies in a safe microcosm. As the symbolic institution of Madison's theory was Deseret, the armed Mormon enclave, so the symbolic institution of the modern theory is the federal district judge informing the state of South Carolina that it cannot assert the sovereignty of numbers to deprive individual Negro citizens of their fundamental right and liberties. American liberty, in short, has become a positive goal of national public policy rather than a fortuitous consequence of fragmentation, pluralism, and social conflict.

NOTES

1. Louis Hartz, *The Liberal Tradition in America* (New York, 1955), p. 263.

2. George P. Gooch and Harold J. Laski, *English Democratic Ideas in the Seventeenth Century* (London, 1927), p. 19.

3. See, for example, the *De Rege* of Juan de Mariana, precisely analyzed by J. W. Allen, *A History of Political Thought in the Sixteenth Century* (London, 1928), pp. 360–366. A seminal discussion of this problem, which despite certain revisions occasioned by subsequent research still holds up well, is John Neville Figgis's *The Divine Right of Kings* (2nd Ed., Cambridge, 1914).

4. Frederic W. Maitland, *Collected Papers* (Cambridge, 1911), III, 164.

5. Frederic W. Maitland, *English Law and the Renaissance* (Cambridge, 1901). For an analysis of Church-State problems in sixteenth century England that likewise suggests the subordination of theory to political imperatives, see F. M. Powicke, *The Reformation in England* (London, 1941).

6. John Milton, *Aeropagitica*, in *The Works of John Milton* (New York, 1931), IV, 349–350. I disagree completely with David Spitz's view that Milton was a principled defender of freedom of opinion, a position that can be defended only by burking Milton's exceptions. See David Spitz, "Milton's Testament," *Antioch Review*, Fall issue 1953, pp. 290–302.

7. Milton, *op. cit.* (italics added).

8. See Richard B. Morris, *Studies in the History of American Law* (New York, 1930), pp. 9–68; Clinton L. Rossiter, *Seedtime of the Republic* (New York, 1953), pp. 3–147; Louis Hartz, *op. cit.*, pp. 3–86.

9. Thomas J. Wertenbaker, *The Puritan Oligarchy* (New York, 1947), p. 32.

10. Williams was a clerk in orders, though of pronounced nonconformist tendencies, in England. He avoided trouble by serving as chaplain to Sir Edward Masham, a Puritan gentleman of Essex. In practical terms, this put him virtually beyond the reach of the High Commission, which largely confined its visitations and inquisitions to members of the formal religious hierarchy, and tended to ignore holders of endowed chapelries or other private benefices. Williams's separatist tendencies emerged full-blown on his arrival in Boston in 1631, when he immediately became a controversial figure by refusing a pulpit on the ground that the congregation had not separated from the Establishment. Rossiter, *Seedtime*, pp. 180–183; Perry Miller, *Roger Williams* (Indianapolis, 1953) pp. 19–20.

11. Leo Pfeffer, *Church, State, and Freedom* (Boston, 1953), p. 81.

12. Cited in Charles M. Andrews, *The Colonial Period of American History* (New Haven, 1936), II, 55.

13. Thomas Jefferson, *Notes on Virginia* (Peden Edition, Chapel Hill, 1955), p. 159.

14. Letter of Feb. 3, 1825, in *The*

Early History of the University of Virginia as Contained in the Letters of Thomas Jefferson and Joseph C. Cabell (Richmond, 1856), p. 339. See Gordon E. Baker, "Thomas Jefferson on Academic Freedom," *Bulletin, American Association of University Professors*, Vol. 39 (1953), pp. 377–387. In the shrewd observation of Howard K. Beale, "Men usually 'tolerate' opposing views on subjects they do not regard as important, and then rationalize 'intolerance' into necessity when disagreement involves a matter vital to them."—Beale, *A History of Freedom of Teaching in American Schools* (New York, 1941), p. xii.

15. Andrews, *op. cit.*, III, 242.

16. John Neville Figgis, *Gerson to Grotius* (2nd Ed., Cambridge, 1916), p. 118.

17. Cited by Sidney I. Pomerantz, "The Patriot Newspapers and the American Revolution," in Richard B. Morris, ed., *The Era of the American Revolution* (New York, 1939), p. 136.

18. See Herbert M. Morais, "The Sons of Liberty in New York," in Morris, ed., *ibid.*, pp. 269–289, for a vivid description of the kinds of pressure exerted upon reluctant rebels.

19. Cited by Willard Hurst, "Treason in the United States," in *Harvard Law Review*, Vol. 58, p. 267. This sort of statute was apparently an old Virginia custom: In 1649 the General Assembly provided that anyone who defended the execution of the late Charles I "by reasoning, discourse or argument" was to be deemed a constructive regicide subject to punishment therefor. Moreover, anyone who defamed the memory of the royal martyr could also be suitably punished by the governor and council. Hurst, *ibid.*, pp. 228–229, fn. 6.

20. *Ibid.*, p. 266.

21. Walter Millis, *Arms and Men* (New York, 1956), p. 34.

22. *The Federalist* (Modern Library Edition, New York, 1937), p. 339. This edition still lists Hamilton as a possible author of this number, but it was prepared before the definitive analysis of Douglass Adair had appeared.

23. *Ibid.*, pp. 339–340 (italics added).

24. *Ibid.*, p. 341.

25. Jonathan Elliot, *The Debates in the State Conventions on the Adoption of the Federal Constitution* (Washington, 1836), III, 313.

26. Cited in Zoltán Haraszti, *John Adams and the Prophets of Progress* (Cambridge, 1952), p. 220. This is a marvelous book that has not received the attention it merits. Haraszti has culled out the best of Adams's marginalia and presented them in the form of dialogues between author and critic.

27. *Ibid.*, p. 219.

28. *Ibid.*

29. *Ibid.*, p. 203.

30. For an able and comprehensive examination of this period, see James M. Smith, *Freedom's Fetters* (Ithaca, N. Y., 1956). For a discussion of the Alien and Sedition Acts in the framework of this paper, see my review of Smith, *Harvard Law Review*, Vol. 70 (1957), pp. 946–950.

31. The American Party still awaits its historian, but the full flavor of its anti-Catholicism can be found in Ray A. Billington, *The Protestant Crusade*, 1800–1860 (New York, 1938). A fine piece of nonscholarly analysis that sensitively recalls the ghetto days of the Irish is John Lardner's "The Martyrdom of Bill the Butcher," *The New Yorker*, Vol. 30, March 20, 1954, pp. 41–53; and March 27, 1954, pp. 38–59.

32. See Gustavus Myers, *History of Bigotry in the United States* (New York, 1943), Chap. 12, pp.

129–139, for a concise discussion of the anti-Masonic upheaval.

33. An extremely useful work with the significant drawback that Myers's approach to bigotry was so evangelical that few fine distinctions emerge from his analysis. He appears to have believed that no one of intelligence or integrity could possibly be bigoted; thus the problem of dealing with intolerance was a simple one of disposing of "bad men" and "bad ideas."

34. See Kenneth Stampp, *The Peculiar Institution* (New York, 1956); Clement Eaton, *Freedom of Thought in the Old South* (Durham, N.C., 1940); Howard K. Beale, *A History of Freedom of Teaching in American Schools*, pp. 111–167.

35. Michigan State College Press, 1949. For another facet of this situation, see the study of the "garrison state" aspects of southern culture, John Hope Franklin, *The Militant South, 1800–1861* (Cambridge, 1956).

36. For a discussion of this point that has been a major influence on my viewpoint, see Alexander Pekelis, *Law and Social Action* (Ithaca, N.Y., 1950), pp. 42–90.

37. Exceptions were litigation arising under the Fugitive Slave Laws, particularly cases arising out of conflicts between the national law and state "personal liberty laws." See, generally, Charles Warren, *The Supreme Court in United States History* (Rev. Ed., Boston, 1947), II, 206–357. Some specific episodes are vividly discussed by Leonard W. Levy in "The 'Abolition Riot': Boston's First Slave Rescue," *New England Quarterly*, Vol. 25 (1952), pp. 85–92; and "Sims' Case: The Fugitive Slave Law in Boston in 1851," *Journal of Negro History*, Vol. 25 (1950), pp. 39–74. Occasionally a case would appear before the High Court under some other rubric of the Constitution that might be con-

strued to protect individual political liberty, e.g., the *ex post facto* clause, but these were rare. Such laws as those passed by the southern states banishing a manumitted slave from the state and prohibiting the immigration of free Negroes were never brought under constitutional scrutiny by the Supreme Court.

38. Alexis de Tocqueville, *Democracy in America* (Bradley Ed., New York, 1945), I, 264–280.

39. 7 Pet. 243 (1833).

40. In the Elizabethan sense of the word; this phrase has been borrowed from a private communication from Howard Jay Graham.

41. *Annals of Congress*, 5th Congress, 2nd Session, Column 1789 (1798).

42. See his "Early Anti-Slavery Backgrounds of the Fourteenth Amendment," *Wisconsin Law Review*, Vol. 1950 (1950), pp. 483–503, 610–661; "Procedure to Substance— Extra-Judicial Rise of Due Process, 1830–1860," *California Law Review*, Vol. 40 (1952–53), pp. 483–500; "Our 'Declaratory' Fourteenth Amendment," *Stanford Law Review*, Vol. 7 (1954), pp. 3–39; see also, Jacobus ten Broek, *The Anti-Slavery Origins of the Fourteenth Amendment* (Berkeley, Calif., 1951). The classic statement of the old view—which it should be emphasized has been amended, not repudiated—is Edward S. Corwin, "The Doctrine of Due Process of Law Before the Civil War," reprinted in *Selected Essays in Constitutional Law* (Chicago, 1938), I, 203–235.

43. Cited by Graham, "Procedure to Substance," *op. cit.*, p. 484.

44. *Scott* v. *Sandford*, 19 Howard 393 (1857).

45. Graham, "Early Anti-Slavery Backgrounds . . . ," *op. cit., passim.*

46. The history of this civil rights legislation is set forth in brief compass in Maslow and Robison, "Civil

Rights Legislation and the Fight for Equality, 1862–1952," *University of Chicago Law Review*, Vol. 20 (1953), p. 363. Technically the first Civil Rights Act was passed before the Fourteenth Amendment was ratified.

47. Notably in the *Slaughterhouse* cases, 16 Wall. 36 (1873), and the *Civil Rights* cases, 109 U.S. 3 (1883).

48. In Britain, royal justice was initially a property of the Crown that was dispensed to subjects for appropriate remuneration. Subsequently the remuneration became ritualized with respect to certain actions; upon payment of standard fees, writs *de cursu* could be obtained. Similarly, an individual's "liberties" were his property rights in himself. See Frederic Maitland, *The Forms of Action at Common Law* (Cambridge, 1948).

49. See C. Vann Woodward, *Reunion and Reaction* (Boston, 1951).

50. I would contend that even the repression that accompanied American participation in World War I was thoroughly decentralized. The Wilson Administration encouraged it in part and discouraged it in part, but the national government and its instruments played a minor role in the actual festivities when compared with state and local governments and private vigilante movements such as the American Protective League.

51. Gaetano Mosca, *The Ruling Class* (New York, 1939), pp. 120–152.

52. See, *e.g.*, *Herndon* v. *Lowry*, 301 U.S. 242 (1937); *De Jonge* v. *Oregon*, 299 U.S. 353 (1937).

53. 254 U.S. 325 (1920).

54. 268 U.S. 652 (1925).

55. 274 U.S. 357 (1927). For details on these cases, see Zechariah Chafee, Jr., *Free Speech in the United States* (Cambridge, 1946).

56. See Eleanor Bontecou, *The*

Federal Loyalty-Security Program (Ithaca, N.Y., 1953), pp. 239–240.

57. See generally, Walter Gellhorn, *The States and Subversion* (Ithaca, N.Y., 1952). For specific studies, see Lawrence H. Chamberlain, *Loyalty and Legislative Action* (Ithaca, N.Y., 1951); Edward L. Barrett, Jr., *The Tenney Committee* (Ithaca, N.Y., 1951); Vern Countryman, *Un-American Activities in the State of Washington* (Ithaca, N.Y., 1951).

58. See *Konigsberg* v. *State Bar of California*, 77 S. Ct. 722 (1957); and *Schware* v. *Board of Bar Examiners of the State of New Mexico*, 77 S. Ct. 752 (1957).

59. *Sweezy* v. *State of New Hampshire by Wyman*, 77 S. Ct. 1203 (1957).

60. *Slaughterhouse* cases, 16 Wall. 36 (1873); *Munn* v. *Illinois*, 94 U.S. 113 (1877); *Hurtado* v. *California*, 110 U.S. 516 (1884). In the *Hurtado* opinion the shift toward substantive due process is already noticeable.

61. See the fine analysis of Field's influence in Howard Jay Graham, "Justice Field and the Fourteenth Amendment," *Yale Law Journal*, Vol. 52 (1943), p. 851.

62. See *Chicago, M. & St. P. Ry.* v. *Minnesota*, 134 U.S. 418 (1890); *Smyth* v. *Ames*, 169 U.S. 466 (1898); *Lochner* v. *New York*, 198 U.S. 45 (1905); Benjamin Twiss, *Lawyers and the Constitution* (Princeton, 1942).

63. Holmes clearly did not reject substantive due process as a limitation on the police power of the states, but refused to join the elaborate, thoroughly documented dissent of Justice Harlan in *Lochner* v. *New York* to the point that *this* restriction on liberty of contract was justified. Instead, he went off on an intellectual buccaneering expedition that was as epigrammatic as it was irrelevant.

64. I find McReynolds's opinion suffused with substantive due process; it is not merely that the state law deprived teachers of their jobs, thus infringing their economic rights, but also that the law was an unconstitutional attempt to invade the educational freedom of the people of the state, 262 U.S. 390 (1923).

65. 268 U.S. 652 (1925).

66. Succinctly told by Edward S. Corwin, *Liberty Against Government* (Baton Rouge, La., 1948), pp. 116–168.

67. 302 U.S. 319 (1937).

68. *Cooley* v. *Board of Wardens of Port of Philadelphia*, 12 How. 299 (1851). See F. D. G. Ribble, *State and National Power over Commerce* (New York, 1937), for an elaborate discussion of this doctrine.

69. *Hines* v. *Davidowitz*, 312 U.S. 52 (1941).

70. *Commonwealth of Pennsylvania* v. *Nelson*, 350 U.S. (1956).

71. *United States* v. *South-Eastern Underwriters Ass'n*, 322 U.S. 533 (1944); immediately reversed by Congress in the McCarran Act, 15 U.S.C.. 1011–15, which delegated the authority to regulate insurance to the states.

72. See the thoughtful and penetrating essay by Clark Kerr, "Industrial Relations and the Liberal Pluralist," *Proceedings* of the Seventh Annual Meeting (reprinted, Industrial Relations Association, Berkeley, Calif., 1955).

73. For a discussion of the varying patterns of judicial liberalism that the Roosevelt Court incorporated, see my "The Utopian Pilgrimage of Mr. Justice Murphy," *Vanderbilt Law Review*, Vol. 10 (1957), p. 369.

74. One gets some insight into the influence of an able clerk on a Justice in Alpheus T. Mason's monumental biography of Chief Justice Stone, *Harlan Fiske Stone: Pillar of the Law* (New York, 1956), especially at pp. 505, 513, 528.

75. Alexis de Tocqueville, *op. cit.*, I, 282 ff.

76. 77 S. Ct. 752 (1957).

77. There was some ambiguity about Biddle's position. When the representatives of the War and Justice departments met on Feb. 17, 1942, and the Army spokesman sprung the evacuation plan, Biddle, over the objections of his colleagues present, Edward Ennis and James H. Rowe, Jr., apparently agreed in principle to the proposal. See Jacobus Ten Broek *et al., Prejudice, War and the Constitution* (Berkeley, Calif., 1954), pp. 111–112. But despite this concession, Biddle made it quite clear that he "thought the Justice Department simply should not be a party to a program in which citizens were to be deprived of their liberties."— *Ibid*, p. 358, fn. 65.

78. Private conversation.

79. This is based on personal experience as an observer and heckler of Mr. McWilliams; the bellicose young man who received the admonition from the policeman was a personal friend.

80. See my brief discussion of this interesting phenomenon in "Sgt. McKeon and the Cult of Violence," *The New Republic*, Aug. 27, 1956, pp. 16–17. (Reprinted on pp. 370–373 of this book.)

We've Never Had More Freedom

About a year ago, the editors of *The New Republic* asked me to prepare a series of articles on the "State of Our Liberties." When we discussed the scope and direction of the series, it was my conviction that American freedom was on the downgrade, that our liberties today are considerably more circumscribed than they were, say, a century or a half-century ago, and the articles as then conceived were to reflect this viewpoint.

However, as I began working through material on the issues under examination, I became increasingly uncertain about my original framework of analysis. In fact, I began to wonder if the "Golden Age of American Freedom," which civil libertarians so confidently locate in the indefinite American past, were not just a myth. At this point, I started to stall off the editors' importunate requests for my manuscript and launched an intensive investigation into the history of American nonconformism.

The outcome of this investigation is the series of three articles which follows. Although I make no claim to originality, the net result is a substantial revision of much current liberal thinking on the subject of civil liberties. The core of my thesis is that American freedom has never been as firmly established or as broadly shared as is the case today. This thesis will seem overly sanguine to some. And so I should make it clear at once that I am not suggesting that the American Civil Liberties Union close up shop, nor am I justifying for one minute the many abuses of civil liberty that do occur. My optimism about the present, if

Reprinted, with permission, from *The New Republic*, January 23, 1956.

"optimism" is the appropriate word, is founded on a pessimistic estimate of the past rather than on any conviction that we have achieved nirvana. We still have a long way to go, and it will take continued struggle by thousands of dedicated individuals to keep the standard of freedom moving forward. Yet, there is no need to travel under the illusion that we are moving downhill from a mystical, unfettered past; on the contrary, it seems to me demonstrable that we are moving up the road from the lynching and the tarpot toward the aspiration of impartial justice and the rule of law.

We are accustomed, when we consider our civil liberty, to extolling the "grass-roots" freedom of the early American scene— the New England town meeting, the spontaneous democracy of the frontier. We bewail the fact that the growth of the industrial state and the increasing bureaucratization of life have created an impersonal civilization in which individualism and liberty wither. Too often we forget that the other side of the direct democracy of the town meeting was the direct democracy of the lynching. That brilliant political sociologist Alexis de Tocqueville noted this ambivalence in his penetrating treatment of "The Unlimited Power of the Majority and Its Consequences" in *Democracy in America*. Indeed, if one accepts majority rule as the touchstone of democracy, he must accept the lynching as a democratic institution, for in it we find the sovereignty in its starkest form.

Yet, until quite recently, democracy in the United States on the basic level of political decisions was rule of numbers pure and simple. True, this rule of numbers was frequently disguised by the forms of due process of law—"Give him a fair trial and hang him!" as the California goldfield slogan put it—but, unlike the situation in economic matters where the courts threw roadblocks in the way of direct democracy, there was little to protect the unpopular citizen from the wrath of his enraged neighbors. If worst came to worst, and attempts were made to enforce individual rights on behalf of the nonconformist, a jury drawn from the vicinity could generally be counted upon (as in recent Southern cases) to redress the balance in favor of community sentiment.

What has confused historians looking back at the intellectual and social history of the United States is the fact that great diversity of opinion indubitably existed in the nation. From this they have drawn the erroneous conclusion that there was toleration of divergent opinions among the populace at large. It is my contention that the diversity of views was a consequence, not of tolerance and mutual respect, but of the existence of many communities within the society each with its own rigid canons of orthodoxy.

In other words, if a man looked hard enough, he could probably find a community within the United States that shared his own peculiar views, and joining it, he could help impose his eccentricities on all within reach. The United States was the happy hunting ground of what David Riesman has acutely termed "vested heresies." There was no monolithic centralized state to fulfill the European model of authoritarianism, but there was decentralized authoritarianism aplenty. Of libertarianism, the respect for views considered fundamentally "wrong," there was little: the Populists, for example, were as ready to suppress economic orthodoxy as the economically orthodox were to expunge Populism. . . .

Some confusion is created by the fact that our forefathers certainly seem more tolerant than we are. In part that may be because they did not necessarily share our convictions as to what was important. Thus from Jefferson's broad tolerance in religious matters is deduced a full belief in freedom of opinion. It would seem more accurate to say that Jefferson considered religion unimportant and was therefore willing to permit any nonsense to be spoken from a pulpit. However, in an area that Jefferson did consider important, he was prepared to excommunicate ideas. For example, in his capacity as *deus ex machina* of the University of Virginia, Jefferson insisted that the trustees (Board of Visitors, to be exact) should have the power to select textbooks in the field of government. . . . In short, freedom of ideas stopped when the insidious poisons of Marshall, Kent, and Story came into the picture, and it is not surprising that a year later we find Jefferson much concerned lest an unorthodox, that is, Federalist-Nationalist, jurist be appointed to the chair of law at the university.

Some may object that this example has been taken from Jefferson's dotage; therefore another example, taken from his political prime, is apposite. It is seldom appreciated that Jefferson's fundamental objection to the Sedition Act of 1798 was based on his states'-rights outlook. He was not necessarily opposed to sedition actions on principle; rather he was opposed to Federalist-dominated courts enforcing the wrong orthodoxy on the press. In this spirit we find President Jefferson in 1803 writing to Governor McKean of Pennsylvania:

The federalists having failed in destroying the freedom of the press with their gag-law, seem to have attacked it in an opposite direction; that is by pushing its licentiousness and its lying to such a degree of prostitution as to deprive it of all credit. . . . This is a dangerous state of things, and the press ought to be restored to its credibility if possible. The restraints provided by the laws of the States are sufficient for this, if applied. And I have therefore long thought that a few prosecutions of the most prominent offenders would have a wholesome effect in restoring the integrity of the presses. Not a general prosecution, for that would look like persecution; but a selected one.

I have quoted from Jefferson at some length, not with the intention of defaming his character. (He was a great American politician, which almost by definition means that he would be willing to use any stick to beat a dog.) On the contrary, he was a militant believer in freedom *as he defined it*, which makes the key point of this analysis.

Sincere obeisance has always been paid to the principles of freedom of speech, press, assembly, and opinion by the great majority of Americans. But few generations have looked with kindness upon those who challenged the established order. There have always been incisive differences of viewpoint as to what constituted speech and opinion and what constituted subversive action. The general outcome of this conflict, which was seldom publicly articulated, was that each community established certain key symbols to which it demanded unqualified allegiance of both idea and action. Outside this myth sector, broad differences of opinion were taken for granted. In the Old South, for example, there were few limitations on freedom of speech or press if the individual concerned accepted the validity of slavery, but the nonconformist was shown no mercy. It is often forgotten that the first Jew (Judah P. Benjamin) and the third Catholic

(Stephen Mallory) to hold Cabinet rank in this country took their seats around the table with Jefferson Davis in 1861!

Freedom of opinion in general has thus been recognized and honored, but woe unto the nonconformist who laid profane hands on the Ark of the Covenant, who rejected a key myth, for by his action he has transmuted his offense from permissible difference of opinion to forbidden conspiracy against the lares and penates of the community. The house gods may vary from community to community, as they often did in the era before the economic consolidation of the nation and the communications revolution, but the reaction was the same: tar and feathers, the knout, the club, the noose—the latter sometimes reinforced by the ritual of trial by jury. The Nonpartisan League organizer in Minnesota, the Wobbly in Colorado, the Abolitionist in Georgia, the Socialist in Oklahoma, the Catholic in Know-Nothing territory, and other crusaders for now forgotten enthusiasms, all felt the scourge of the great god Numbers. Indeed, a close reading of American social history leaves one with the ineradicable conviction that tar and feathers was standard armament for "grass-roots democracy."

Nor is the decentralized authoritarianism in our past limited to political and religious agitation. It is one of the ironies of history that the academic freedom of which the French and British are so proud is the consequence in the British instance of the virtually complete autonomy of the educational system from local pressures, and in the French instance, of the complete centralization of authority over the national educational system in an irresponsible bureaucracy. It is American "grass-roots democracy" that has put public educational institutions at the mercy of local pressure groups. Here as in all issues we pay our money and take our choice, for if local communities are restrained from doing evil, they can also be restrained from doing good.

In recent years, however, there has been a distinct letup in the force of direct democracy in the United States, and with it an easing of pressure against nonconformity. The Negro, the trade-union organizer, the radical, even the Communist, have rights today that were nonexistent, or at best fragmentary, thirty years ago.

It is my contention that two major developments are responsible. The first is the increasing power and jurisdiction of the national government over national life which has taken place as a concomitant, if not as a consequence, of the increasing industrialization and urbanization of the nation. The second is the rise of civil-liberty elites, leadership groups, in American society that have initiated unceasing legal and educational campaigns on behalf of the rights of nonconformists. Let us examine these two propositions in some detail.

The national government was insulated against "direct democracy"—and by design. The Framers of the Constitution were superbly successful experimenters, but they sought to bar mob rule. The instrument of government they created was contrived above all to exorcise passion from political decision-making, to make impossible the sudden seizure of power by any faction, however well motivated. It is not accidental, then, that the United States—a nation historically characterized by violent tides of political extremism—has never fallen into the hands of extremist politicians. . . . The constitutional framework, the diffusion of the power to govern among competing power centers, cannot frustrate indefinitely the demand for change, but it can ensure that whatever changes do become incorporated in public policy will rest on the "sober second thought" of the American community rather than on the pitch of frantic passion.

But an even more important factor is the social and economic consolidation that underlies this increase in national power. Here the outstanding characteristic is urbanization and the impersonalization of life that accompanies life in the metropolis and its suburbs. The growth of the city saw the disintegration of the rural system of social control, centered usually on that highly efficient intelligence service, the rural church. In the city it is quite possible to live differently, and believe differently, from one's neighbors without their even knowing, much less caring, about the deviation. While associations may be formed on a neighborhood basis, more frequently there are functional alignments: one's friends are the people one works with, who may be scattered all over town. . . .

For obvious reasons—the inherent impotence of city man in

the face of food, water, electricity, transportation crises, the recognition that his destiny is controlled by factors beyond his reach—urban politics has been government-minded. Probably because most state legislatures are controlled firmly by nonurban forces, he has turned to the national government for his salvation. But urban man has not only turned over to Washington his economic destiny, he has also waived in favor of the federal government his ancestral right to take direct action against the desecrators of his house gods: *Enter*—the Smith Act.

To assert this is, of course, to oversimplify the background of the Smith Act, which was part and parcel of the national defense program, but I think it is interesting to compare the treatment of "subversives" in the 1940's and 1950's with that of 1917, 1863, or even 1776. Personally, I consider the Smith Act and its subsidiary legislation unwise and unnecessary—in my view, existing statutes were adequate to the danger—but in the long view I have little sympathy for the imprisoned Communists. Compared with the treatment handed out to authentic radicals in 1918, they have merely attended a compulsory tea party. I wish no human being any hard luck, but I save my tears for those who suffered genuine martyrdom in the cause of human freedom. Few people [a total of 109 by 1964] have fallen under the arm of the Smith Act—probably about enough to fill Tom Mooney Hall. In fact, they are probably holding a protest meeting against the "police state" there this week, for most of those convicted are out on bail.

And yet if civil liberty has gained from this process of urbanization and nationalization of political decision-making the gain has been accidental, a mere by-product of impersonal historical developments. In contrast, the second factor in my analysis, the growth of civil-liberty elites, involves human action and volition. Outstanding in this category of opinion-leaders have been the lawyers, closely followed by ministers, teachers, editors, and businessmen. . . .

More important, perhaps, has been the infiltration of national government decision-making groups by the legal elite. The great legal migration to Washington that took place in the thirties as the consequence of the mushroom-like growth of the national administration resulted in thousands of key jobs being held by firm advocates of due process of law and civil rights. The full impact of this legal colonization on the civil rights climate of the national government can only be imagined; in practice it meant that the thousands of basic, mundane decisions in which human rights were involved were suffused with a new direction. . . . As de Tocqueville saw the legal profession of his day as a real check on the excesses of local democracy, so today we can see the lawyers as a force for regularized—even pettifogged—procedures of national governmental operation and for the maintenance of the myth of impartial justice, a myth never fully fleshed, but nonetheless vital as a goal for collective aspirations.

But the improvement of the civil-liberties climate has also been due to the passionate efforts of crusading individuals and groups. It is almost true to say that the American Civil Liberties Union invented civil rights, for before this organization came on the scene after World War I, there was little articulated interest in or concern for the problem except among the oppressed. Much the ACLU did directly, but above all, it supplied a formula—a public relations "package"—a body of civil rights doctrine, around which could be mobilized the teachers, trade unionists, ministers, editors, and others who had previously lived in atomized impotence. Roger Baldwin, a Madison Avenue advertising genius who somehow located on the wrong street, supplied the organization an impetus and a direction that gave the union a nationwide reputation in an incredibly short space of time. For every dues-paying member, there were probably a hundred non-members, frequently in key opinion-forming positions in their communities, who followed the union's leadership, rallied to its campaigns, and passed on its position to their opinion constituents.

In this article, I have suggested that the concept of civil liberties as we think of it today is a modern development on the American scene. Roughly prior to World War I, an American's civil rights were a coefficient of his subculture. If he remained among his co-believers, his rights were secure (and he was secure in his right to enforce his opinions on nonbelievers in his bailiwick), while if he traveled among heathens, he expressed himself at his peril. In practice, the great bulk of Americans had substantial freedom because they lived and died among their co-opinionists in a context where unquestioned and unquestioning allegiance was rendered to the vital myths of the group.

Some may question this thesis on the ground that it rests on the analysis of extreme cases, of radically deviant opinions, and is therefore unrepresentative. But in a discussion of civil liberties, it is the extreme situations which determine the theoretical framework; the fact that Democrats respect the rights of Republicans is not analytically meaningful, for neither group challenges the vital myths of the other—indeed, they share the same body of myths with minor variations. The touchstone of an authentic civil libertarian is his attitude toward one who denigrates the house gods. Unless one is willing to defend the rights of the person whose views (and this is a discussion of views, not overt acts) are not ranked as "opinion," but as subversion or sacrilege, he cannot in justice claim to defend civil liberty.

New-Fashioned American Radicals

Although Americans pride themselves on their patriotism, and vigilant state legislatures have made it virtually impossible for the young to escape some exposure to the facts of the American past, the average American is nonetheless singularly deficient in historical sense. Born without a historical umbilical cord, *Homo Americanus* tramps from situation to situation through time, hardly concerning himself with the historical antecedents of his reactions, or with their probable historical consequences. His concern is with Hard Facts; he makes his judgments On The Merits; and his disregard, even scorn, for abstract thinking— and the intellectuals who engage in this peculiar avocation—is manifested in the public policy of the nation.

A striking instance of this American lack of a sense of history has been the contrast between American and French attitudes toward the rearming of Germany. Having reached the conclusion that a German army is necessary, American policy-makers have exorcised the past and acted as though Nazism and World War II were just a bad dream. The French, in contrast, living in an atmosphere of brooding historicism, have acted as though the main task today is to remedy certain procedural defects in the Treaty of Westphalia of 1648. Similarly in the Pacific, anti-Japanese sentiment is far stronger in Indonesia than among Americans, although the United States bore the main brunt of Japanese militarism. In short, Americans begin each evaluation by setting the scales at zero.

Reprinted, with permission, from *The New Republic*, January 30, 1956.

Recognizing the merits of this flexible technique, it is also important to note the defects that it contains. Each crisis is approached as though nothing like it had never before occurred on this planet. McCarthy was treated by the liberal press as though Watson, Long, Coughlin, and other leading specimens of the genus demagogue had never trod the American stage; the conservative press perpetually screams about the imminent murder of American liberty, as though the business community had suffered at the hands of Roosevelt and Truman, instead of prospering and surviving to bellow *Tyranny!* another day. The Reign of Terror is always upon us; the Jacobins—or the men of Thermidor—are ever on the verge of power.

Perhaps I am unduly skeptical about reigns of terror, but I have in my short life been alerted to many that never came off. In fact, my political weaning took place in the shadow of Roosevelt's guillotine, for in 1936 I was the only Democrat in my high school class. My classmates, from good Liberty League families, assured me that F.D.R.'s reelection would bring an end to human freedom. To emphasize the point they engaged in a campaign to "beat hell out of that little mick Roche," and I must confess that I deeply regretted the fact that heads did *not* subsequently roll. By 1940, I was convinced that the authentic terror was in the offing if the United States entered World War II, and with my Socialist and pacifist cohorts, I grimly applauded Norman Thomas's pronouncement that 1940 would see our last free election unless we repudiated the Democratic and Republican warmongers. Elections came and went, and I suspect that some of us were quite disappointed, since we felt that our potent opposition to the regime merited at least a *little* persecution. There is nothing so psychologically humiliating as to steel oneself for martyrdom, and be ignored.

The point of this autobiographical diversion is that the reign of terror is a constant occupant of some area of the American political tradition. As today the *Daily Worker* and *Political Affairs* live in full expectation of suppression, so in the past the organs of the abolitionists, the Socialists, the I.W.W., the pacifists, the Nonpartisan League, the anti-Masons, the Jeffersonians —and perhaps the Virginia Federalists!—and countless other embattled zealots published regular forecasts of the death of American liberty at the hands of their enemies. Moreover, the point of this article is that in an earlier period one could often speak accurately of a reign of terror, whereas today, in view of the changes in American life discussed in the previous article, the terrorists are usually equipped with a papier-mâché guillotine.

Authentic reigns of terror were launched in the nineteenth century, to say nothing of such earlier campaigns as those conducted by God's Massachusetts agents against the Quakers in the colonial period. The dominant white, rural, Protestant subculture was constantly at war with other subcultures who rejected their key social symbols. Take, for instance, the nativist movement which in the 1840's and 1850's spawned a powerful political wing in the Know-Nothings, with a platform of virulent anti-Catholic sentiments. The nativists did not simply propagandize for their viewpoint; they organized murderous and destructive riots in the major eastern cities, directed, interestingly enough, against the one immigrant Catholic group that demonstrated political talent, the Irish. The Protestant elements of the *Lumpenproletariat* organized into street gangs with such names as the Plug Uglies, Black Snakes, Rough Skins, and Blood Tubs, and carried on guerrilla street warfare with Irish home guards—top standing in the league went to those successful enough to burn down a church or a nunnery.

At about the same time, the abolitionists were receiving brutal treatment from "Vigilance Committees" in various southern communities. These committees of leading citizens actually offered rewards for delivery to the magistrates, that is, for kidnapping, of leading abolitionists. New Orleans, in fact, topped the list with an offer of $100,000 for Arthur Tappan and LaRoy Sunderland. William Lloyd Garrison estimated that three hundred abolitionist agents were lynched, and recently a careful student of the period, Russel B. Nye, agreed that this was not an unreasonable figure. Most, though not all, of these antislavery advocates were unarmed fanatics who sought to exercise their freedom of speech in the South.

But for every lynching, there were hundreds of lesser penalties meted out. The tarpot was constantly simmering, and the whip was kept limber. "Four Ohioans . . . whipped," "Rev. Aaron Kitchell . . . tarred and feathered," "Amos Dresser . . . 20 lashes in the marketplace and confiscation of belongings," "Rev. T. S. Kendall . . . tarred and ejected from town"—so runs the gloomy catalogue of pain in Nye's book *Fettered Freedom*, and it goes on for page after page.

Similarly, the organizer for the I.W.W., the Socialist Party, or other economically unorthodox organizations was liable to encounter genuine repression from the communities in which he spread his gospel, and there is hardly a trade union in the country whose history is not spotted with the blood of its pioneers.

In another sector, Walter Metzger and Richard Hofstadter have recently demonstrated that academic freedom, as a viable proposition, cannot be found operating in American colleges and universities much before World War I. Although there were shining exceptions, the teacher was generally at the mercy of his administrators, and if there were comparatively few outright dismissals, great care was taken to see that the unorthodox did not get hired in the first place. (In examining civil-liberties issues, the incidence of cases can be a deceptive guide. Far from necessarily indicating a high level of oppression, a high case rate *can* symbolize the opposite—that acts formerly taken for granted are being resisted.)

An instance-by-instance discussion of the treatment of dissenters in the nineteenth and early twentieth centuries could easily fill a whole issue of this journal, but there is no need for such a detailed analysis. It is patent that real reigns of terror against deviant subcultures were the rule rather than the exception, with the ironic corollary that the persecuted were themselves often quite willing to persecute those more helpless than themselves—see the Irish attitude toward the Jews. But what has tended to conceal this reality from later analysts of American social history is the fact that these persecutions were local rather than national in scope. The model Reign of Terror was built by the French Jacobins on a national scale, and when applied to the heterogeneous United States, this model was clearly irrelevant.

In the first article in this series I suggested several reasons for the decline of direct democracy in the United States. One of the points mentioned but passed over lightly in the discussion was the growth in power of the national government—national government, moreover, which was carefully insulated against political extremism. Evidence suggests that only once have we approached a national reign of terror: in the era of Woodrow Wilson and his Grand Vizier A. Mitchell Palmer. However, while Palmer and his assistants contributed manfully to the great Red Scare and the concomitant assaults on radicals of all shades, careful analysis of the period 1917-21 indicates that the great bulk of the actions taken against deviants were locally sponsored. In effect, the facilities of the Departments of Justice and Labor were put at the disposal of local extremists—American Legionnaires, American Protective Leagues, and so on—and the national government looked on benignly.

In this regard, the difference between World War I and World War II is immediately apparent. In the latter conflict, Attorney General Francis Biddle employed the Department of Justice as a buffer against local extremism, refusing, for example, to permit local United States attorneys to prosecute alleged disloyal or subversive elements without prior permission from Washington. This should be compared with the policy of Wilson's two Attorneys General, who gave full discretion to the local United States officials to deal with these matters as they saw fit. Attorney General Thomas W. Gregory disapproved of the indictment of Eugene Debs, for instance, but allowed the United States Attorney for the Northern District of Ohio, E. S. Wertz, to follow his own tack in dealing with the Socialist leader.

Biddle's policy was extremely important for two main reasons: first, because willy-nilly the national government tends to establish institutional behavior patterns which other governments in the nation imitate; and, second, because United States prosecutors were withdrawn from bureaucratic competition with local officials. To be specific, if the United States Attorney for the Western District of Pennsylvania begins to hunt subversives, with all the publicity that such diversions receive, it becomes extremely difficult for analagous state officials not to join in and stage a safari of their own. Given the nature of the patronage system, local federal officials are always potential candidates for state office; so state officeholders must never permit them to get a unique hold on the public attention. This is true even when the same party controls both the state and national government, for then factional battles in primaries have to be reckoned with; it is more true when different parties control these two governments. Needless to add, once this institutional competition gets under way, there is no effective check on how extreme it will become except the danger of committing the mortal sin of American politics—boring the sovereign people.

Another factor to be considered is that the national government is far more responsive to the views of civil-liberty elites than are state and local governments. This is not necessarily due to superior enlightenment (although the high precentage of "enlightened" lawyers in key jobs in Washington discussed in my first article fits into the picture here); superior vulnerability is probably a better explanation. When the *New York Times* thunders editorially against the Veterans Administration for depriving legless veteran James Kutcher of his disability pension, the VA quakes, but all the admonitory *Times* pronouncements in the world will hardly disturb the Board of Selectmen of East Siwash. There is *one* national government; there are thousands of local governments. Although it may seem that I am here contradicting my earlier assertion that the national government is more insulated from extremism than other governments, in fact the two propositions are supplementary rather than opposed. The various segments of the national government are highly vulnerable to pressure, the administration being the most poorly insulated, but it is virtually impossible for the same pressure complex to dominate *all* segments—the President, the Congress, and the courts.

It seems clear that today the old-fashioned American reign of terror is a disappearing phenomenon. Direct democracy—citizens taking the law into their own hands—is not completely dead, but except in the South it lives a fitful and anemic existence. A casualty that has been unreported, but which seems to me to have accompanied it, is the old-fashioned American radical. In place of the wild-eyed enthusiast, prepared to tell judge, jury, and community to go to hell, we have the Nonconformist in the Brooks Brothers suit. He prides himself on his Nonconformity, but, as the capital letters indicate, the deviant values which he holds are now an orthodoxy and he a bureaucrat. While the old-style radical stuck out his chin and took his licks, never expecting that the reward for apostasy would be good fellowship, our Nonconformist is hurt when society retaliates for his deviation, for he feels that he deserves a medal. He frequently lives well, probably in what Russell Lynes called "Upper Bohemia," has a Volkswagen and *no* televison set, and meets his fellow sectarians at cocktail parties to discuss ominous portents of impending American totalitarianism. He may be identified by the opening notes of his song: "*Everyone* these days is afraid. . . ."

Let me give two examples. There are lawyers whom I know who work hard and well for unpopular causes (and I am *not* referring to legal defense of unpopular people, which is a different proposition) and yet are constantly disturbed because conservative businessmen refuse to purchase their services. Recently I had lunch with a group of these gentlemen. The first half of the conversation concerned the immoral character of the business community, and the second half was a lamentation that these attorneys were being discriminated against for their opinions. When I gently suggested that businessmen were hardly violating their civil rights by refusing to purchase their services, there was stunned silence. I was a fake liberal!

The second example is that group of alleged radicals who, when officially queried on their political beliefs, plead the Fifth Amendment. I am not suggesting for a second that they are not within their legal rights in doing so; what I am suggesting is that by taking this way out they waive their moral status as radicals. "I refuse to testify on the ground that my testimony may incriminate me"—for a radical was there ever a starker summation of moral bankruptcy? Can one conceive of Gene Debs taking the Fifth? Debs, the Wobblies, and their radical brethren never lost an opportunity to tell the world exactly what they thought.

There is a famous anecdote about a Socialist agitator who had been treated to tar and feathers by a town in Oklahoma and was being ridden out on a rail. Asked by one of his tormentors how he liked the ride, he replied, "If it wasn't for the honor of the thing, I'd just as soon walk." While there are still some militants of this caliber in circulation—A. J. Muste comes to mind immediately—they tend to make the Nonconformist nervous— "Certainly I *respect* Muste, but don't you think he suffers from a martyr complex?" No, I don't. What arouses my indignation is not human fallibility, but human sham: the hypocrisy of those who claim for themselves the tradition of radicalism but who quail from the social and economic repercussions of defying the community. As an early Quaker, haled into court for nonviolent resistance to a "wicked law," told a magistrate who was reluctant to jail him and asked instead for a promise of future good behavior: "Friend, my Light makes me stand against thee, and thy Light makes thee imprison me—let us each then affirm the Light as God has given us to see it."

While today most of the sting has gone from direct democracy, and nothing of equal coercive impact has developed on the national scene to replace it, the character of persecution has also changed. Typically, the deviant in contemporary America faces restrictions of a bureaucratic nature: he is denied security clearance, he is discharged without honor from the army, and so on. It is surely no consolation to the employee discharged from government in a Kafkaesque proceeding to hear that in 1919 he might have been beaten to death with a tire chain. And yet, compared with the segment of American society that lived in rightless limbo half a century ago, the segment that is today maltreated is minute, and this segment has a good chance of receiving at least the elements of due process of law.

But if the present position of the nonconformist has improved, his future situation is not necessarily so cheerful. As was suggested earlier, the decline of local democracy has ameliorated the condition of the individual deviant, but it has also contributed to an increasing concentration of power in the central government. It is now conceivable that we could have a nationwide reign of terror, whereas in the nineteenth century this was literally impossible. While no prophet of gloom, and certainly no advocate of such an anachronism as states' rights, I think we should notice carefully one instance of what the national government can do:

the "unconstitutional" imprisonment in concentration camps of the West Coast American-Japanese in World War II. (I put "unconstitutional" in quotes because the Supreme Court, Justice Black speaking, found the Constitution flexible enough to permit this incarceration.) This was a case in which the fragmentation of power which normally operates in the national government went into hibernation, and President Roosevelt, the Congress *without dissent*, and the courts put the nisei away for possessing, not enemy beliefs, but enemy chromosomes.

A similar potential can be seen in the security program. During the Civil War, northern "security risks" could flee to honor in the South, and vice versa, but today a man found to be a risk in New York is barred from broad categories of employment throughout the nation. He can no longer find security in a sympathetic subculture. The great power for good of the national government has as an inevitable concomitant a great power for evil. From my point of view there are no inexorable forces at work moving the United States toward authoritarianism, but the liberal community must realize that the instruments of national power it so casually bestowed upon the national government in the period 1935–1952 are capable of employment against its interests. "The sword cares not who wields it, nor whose blood it sheds." It is perhaps at this point that an impartial sociological observer might regret the domestication of American nonconformists, alluded to above: so large a proportion of the American reform elite was taken into the firm in the 1930's and 1940's that few voices but those of the crackpot Right are disposed to criticize and attack.

A Sane View of Nonconformity

In the first article of this series, I suggested that the United States is today a freer nation, from the standpoint of the individual nonconformist, than ever before in its history. In the second article, I discussed that American perennial, the reign of terror, concluding that the situation today, when compared with the reigns of terror that have on a local basis bloodied up the American past, augurs well for the life expectancy of the nonconformist. The bulk of punishments for nonconformity today are less severe than was the case in the nineteenth century: typically, deviations are punished on a bureaucratic rather than on a direct level; that is, a "security risk" is dismissed from his job, not hanged to a lamppost or tarred and feathered.

In these articles, I attempted to divorce my convictions from my analysis, to examine the past on its merit. I am certain that my prejudices did from time to time seep into the interstices of the argument; yet it is essential, if we are to learn anything from the experience of our ancestors, that we refuse to treat the past as a retrospective proving ground for our convictions about the present. However, in this final article, I am free to present my convictions about the present, and I shall examine what seem to me to be the major threats to our liberties.

The literature about individual violations of rights is abundant, so I shall not attempt an instance-by-instance, area-by-area study. What I plan to do is investigate two major tendencies in American public policy. First, the enlargement of the political sector;

Reprinted, with permission, from *The New Republic*, February 6, 1956.

and, second, the withering of decency. However, before I begin the discussion of these trends, it is essential that I define what I mean by democracy, for this definition is fundamental to my subsequent analysis.

Democratic government is by far the most difficult system to implement and operate ever conceived. The supreme danger that confronts it is a perpetual tendency to drift in the direction of majoritarianism. But majority rule is not democracy; to identify the two is to confuse the instrument with the premise. Once one identifies the two, he divorces himself from the democratic tradition and enters another which either overtly or covertly asserts that power is its own justification. The essence of this approach to democracy is that the fists of the majority, like Frederick the Great's cannon, are inscribed *ultima ratio regum*—the ultimate justification of the sovereign.

To the democrat, power is not self-legitimatizing. On the contrary, power is legitimate only to the extent that it forwards certain ethical, philosophical, or religious ends. The basic purpose of power is to make possible a maximum development of human potentialities, and this purpose is in turn founded upon the unverifiable assumption that men are capable of rising to a level of unselfish dedication to one another and to the common weal.

Moreover, the democrat is denied the comforting crutch of certainty. While he holds his convictions *on the level of action* firmly enough to die for them on occasion, *on the level of thought* he is constantly engaged in questioning, in searching for better answers. It is his fate to be constantly battling for what he knows to be at best a half-truth, to be making a full action commitment on the basis of incomplete evidence.

To achieve working answers to everyday problems, the democrat accepts majority decisions as binding on the actions of the community. However, no decision is ever final. In the event that new evidence appears, a new trial is in order, and it is the dynamic function of the nonconformist to urge new trials, to submit new evidence, to demand a public hearing for a different view. Thus, in a healthy democracy the majority and the nonconformist depend upon each other, and each supplies a vital component to the whole. Stability is provided by the majority, while vitality flows from the nonconformist. Consequently, the democrat protects the rights of the nonconformist not merely as an act of decency, but more significantly as an imperative for himself and the whole society.

This is the idea, and if, as I have suggested, we in the United States have tarnished it somewhat, even tarnished it has a grandeur which no elitist theory can approach. It is toward this great dream of power as the ethical instrument of a self-governing community—not as the whim of a prince, a priest, or a proletariat, or the passions of a majority—that I believe American public policy must be directed.

A major threat to the achievement of this goal seems to me to stem from the enlargement of the political sector. It is characteristic of totalitarian states that no sector of national life can exist free from political control. Everything from stamp clubs and bowling leagues to political parties and pressure groups must pay obeisance to political objectives, must, if demanded, purge themselves of Jews, kulaks, Trotskyites, or other deviants. The state becomes the only *real* organization, and all other groups are subservient to it. When this occurs, political criteria are injected into judgments where they have no rational meaning: chess players are evaluated in terms of their politics, not their chess; great physicists are condemned for their religion, while their scientific merit goes unevaluated.

The Soviet Union has pushed this tendency almost to its logical conclusion, and faced with worldwide assault from Communism, free societies have been forced to review their own definition of "political." For example, it is patent that nineteenth century clichés about freedom of organization cannot suffice to deal with a political party that is also a foreign intelligence service and a potential rebel army. Similarly, insurance companies, sport clubs, trade unions, children's camps, have turned up which defy the classic definition of these organizations by having political rather than private objectives.

Faced with this strange and frightening phenomenon, the American people have moved in two directions to counteract the dangers they fear: first, they have rushed to set up a security program, or programs, based more on principles of vengeance

than on security; and, second, they have injected political criteria into areas where these principles have no meaning. In short,
they have tended to defend themselves by imitating the tactics of
the enemy, by enlarging the political sector.

Governments have the right to protect themselves from disloyal servants, and I heartily approve of rigid standards of loyalty
for all persons in sensitive positions. But our national security
programs proceed, by methods that vary from careful scrutiny
to malevolent idiocy (compare Wolf Ladejinsky), to dismiss
from governmental positions of every description persons of
"doubtful" loyalty.

This is "getting Commies" with a vengeance, but it does not
necessarily add one iota to the security of the United States. The
great bulk of government jobs are of a nonsensitive character,
and it seems to me that a meaningful security program with respect to these posts would require only old-fashioned civil service
techniques with the burden of proof on the United States to
demonstrate the malfeasance of the individual.

The second direction in which we have moved is toward applying political criteria in areas where they are senseless, if not
pernicious. Many examples of this sort can be found on the
American scene: harmonica players are denied a hall because of
alleged subversive connections; boxers are required to take loyalty oaths before putting on the gloves; unemployed workers are
refused compensation because of ties with Communist unions,
and so on. Most actions of this sort are merely silly, and—as I
suggested in an earlier article—there is certainly no reign of
terror loose in the nation; but, silly or not, their cumulative effect
is dangerous.

Consequently we should make all possible efforts to limit the
political sector. In dealing, for example, with Communist public
school teachers, I feel the key level of examination is not that
of Party membership but that of teaching. It is my personal conviction that Communists make bad teachers because of the closed
quality of their minds, to say nothing of their penchant for illegitimate extracurricular activities such as organizing secret student cells, but this proposition is a matter to be tested and
adjudicated in individual instances.

The second broad tendency which seems to me to threaten our liberties is what I have called the withering of decency. The assault against Communism has in the United States begun to resemble a campaign against rabid foxes—in word, if not in deed —and many seem to have forgotten a basic truth that can be overlooked only at great peril to an individual and a national soul: that Communists are human beings.

It has always been characteristic of public hysteria, reigns of terror, purges, and the like, that the enemy is dehumanized; he becomes a *thing.* The basic philosophical and theological case for human slavery from Aristotle down to our own times has rested on the premise that slaves are subhuman, and Hannah Arendt has pointed out the use to which modern totalitarianism has put this sophistry. How totalitarian regimes strip their opposition groups of humanity has also been recorded in such superb literary works as Arthur Koestler's *Darkness at Noon,* George Orwell's *1984,* and Czeslaw Milosz's *Captive Mind.* Viewed from this perspective, the Moscow Trials were merely the disposal by the Stalinist state of some inadequate tools that had not fulfilled their tasks properly.

Let us take a case with which I have some personal experience, the "Fifth Amendment librarian" of Plymouth Meeting, Pennsylvania. The background of this case is well known: Mary Knowles pleaded the Fifth Amendment before a congressional committee some years ago in Boston after having been named by Herbert Philbrick as a Communist. She was dismissed from a public library in Massachusetts, but no indictment was lodged against her for any criminal offense. Moving to Wayne, Pennsylvania, she took a position with a little library run by a Quaker organization, and also in part subsidized from public funds. Her performance as librarian has been from all accounts excellent—there has been no evidence adduced to suggest that she has been using her job to forward the Communist Party.

However, in the neighboring area a group has organized to "get" Mrs. Knowles with the engaging title of "Citizens for Philbrick." I surely have no objections to citizens organizing peacefully for anything they choose, but this group has instituted a real campaign of hate against the librarian—a campaign which was intensified when the Fund for the Republic announced a $5,000 grant to the Quaker Meeting for standing fast against the lynch mob—and will apparently be satisfied with nothing less than her head on a platter. In the course of the affair, it has apparently been overlooked that Mrs. Knowles, a person against whom no criminal accusations have been lodged, is a human being who must eat.

On a broader level, probably no episode has left such a spoor of hate in its wake as the *Rosenberg* case. When human beings talk of other human beings as "rats"—"Kill the rats!"—I feel an overpowering urge to abdicate from the human race.

We all know from personal experience how easy it is to be carried away by frenzy and join the haters—the human capacity to hate is proof of a sort for the doctrine of Original Sin—and we all have regretted our dalliance. It is probably to prevent our hasty judgments from haunting us forever that we have built elaborate procedural labyrinths into our law, and it is to prevent such frenzied aberrations from poisoning the future that we have built delay into our political institutions. As the Massachusetts *Body of Liberties* (1641) succinctly put the matter: "Our duty and desire is to do nothing suddainlie which fundamentally concerne us."

However, we cannot expect our institutions alone to preserve our spiritual chastity; on the contrary, these institutions can in the long haul be no stronger than the morality that supports them. This is why it is so important that our political leaders *be* leaders, be willing to stick their necks out in the cause of decency. While I have never been a devotee of Dean Acheson's foreign policy, he stands at the top of my list for his courageous decency. Tactically it was a blunder to state that he would not "turn his back on Alger Hiss," but in a moral sense it was an affirmation of humanity against the blood cultists.

A final aspect of this withering of decency that deserves mention is the tendency that accompanies it to turn life into a conspiracy: No blunder is ever accidental, no policy-maker is ever stupid. This approach to life supplies logical justification for exorcising decency from political relations, for if one assumes that individuals are mere instruments of alien forces, ideological automata, as it were, he is consistent when he treats his enemies as objects to be destroyed. A blunderer in the State Department loses his character as a fallible human being, perhaps deserving dismissal for incompetence, and becomes an enemy knight on a cosmic chessboard, an object to be eliminated.

In evaluating errors in policy, we should always assume that bad judgment is at fault until the contrary can be conclusively demonstrated. In general, we should act upon the assumption that in politics, as in interpersonal relations, the simplest explanation is usually the best. If we abandon this common-sense rule, we enter a universe in which logic triumphs over life, and decency is a superfluous, if not a dangerous, quality.

I have concentrated in this article on the two main trends in contemporary American life that seem to me to threaten the long-run development of our liberties. There are, of course, others which a longer analysis would have to take into account, notably the resurgence of direct democracy in the South since the Supreme Court's desegregation holding. It is my conviction that the law-abiding majority in the South will eventually rally to the Constitution and that, perhaps with great delays, white and Negro children will at last be granted full equality. However, before that day dawns, the Negro community in the South is going to have some rough sledding at the hands of the local forces of "law and order." To the extent that "Citizens' Councils" merely agitate against the Constitution—even if their agitation is of a despicable character—they are within their rights, but every resource that the national government can legitimately command should be employed against them if they employ force and violence to subvert the Constitution.

I have attempted an overall appraisal of the state of American liberties as of 1956. Perhaps because I do not share the conviction of many American historians that the history of the United States has been the unfolding of Anglo-Saxon virtues and the assimilation to them of benighted Irish, Jews, Poles, or Asians, I take a somewhat more jaundiced view in these articles of the American past than is customary. As a descendant of immigrants who were *not* greeted by Grover Whalen, but by signs reading "No Irish Need Apply," I may have an unduly prejudiced view of intergroup relations in the nineteenth century. But whatever biases I may have, I submit that the evidence is clear: in the United States today, ethnic, political, religious nonconformists have more leeway, have a better life expectancy, than was ever before the case. As the United States has emerged from the radical internal transformations that accompanied the Industrial Revolution, we seem to have achieved a new maturity, a willingness to live and let live, and a growing acceptance of legal procedures. As I have suggested in this final article, great dangers confront us; and those who cherish liberty must fight a many-fronted war if we are to maintain and enlarge our heritage. But in these fights we can draw some comfort from looking back at the great distance we have traveled and from the knowledge that while the American standard may be tattered, we have achieved a level of individual freedom that hundreds of millions of human beings can conceive of only as a remote, impossible aspiration.

The Curbing of the Militant Majority:
A Dissent from the Classic Liberal
Interpretation of Civil Liberties
in America

For some curious reason, historians and political scientists have largely bypassed the history of civil liberties in the United States before World War I. The consequence of this neglect has been the prevalence of an amazing set of clichés about the character of contemporary American society and the historic position of civil liberty in the American political tradition.

Once upon a time, so the story runs, the United States was a land of militant, inner-directed nonconformists, men who were as sensitive to the rights of others as they were fierce in the defense of their own autonomy. Then slowly over this green and pleasant land crept the miasma of orthodoxy, an enervating spirit of conformity which left in its wake an atomized population of other-directed status seekers gibbering the slogans of the moment, terrified of the FBI, and finding ultimate consolation only in the narcosis of mass culture. A nation of Thoreaus has in some subtle fashion been transformed into an anomic mass of dying salesmen.

Underlying all this nonsense, of course, is the myth of bucolic virtue which Richard Hofstader so sensitively limned in *The Age of Reform:* the notion, profoundly Jeffersonian, that the rural yeoman is the paradigmatic Democratic Citizen and that cities are a source of civic degeneracy, a malignant cancer on the body politic. With this agrarian nostalgia is combined a heavy dose of sociological paranoia: a self-anointed intellectual elite has simply lost patience with a mass society that persists in spending its new-found leisure bowling or watching TV rather than reading Kafka,

Reprinted, with permission, from *The Reporter*, July 18, 1963.

a society where the masses refuse to genuflect to their Cultural Betters. So the critics talk morosely of "the eclipse of community" and "the lonely crowd," conveniently forgetting that a mere half-century ago it was precisely the firmly integrated rural community and the accompanying "idiocy of rural life" that set off the mad rush to urban anonymity.

Few historians, political scientists, or sociologists seem to love cities; the medieval German aphorism *"Stadt Luft macht frei"*— City air nourishes freedom—has seldom been echoed by American students of the process of urbanization. Suffice it here to note my conviction that it has been a major factor in the growth of liberty in the United States by bringing about the collapse of that "natural community" which brings nostalgic tears to the eyes of sociological critics of contemporary American culture. Within the cities the breakdown of ethnic ghettos—"natural communities" par excellence—has paralleled the demise of a rurally based, authoritarian social structure.

There is a singular durability in the myth that at some undesignated time in the past there was in the United States a golden age of individual freedom. Vernon L. Parrington (*Main Currents in American Thought*) and his followers probably established this tradition so far as modern American historians are concerned, although it should be added that the filio-patristic nationalistic writers, for their own reasons, assigned extraordinary virtue to the founders of the Republic. Parrington was quite explicit: American liberty hit its apogee with the Declaration of Independence, and has been on the decline ever since. Jefferson is the folk hero of this tradition, and the basic analytic proposition on which the whole Parringtonian superstructure rests is that the centralized state is the enemy of freedom. The Hamiltonians thus become the sappers under the fortress of liberty, and it follows (quite properly in logical terms) that the increase in the power of the state has automatically led to a decline in the rights of the individual. The better to preserve the pristine ideal, Parringtonians regularly overlook the inconvenient facts that Jefferson opposed both John Adams's Sedition Law and Hamilton's mercantilism on *states'-rights* grounds. Here, for example, is Jefferson's Second Inaugural Address on the subject of religious freedom:

In matters of religion I have considered that its free exercise is placed by the Constitution independent of the powers of the General Government. I have therefore undertaken on no occasion to prescribe the religious exercises suited to it, but have left them, as the Constitution found them, under the direction and discipline of the church *or state* authorities acknowledged by the several religious societies. [Italics added.]

A few paragraphs later, he made the same differentiation between state and national *vires* in connection with the handling of seditious libels.

How can we account for this curious refusal to confront historical reality on its own terms? A generation that ruthlessly suppressed Tory speech and Tory press (not merely "overt" Tory acts), confiscated Tory property with a zeal and efficiency a Bolshevik could admire, and populated the wilds of Canada with its opposition, has somehow been acclaimed as "conservative." A generation that employed loyalty oaths and disclaimer affidavits in a fashion that would bring joy to the heart of a Joseph R. McCarthy has similarly been credited with establishing civil liberties in the United States. The forty-second and latest *Annual Report* of the American Civil Liberties Union, for example, gives a stirring quotation from Jefferson, and bemoans "our twentieth century resurrection of official orthodoxy," with the clear implication that "official orthodoxy" was a foreign product that Jefferson and his fellow libertarians barred from the United States.

Still Fighting the King

If there was one thing on which John Adams and Thomas Jefferson always agreed, it was with respect to what has been called the doctrine of "American exceptionalism," the view that the truths of the Old World were not necessarily applicable to the realities of the New. It seems to me that, oddly enough, the source of historical confusion about civil rights has largely arisen from a refusal to recognize the validity of this insight. To put the point precisely, a set of analytic categories devised in Europe to cope with European development has been unthinkingly applied to the American scene. Thus because the political leaders of the American Revolution were not "Jacobins," they must have been "conservatives." Similarly the often terrifying realities of a savage, brawling frontier society and the brutal confrontations in the great Civil War and the lesser civil wars (between labor and management, white and Negro, Mormon and "gentile," Irish and nativist) have been converted into exercises in consensual group therapy because they refuse to fit the standards of European social theory.

What this means in concrete terms is that the European liberal doctrine that the centralized state is the natural enemy of freedom was simply transplanted to the American scene—where, I submit, it was essentially irrelevant. The centralized state, that "Mortall God" which in Europe emerged triumphant over the centrifugal tendencies of feudalism and the religious wars and in the process destroyed the "liberties" of the subject, of the town, and of the province or shire alike, never developed on this side of the water. To the European liberals, Thomas Hobbes was the enemy incarnate, and bravely they fought to put chains on Leviathan, to curb the power of a centralized bureaucracy, to mobilize the power of the community against the artificial "engines of tyranny" created at Paris or Westminster. But the "engines of oppression" were not successfully exported to the American colonies; British efforts to establish centralized colonial administration foundered—as young John Adams pointed out to a Boston discussion group almost two centuries ago—on the stubborn realities of local sovereignty (and, it should be added, on British inefficiency).

The American Revolution was—as Adams also pointed out—fought to retain de facto local sovereignty against British efforts to establish Leviathan on an international basis. It was fought to maintain the civil liberties of Americans, that is, the right of Americans to define their rights for themselves. No one ever suggested that a Tory could assert his rights against his patriot neighbors, and there was certainly no operating concept of "vested individual rights" against the community. John Locke was interpreted, as indeed he had been in his own day, as the theoretician of majority rule, as the tribune of the community in its resistance to arbitrary, capricious, and above all unrepresentative governmental institutions. There was no appeal to "natural law" against the responsible decisions of the society: for Locke and the Americans who set to work building their own governments, it was simply taken for granted that civil law defined natural law in any truly representative system. Bills of rights were thus designed to protect the citizen from the possible usurpations of the government, not from the decisions of his neighbors.

The federal Bill of Rights, from this viewpoint, was not designed to preserve the liberty of the individual but to guarantee that *local* definitions of liberty would prevail. If one reads carefully the Amendments dealing with criminal procedure (IV through VIII), he will appreciate the institutional sagacity of their sponsors: literally enforced, they would make impossible the development in the United States of a Tudor judiciary, that marvelous mechanism of centralization where the royal judge became in effect a local viceroy. (Those who noted the failure of the federal government to indict former Major General Edwin Walker for incitement to riot against national authority in the wake of the Mississippi crisis last year will admire the effectiveness of the authors of the Fifth Amendment: a Mississippi grand jury refused to turn in a true bill, and the United States government was helpless.)

The community, then, is charged with protecting civil liberties from any perversion by the state. But, returning to the concept of American exceptionalism, has this curbing of the federal government ever really been the problem in the United States? It is my contention that since the seventeenth century the basic civil-liberties problem has been not the arbitrary exercise of centralized power but the despotism of the militant majority. Thus while the growth of bureaucracy, particularly of the national government, and the expansion of national law proves to the Parringtonians that liberty is in decline, I look upon the same set of historical developments and find a growing tradition of impersonal bureaucratized justice and a withering away of decentralized authoritarianism. Moreover, I am prepared to argue that something "impossible" has happened, impossible, that is, in terms of the premises of European liberalism: the national government has become an instrument for protecting individual freedom.

An Invisible Terror

Since this involves some drastic shifts in definition, let me set forth in more detail what I mean by the despotism of the militant majority. Until roughly World War I, excluding the Sedition Act of 1798, it is difficult to find any national laws penalizing dissenting *opinion*. And until the great epidemic of criminal-anarchy laws touched off by the assassination of President McKinley, the states had little legislation on the subject. It would, however, be a drastic error to draw from this absence of legislation the conclusion that freedom of opinion was universally respected. Or, if one wishes to quibble with this generalization, we can concede that freedom of opinion was everywhere respected—with the right to define *opinion* reserved to local juries. There was nothing "individualistic" about the common law, and in most states the old common-law remedies for nonconformity were adequate to the needs of the time. Thus a citizen who advocated birth control would find himself in court charged with "lewd behavior" and "breach of the peace," and, unless he could convince stalwart juryman of the virtue of his cause, would wind up in the workhouse for six months. His opinions were not at issue; it was his "lewd behavior" that got him into trouble—and no one, anywhere, has a constitutional right to behave lewdly. If his opinions were the source of his behavior, that was his problem; his objective actions alone were involved in the trial. He might think whatever he wanted, but he might not behave lewdly.

Let us take another area—freedom of conscience, which most bills of rights guaranteed absolutely. Here we have a classic example in the legal assault on the Church of Jesus Christ, Latter-day Saints, by which the Mormons were savagely persecuted in Missouri and Illinois and eventually besieged and beaten in their Utah fortress. The Mormons, claiming divine inspiration, incorporated as part of their creed the doctrine of "celestial marriage," that is, polygamy. Their neighbors, suffering perhaps from prurient envy, denounced them as bigamists, and the majesty of the law was invoked. To their claim of freedom of religion, the judges and juries uniformly replied that bigamy was a crime, not an exercise of freedom of conscience. Freedom of religion stopped at the outer limits of the Criminal Code. (In Utah and Idaho, however, the jury system failed in its obligations: Mormon jurors acquitted Mormons. The consequence was that Congress, which had refused to act in defense of southern Negroes who had been returned to virtual slavery by a militant majority, their white neighbors, passed a bill barring "bigamists," "polygamists," and "any person cohabiting with more than one woman" from voting or serving on juries and thus got the local majority back in sound hands!) A Mormon in jail for bigamy could hardly claim that his religious freedom had been violated; by definition (of twelve good men, well chosen and true), religious freedom had been held not to include the right to be a bigamist.

To abbreviate a long story, I have been searching for some years for an early (say pre-1900) case in which a state court overruled a decision of a lower court on civil rights grounds, that is, invoked a provision of a state bill of rights as a bar to prosecution. There are cases that conform to the Parringtonian ideal— where state courts have thrown out *statutes* as violative of a state bill of rights—but I have yet to find an instance in which an appellate state tribunal threw out the decision of a local jury on libertarian grounds. There must be some cases in this category somewhere, but they are fairly well concealed. Perhaps elected judges took a dim view of reversing and remanding the decisions of their constituents.

One of the marvels of the common law in this context was (and is) its invisibility. No centralized state apparatus had been mobilized; the sheriff or chief of police handled the burden of prosecution; no statute was normally invoked; and the defendant was never put away for sedition but simply for "unlawful assembly" or "breach of the peace"—legal rubrics that are still, as recent Freedom Rider and sit-in litigation demonstrates, extremely difficult to handle at the appellate level. For technical reasons that need not concern us here, appellate courts have always been limited in their ability to go "behind" the record—to investigate *de novo* the facts in a case—so that to this day it is extraordinary to find an instance where sufficient legal sophistication is employed at the trial level to make possible an appellate reversal of a conviction for "breach of the peace." (The N.A.A.C.P. has been infuriating southern prosecutors by providing precisely this expertise, carefully introducing into the trial record material that opens up the possibility of broad appeal.)

Although one can condemn the consequences of this system as "undemocratic," the system itself seems to have reflected the "will of the people." This pluralism of decentralized authoritarianism made it possible, of course, for a wide range of views to exist, each in its own haven of orthodoxy. "Law and order" in this milieu clearly meant what the local majority defined as such. A sheriff elected on a clean-up program in Nevada gave this position its finest expression: Anyone who rejected the principles of "law and order," he proclaimed, would be "summarily hanged."

Now, all of this—like the local campaign of extermination in the antebellum South against the abolitionists—took place below the threshold of classic liberal sensitivity. Civil rights in the United States were secure, an Albert Jay Nock or William Graham Sumner would argue, adducing the absence of centralized, bureaucratized despotism. Also below their threshold were the exercises of sovereign power by economic feudalities, the great private governments of the last quarter of the nineteenth century and the first three decades of the twentieth. While the New York Central Railroad or the United States Steel Corporation, *inter alia*, fulfilled every definition of sovereignty except issuing postage stamps, the restrictions they imposed on their subjects were not violations of individual liberty. On the contrary, from this vantage point they were merely contractual obligations freely accepted as a precondition for making a living. A man might receive the economic equivalent of the death sentence—dismissal and blacklisting—for joining a union, and a union organizer might be forbidden even to discuss the merits of organization with workers who had signed "yellow-dog" contracts (a limitation on freedom of speech which the Supreme Court accepted on the grounds that such a speech constituted incitement to breach of contract!), but none of the classic civil rights issues were involved.

Indeed, civil rights issues did not arise in this area unless the state attempted to intervene on behalf of the workers—by, say, banning the yellow-dog contract, or requiring payment in coin of the realm rather than scrip, or limiting the workweek. The minute the state was sighted on the horizon, classical civil libertarians marshaled their forces for Armageddon.

Mob Rule and the Law

To summarize an elaborate argument, if we examine the "state of civil liberties" in 1900 from the classical liberal viewpoint, we find that the United States was clearly the freest nation in the world (the otherwise sound British had a bad habit of passing Factory Acts and other invasions of freedom of contract). There was no centralized bureaucracy, no national police, no income tax, no national control of state and local government—the nation was a libertarian paradise. Yet, if one analyzed the same data from another angle, he might contend that the United States was a nation where the workers were at the mercy of their employers, Negroes were living in serfdom, religious and ethnic minorities were subjected to blatant discrimination, and the "rights of the individual" were those specified by a militant majority of his neighbors.

Patently it is a question of what "model" one employs. In the United States there existed both a weak and decentralized governmental apparatus and a fundamental absence of individual freedom for those to whom it was important: those who differed on basic issues with the rural white, predominantly Anglo-Saxon Protestant majority. The majority was free—it held views approved by the majority, or by those local majorities which characterized a country still strongly regional in emphasis. Community authoritarianism also permeated those subcultures that were under attack by the great society: Brooklyn Jews who sponsored a Yom Kippur ball to demonstrate their liberation from the "superstitions" of the Orthodox were mobbed by their neighbors in the ghetto, and a hard-rock miner in Colorado who refused to respond to the bugle of the Western Federation of Miners could expect little sympathy on his painful ride out of town.

One final example may illuminate the shadowy place in my argument. On April 26, 1913, a tragic sequence of events began in Atlanta, Georgia, when Mary Phagan was found raped and murdered in the basement of Moses Frank's pencil factory, managed by his nephew Leo. Leo Frank was accused of the crime, indicted, tried, and convicted of murder. The evidence was flimsy and wholly circumstantial; the prosecution's key witness, Jim Conley, was certainly himself the murderer. But in no real sense was Frank on trial: the Jews were in the cage. "Our little girl—*ours* by the eternal God!" bellowed Tom Watson, the agrarian demagogue who was to be elected to the Senate in 1920 on a program that mixed equal parts of antiwar Populism, anti-Semitism, and anti-Catholicism, "has been pursued to a hideous death and bloody grave by *this filthy perverted Jew of New York*." Frank's lawyer was told bluntly, "If they don't hang that Jew, we'll hang you." In this atmosphere Frank was sentenced to hang (Watson editorially licked his chops at the prospect of vengeance on this "lascivious Jew.") Eventually, after successive appeals, the United States Supreme Court rejected Frank's contention that the State of Georgia had denied him due process of law. Oliver Wendell Holmes, Jr., joined by Charles Evans Hughes, dissented brutally from the seven-Justice majority which implicitly ruled (technically they declined jurisdiction) that Frank had been granted his full legal remedies under the Constitution. "Mob rule," said Holmes, expounding a position taken for granted by today's Court, "does not become due process of law by securing the assent of a terrorized jury. . . . it is our duty [to declare] lynch law as little valid when practiced by a regularly drawn jury as when administered . . . by a mob intent on death."

It appears that by this time the Georgia judges were well aware of Frank's innocence. Conley had confessed to his lawyer, who, bound by the lawyer-client relationship, could not reveal the information. Finally, incapable of standing silent while Frank was railroaded to the gallows, the counsel confided the matter to Judge Arthur Powell, who was his intimate friend. The latter apparently passed the information on to Governor John Slaton, though still under the seal of secrecy. But with Watson on the warpath, no one wished to assume responsibility for letting "the Jew" go free, or even for ordering a new trial. Finally, with Frank about to hang, Governor Slaton risked his own neck and commuted the sentence to life imprisonment. Frank, secretly removed from Atlanta to Milledgeville Prison Farm, was immediately knifed by a fellow convict and was soon seized by a mob, and lynched. "We regard the hanging of Leo Frank as an act of law-abiding citizens," observed the Marietta *Journal*, and Tom Watson chortled, "Jew libertines take notice!"

Back at the statehouse in Atlanta, only the intervention of armed troops prevented a frenzied mob from hanging Governor Slaton and dynamiting his home. When Slaton left office, and Georgia, three days after commuting Frank's sentence, his once-promising political career was over. And when Tom Watson died in 1922, Eugene V. Debs sent his widow a letter praising this "heroic soul who fought the power of evil his whole life long." More appropriately, the Ku Klux Klan sent a huge floral cross.

The Sources of Freedom

This was the militant majority in action, and one can find other episodes that equally demonstrate the unfettered passion of mob rule operating under the procedural formulas of "due process of law"—the extirpation of opposition during World War I presents the interested student with an endless accumulation of relevant data. But the classical liberal would theoretically remain unmoved: the centralized state, that civil abstraction, played a minor role or none. The absence of a star chamber has been taken as proof of the existence of freedom of opinion, the lack of an FBI or a "security program" as evidence of unfettered individual freedom.

Actually, in the transformation of American life from the condign direct democracy of the "old order" to the regularized tradition of due process of law, enforced by national courts, a major share of the credit for converting civil liberties from privileges a community granted to its members to rights which can be defended against a militant local majority must be accorded to the intervention of the centralized state. The passage of the Wagner Act, for example, was one of the greatest acts of liberation in American history; decisions of the Supreme Court in school segregation, reapportionment, search and seizure, right to counsel, and other cases have played a notable part in the expansion of individual freedom; and one should not overlook in this context the work of the national executive, such as President Truman's desegregation orders for the federal administration and the Armed Forces and President Kennedy's housing order. The same pattern of governmental action has been instituted in many states.

And yet this state action for individual freedom—not group freedom, not majority freedom—still arouses the wrath of classical liberals; and contemporary liberals, who hold no general brief against the state, often seem hypnotized by the litany. Last December, for instance, the Center for the Study of Democratic Institutions held a potlatch in New York where speaker after speaker, mostly from civil-liberties circles, echoed the mordant warning that American liberty was in unprecedented jeopardy. (Indeed, the refrain was so persistent that it almost seemed as though the participants had been selected for their liturgical conformity.) No sane man will deny that the *potential* threats to American freedom from *possible* state action are far greater in 1963 than they were in 1833 or 1913. The great apparatus of federal power *could* be employed for evil ends as well as for good ones, and the real possibility of resistance to centralized power has vanished. But what indications are there that our modern Leviathan is driven by totalitarian compulsions? One hundred and nine once-jailed Communists, many now busy lecturing to liberal-arts colleges? Without suggesting that one can adopt a quantitative scale in matters of this sort, I would submit that any sober evaluation of the contribution of the national government to the improvement or the decline of civil liberty must conclude on the basis of the evidence to date with a decision in favor of federal intervention.

Anyone who cherishes the ideals of individual freedom and justice can never relax his efforts to push forward the frontiers of liberty. But the historian of civil liberty in the United States (though himself a civil libertarian who realizes that history can grant no absolution) has the obligation to assert the relative proposition that the contemporary American, despite the existence of a huge centralized state, is today free to enjoy a range of personal liberty unknown to his ancestors.

A Review of *Freedom's Fetters:*
The Alien and Sedition Laws and
American Civil Liberties
by James Morton Smith

Three times in the history of the Republic the American body politic has undergone what might be described as "acute circulatory crises." Each time—in 1800, 1860, and 1876—an entrenched political class, elite, or *politeuma*, was faced with the prospect of "circulating": of yielding its power to its political opponents; to opponents, moreover, whom it considered ideological enemies rather than mere rivals for office. Rather than falling into the usual pattern of American politics, the elections of these years were ideological confrontations: whichever perspective one took, he aligned himself with political Truth and peered over the barricades at the forces of Evil.

Civil war ensued from the refusal of the southern Democratic elite to circulate; massive economic and social bribery ended the deadlock of 1876; and in 1800 the plans of the Federalist fanatics foundered on the indomitable integrity of a man equally notable for his choleric pettiness, President John Adams. From a historical perspective the crisis of 1800 was probably the most ominous of the three, for the institutions of freedom could easily have died in the cradle. Yet, while shelves have been filled with Civil War studies, and an authoritative analysis of the crisis of 1876 has recently appeared,[1] the thrombosis that threatened the infant nation in the years 1796–1800 has yet to be adequately diagnosed.[2]

James Morton Smith's [3] fine study of the Alien and Sedition

Reprinted, with permission, from *Harvard Law Review*, Volume 70, Number 5, March, 1957, pages 946–950.

Acts and the peripheral legislation that accompanied them in the statute books has filled a great gap in our knowledge of the period.[4] His painstaking research, which has encompassed every conceivable aspect of the problem, is of a caliber that should bring kudos from even such masters of legal history as Howard Jay Graham and Charles Fairman. Like all good history, this book transports the reader back into the past, where, with the exercise of a little empathy, he can relive the desperate flailings of the Federalists, full of hubris and of contempt for the people who refused to recognize and honor virtue, and the desperation of the Jeffersonian attempts to counter the *coup d'état* that seemingly was in the offing, a desperation that led them in the Virginia and Kentucky Resolutions to plant the dragon seed of interposition.[5] One can hear Mr. Justice Chase bullying Jeffersonian counsel and visualize the predicament of the editor accused of sedition, confronted by a judge dedicated to the principle that seditions must not go unpunished and by a jury picked and packed by a Federalist United States marshal.

Smith has done exhaustive research on the passage and enforcement of the Sedition Act and has also discussed in detail the history of other xenophobic enactments, which were, however, of little practical consequence. I was particularly impressed by his analysis of the development of the Federalist doctrine of seditious libel, in which he indicates the extent to which the promulgators of the law leaned upon contemporary British practice. He has also entombed once for all (I hope) the myth that Alexander Hamilton was a "moderate" Federalist, that he "did coolheadedly oppose such hysterical transports as the Alien and Sedition Acts." [6]

While Hamilton was probably incapable of hysteria, and did not foam at the mouth at the thought of Jefferson, the *Aurora*, or the Irish, as did his cohorts, Robert Goodloe Harper, Harrison Gray Otis, or John Allen, it was because he was a far abler tactician than they. Hamilton realized that if the zealots overplayed their hand, a rebellion might occur, while if they played their cards coolly and deliberately they might in piecemeal fashion destroy the sources of Jeffersonian strength. With the Jefferson press muzzled, anti-Federalist militants (including congressmen) in jail for *lèse Adams*, a special electoral commission prepared to deliver the election of 1800 to the Federalist candidates, and a full-scale war with France to justify both the creation of a sizable standing army and the suppression of "domestik Jacobins," the seemingly inexorable movement of public opinion toward Jefferson might be checked once for all. No, Hamilton was no "moderate"; [7] indeed, the only first-line Federalist who emerged with clean hands from the period was John Marshall (p. 151).

The one piece of legislation that was vigorously implemented was the Sedition Act. Under its provisions a few individuals were prosecuted for their attacks on the Adams administration—for example, Thomas Cooper, Congressman Matthew Lyon, and Luther Baldwin—but the real impact of the statute was upon the anti-Federalist press. To understand the full implications of the Act, it is necessary briefly to examine the function of the press in the Federal period, indeed, in the whole era before the communications revolution. One searches the newspaper files of the period 1795–1800 in vain if he seeks an impartial journal; the papers were without exception militant partisan organs which served their readers with both *ex parte* interpretations of the events of the time and injunctions to mobilize against the political enemy. The typical circulation was small, but each copy might well pass through several sets of hands, be read aloud at a political-club meeting, and perhaps terminate its career posted in a public place outside a tavern for the curious to read. The press was, in short, the primary organ of political communication, and the leaders of both emergent factions utilized friendly journals to publicize their views and combat those of their opponents. Disputes often raged for months, as did, for example, the argument between Hamilton as "Pacificus" and Madison as "Helvidius" over the constitutionality of the 1793 Proclamation of Neutrality. Jefferson was extremely conscious of the power of the press, and in this instance urged Madison to take up the cudgels against Hamilton lest the latter's views gain public acceptance.

By 1796 each faction had its outstanding journal: the Federalists, John Fenno's *Gazette of the United States;* the Jeffersonians, Benjamin Franklin Bache's *Aurora*—published in Philadelphia, the seat of the government. These papers served as ideological bellwethers, their articles being widely republished in lesser factional papers throughout the country. The level of political controversy was uniformly low: the Jeffersonian journals never missed an opportunity to refer to Colonel Hamilton as a self-confessed adulterer, while the Federalist editors treated Vice-President Jefferson as a French agent and subversive atheist. A successful editor such as Fenno or Bache was a master of calumny, while the Federalist editor William Cobbett and the anti-Federalist James T. Callender were unbelievably vituperative even by the lax standards of that day. On neither side of the ideological fence was there any respect for truth or decency.

But while the Federalists smarted under the indictment they received from the *Aurora* and its allies, their discontent had deeper roots than mere chagrin. From the Federalist viewpoint, watching their national electoral strength dwindle while anti-Federalism was burgeoning, it was clear that public defection was a direct consequence of meretricious Jeffersonian propaganda which had seduced simple, naïve people from the path of political righteousness. The Jeffersonian press, they realized, was the cutting edge of the party blade which must be blunted if Federalism was to survive. Moreover, suppression of the anti-Federalist organs would have the additional merit of destroying the opposition's communication net, its coordinating mechanism, for no longer could the "party line" be disseminated from the chief journals to subsidiary papers and to party cadres throughout the nation.

Even before the Sedition Act went into effect, a common-law prosecution was lodged in federal court against Bache and the *Aurora*. Before the unhappy business was ended, every leading Jeffersonian editor, and several lesser lights as well, had been haled into federal court to answer for his seditions. By way of comparison it should be noted that no legal action was instigated against those papers which confined their abuse to the Vice-President and his friends, though an impartial observer can discover no legal distinction between the obloquy heaped on Jefferson by Fenno and Cobbett and that directed at Adams by Bache, Callender, and William Duane.

In a broad sense, although several Jeffersonian papers were destroyed, suppression was a failure. Indeed, if anything, the government's legal actions seemed to drive the prosecuted editors, both in jail and out, to new heights of abusiveness. More significantly, the prosecutions, by arousing intense public sympathy for the accused, worked to the political disadvantage of the Federalists. Yet this failure should not hide the fact that this attempt at suppression, and its companion legislation both enacted and contemplated, is unique in our history. The Federalist program was qualitatively different from the anti-Communist legislation that currently fattens the statute books: the former was aimed at eliminating a major-party opposition, while the latter is directed at a minute minority in American society. Thus, I submit, the Federalist program did not raise a civil-liberty issue in the usual sense of the phrase; on the contrary, it was a revolutionary effort to put the opposition out of business and to create a one-party state under the beneficent aegis of "the wise and good and rich."

My only real complaint about *Freedom's Fetters* is that Smith at no point really draws in the full context of Federalist actions. He is quite aware that the Alien and Sedition Acts were part of a revolutionary strategy—in fact, all the points made above are made by him somewhere in his book. Specifically, it seems to me unfortunate that he devotes his final chapter to a superficial discussion of the impact of the Alien and Sedition Acts on the American tradition rather than to a full examination of the framework within which they were designed to operate and the function they were planned to fulfill.

As a consequence of his narrow perspective, Smith has, I suggest, done John Adams a grievous injustice. Viewed only in the context of the Sedition Act, President Adams appears as a traitor to the principles upon which he and his generation founded the Republic—as a petty, vindictive man who was prepared to stifle a free press for the greater glorification of his ego. Now, within limits this is valid: Adams was a vain, splenetic, pompous little martinet who writhed under the slightest criticism. But when the chips were down and the future of our free institutions was in the balance, Adams demonstrated that beneath that inordinate ego and pouter-pigeon comportment there remained an iron core of democratic conviction. By rejecting Hamilton's war with France and by firing Hamilton's lackey, Secretary of State Timothy Pickering, Adams split his party and guaranteed a Jeffersonian victory in 1800. Yet his knowledge that this was a certain consequence of his action in no way stayed his hand, for the Adams wing of the Federalist elite was willing to circulate. This, while hardly justifying a full pardon for his unseemly role in the Sedition Act prosecutions, surely warrants a mitigation of the sentence that Smith has laid upon him.

Aside from this—and a pair of technical complaints about his remarks on the Naturalization Act of 1798 [8]—I think Smith has turned in a remarkable performance. If his forthcoming study of the Virginia and Kentucky Resolutions matches the caliber of this work, it seems probable that we shall at last have a definitive study of the political metabolism of the Federal period.

NOTES

1. Director of Publications, Institute of Early American History and Culture, Williamsburg, Va.

2. C. Vann Woodward, *Reunion and Reaction* (1951).

3. The best single study is Manning J. Dauer, *The Adams Federalists* (1953).

4. See John Miller, *Crisis in Freedom* (1951), for a popular treatment of the Alien and Sedition Acts which, though useful, is not adequate for scholarly purposes.

5. I have used "interposition" rather than "nullification" here because it seems clear to me that these resolutions did not pretend to reach as far as nullification. See Arthur Miller and Ronald Howell, "Interposition, Nullification and the Delicate Division of Power in a Federal System," *Journal of Public Law*, Vol. 5 (1956), pp. 2, 12-13.

6. Robert G. McCloskey, "Conservatives, Businessmen, and Blath-

erskites," *Harvard Business Review*, Sept.–Oct., 1956, p. 41.

7. J. M. Smith has handled this problem most concisely in his article "Alexander Hamilton, the Alien Law, and Seditious Libels," *Review of Politics*, Vol. 16 (1954), p. 305. The material in this article is used at various points in the book. See also C. Rossiter, *Conservatism in America* (1955), for a perceptive discussion of the subject.

8. J. M. Smith suggests that the Naturalization Act of 1798, which established a fourteen-year-residence requirement, acted as an automatic curb on the franchise. "[T]his restriction on the enfranchisement of immigrants dealt the Democratic-Republican party a heavy blow by robbing it of an important element of its support" (p. 34). I can find no evidence to support this contention, and since the states had the right to establish their own fran-

chise requirements, usually based on state citizenship with varying but generally brief residence periods as a prerequisite, disfranchisement was in no sense automatic. See John P. Roche, *Early Development of United States Citizenship* (1949), pp. 12–13. Furthermore, Smith seems confused about the citizenship status of Albert Gallatin. While Gallatin was barred from taking his seat in the Senate in 1793 on the spurious ground that he had not been a citizen for nine years, in fact, he—and for that matter Alexander Hamilton —was by 1796 a full citizen, qualified under the Constitution even for the high office of President of the United States. Both were citizens of the United States at the time the new Republic was launched, and Hamilton had become a resident of New York in 1772, while Gallatin arrived in Massachusetts in 1780, so each had fulfilled the fourteen-year residence required of Presidents by the Constitution.

A Review of *The Lean Years:*
A Philosophy of the
American Worker, 1920-1933
by Irving Bernstein

The 1930's—the Era of Roosevelt—have attracted the attention of countless commentators and historians. There was a dynamism about the New Deal and a charismatic elusiveness about its central figure which have stimulated such cogent and provocative studies as Arthur Schlesinger, Jr.'s, *Age of Roosevelt* (also known as *Summa Contra Republicanos*), Mario Einaudi's *Roosevelt Revolution*, and James M. Burns's *Roosevelt: The Lion and the Fox*. In a sense, art has reflected life: A turbulent and paradoxical period has received evocative and vigorous delineation.

The 1920's, in contrast, have traditionally received the historical brushoff. To the extent that historians of the New Deal discuss the previous decade, they tend to treat it as the first act of a medieval passion play. Satan and his imps run rampant over the forces of righteousness, but—as the curtain drops—are seen quaking at the sound of a distant trumpet. To put it another way, the twenties are treated schematically as the prelude to the thirties rather than integrally on their own merits. This is a common and legitimate historical technique, but it has led to an unfortunate gap with respect to a crucial decade in the history of modern America.

Irving Bernstein has written a superb book which goes a long way toward filling this gap. Although the analytical viewpoint is narrow—Bernstein adheres rightly to his purpose of presenting, as it were, the worm's-eye view of American society—the book is something of a *tour de force*. It is as if we had a view of the

Reprinted, with permission, from *The New Leader*, January 23, 1961.

pre–Civil War South from the viewpoint of a slave, or a history of the Indian Wars written by an articulate Sioux. In effect, one enters a different world, a universe literally standing on its head. From the vantage point of 1960, the twenties *were* the first act in a great drama of liberal reform and social redemption; viewed from the bottom of the contemporary heap, the twenties were an age of hate, disaster, and repression totally lacking in omens of impending succor.

This was a terrible decade, one of acute social dislocation and violent conflict. In the period between the end of World War I and the Great Depression, the whole value structure of rural, pre-industrial America collided with the dingy realities of an urban, industrial society. The 1920 Census was the watershed: For the first time more Americans lived in cities than in the expanses of rural, agricultural terrain. And the ancient masters of the house took arms both literally and figuratively to put down the upstart, often foreign, invaders, and restore the pristine vision of small-town, white, Anglo-Saxon, Protestant America. The consequences? The Ku Klux Klan, the Palmer Raids, Sacco-Vanzetti, immigration restriction, the Scopes Trial, the campaign of 1928, Prohibition, the American Plan, and the yellow-dog contract.

It was a savage decade, one that left a permanent impression on the young who fought back. The intellectuals of the twenties, and those who then were molded, carried or will carry the impress to their graves. Contrast the cliché-ridden intellectual collectivity of the thirties with the prophets or products of the twenties: the vitalism of Hemingway, the bitter-sweet alienation of F. Scott Fitzgerald, the ferocious iconoclasm of Robert M. Hutchins (in some ways a character from the pen of Fitzgerald), the intellectual freebooting of Max Eastman, the libertarian passion of John Dos Passos. The men of the twenties lusted for life and experience; the men of the thirties itched for power and status. The men of the twenties fought; the men of the thirties organized.

Irving Bernstein has chronicled in masterly detail the inept, tragic saga of the suppression of the American worker by the masters of the American economy. It is, stripped of its human implications, an ironic story, a parody of the "American way." The bosses, operating as if they had received their instructions, their historical compass, from Karl Marx himself, insisting on their absolute right to treat labor as a commodity; the workers, in contrast, taking licking after licking, but refusing to commit their destiny to a radical political or industrial movement, still believing in their hearts that injustice could not triumph in a free country. There was violence (*The New Republic* in 1931 listed 3 miners killed, 55 hospitalized, and over 2,000 gassed, injured, or wounded in recent Pennsylvania coal disputes); there was pathos (the flag-waving veterans of the Bonus Army viewing with stunned disbelief the Army deploying against them); but somehow the country held together. The revolutionaries, who had a first-class brief for revolution, never really got to first base. (If Bernstein had seen Theodore Draper's *American Communism and Soviet Russia*, his discussion of the failure of the radicals would have profited—he does not appreciate the degree to which the radical thrust was weakened by left-wing factionalism.)

This volume ends with the American workers sunk in the Great Depression, the unions broken and powerless, the authority of the state and the condition of the economy massed against them. An old order was moribund and incapable of governing in any positive sense; a new order was yet to be born. Those who have read the last chapter of the mystery know the outcome (which can easily be made inevitable by the application of some retrospective omniscience); the great virtue of Bernstein's book is that throughout he writes as if he really did not know of the ineluctable Happy Ending.

II. The Theory and Practice of American Constitutionalism

The Founding Fathers:
A Reform Caucus in Action

Over the last century and a half, the work of the Constitutional Convention and the motives of the Founding Fathers have been analyzed under a number of different ideological auspices. To one generation of historians, the hand of God was moving in the assembly; under a later dispensation, the dialectic (at various levels of philosophical sophistication) replaced the Deity: "relationships of production" moved into the niche previously reserved for Love of Country. Thus, in counterpoint to the Zeitgeist, the Framers have undergone miraculous metamorphoses: at one time acclaimed as liberals and bold social engineers, today they appear in the guise of sound Burkean conservatives, men who in our time would subscribe to *Fortune*, look to Walter Lippmann for political theory, and chuckle patronizingly at the antics of Barry Goldwater. The implicit assumption is that if James Madison were among us, he would be President of the Ford Foundation, while Alexander Hamilton would chair the Committee for Economic Development.

The "Fathers" have thus been admitted to our best circles; the revolutionary ferocity which confiscated all Tory property in reach and populated New Brunswick with outlaws has been converted by the "Miltown School" of American historians into a benign dedication to "consensus" and "prescriptive rights." The Daughters of the American Revolution have, through the ministrations of Professors Boorstin, Hartz, and Rossiter, at last found

Reprinted, with permission, from *The American Political Science Review,* Volume LV, Number 4, December, 1961, pages 799–816.

ancestors worthy of their descendants. It is not my purpose here
to argue that the "Fathers" were, in fact, radical revolutionaries;
that proposition has been brilliantly demonstrated by Robert R.
Palmer in his *Age of the Democratic Revolution*. My concern
is with the further position that not only were they revolutionaries; they were also democrats. Indeed, in my view, there is one
fundamental truth about the Founding Fathers that *every* generation of Zeitgeisters has done its best to obscure: they were
first and foremost superb democratic politicians. I suspect that
in a contemporary setting, James Madison would be Speaker of
the House of Representatives and Hamilton would be the *émi-
nence grise* dominating (*pace* Theodore Sorenson or Sherman
Adams) the Executive Office of the President. They were, with
their colleagues, *political men*—not metaphysicians, disembodied
conservatives or Agents of History—and as recent research into
the nature of American politics in the 1780's confirms,[1] they were
committed (perhaps willy-nilly) to working within the democratic framework, within a universe of public approval. Charles
Beard *and* the filiopietists to the contrary notwithstanding, the
Philadelphia Convention was not a College of Cardinals or a
council of Platonic guardians working within a manipulative,
predemocratic framework; it was a *nationalist* reform caucus
which had to operate with great delicacy and skill in a political
cosmos full of enemies to achieve the one definitive goal—popular
approbation.

Perhaps the time has come, to borrow Walton Hamilton's fine
phrase, to raise the Framers from immortality to mortality, to
give them credit for their magnificent demonstration of the art
of democratic politics. The point must be reemphasized; they
made history, and did it within the limits of consensus. There was
nothing inevitable about the future in 1787; the *Zeitgeist*, that
fine Hegelian technique of begging causal questions, could be
discerned only in retrospect. What they did was to hammer out
a pragmatic compromise which would both bolster the "national
interest" and be acceptable to the people. What inspiration they
got came from their collective experience as professional politicians in a democratic society. As John Dickinson put it to his

fellow delegates on August 13th: "Experience must be our guide. Reason may mislead us."

In this context, let us examine the problems they confronted and the solutions they evolved. The Convention has been described picturesquely as a counterrevolutionary junta and the Constitution as a *coup d'état*,[2] but this has been accomplished by withdrawing the whole history of the movement for constitutional reform from its true context. No doubt the goals of the constitutional elite were "subversive" to the existing political order, but it is overlooked that their subversion could have succeeded only if the people of the United States endorsed it by regularized procedures. Indubitably they were "plotting" to establish a much stronger central government than existed under the Articles, but only in the sense in which one could argue equally well that John F. Kennedy was, from 1956 to 1960, "plotting" to become President. In short, on the fundamental *procedural* level, the Constitutionalists had to work according to the prevailing rules of the game. Whether they liked it or not is a topic for spiritualists—and is irrelevant: one may be quite certain that had Washington agreed to play the De Gaulle (as the Cincinnati once urged), Hamilton would willingly have held his horse, but such fertile speculation in no way alters the actual context in which events took place.

[1]

When the Constitutionalists went forth to subvert the Confederation, they utilized the mechanisms of political legitimacy. And the roadblocks which confronted them were formidable. At the same time, they were endowed with certain potent political assets. The history of the United States from 1786 to 1790 was largely one of a masterful employment of political expertise by the Constitutionalists as against bumbling, erratic behavior by the opponents of reform. Effectively, the Constitutionalists had to induce the states, by democratic techniques of coercion, to emasculate themselves. To be specific, if New York had refused to join the new Union, the project was doomed; yet before New York was safely in, the reluctant state legislature had *sua sponte* to take the following steps: (1) agree to send delegates to the Philadelphia Convention; (2) provide maintenance for these delegates (these were distinct stages: New Hampshire was early in naming delegates, but did not provide for their maintenance until July); (3) set up the special *ad hoc* convention to decide on ratification; and (4) concede to the decision of the *ad hoc* convention that New York should participate. New York admittedly was a tricky state, with a strong interest in a *status quo* which permitted her to exploit New Jersey and Connecticut, but the same legal hurdles existed in every state. And at the risk of becoming boring, it must be reiterated that the *only* weapon in the Constitutionalist arsenal was an effective mobilization of public opinion.

The group which undertook this struggle was an interesting amalgam of a few dedicated nationalists with the self-interested spokesmen of various parochial bailiwicks. The Georgians, for example, wanted a strong central authority to provide military protection for their huge, underpopulated state against the Creek Confederacy; Jerseymen and Connecticuters wanted to escape from economic bondage to New York; the Virginians hoped to establish a system which would give that great state its rightful place in the councils of the republic. The dominant figures in the politics of these states therefore cooperated in the call for the Convention.[3] In other states, the thrust toward national reform was taken up by opposition groups who added the "national interest" to their weapons system; in Pennsylvania, for instance, the group fighting to revise the Constitution of 1776 came out foursquare behind the Constitutionalists, and in New York, Hamilton and the Schuyler ambience took the same tack against George Clinton.[4] There was, of course, a large element of personality in the affair: there is reason to suspect that Patrick Henry's opposition to the Convention and the Constitution was founded on his conviction that Jefferson was behind both, and a close study of local politics elsewhere would surely reveal that others supported the Constitution for the simple (and politically quite sufficient) reason that the "wrong" people were against it.

To say this is not to suggest that the Constitution rested on a foundation of impure or base motives. It is rather to argue that in politics there are no immaculate conceptions and that in the drive for a stronger general government, motives of all sorts played a part. Few men in the history of mankind have espoused a view of the "common good" or "public interest" that militated against their private status; even Plato with all his reverence for disembodied reason managed to put philosophers on top of the pile. Thus it is not surprising that a number of diversified private interests joined to push the nationalist public interest; what would have been surprising was the absence of such a pragmatic united front. And the fact remains that, however motivated, these men did demonstrate a willingness to compromise their parochial interests in behalf of an ideal which took shape before their eyes and under their ministrations.

As Stanley Elkins and Eric McKitrick have suggested in a perceptive essay,[5] what distinguished the leaders of the Constitutionalist caucus from their enemies was a "Continental" approach to political, economic and military issues. To the extent that they shared an institutional base of operations, it was the Continental Congress (thirty-nine of the delegates to the Federal Convention had served in Congress),[6] and this was hardly a locale which inspired respect for the state governments. Robert de Jouvenal observed French politics half a century ago and noted that a revolutionary deputy had more in common with a nonrevolutionary deputy than he had with a revolutionary nondeputy;[7] similarly one can surmise that membership in the Congress under the Articles of Confederation worked to establish a Continental frame of reference, that a congressman from Pennsylvania and one from South Carolina would share a universe of discourse which provided them with a conceptual common denominator *vis à vis* their respective state legislatures. This was particularly true with respect to external affairs: the average state legislator was probably about as concerned with foreign policy then as he is today, but congressmen were constantly forced to take the broad view of American prestige, were compelled to listen to the reports of Secretary John Jay and to the dispatches and pleas from their frustrated envoys in Britain, France, and Spain.[8] From considerations such as these, a "Continental" ideology developed which seems to have demanded a revision of our domestic institutions primarily on the ground that only by invigorating our general government could we assume our rightful place in the international arena. Indeed, an argument with great force—particularly since Washington was its incarnation—urged that our very survival in the Hobbesian jungle of world politics depended upon a reordering and strengthening of our national sovereignty.[9]

Note that I am not endorsing the "Critical Period" thesis; on the contrary, Merrill Jensen seems to me quite sound in his view that for most Americans, engaged as they were in self-sustaining agriculture, the "Critical Period" was not particularly critical.[10] In fact, the great achievement of the Constitutionalists was their ultimate success in convincing the elected representatives of a majority of the white male population that change was imperative. A small group of political leaders with a Continental vision and essentially a consciousness of the United States' *international* impotence, provided the matrix of the movement. To their standard other leaders rallied with their own parallel ambitions. Their great assets were (1) the presence in their caucus of the one authentic American "father figure," George Washington, whose prestige was enormous;[11] (2) the energy and talent of their leadership (in which one must include the towering intellectuals of the time, John Adams and Thomas Jefferson, despite their absence abroad); and their communications "network," which was far superior to anything on the opposition side;[12] (3) the preemptive skill which made "their" issue The Issue and kept the locally oriented opposition permanently on the defensive; and (4) the subjective consideration that these men were spokesmen of a new and compelling credo: *American* nationalism, that ill-defined but nonetheless potent sense of collective purpose that emerged from the American Revolution.

Despite great institutional handicaps, the Constitutionalists managed in the mid-1780's to mount an offensive which gained momentum as years went by. Their greatest problem was lethargy, and paradoxically, the number of barriers in their path may have proved an advantage in the long run. Beginning with the initial battle to get the Constitutional Convention called and delegates appointed, they could never relax, never let up the pressure. In practical terms, this meant that the local "organizations" created by the Constitutionalists were perpetually in movement building up their cadres for the next fight. (The word "organization" has to be used with great caution: a political organization in the United States—as in contemporary England [13] —generally consisted of a magnate and his following, or a coalition of magnates. This did not necessarily mean that it was "undemocratic" or "aristocratic," in the Aristotelian sense of the word: while a few magnates such as the Livingstons could draft their followings, most exercised their leadership without coercion on the basis of popular endorsement. The absence of organized opposition did not imply the impossibility of competition any more than low public participation in elections necessarily indicated an undemocratic suffrage.)

The Constitutionalists got the jump on the "opposition" (a collective noun: opposition*s* would be more correct) at the outset with the demand for a Convention. Their opponents were caught in an old political trap: they were not being asked to approve any specific program of reform, but only to endorse a meeting to discuss and recommend needed reforms. If they took a hard line at the first stage, they were put in the position of glorifying the *status quo* and of denying the need for *any* changes. Moreover, the Constitutionalists could go to the people with a persuasive argument for "fair play"—"How can you condemn reform before you know precisely what is involved?" Since the state legislatures obviously would have the final say on any proposals that might emerge from the Convention, the Constitutionalists were merely reasonable men asking for a chance. Besides, since they did not make any concrete proposals at that stage, they were in a position to capitalize on every sort of generalized discontent with the Confederation.

Perhaps because of their poor intelligence system, perhaps because of overconfidence generated by the failure of all previous efforts to alter the Articles,[14] the opposition awoke too late to the dangers that confronted them in 1787. Not only did the Constitutionalists manage to get every state but Rhode Island (where politics was enlivened by a party system reminiscent of the "Blues" and the "Greens" in the Byzantine Empire) [15] to appoint delegates to Philadelphia, but when the results were in, it appeared that they dominated the delegations. Given the apathy of the opposition, this was a natural phenomenon: in an ideologically nonpolarized political atmosphere, those who get appointed to a special committee are likely to be the men who supported the movement for its creation. Even George Clinton, who seems to have been the first opposition leader to awake to the possibility of trouble, could not prevent the New York Legislature from appointing Alexander Hamilton—though he did have the foresight to send two of his henchmen to dominate the delegation. Incidentally, much has been made of the fact that the delegates to Philadelphia were not elected by the people; some have adduced this fact as evidence of the "undemocratic" character of the gathering. But put in the context of the time, this argument is wholly specious: the central government under the Articles was considered a creature of the component states; and in all the states but Rhode Island, Connecticut, and New Hampshire, members of the national Congress were chosen by the state legislatures. This was not a consequence of elitism or fear of the mob; it was a logical extension of states'-rights doctrine to guarantee that the national institution did not end-run the state legislatures and make direct contact with the people.[16]

[2]

With delegations safely named, the focus shifted to Philadelphia. While waiting for a quorum to assemble, James Madison got busy and drafted the so-called Randolph or Virginia Plan with the aid of the Virginia delegation. This was a political masterstroke. Its consequence was that once business got under way, the framework of discussion was established on Madison's terms. There was no interminable argument over agenda; instead the delegates took the Virginia Resolutions—"just for purposes of discussion"—as their point of departure. And along with Madison's proposals, many of which were buried in the course of the summer, went his major premise: a new start on a Constitution rather than piecemeal amendment. This was not necessarily revolutionary—a little exegesis could demonstrate that a new Constitution might be formulated as "amendments" to the Articles of Confederation—but Madison's proposal that this "lump sum" amendment go into effect after approval by nine states (the Articles required unanimous state approval for any amendment) was thoroughly subversive.[17]

Standard treatments of the Convention divide the delegates into "nationalists" and "states'-righters," with various improvised shadings ("moderate nationalists," and so on), but these are *a posteriori* categories which obfuscate more than they clarify. What is striking to one who analyzes the Convention as a case study in democratic politics is the lack of clear-cut ideological divisions in the Convention. Indeed, I submit that the evidence —Madison's *Notes*, the correspondence of the delegates, and debates on ratification—indicates that this was a remarkably homogeneous body on the ideological level. Yates and Lansing, Clinton's two chaperons for Hamilton, left in disgust on July 10th. (Is there anything more tedious than sitting through endless disputes on matters one deems fundamentally misconceived? It takes an iron will to spend a hot summer as an ideological *agent provocateur*.) Luther Martin, Maryland's bibulous narcissist, left on September 4th in a huff when he discovered that others did not share his self-esteem; others went home for personal reasons. But the hard core of delegates accepted a grinding regimen throughout the attrition of a Philadelphia summer precisely because they shared the Constitutionalist goal.

Basic differences of opinion emerged, of course, but these were not ideological; they were *structural*. If the so-called "states'-rights" group had not accepted the fundamental purposes of the Convention, they could simply have pulled out and by doing so have aborted the whole enterprise. Instead of bolting, they returned day after day to argue and to compromise. An interesting symbol of this basic homogeneity was the initial agreement on secrecy: these professional politicians did not want to become prisoners of publicity; they wanted to retain that freedom of maneuver which is possible only when men are not forced to take public stands in the preliminary stages of negotiation.[18] There was no legal means of binding the tongues of the delegates: at any stage in the game a delegate with basic principled objections to the emerging project could have taken the stump (as Luther Martin did after his exit) and denounced the Convention to the skies. Yet Madison did not even inform Thomas Jefferson in Paris of the course of the deliberations,[19] and available correspondence indicates that the delegates generally observed the injunction. Secrecy is certainly uncharacteristic of any assembly marked by strong ideological polarization. This was noted at the time: the *New York Daily Advertiser*, August 14, 1787, commented that the ". . . profound secrecy hitherto observed by the Convention [we consider] a happy omen, as it demonstrates that the spirit of party on any great and essential point cannot have arisen to any height." [20]

Commentators on the Constitution who have read *The Federalist* in lieu of reading the actual debates have credited the Fathers with the invention of a sublime concept called "Federalism." [21] Unfortunately, *The Federalist* is probative evidence for only one proposition: that Hamilton and Madison were inspired propagandists with a genius for retrospective symmetry. Federalism, as the theory is generally defined, was an improvisation which was later promoted into a political theory. Experts on "Federalism" should take to heart the advice of David Hume, who warned in his *Of the Rise and Progress of the Arts and Sciences* that ". . . there is no subject in which we must proceed with more caution than in [history], lest we assign causes which never existed and reduce what is merely contingent to stable and universal principles." In any event, the final balance in the Constitution between the states and the nation must have come as a great disappointment to Madison, while Hamilton's unitary views are too well known to need elucidation.

It is indeed astonishing how those who have glibly designated James Madison the "father" of Federalism have overlooked the solid body of fact which indicates that he shared Hamilton's quest for a unitary central government. To be specific, they have avoided examining the clear import of the Madison-Virginia Plan,[22] and have disregarded Madison's dogged inch-by-inch retreat from the bastions of centralization. The Virginia Plan envisioned a unitary national government effectively freed from and dominant over the states. The lower house of the national legislature was to be elected directly by the people of the states with membership proportional to population. The upper house was to be selected by the lower, and the two chambers would elect the executive and choose the judges. The national government would be thus cut completely loose from the states.[23]

The structure of the general government was freed from state control in a truly radical fashion, but the scope of the authority of the national sovereign as Madison initially formulated it was breathtaking—it was a formulation worthy of the Sage of Malmesbury himself. The national legislature was to be empowered to disallow the acts of state legislatures,[24] and the central government was vested, in addition to the powers of the nation under the Articles of Confederation, with plenary authority wherever ". . . the separate States are incompetent or in which the harmony of the United States may be interrupted by the exercise of individual legislation." [25] Finally, just to lock the door against state intrusion, the national Congress was to be given the power to use military force on recalcitrant states.[26] This was Madison's "model" of an ideal national government, though it later received little publicity in *The Federalist*.

The interesting thing was the reaction of the Convention to this militant program for a strong autonomous central government. Some delegates were startled, some obviously leery of so comprehensive a project of reform,[27] but nobody set off any fireworks and nobody walked out. Moreover, in the two weeks that followed, the Virginia Plan received substantial endorsement *en principe*; the initial temper of the gathering can be deduced from the approval "without debate or dissent," on May 31st, of the Sixth Resolution, which granted Congress the authority to disallow state legislation ". . . contravening *in its opinion* the Articles of Union." Indeed, an amendment was included to bar states from contravening national treaties.[28]

The Virginia Plan may therefore be considered, in ideological terms, as the delegates' Utopia, but as the discussions continued and became more specific, many of those present began to have second thoughts. After all, they were not residents of Utopia or guardians in Plato's Republic who could simply impose a philosophical ideal on subordinate strata of the population. They were practical politicians in a democratic society, and no matter what their private dreams might be, they had to take home an acceptable package and defend it—and their own political futures—against predictable attack. On June 14th the breaking point between dream and reality took place. Apparently realizing that under the Virginia Plan, Massachusetts, Virginia, and Pennsylvania could virtually dominate the national government—and probably appreciating that to sell this program to the "folks back home" would be impossible—the delegates from the small states dug in their heels and demanded time for a consideration of alternatives. One gets a graphic sense of the inner politics from John Dickinson's reproach to Madison: "You see the consequences of pushing things too far. Some of the members from the small States wish for two branches in the General Legislature and are friends to a good National Government; but we would sooner submit to a foreign power than . . . be deprived of an equality of suffrage in both branches of the Legislature, and thereby be thrown under the domination of the large States." [29]

The bare outline of the *Journal* entry for Tuesday, June 14th, is suggestive to anyone with extensive experience in deliberative bodies. "It was moved by Mr. Patterson [*sic*, Paterson's name was one of those consistently misspelled by Madison and everybody else] seconded by Mr. Randolph that the further consideration of the report from the Committee of the whole House [endorsing the Virginia Plan] be postponed til tomorrow, and before the question for postponement was taken. It was moved by Mr. Randolph seconded by Mr. Patterson that the House adjourn." [30] The House adjourned by obvious prearrangement of the two principals: since the preceding Saturday when David Brearley and Paterson of New Jersey had announced their fundamental discontent with the representational features of the Virginia Plan, the informal pressure had certainly been building up to slow down the steamroller. Doubtless there were extended arguments at the Indian Queen between Madison and Paterson, the latter insisting that events were moving rapidly toward a probably disastrous conclusion, toward a political suicide pact. Now the process of accommodation was put into action smoothly

—and wisely, given the character and strength of the doubters. Madison had the votes, but this was one of those situations where the enforcement of mechanical majoritarianism could easily have destroyed the objectives of the majority: the Constitutionalists were in quest of a qualitative as well as a quantitative consensus. This was hardly from deference to local Quaker custom; it was a political imperative if they were to attain ratification.

[3]

According to the standard script, at this point the "states'-rights" group intervened in force behind the New Jersey Plan, which has been characteristically portrayed as a reversion to the *status quo* under the Articles of Confederation with but minor modifications. A careful examination of the evidence indicates that only in a marginal sense is this an accurate description. It is true that the New Jersey Plan put the states back into the institutional picture, but one could argue that to do so was a recognition of political reality rather than an affirmation of states' rights. A serious case can be made that the advocates of the New Jersey Plan, far from being ideological addicts of states' rights, intended to substitute for the Virginia Plan a system which would both retain strong national power and have a chance of adoption in the states. The leading spokesman for the project asserted quite clearly that his views were based more on counsels of expediency than on principle; said Paterson on June 16th: "I came here not to speak my own sentiments, but the sentiments of those who sent me. Our object is not such a Governmt. as may be best in itself, but such a one as our Constituents have authorized us to prepare, and as they will approve." [31] This is Madison's version; in Yates's transcription, there is a crucial sentence following the remarks above: "I believe that a little practical virtue is to be preferred to the finest theoretical principles, which cannot be carried into effect." [32] In his preliminary speech on June 9th, Paterson had stated ". . . to the public mind we must accommodate ourselves," [33] and in his notes for this and his later effort as well, the emphasis is the same. The *structure* of government under the Articles should be retained:

   2. Because it accords with the Sentiments of the People
     [Proof:] 1. Coms. [Commissions from state legislatures defining
            the jurisdiction of the delegates]
          2. News-papers—Political Barometer. Jersey never
            would have sent Delegates under the first [Virginia]
            Plan—
Not here to sport Opinions of my own. Wt. [What] can be done.
A little practicable Virtue preferrable to Theory.[34]

This was a defense of political acumen, not of states' rights. In fact, Paterson's notes of his speech can easily be construed as an argument for attaining the substantive objectives of the Virginia Plan by a sound political route, that is, pouring the new wine into the old bottles. With a shrewd eye, Paterson queried:

Will the Operation and Force of the [central] Govt. depend upon the mode of Representn.—No—it will depend upon the Quantum of Power lodged in the leg. ex. and judy. Departments—Give [the existing] Congress the same Powers that you intend to give the two Branches, [under the Virginia Plan] and I apprehend they will act with as much Propriety and more Energy. . . .[35]

In other words, the advocates of the New Jersey Plan concentrated their fire on what they held to be the *political liabilities* of the Virginia Plan—which were matters of institutional structure—rather than on the proposed scope of national authority. Indeed, the Supremacy Clause of the Constitution first saw the light of day in Paterson's Sixth Resolution; the New Jersey Plan contemplated the use of military force to secure compliance with national law; and finally Paterson made clear his view that under either the Virginia or the New Jersey systems, the general government would ". . . act on individuals and not on states." [36] From the states'-rights viewpoint, this was heresy: the fundament of that doctrine was the proposition that any central government had as its constituents the states, not the people, and could reach the people only through the agency of the state government.

Paterson then reopened the agenda of the Convention, but he did so within a distinctly nationalist framework. Paterson's position was one of favoring a strong central government in principle, but opposing one which in fact *put the big states in the saddle*. (The Virginia Plan, for all its abstract merits, did very well by Virginia.) As evidence for this speculation, there is a curious and intriguing proposal among Paterson's preliminary drafts of the New Jersey Plan:

Whereas it is necessary in Order to form the People of the U.S. of America in to a Nation, that the States should be consolidated, by which means all the Citizens thereof will become equally intitled to and will equally participate in the same Privileges and Rights. . . . it is therefore resolved, that all the Lands contained within the Limits of each state individually, and of the U.S. generally be considered as constituting one Body or Mass, and be divided into thirteen or more integral parts.

Resolved, That such Divisions or integral Parts shall be styled Districts.[37]

This makes it sound as though Paterson was prepared to accept a strong unified central government along the lines of the Virginia Plan if the existing states were eliminated. He may have got the idea from his New Jersey colleague Judge David Brearley, who on June 9th had commented that the only remedy to the dilemma over representation was ". . . that a map of the U. S. be spread out, that all the existing boundaries be erased, and that a new partition of the whole be made into 13 equal parts."[38] According to Yates, Brearley added at this point, ". . . then a government on the present [Virginia Plan] system will be just."[39]

This proposition was never pushed—it was patently unrealistic—but one can appreciate its purpose: it would have separated the men from the boys in the large-state delegations. How attached would the Virginians have been to their reform principles if Virginia were to disappear as a component geographical unit (the largest) for representational purposes? Up to this point, the Virginians had been in the happy position of supporting high ideals with that inner confidence born of knowledge that the "public interest" they endorsed would nourish their private interest. Worse, they had shown little willingness to compromise. Now the delegates from the small states announced that they were unprepared to be offered up as sacrificial victims to a "national interest" which reflected Virginia's parochial ambition. Caustic Charles Pinckney was not far off when he remarked sardonically that ". . . the whole [conflict] comes to this: Give N. Jersey an equal vote, and she will dismiss her scruples, and concur in the Natl. system." [40] What he rather unfairly did not add was that the Jersey delegates were not free agents who could adhere to their private convictions; they had to take back, sponsor, and risk their reputations on the reforms approved by the Convention—and in New Jersey, not in Virginia.

Paterson spoke on Saturday, and one can surmise that over the weekend there was a good deal of consultation, argument, and caucusing among the delegates. One member at least prepared a full-length address: on Monday, Alexander Hamilton, previously mute, rose and delivered a six-hour oration.[41] It was a remarkably apolitical speech; the gist of his position was that *both* the Virginia and New Jersey plans were inadequately centralist, and he detailed a reform program which was reminiscent of the Protectorate under the Cromwellian *Instrument of Government* of 1653. It has been suggested that Hamilton did this in the best political tradition to emphasize the moderate character of the Virginia Plan,[42] to give the cautious delegates something *really* to worry about; but this interpretation seems somehow too clever, particularly since the sentiments Hamilton expressed happened to be completely consistent with those he privately —and sometimes publicly—expressed throughout his life. He wanted, to take a striking phrase from a letter to George Washington, a "strong well mounted government"; [43] in essence, the Hamilton Plan contemplated an elected life monarch, virtually free of public control, on the Hobbesian ground that only in this fashion could strength and stability be achieved. The other alternatives, he argued, would put policy-making at the mercy of the passions of the mob; only if the sovereign was beyond the reach of selfish influence would it be possible to have government in the interests of the whole community.[44]

From all accounts, this was a masterful and compelling speech, but (aside from furnishing John Lansing and Luther Martin with ammunition for later use against the Constitution) it made little impact. Hamilton was simply transmitting on a different wavelength from the rest of the delegates; the latter adjourned after his great effort, admired his rhetoric, and then returned to business.[45] It was rather as if they had taken a day off to attend the opera. Hamilton, never a particularly patient man or much of a negotiator, stayed for another ten days, and then left, in considerable disgust, for New York.[46] Although he came back to Philadelphia sporadically and attended the last two weeks of the Convention, Hamilton played no part in the laborious task of hammering out the Constitution. His day came later when he led the New York Constitutionalists into the savage imbroglio over ratification—an arena in which his unmatched talent for dirty political infighting may well have won the day. For instance, in the New York Ratifying Convention, Lansing threw back into Hamilton's teeth the sentiments the latter had expressed in his June 18th oration in the Convention. However, having since retreated to the fine defensive positions immortalized in *The Federalist*, the Colonel flatly denied that he had ever been an enemy of the states, or had believed that conflict between states and nation was inexorable! As Madison's authoritative *Notes* did not appear until 1840, and there had been no press coverage, there was no way to verify his assertions, so in the words of the reporter, ". . . a warm personal altercation between [Lansing and Hamilton] engrossed the remainder of the day [June 28, 1788]." [47]

[4]

On Tuesday morning, June 19th, the vacation was over. James Madison led off with a long, carefully reasoned speech analyzing the New Jersey Plan which, while intellectually vigorous in its criticisms, was quite conciliatory in mood. "The great difficulty," he observed, "lies in the affair of Representation; and if this could be adjusted, all others would be surmountable." [48] (As events were to demonstrate, this diagnosis was correct.) When he finished, a vote was taken on whether to continue with the Virginia Plan as the nucleus for a new constitution: seven states voted "Yes"; New York, New Jersey, and Delaware voted "No"; and Maryland, whose position often depended on which delegates happened to be on the floor, divided.[49] Paterson, it seems, lost decisively; yet in a fundamental sense he and his allies had achieved their purpose: from that day onward, it could never be forgotten that the state governments loomed ominously in the background and that no verbal incantations could exorcise their power. Moreover, nobody bolted the convention: Paterson and his colleagues took their defeat in stride and set to work to modify the Virginia Plan, particularly with respect to its provisions on representation in the National Legislature. Indeed, they won an immediate rhetorical bonus; when Oliver Ellsworth of Connecticut rose to move that the word "national" be expunged from the Third Virginia Resolution ("Resolved that a *national* Government ought to be established consisting of a *supreme* Legislative, Executive and Judiciary"),[50] Randolph agreed, and the motion passed unanimously.[51] The process of compromise had begun.

For the next two weeks, the delegates circled around the problem of legislative representation. The Connecticut delegation appears to have evolved a possible compromise quite early in the debates, but the Virginians and particularly Madison (unaware that he would later be acclaimed as the prophet of "Federalism") fought obdurately against providing for equal representation of states in the second chamber. There was a good deal of acrimony, and at one point Benjamin Franklin—of all people —proposed the institution of a daily prayer; practical politicians in the gathering, however, were meditating more on the merits of a good committee than on the utility of divine intervention. On July 2nd, the ice began to break when through a number of fortuitous events [52]—and one that seems deliberate [53]—the majority against equality of representation was converted into a dead tie. The Convention had reached the stage where it was "ripe" for a solution (presumably all the therapeutic speeches had made), and the South Carolinians proposed a committee. Madison and James Wilson wanted none of it, but with only Pennsylvania dissenting, the body voted to establish a working party on the problem of representation.

The members of this committee, one from each state, were elected by the delegates—and a very interesting committee it was. Despite the fact that the Virginia Plan had held majority support up to that date, neither Madison nor Randolph was selected (Mason was the Virginian), and Baldwin of Georgia, whose shift in position had resulted in the tie, was chosen. From the composition, it was clear that this was not to be a "fighting" committee: the emphasis in membership was on what might be described as "second-level political enterpreneurs." On the basis of the discussions up to that time, only Luther Martin of Maryland could be described as a "bitter-ender." Admittedly, some divination enters into this sort of analysis, but one does get a sense of the mood of the delegates from these choices—including the interesting selection of Benjamin Franklin, despite his age and intellectual wobbliness, over the brilliant and incisive Wilson or the sharp, polemical Gouverneur Morris, to represent Pennsylvania. His passion for conciliation was more valuable at this juncture than Wilson's logical genius, or Morris's acerbic wit.

There is a common rumor that the Framers divided their time between philosophical discussions of government and reading the classics in political theory. Perhaps this is as good a time as any to note that their concerns were highly practical, that they spent little time canvassing abstractions. A number of them had some acquaintance with the history of political theory (probably gained from reading John Adams's monumental compilation *A Defence of the Constitutions of Government*,[54] the first volume of which appeared in 1786), and it was a poor rhetorician indeed who could not cite Locke, Montesquieu, or Harrington *in support* of a desired goal. Yet up to this point in the deliberations, no one had expounded a defense of states' rights or the "separation of powers" on anything resembling a theoretical basis. It should be reiterated that the Madison model had no room either for the states or for the "separation of powers": effectively *all* governmental power was vested in the national legislature. The merits of Montesquieu did not turn up until *The Federalist*; and although a perverse argument could be made that Madison's ideal was truly in the tradition of John Locke's *Second Treatise of Government*,[55] the Locke whom the American rebels treated as an honorary president was a pluralistic defender of vested rights,[56] not of parliamentary supremacy.

It would be tedious to continue a blow-by-blow analysis of the work of the delegates; the critical fight was over representation of the states, and once the Connecticut Compromise was adopted, on July 17th, the Convention was over the hump. Madison, James Wilson, and Gouverneur Morris of New York (who was there representing Pennsylvania!) fought the compromise all the way in a last-ditch effort to get a unitary state with parliamentary supremacy. But their allies deserted them, and they demonstrated after their defeat the essentially opportunist character of their objections—using "opportunist" here in a nonpejorative sense, to indicate a willingness to swallow their objections and get on with the business. Moreover, once the compromise had carried (by five states to four, with one state divided), its advocates threw themselves vigorously into the job of strengthening the general government's substantive powers—as might have en predicted, indeed, from Paterson's early statements. It nourishes an increased respect for Madison's devotion to the art of politics, to realize that this dogged fighter could sit down six months later and prepare essays for *The Federalist* in contradiction to his basic convictions about the true course the Convention should have taken.

[5]

Two tricky issues will serve to illustrate the later process of accommodation. The first was the institutional position of the executive. Madison argued for an executive chosen by the National Legislature, and on May 29th this had been adopted with a provision that after his seven-year term was concluded, the chief magistrate should not be eligible for reelection. In late July this was reopened, and for a week the matter was argued from several different points of view. A good deal of desultory speechmaking ensued, but the gist of the problem was the opposition from two sources to election by the legislature. One group felt that the states should have a hand in the process; another small but influential circle urged direct election by the people, election by state governors, by electors chosen by state legislatures, by the National Legislature (James Wilson, perhaps ironically, proposed at one point that an electoral college be chosen by lot from the National Legislature!), and there was some resemblance to three-dimensional chess in the dispute because of the presence of two other variables, length of tenure and re-eligibility. Finally, after opening, reopening, and re-reopening the debate, the thorny problem was consigned to a committee for resolution.

The Brearley Committee on Postponed Matters was a superb aggregation of talent, and its compromise on the executive was a masterpiece of political improvisation. (The Electoral College, its creation, however, had little in its favor as an *institution*—as the delegates well appreciated.) The point of departure for all discussion about the Presidency in the Convention was that in immediate terms, the problem was nonexistent; in other words, everybody present knew that under any system devised, George Washington would be President. Thus they were dealing in the future tense, and to a body of working politicians the merits of the Brearley proposal were obvious: everybody got a piece of cake. (Or, to put it more academically, each viewpoint could leave the Convention and argue to its constituents that it had *really* won the day.) First, the state legislatures had the right to determine the mode of selection of the electors; second, the small states received a bonus in the Electoral College in the form of a guaranteed minimum of three votes, while the big states got acceptance of the principle of proportional power; third, if the state legislatures agreed (as six did in the first presidential election), the people could be involved directly in the choice of electors; and finally, if no candidate received a majority in the College, the right of decision passed on to the National Legislature, with each state exercising equal strength. (In the Brearley recommendation, the election went to the Senate, but a motion from the floor substituted the House; this was accepted on the ground that the Senate already had enough authority over the executive in its treaty and appointment powers.)

This compromise was almost too good to be true, and the Framers snapped it up with little debate or controversy. No one seemed to think well of the College as an *institution*; indeed, what evidence there is suggests that there was an assumption that once Washington had finished his tenure as President, the electors would cease to produce majorities and that the Chief Executive would usually be chosen in the House. George Mason observed casually that the selection would be made in the House nineteen times in twenty, and no one seriously disputed this point. The vital aspect of the Electoral College was that it got the Convention over the hurdle and protected everybody's interests. The future was left to cope with the problem of what to do with this Rube Goldberg mechanism.

In short, the Framers did not in their wisdom endow the United States with a College of Cardinals—the Electoral College was neither an exercise in applied Platonism nor an experiment in indirect government based on elitist distrust of the masses. It was merely a jerry-rigged improvisation which has subsequently been endowed with a high theoretical content. When an elector from Oklahoma in 1960 refused to cast his vote for Nixon (naming Byrd and Goldwater instead) on the ground that the Founding Fathers intended him to exercise his great independent wisdom, he was indulging in historical fantasy. If one were to indulge in counterfantasy, he would be tempted to suggest that the Fathers would be startled to find the College still in operation—and perhaps even dismayed at their descendants' lack of judgment or inventiveness.[57]

The second issue on which some substantial practical bargaining took place was slavery. The morality of slavery was, by design, not at issue;[58] but in its other concrete aspects, slavery colored the arguments over taxation, commerce, and representation. The "Three-Fifths Compromise," that three-fifths of the slaves would be counted both for representation and for purposes of direct taxation (which was drawn from the past—it was a formula of Madison's utilized by Congress in 1783 to establish the basis of state contributions to the Confederation treasury), had allayed some northern fears about southern over-representation (no one then foresaw the trivial role that direct taxation would play in later federal financial policy), but doubts still remained. The Southerners, on the other hand, were afraid that congressional control over commerce would lead to the exclusion of slaves or to their excessive taxation as imports. Moreover, the Southerners were disturbed over "navigation acts," that is, tariffs, or special legislation providing, for example, that exports be carried only in American ships; as a section depending upon exports, they wanted protection from the potential voracity of their commercial brethren of the eastern states. To achieve this end, Mason and others urged that the Constitution include a proviso that navigation and commercial laws should require a two-thirds vote in Congress.

These problems came to a head in late August and, as usual, were handed to a committee in the hope that, in Gouverneur Morris's words, ". . . these things may form a bargain among the Northern and Southern states." [59] The committee reported its measures of reconciliation on August 25th, and on August 29th the package was wrapped up and delivered. What occurred can best be described in George Mason's dour version (he anticipated Calhoun in his conviction that permitting navigation acts to pass by majority vote would put the South in economic bondage to the North—it was mainly on this ground that he refused to sign the Constitution):

The Constitution as agreed to till a fortnight before the Convention rose was such a one as he would have set his hand and heart to. . . . [Until that time] The 3 New England States were constantly with us in all questions . . . so that it was these three States with the 5 Southern ones against Pennsylvania, Jersey and Delaware. With respect to the importation of slaves, [decision-making] was left to Congress. This disturbed the two Southernmost States who knew that Congress would immediately suppress the importation of slaves. Those two States therefore struck up a bargain with the three New England States. If they would join to admit slaves for some years, the two Southern-most States would join in changing the clause which required the ⅔ of the Legislature in any vote [on navigation acts]. It was done.[60]

On the floor of the Convention there was a virtual love feast on this happy occasion. Charles Pinckney, of South Carolina, attempted to overturn the committee's decision, when the compromise was reported to the Convention, by insisting that the South needed protection from the imperialism of the northern states. But his southern colleagues were not prepared to rock the boat, and General C. C. Pinckney arose to spread oil on the suddenly ruffled waters; he admitted that:

It was in the true interest of the S[outhern] States to have no regulation of commerce; but considering the loss brought on the commerce of the Eastern States by the Revolution, their liberal conduct towards the views of South Carolina [on the regulation of the slave trade] and the interests the weak Southn. States had in being united with the strong Eastern states, he thought it proper that no fetters should be imposed on the power of making commercial regulations; *and that his constituents, though prejudiced against the Eastern States, would be reconciled to this liberality*. He had himself prejudices agst the Eastern States before he came here, but would acknowledge that he had found them as liberal and candid as any men whatever. [Italics added] [61]

Pierce Butler took the same tack, essentially arguing that he was not too happy about the possible consequences but that a deal was a deal.[62] Many southern leaders were later—in the wake of the "Tariff of Abominations"—to rue this day of reconciliation; Calhoun's *A Disquisition on Government* was little more than an extension of the argument in the Convention against permitting a congressional majority to enact navigation acts.[63]

[6]

Drawing on their vast collective political experience, utilizing every weapon in the politician's arsenal, looking constantly over their shoulders at their constituents, the delegates put together a Constitution. It was a makeshift affair; some sticky issues (for example, the qualification of voters) they ducked entirely; others they mastered with that ancient instrument of political sagacity, studied ambiguity (for example, citizenship), and some they just overlooked. In this last category, I suspect, fell the matter of the power of the federal courts to determine the constitutionality of acts of Congress. When the judicial article was formulated (Article III of the Constitution), deliberations were still in the stage where the legislature was endowed with broad power under the Randolph formulation, authority which by its own terms was scarcely amenable to judicial review. In essence, courts could hardly determine when ". . . the separate States are incompetent or . . . the harmony of the United States may be interrupted"; the National Legislature, as critics pointed out, was free to define its own jurisdiction. Later the definition of legislative authority was changed into the form we know, a series of stipulated powers, *but the delegates never seriously reexamined the jurisdiction of the judiciary under this new limited formula-*

tion.[64] All arguments on the intention of the Framers in this matter are thus deductive and *a posteriori*, though some obviously make more sense than others.[65]

The Framers were busy and distinguished men, anxious to get back to their families, their positions, and their constituents, not members of the French Academy devoting a lifetime to a dictionary. They were trying to do an important job, and do it in such fashion that their handiwork would be acceptable to very diverse constituencies. No one was rhapsodic about the final document, but it was a beginning, a move in the right direction, and one they had reason to believe the people would endorse. In addition, since they had modified the impossible amendment provisions of the Articles (the requirement of unanimity which could always be frustrated by "Rogues Island") to one demanding approval by only three-quarters of the states, they seemed confident that gaps in the fabric which experience would reveal could be rewoven without undue difficulty.

So with a neat phrase introduced by Benjamin Franklin (but devised by Gouverneur Morris) [66] which made their decision sound unanimous, and an inspired benediction by the Old Doctor urging doubters to doubt their own infallibility, the Constitution was accepted and signed. Curiously, Edmund Randolph, who had played so vital a role throughout, refused to sign, as did his fellow Virginian George Mason and Elbridge Gerry of Massachusetts. Randolph's behavior was eccentric, to say the least—his excuses for refusing his signature have a factitious ring even at this late date; the best explanation seems to be that he was afraid that the Constitution would prove to be a liability in Virginia politics, where Patrick Henry was burning up the countryside with impassioned denunciations. Presumably, Randolph wanted to check the temper of the populace before he risked his reputation, and perhaps his job, in a fight with both Henry and Richard Henry Lee.[67] Events lend some justification to this speculation: after much temporizing and use of the conditional subjunctive tense, Randolph endorsed ratification in Virginia and ended by getting the best of both worlds.

Madison, despite his reservations about the Constitution, was the campaign manager in ratification. His first task was to get the Congress in New York to light its own funeral pyre by approving the "amendments" to the Articles and sending them on to the state legislatures. Above all, momentum had to be maintained. The anti-Constitutionalists, now thoroughly alarmed and no novices in politics, realized that their best tactic was attrition rather than direct opposition. Thus they settled on a position expressing qualified approval but calling for a second Convention to remedy various defects (the one with the most demagogic appeal was the lack of a Bill of Rights). Madison knew that to accede to this demand would be equivalent to losing the battle, nor would he agree to conditional approval (despite wavering even by Hamilton). This was an all-or-nothing proposition: national salvation or national impotence with no intermediate positions possible. Unable to get congressional approval, he settled for second best: a unanimous resolution of Congress transmitting the Constitution to the states for whatever action they saw fit to take. The opponents then moved from New York and the Congress, where they had attempted to attach amendments and conditions, to the states for the final battle.[68]

At first the campaign for ratification went beautifully: within eight months after the delegates set their names to the document, eight states had ratified. Only in Massachusetts had the result been close (187–168). Theoretically, a ratification by one more state convention would set the new government in motion, but in fact until Virginia and New York acceded to the new Union, the latter was a fiction. New Hampshire was the next to ratify; Rhode Island was involved in its characteristic political convulsions (the legislature there sent the Constitution out to the towns for decision by popular vote and it got lost among a series of local issues); [69] North Carolina's convention did not meet until July, and then postponed a final decision. This is hardly the place for an extensive analysis of the conventions of New York and Virginia. Suffice it to say that the Constitutionalists clearly outmaneuvered their opponents, forced them into impossible political positions, and won both states narrowly. The Virginia Convention could serve as a classic study in effective floor management: Patrick Henry had to be contained, and a reading of the debates discloses a standard two-stage technique. Henry would give a four- or five-hour speech denouncing some section of the Constitution on every conceivable ground (the federal district, he averred at one point, would become a haven for convicts escaping from state authority!).[70] When Henry subsided, "Mr. Lee of Westmoreland" would rise and poleax him with sardonic invective. (When Henry complained about the militia power, "Lighthorse Harry" really punched below the belt: observing that while the former governor had been sitting in Richmond during the Revolution, *he* had been out in the trenches with the troops and thus felt better qualified to discuss military affairs.)[71] Then the gentlemanly Constitutionalists (Madison, Pendleton, and Marshall) would pick up the matters at issue and examine them in the light of reason.

Indeed, modern Americans who tend to think of James Madison as a rather desiccated character should spend some time with this transcript. Probably Madison put on his most spectacular demonstration of nimble rhetoric in what might be called the "Battle of the Absent Authorities." Patrick Henry in the course of one of his harangues alleged that Jefferson was known to be opposed to Virginia's approving the Constitution. This was clever: Henry hated Jefferson, but was prepared to use any weapon that came to hand. Madison's riposte was superb: First, he said that with all due respect to the great reputation of Jefferson, he was not in the country and therefore could not formulate an adequate judgment; second, no one should utilize the reputation of an outsider—the Virginia Convention was there to think for itself; third, if there were to be recourse to outsiders, the opinions of George Washington should certainly be taken into consideration; and, finally, he knew from privileged personal communications from Jefferson that in fact the latter *strongly favored* the Constitution.[72] To devise an assault route into this rhetorical fortress was literally impossible.

[7]

The fight was over; all that remained now was to establish the new frame of government in the spirit of its Framers. And who were better qualified for this task than the Framers themselves? Thus victory for the Constitution meant simultaneous victory for the Constitutionalists; the anti-Constitutionalists either capitulated or vanished into limbo—soon Patrick Henry would be offered a seat on the Supreme Court [73] and Luther Martin would be known as the Federalist "bull-dog." [74] And, irony of ironies, Alexander Hamilton and James Madison would shortly accumulate a reputation as the formulators of what is often alleged to be our political theory, the concept of "Federalism." Also, on the other side of the ledger, the arguments would soon appear over what the Framers "really meant"; while these disputes have assumed the proportions of a big scholarly business in the last century, they began almost before the ink on the Constitution was dry. One of the best early ones featured Hamilton versus Madison on the scope of presidential power, and other Framers characteristically assumed positions in this and other disputes on the basis of their political convictions.

Probably our greatest difficulty is that we know so much more about what the Framers *should have meant* than they themselves did. We are intimately acquainted with the problems that their Constitution should have been designed to master; in short, we have read the mystery story backward. If we are to get the right "feel" for their time and their circumstances, we must, in Maitland's phrase, ". . . think ourselves back into a twilight." Obviously, no one can pretend completely to escape from the solipsistic web of his own environment, but if the effort is made, it is possible to appreciate the past roughly on its own terms. The first step in this process is to abandon the academic premise that because we can ask a question, there must be an answer.

Thus we can ask what the Framers meant when they gave Congress the power to regulate interstate and foreign commerce, and we emerge, reluctantly perhaps, with the reply that (Professor Crosskey to the contrary notwithstanding) [75] they may not have known what they meant, that there may not have been any semantic consensus. The Convention was not a seminar in analytic philosophy or linguistic analysis. Commerce was *commerce*—and if different interpretations of the word arose, later generations could worry about the problem of definition. The delegates were in a hurry to get a new government established; when definitional arguments arose, they characteristically took refuge in ambiguity. If different men voted for the same proposition for varying reasons, that was politics (and still is); if later generations were unsettled by this lack of precision, that would be their problem.

There was a good deal of definitional pluralism with respect to the problems the delegates did discuss, but when we move to the question of extrapolated intentions we enter the realm of spiritualism. When men in our time, for instance, launch into elaborate talmudic exegesis to demonstrate that federal aid to parochial schools is (or is not) in accord with the intentions of the men who established the Republic and endorsed the Bill of Rights, they are engaging in historical extrasensory perception. (If one were to join this E.S.P. contingent for a minute, he might suggest that the hard-boiled politicians who wrote the Constitution and Bill of Rights would chuckle scornfully at such an invocation of authority: obviously a politician would chart his course on the intentions of the living, not of the dead, and count the number of Catholics in his constituency.)

The Constitution, then, was not an apotheosis of "constitutionalism," a triumph of architectonic genius; it was a patchwork sewn together under the pressure of both time and events by a group of extremely talented democratic politicians. They refused to attempt the establishment of a strong, centralized sovereignty on the principle of legislative supremacy, for the excellent reason that the people would not accept it. They risked their political fortunes by opposing the established doctrines of state sovereignty because they were convinced that the existing system was leading to national impotence and probably foreign domination. For two years they worked to get a convention established. For over three months, in what must have seemed to the faithful participants an endless process of give-and-take, they reasoned, cajoled, threatened, and bargained amongst themselves. The result was a Constitution which the people, in fact, by democratic processes, did accept, and a new and far better national government was established.

Beginning with the inspired propaganda of Hamilton, Madison, and Jay, the ideological buildup got under way. *The Federalist* had little impact on the ratification of the Constitution, except perhaps in New York, but this volume had enormous influence on the image of the Constitution in the minds of future generations, particularly on historians and political scientists who have an innate fondness for theoretical symmetry. Yet, while the shades of Locke and Montesquieu *may* have been hovering in the background and the delegates *may* have been unconscious instruments of a transcendent *telos*, the careful observer of the day-to-day work of the Convention finds no overarching principles. The "separation of powers" to him seems to be a by-product of suspicion, and "Federalism" he views as a *pis aller*, as the farthest point the delegates felt they could go in the destruction of state power without themselves inviting repudiation.

To conclude, the Constitution was neither a victory for abstract theory nor a great practical success. Well over half a million men had to die on the battlefields of the Civil War before certain constitutional principles could be defined—a baleful consideration which is somehow overlooked in our customary tributes to the farsighted genius of the Framers and to the supposed American talent for "constitutionalism." The Constitution was, however, a vivid demonstration of effective democratic political action, and of the forging of a national elite which literally persuaded its countrymen to hoist themselves by their own boot straps. American pro-consuls would be wise not to translate the Constitution into Japanese, or Swahili, or treat it as a work of semi-Divine origin; but when students of comparative politics examine the process of nation-building in countries newly freed from colonial rule, they may find the American experience instructive as a classic example of the potentialities of a democratic elite.

NOTES

1. The view that the right to vote in the states was severely circumscribed by property qualifications has been thoroughly discredited in recent years. See Chilton Williamson, *American Suffrage from Property to Democracy, 1760–1860* (Princeton, 1960). The contemporary position is that John Dickinson actually knew what he was talking about when he argued that there would be little opposition to vesting the right of suffrage in freeholders, since, "The great mass of our Citizens is composed at this time of freeholders, and will be pleased with it." Max Farrand, *Records of the Federal Convention* (New Haven, 1911),

II, 202 (henceforth cited as *Farrand*).

2. The classic statement of the *coup d'état* theory is, of course, Charles A. Beard, *An Economic Interpretation of the Constitution of the United States* (New York, 1913), and this theme was echoed by Vernon L. Parrington, Merrill Jensen, and others in the "populist" historiographical tradition. For a sharp critique of this thesis, see Robert E. Brown, *Charles Beard and the Constitution* (Princeton, 1956). See also Forrest McDonald, *We the People* (Chicago, 1958); the trailblazing work in this genre was Douglass Adair, "The Tenth Federalist Revisited," *William and Mary Quarterly*, Third Series, Vol. 8 (1951), pp. 48–67.

3. A basic volume, which, like other works by Warren, provides evidence with which one can evaluate the author's own opinions, is Charles Warren, *The Making of the Constitution* (Boston, 1928). The best brief summary of the forces behind the movement for centralization is Chapter 1 of *Warren* (as it will be cited hereafter).

4. On Pennsylvania see Robert L. Brunhouse, *Counter-Revolution in Pennsylvania* (Harrisburg, 1942), and Charles P. Smith, *James Wilson* (Chapel Hill, 1956), Chap. 15. For New York, which needs the same sort of microanalysis Pennsylvania has received, the best study is E. Wilder Spaulding, *New York in the Critical Period, 1783–1789* (New York, 1932).

5. Stanley Elkins and Eric McKitrick, "The Founding Fathers: Young Men of the Revolution," *Political Science Quarterly*, Vol. 76 (1961), p. 181.

6. *Warren*, p. 55.

7. In *La République des Camarades* (Paris, 1914).

8. See Frank Monaghan, *John Jay*

(New York, 1935), Chapter 13.

9. "[T]he situation of the general government, if it can be called a government, is shaken to its foundation, and liable to be overturned by every blast. In a word, it is at an end; and, unless a remedy is soon applied, anarchy and confusion will inevitably ensue." Washington to Jefferson, May 30, 1787, *Farrand*, III, 31. See also Irving Brant, *James Madison, The Nationalist* (New York, 1948), Chap. 25.

10. Merrill Jensen, *The New Nation* (New York, 1950). Interestingly enough, Professor Jensen virtually ignores international relations in his laudatory treatment of the government under the Articles of Confederation.

11. The story of James Madison's cultivation of Washington is told by Brant, *op. cit.*, pp. 394–397.

12. The "message center" being the Congress; nineteen members of Congress were simultaneously delegates to the Convention. One gets a sense of this coordination of effort from Broadus Mitchell, *Alexander Hamilton: Youth to Maturity* (New York, 1957), Chap. 22.

13. See Sir Lewis Namier, *The Structure of Politics at the Accession of George III*, 2nd ed. (New York, 1957); *England in the Age of the American Revolution* (London, 1930).

14. The Annapolis Convention, called for the previous year, turned into a shambles: only five states sent commissioners, only three states were legally represented, and the instructions to delegates named varied quite widely from state to state. Clinton and others of his persuasion may have thought this disaster would put an end to the drive for reform. See Mitchell, *op. cit.*, pp. 362–367; Brant, *op. cit.*, pp. 375–387.

15. See H. M. Bishop, *Why Rhode Island Opposed the Federal Consti-*

tution (Providence, 1950), for a careful analysis of the labyrinthine political course of Rhode Island. For background see David S. Lovejoy, *Rhode Island Politics and the American Revolution* (Providence, 1958).

16. The terms "radical" and "conservative" have been bandied about a good deal in connection with the Constitution. This usage is nonsense if it is employed to distinguish between two economic "classes"—*e.g.*, radical debtors versus conservative creditors, radical farmers versus conservative capitalists, etc.—because there was no polarization along this line of division; the same types of people turned up on both sides. And many were hard to place in these terms: Does one treat Robert Morris as a debtor or a creditor? or James Wilson? See Brown, *op. cit.*, *passim*. The one line of division that holds up is between those deeply attached to states' rights and those who felt that the Confederation was bankrupt. Thus, curiously, some of the most narrow-minded, parochial spokesmen of the time have earned the designation "radical," while those most willing to experiment and alter the *status quo* have been dubbed "conservative"! See Cecelia Kenyon, "Men of Little Faith," *William and Mary Quarterly*, Vol. 12 (1955), p. 3.

17. Yet there was little objection to this crucial modification from any quarter—there almost seems to have been a gentlemen's agreement that Rhode Island's *liberum veto* had to be destroyed.

18. See Mason's letter to his son, May 27, 1787, in which he endorsed secrecy as "a proper precaution to prevent mistakes and misrepresentation until the business shall have been completed, when the whole may have a very different complexion from that in which the several crude and indigested parts might in their first shape appear if submitted

to the public eye." *Farrand*, III, 28.

19. See Madison to Jefferson, June 6, 1787, *Farrand*, III, 35.

20. Cited in *Warren*, p. 138.

21. See, *e.g.*, Gottfried Dietze, *The Federalist: A Classic on Federalism and Free Government* (Baltimore, 1960); Richard Hofstadter, *The American Political Tradition* (New York, 1948); and John P. Roche, "American Liberty," in M. Konvitz and C. Rossiter, eds., *Aspects of Liberty* (Ithaca, 1958).

22. "I hold it for a fundamental point, that an individual independence of the states is utterly irreconcilable with the idea of an aggregate sovereignty," Madison to Randolph, cited in Brant, *op. cit.*, p. 416.

23. The Randolph Plan was presented on May 29th (see *Farrand*, I, 18–23); the state legislatures retained only the power to *nominate* candidates for the upper chamber. Madison's view of the appropriate position of the states emerged even more strikingly in Yates's record of his speech on June 29th: "Some contend that states are sovereign when in fact they are only political societies. There is a gradation of power in all societies, from the lowest corporation to the highest sovereign. The states never possessed the essential rights of sovereignty. .⋅. The states, at present, are only great corporations, having the power of making by-laws, and these are effectual only if they are not contradictory to the general confederation. The states ought to be placed under the control of the general government—at least as much so as they formerly were under the king and British parliament." *Farrand*, I, 471. Forty-six years later, after Yates's "Notes" had been published, Madison tried to explain this statement away as a misinterpretation: he did not flatly deny the authenticity of Yates's record, but at-

tempted a defense that was half justification and half evasion. Madison to W. C. Rives, Oct. 21, 1833. *Farrand*, III, 521–524.

24. Resolution 6 gave the National Legislature this power subject to review by the Council of Revision proposed in Resolution 8.

25. Resolution 6.

26. *Ibid.*

27. See the discussions on May 30th and 31st. "Mr. Charles Pinkney wished to know of Mr. Randolph whether he meant to abolish the State Governts. altogether. . . . Mr. Butler said he had not made up his mind on the subject and was open to the light which discussion might throw on it. . . . Genl. Pinkney expressed a doubt. . . . Mr. Gerry seemed to entertain the same doubt." *Farrand*, I, 33–34. There were no denunciations—though it should perhaps be added that Luther Martin had not yet arrived.

28. *Farrand*, I, 54 (italics added).

29. *Ibid.*, p. 242. Delaware's delegates had been instructed by their general assembly to maintain in any new system the voting equality of the states. *Farrand*, III, 574.

30. *Ibid.*, p. 240.

31. *Ibid.*, p. 250.

32. *Ibid.*, p. 258.

33. *Ibid.*, p. 178.

34. *Ibid.*, p. 274.

35. *Ibid.*, pp. 275–276.

36. "But it is said that this national government is to act on individuals and not on states; and cannot a federal government be so framed as to operate in the same way? It surely may." *Ibid.*, pp. 182–183; also *ibid.* at p. 276.

37. *Farrand*, III, 613.

38. *Farrand*, I, 177.

39. *Ibid.*, p. 182.

40. *Ibid.*, p. 255.

41. J. C. Hamilton, cited *ibid.*, p. 293.

42. See, *e.g.*, Mitchell, *op. cit.*, p. 381.

43. Hamilton to Washington, July 3, 1787. *Farrand*, III, 53.

44. A reconstruction of the Hamilton Plan is found in *Farrand*, III, 617–630.

45. Said William Samuel Johnson on June 21st: "A gentleman from New-York, with boldness and decision, proposed a system totally different from both [Virginia and New Jersey]; and though he has been praised by every body, he has been supported by none." *Farrand*, I, 363.

46. See his letter to Washington cited *supra*, Note 43.

47. *Farrand*, III, 338.

48. *Farrand*, I, 321.

49. Maryland's politics in this period were only a bit less intricate than Rhode Island's: the rural gentry, in much the same fashion that Namier described in England, divided up among families—Chases, Carrolls, Pacas, Lloyds, Tilghmans, etc.—and engaged in what seemed, to the outsider, elaborate political Morris dances. See Philip A. Crowl, *Maryland During and After the Revolution* (Baltimore, 1943). The Maryland General Assembly named five delegates to the Convention, and provided that "the said Deputies or such of them as shall attend . . . shall have full Power to represent this State," *Farrand*, III, 586. The interesting circumstance was that three of the delegates were Constitutionalists (Carroll, McHenry, and Jenifer), while two were opposed (Martin and Mercer); and this led to an *ad hoc* determination of where Maryland would stand when votes were taken. The vote on equality of representation, to be described *infra*, was an important instance of this eccentricity.

50. This formulation was voted into the Randolph Plan on May 30, 1787, by a vote of six states to none, with one divided. *Farrand*, I, 30.

51. *Farrand*, I, 335–336. In agreeing, Randolph stipulated his disagree-

ment with Ellsworth's rationale, but said he did not object merely to changing an "expression." Those who subject the Constitution to minute semantic analysis might do well to keep this instance in mind; if Randolph could so concede the deletion of "national," one may wonder if any word changes can be given much weight.

52. According to Luther Martin, he was alone on the floor and cast Maryland's vote for equality of representation. Shortly thereafter, Jenifer came on the floor, and "Mr. King, from Massachusetts, valuing himself on Mr. Jenifer to divide the State of Maryland on this question . . . requested of the President that the question might be put again; however, the motion was too extraordinary in its nature to meet with success." Cited from "The Genuine Information, . . ." *Farrand*, III, 188.

53. Namely Baldwin's vote *for* equality of representation which divided Georgia—with Few absent and Pierce in New York fighting a duel, Houston voted against equality, and Baldwin shifted to tie the state. Baldwin was originally from Connecticut, and attended and tutored at Yale, facts which have led to much speculation about the pressures the Connecticut delegation may have brought on him to save the day (Georgia was the last state to vote) and open the way to compromise. To employ a good Russian phrase, it was certainly not an accident that Baldwin voted the way he did. See *Warren*, p. 262.

54. For various contemporary comments, see *Warren*, pp. 814–818. On Adams's technique, see Zoltán Haraszti, "The Composition of Adams' Defense," in *John Adams and the Prophets of Progress* (Cambridge, 1952), Chap. 9. In this connection it is interesting to check the

Convention discussions for references to the authority of Locke, Montesquieu, and Harrington, the theorists who have been assigned various degrees of paternal responsibility. There are no explicit references to James Harrington; one to John Locke (Luther Martin cited him on the state of nature, *Farrand*, I, 437); and seven to Montesquieu, only one of which related to the "separation of powers" (Madison in an odd speech, which he explained in a footnote was given to help a friend rather than to advance his own views, cited Montesquieu on the separation of the executive and legislative branches, *Farrand*, II, 34). This, of course, does not prove that Locke and Co. were without influence; it shifts the burden of proof, however, to those who assert ideological causality. See Benjamin F. Wright, "The Origins of the Separation of Powers in America," *Economica*, Vol. 13 (1933), p. 184.

55. I share Willmoore Kendall's interpretation of Locke as a supporter of parliamentary supremacy and majoritarianism; see Kendall, *John Locke and the Doctrine of Majority Rule* (Urbana, 1941). Kendall's general position has recently received strong support in the definitive edition and commentary of Peter Laslett, *Locke's Two Treatises of Government* (Cambridge, 1960).

56. The American Locke is best delineated in Carl Becker, *The Declaration of Independence* (New York, 1948).

57. See John P. Roche, "The Electoral College: A Note on American Political Mythology," *Dissent* (Spring, 1961), pp. 197–199. The relevant debates took place July 19–26, 1787, *Farrand*, II, 50–128, and Sept. 5–6, 1787, *ibid.*, pp. 505–531.

58. See the discussion on Aug. 22, 1787, *Farrand*, II, 366–375; King seems to have expressed the sense

of the Convention when he said that "the subject should be considered in a political light only." *Ibid.* at 373.

59. *Farrand*, II, 374. Randolph echoed his sentiment in different words.

60. Mason to Jefferson, cited in *Warren*, p. 584.

61. Aug. 29, 1787, *Farrand*, II, 449–450.

62. *Ibid.*, p. 451. The plainest statement of the matter was put by the three North Carolina delegates (Blount, Spaight, and Williamson) in their report to Governor Caswell, Sept. 18, 1787. After noting that "no exertions have been wanting on our part to guard and promote the particular interest of North Carolina," they went on to explain the basis of the negotiations in cold-blooded fashion: "While we were taking so much care to guard ourselves against being over reached and to form rules of Taxation that might operate in our favour, it is not to be supposed that our Northern Brethren were Inattentive to their particular Interest. A navigation Act or the power to regulate Commerce in the Hands of the National Government . . . is what the Southern States have given in Exchange for the advantages we Mentioned." They concluded by explaining that while the Constitution did deal with other matters besides taxes—"there are other Considerations of great Magnitude involved in the system"—they would not take up valuable time with boring details! *Farrand*, III, 83–84.

63. See John C. Calhoun, *A Disquisition on Government* (New York, 1943), pp. 21–25, 38. Calhoun differed from Mason and others in the Convention who urged the two-thirds requirement, by advocating a functional or interest veto rather than some sort of special majority; *i.e.*, he abandoned the search for

quantitative checks in favor of a qualitative solution.

64. The Committee on Detail altered the general grant of legislative power envisioned by the Virginia Plan into a series of specific grants; these were examined closely between August 16th and August 23rd. One day only was devoted to the Judicial Article, August 27th, and since no one raised the question of judicial review of *federal* statutes, no light was cast on the matter. A number of random comments on the power of the judiciary were scattered throughout the discussions, but there was another variable which deprives them of much probative value: the proposed Council of Revision which would have joined the executive with the judges in *legislative* review. Madison and Wilson, for example, favored this technique—which had nothing in common with what we think of as judicial review except that judges were involved in the task.

65. For what it may be worth, I think that judicial review of congressional acts was logically on all fours with review of state enactments and that it was certainly consistent with the view that the Constitution could not be amended by the Congress and President, or by a two-thirds vote of Congress (overriding a veto), without the agreement of three-quarters of the states. *External* evidence from that time supports this view (see Charles Warren, *Congress, the Constitution, and the Supreme Court* [Boston, 1925], pp. 41–128), but the debates *in* the Convention prove nothing.

66. Or so Madison stated, *Farrand*, II, 643. Wilson too may have contributed; he was close to Franklin, and delivered the frail old gentleman's speeches for him.

67. See a very interesting letter, from an unknown source in Phila-

delphia, to Jefferson, Oct. 11, 1787: "Randolph wishes it well, & it is thought would have signed it, but he wanted to be on a footing with a popular rival." *Farrand*, III, 104. Madison, writing Jefferson a full account on Oct. 24, 1787, put the matter more delicately—he was working hard on Randolph to win him for ratification: "[Randolph] was not inveterate in his opposition, and grounded his refusal to subscribe pretty much on his unwillingness to commit himself, so as not to be at liberty to be governed by further lights on the subject." *Ibid.*, p. 135.

68. See Edward P. Smith, "The Movement Towards a Second Constitutional Convention in 1788," in J. F. Jameson, ed., *Essays in the Constitutional History of the United States* (Boston, 1889), pp. 46–115.

69. See Bishop, *op. cit.*, *passim.*

70. See J. Elliot's *Debates on the Federal Constitution* (Washington, 1836), III, 436–438.

71. This should be quoted to give the full flavor: "Without vanity, I may say I have had different experience of [militia] service from that of [Henry]. It was my fortune to be a soldier of my country. . . . I saw what the honorable gentleman did not see—our men fighting. . . ." *Ibid.*, p. 178.

72. *Ibid.*, p. 329.

73. Washington offered him the Chief Justiceship in 1796, but he declined; Charles Warren, *The Supreme Court in United States History* (Boston, 1947), I, 139.

74. He was a zealous prosecutor of seditions in the period 1798–1800; with Justice Samuel Chase, like himself an alleged "radical" at the time of the Constitutional Convention, Martin hunted down Jeffersonian heretics. See James M. Smith, *Freedom's Fetters* (Ithaca, 1956), pp. 342–343.

75. William Crosskey in his sprawling *Politics and the Constitution . . .* (Chicago, 1953), 2 vols., has developed with almost unbelievable zeal and intricacy the thesis that the Constitution *was* designed to establish a centralized unitary state but that the political leadership of the Republic in its formative years betrayed this ideal and sold the pass to states' rights. While he has unearthed some interesting newspaper articles and other material, it is impossible for me to accept his central proposition. Madison and the other delegates, with the exceptions discussed in the text *supra*, did *want* to diminish the power of the states and create a vigorous national government. But they were not fools, and were, I submit, under no illusions when they departed from Philadelphia that this end had been accomplished. The crux of my argument is that *political realities* forced them to water down their objectives, and they settled, like the good politicians they were, for half a loaf. The basic difficulty with Crosskey's thesis is that he knows *too much*—he assumes that the Framers had a perfectly clear idea of the road they were taking: with a semantic machete he cuts blandly through all the confusion on the floor of the meeting to the *real* meanings. Thus, despite all his ornate research apparatus, there is a fundamentally nonempirical quality about Crosskey's work: at crucial points in the argument he falls back on a type of divination which can only be described as cabalistic. He may be right, for example, in stating (without any proof) that Richard Henry Lee did *not* write the "Letters from a Federal Farmer," but in this country spectral evidence has not been admissible since the seventeenth century.

Executive Power and
Domestic Emergency:
The Quest for Prerogative

Introduction

The Supreme Court's decision in the *Steel Seizure* case [1] that President Truman had exceeded his constitutional *vires* when he ordered Secretary of Commerce Sawyer to take over the steel industry is in many ways a unique holding. Although executive prerogative has been a constitutional tradition since the foundation of the Republic, the Court's opinion in the steel case marks the first instance since Lambdin P. Miligan was unnoosed in 1866 that a President has been told that his exercise of prerogative power was unconstitutional. The decision is, of course, entirely without precedent in that Truman, unlike Lincoln, was alive to learn his lesson.

This is not to suggest that Presidents have not been called to task by the Court in earlier decisions, but rather to note that in such cases as *Panama Refining Company* v. *Ryan*,[2] or *Schechter* v. *United States*,[3] the Court included Congress with the President in its interdiction, while in *Rathbun* v. *United States* [4] the Court construed the statute establishing the Federal Trade Commission in such a manner as to forbid Roosevelt's dismissal of Humphreys on the ground utilized. In these instances, the President claimed a statutory basis for his actions, but neither Lincoln, in his original order suspending habeas corpus and establishing military commissions for the trial of disloyal civilians,[5] nor Truman, in

Reprinted, with permission, from *The Western Political Quarterly*, Volume V, Number 4, December, 1952, pages 592–618.

his seizure of the steel industry, offered any statutory foundation for his action. Each felt that he was exercising inherent executive power—prerogative—in combating a domestic emergency.

Consequently, before analyzing what the Supreme Court said about President Truman's seizure, it will be worthwhile to examine in some detail the precedents that exist for presidential exercise of prerogative power in domestic emergencies. Once this has been done, the decision and its implications will be discussed, and finally, certain conclusions will be suggested.

The Quest for Prerogative

The Court's opinion in the *Steel Seizure* case was preceded and accompanied by the most frenetic display of precedent-chopping that the American public has been subjected to since President Roosevelt's 1937 attempt to "pack" the Supreme Court. The supporters of President Truman invoked the shades of Presidents Jefferson, Cleveland, and Franklin D. Roosevelt, with Lincoln and Theodore Roosevelt to give an air of bipartisanship to the undertaking. The steel seizure was equated with the Louisiana Purchase, the Emancipation Proclamation, Franklin D. Roosevelt's "destroyer deal," and other successful exercises of executive authority. On the other hand, President Truman's opponents, while not issuing a call for regicides, compared him unfavorably with Charles I, denied that the United States Constitution endowed the executive with any "prerogative," and maintained that the seizure of the steel companies was one more step on the road to unconstitutional, unlimited government—government of "men and not of laws." However, it is interesting to note that, unlike some of the bitter judicial controversies of the thirties, the division of opinion on the legality of seizure did not fall into the neat categories of "Left" against "Right," or "liberal" versus "reactionary"; individuals and organizations of unquestioned "liberalism," such as Norman Thomas and the American Civil Liberties Union, while not accepting the position of the steel companies on the merits of the dispute, condemned the government's constitutional claims.

One of the major assertions of the steel companies was that the President's seizure order was without constitutional basis or precedent. On the other hand, the solicitor-general of the United States, in his plea before the Supreme Court, maintained that President Truman's action, far from being *sui generis*, was just another exercise of an authority that could be traced back to the administration of President Washington. To a student of constitutional law, this is a major, if not the crucial, issue in the steel-seizure litigation. Which, if any, of these antithetical claims does a dispassionate examination of American constitutional history support?

The question may be formulated in more precise terms: To what extent does an analysis of the American constitutional tradition buttress the assertion that there is, incorporated in the initial phraseology of Article II of the Constitution, an independent grant of executive power? The exhaustive and definitive research of Professors Corwin,[6] Binkley,[7] Hart,[8] and Rossiter[9] has well explored the main lines and byways of the argument. One school of constitutional theorists, accepting the view of prerogative so brilliantly expounded by Alexander Hamilton in 1793, has maintained that the President is endowed by the Constitution with a high degree of autonomy and discretion—with "the executive power of the United States," not with "the executive power herein granted." The other viewpoint, that of Madison in 1793 and of Jefferson-the-philosopher (who must be distinguished from Jefferson-the-President, who was occasionally prepared to "rise above" the principle of strict construction), has urged that the President, like the Congress, has only those powers enumerated in the Constitution, and that there is, consequently, no executive "prerogative."

It would be highly pretentious here to attempt a retread of the scholarship in this area. Suffice it to say that Professor Corwin has concluded that the Framers of the Constitution intended to establish a "balanced constitution," which "carried with it the idea of a divided initiative in the matter of legislation and a broad range of autonomous executive power or 'prerogative.'"[10] However, the intent of the Framers, while of antiquarian interest, does not control the present interpretation of the Constitution.[11] Thus, while one may accept as bona fide the birth certificate of prerogative, it is necessary to examine further the history of executive power in order to determine the usages of prerogative, how this conception has been applied in specific instances, and how it has been received by the Court. More particularly it is important to consider precedents in the field of *domestic emergencies* where the President has taken action independent of any specific constitutional or congressional authorization.

This formulation immediately excludes two rich seams of precedent from consideration: first, those actions taken by the President in the field of foreign affairs which, like the Louisiana Purchase, were not based on any affirmative grant of power; and, second, such actions as various Presidents have taken in domestic emergencies under specific congressional authorization; for example, Wilson's activities under the Overman Act of 1918, or Franklin D. Roosevelt's actions under the War Labor Disputes Act of 1943. The first of these exclusions is automatic; domesticity has been imposed on the author. The second, however, is arbitrary, and requires some justification.

It is patent that most of the President's powers in domestic emergencies have grown out of congressional delegations of power. Nevertheless, there seems to be little point to an elaborate examination of these delegated powers because there are no existent criteria of limitation. In fact, when the President and Congress coordinately and cooperatively recognize the existence of an emergency, there appear to be no limits to the power that the legislature can constitutionally confer upon the executive to cope with the problem. For example, in 1942, when the President and Congress [12] were in agreement that the Japanese-Americans were a threat to the security of the West Coast, seventy thousand American citizens were "relocated" in concentration camps. When, three years later, this unparalleled emergency action finally came under the scrutiny of the Supreme Court, the majority could only observe, in effect, that war was hard on everybody. The Court refused to question, or even to examine, the reality of the emergency.

Along the same line, it should be noted that there is a notable scarcity of cases in which the Court has substituted its evaluation of an emergency for that urged by the executive. In the *Korematsu* case,[13] alluded to above, the Court said that it had to accept the executive definition of emergency. However, in the *Steel Seizure* case, the Supreme Court, far from accepting President Truman's claim that a pressing emergency existed, rhetorically exorcised the menace of a steel shortage and invoked the Constitution against the President. It is submitted that the key difference between the *Korematsu* case and the *Steel Seizure* case was that, in the former, Congress and the President were in full accord on the existence of the emergency, while in the latter there was militant hostility on Capitol Hill toward the President's action. The judiciary is seldom willing, even with an overwhelming body of constitutional precedent behind it, to stand against a united front of the legislative and executive branches. This may sound like a truism, but it is significant in defining the term "emergency." It may be suggested that an emergency is not an emergency if the Court is prepared to do something about it; its reality is more or less subjective. Aided by retrospective omniscience, one may assert that there was no menace of a Spanish invasion in 1898, or of a Japanese rising in California in 1942; but the Court, while it can refuse to come to terms with a problem for a year or two, must judge emergencies in a contemporary frame of reference. And when the Court is asked specifically if *this action* is justified by this emergency, its doubts on the matter will be assuaged or encouraged more by the temper of Congress than by the phraseology of the Constitution.

It may be objected that the Court's activities during Franklin D. Roosevelt's first term, when it defied both President and Congress, disprove this interpretation. They do indeed cast some doubt on its validity. However, the peculiar, antediluvian composition of the Court puts this period in a special category. The heart of the Court's actions at that time seems to have rested on the premise that the Justices represented the best interests of the people and that the striking down of New Deal legislation was what the people *really* wanted. Hence, the Court felt that it was the only truly representative branch of government, or, to put it differently, that it was sustained by real political power. What the Court did was to hold off the tide of radicalism until the electorate had another opportunity to put *real* representatives into office. Thus, the tremendous Roosevelt victory of 1936 seems to have been far more effective than the 1937 "Court-packing" scheme, or the series of Roosevelt appointees (the first of whom, Black, took office after *West Coast Hotel* v. *Parrish* and *Jones-Laughlin* v. *N.L.R.B.*), in forcing the Court to reassess its apprehension of the American climate of opinion.[14]

One more striking instance comes to mind. In 1867 there was considerable—and justified—doubt as to the constitutionality of the Reconstruction Acts. Here was a situation in which President Johnson, who had vetoed the measures on constitutional grounds and seen Congress override his vetoes without paying the slightest attention to his views, undoubtedly hoped that the Court would accept his view of the legislation and strike it down. However, the Court, doubtless realizing that the Radical Congress would stop at nothing in its drive to inflict vengeance on the South, neatly sidestepped—on two rather shabby pretexts—the whole question.[15] The real locus of political power was then in Congress, and the Court, aware that if the myth of judicial supremacy is to be maintained the judiciary must never ride forth on quixotic ventures (compare *Scott* v. *Sandford*), refused to invoke the Constitution against the Radicals.

The Supreme Court then will rarely, if ever, attempt to frustrate the exercise of real political power; and, since in the United States real political power normally is shared between the President and Congress, the Court has shown great respect for emergency powers given to the President by Congress no matter what constitutional substance may be involved. Consequently, there is little point to a lengthy analysis of emergency powers which Congress has put in the President's arsenal. To those who maintain that the Constitution is the same in time of emergency as it is in time of calm, the Court has replied that, indeed, emergencies "do not create power," but that they may create situations in which hitherto unused powers may be exercised.[16] This ingenious sophistry converts the Constitution into a platonic form which exists in its full development somewhere, but which is not fully apprehended by any given generation. As new problems create new constitutional needs, the Constitution is found by the philosopher-Justices to contain adequate instruments to deal with emergent requirements. While some cynics may denounce this process as judicial legislation, it is not the purpose of this paper to engage in that discussion; [17] suffice it to say that, however the process of adjustment may be justified, the Constitution will be found flexible enough to authorize almost any conceivable congressional delegation of emergency powers to the executive.

Once the analysis has been thus narrowed, it may be possible to find a residue of "domestic prerogative," a body of inherent presidential powers which may be utilized in domestic emergencies. That prerogative powers have long existed in the field of foreign affairs hardly needs reiterating; the President's exercise of autonomy in this area can be traced back to Washington's administration, and has repeatedly received endorsement by the Supreme Court. However, as Justice Sutherland pointed out in *United States* v. *Curtiss-Wright Export Corp.*,[18] this "external prerogative" grew out of inherent powers of sovereignty in the field of international relations which could not apply to the domestic scene. Certainly in the view of this Justice, who more than any other man was responsible for the full formulation of the concept of "external prerogative," there could be no "domestic prerogative." The whole point of the *Curtiss-Wright* decision was that the doctrine of the separation of powers, while an active limitation on congressional and presidential action in domestic affairs, was not applicable to foreign affairs where special rules existed. Consequently, it is necessary to seek a different rationale for domestic prerogative from that which serves as constitutional justification for external prerogative. The United States cannot, at least legitimately, offer the Louisiana Purchase as a precedent for the steel seizure.

The conception of domestic prerogative is found in the thought of Alexander Hamilton, and Abel Upshur could observe in 1840 that it had been "gravely asserted in Congress that whatever power is neither legislative nor judiciary, is of course executive, and, as such, belongs to the President under the Constitution. . . ." [19] However, it is the administration of Abraham Lincoln which provides the first full display of nonconstitutional, nonstatutory authority applied to a domestic emergency.

President Lincoln assumed the role of Protector of the Union, and maintained that any and all means were legitimate to sustain the Constitution and the Union.[20] Thus, when mobs of Confederate sympathizers interrupted rail and telegraph communications between Washington, D.C., and Annapolis, Maryland, Lincoln, on April 27, 1861, seized the railroad and telegraph installations.[21] He enlarged the Army, suspended habeas corpus, turned government money over to private individuals, and ordered a naval blockade of southern ports—all without the slightest statutory or specific constitutional warrant, and much in direct violation of the Constitution. To Lincoln, the Constitution was not a set of procedural instructions, but a mystical entity—a corpus of republican principles—and it was in the spiritual sense a betrayal of solemn responsibility for the President—the highest priest of this republican rite—to allow the shadow of procedural legality to undermine the substance of "Sacred Union."

True, Lincoln was prepared to request congressional approval, *a posteriori* for his emergency actions, but he assured himself of a free hand in the immediate crisis by not calling Congress into special session until July 4, 1861—eleven weeks after the bombardment of Fort Sumter. When the Congress of patriotic Unionists did at last assemble, there was little else it could do but provide by statute that "all the acts, proclamations and orders of the President respecting the army and navy of the United States . . . are hereby approved and in all respects made valid . . . as if they had been issued and done under the previous express authority and direction of the Congress of the United States." The implication here was that the powers exercised by Lincoln were the property of Congress, but that Congress in a burst of generosity ratified the President's actions. In effect, the statute asserted that the President was working for Congress all the time. That this was hardly Lincoln's view emerges from an examination of the President's activities as commander in chief of the Armed Forces. While Article I of the Constitution specifically enumerates the power to wage war among the attributes of Congress, Lincoln infused presidential war powers into the commander-in-chief clause of Article II. Although it is doubtful whether the Framers intended anything more than civil control over the military by this provision,[22] Lincoln employed it as the rationale for broad substantive powers of presidential war-waging and, indeed, based the Emancipation Proclamation upon his authority as commander in chief. Similarly, he promulgated General Order 100, incorporating Lieber's *Code of Instructions for the Government of the Armies in the Field*, without any reference to Congress, although the latter body is charged by the Constitution with the establishment of rules and regulations for the Armed Forces.

What did the Supreme Court think of this tremendous exercise of domestic prerogative? In *Ex parte Merrymen*,[23] Chief Justice Taney felt that the suspension of habeas corpus (and by implication the other concomitants of Lincoln's dictatorship) was thoroughly unconstitutional. But Taney's action, undertaken in his capacity as circuit judge, had no follow-up; the copy of the decision that the courageous old Chief Justice sent to Mr. Lincoln apparently did not inhibit the President in the slightest. With the exception of *Ex parte Vallandigham*,[24] which the Court burked by a devious semantic maneuver, the only wartime test of Lincoln's actions to reach the Court was the *Prize* cases,[25] in which the President's power to blockade the South and seize shipping which violated the blockade was questioned. This decision, which was not handed down until March 10, 1863, involved a certain amount of judicial legerdemain, for the Supreme Court—unless it was prepared seriously to embarrass the administration—had to sustain the blockade without in any way according the Confederacy belligerent status. There is no point in here examining the intricate problems in both municipal and international law that were raised in the litigation; suffice it to say that Justice Grier succeeded notably in extricating the Court from its difficult position. With respect to the President's exercise of domestic prerogative, the Justice asserted that it was the duty of the President to resist rebellion with all the force at his command "without waiting for Congress to baptize it with a name," thus in large part ratifying Lincoln's conception of his war powers. As Rossiter has noted, the Court's decision in the *Prize* cases encouraged President Lincoln

to believe that his ever-broadening interpretation of the commander-in-chief clause would encounter no substantial restrictions in the future decisions of the Court. It was a fact of considerable importance for the conduct of the war that the Court, although clearly in a position to do all sorts of legal and moral damage to the cause, did not go out of its way to castigate Lincoln's theory of his powers . . . or invite other challenges to the effective prosecution of the war.[26]

The war over, Lincoln dead, and the need for constitutional protection of individual rights largely passed, the Supreme Court became conscience-stricken. Although the exegesis on *Ex parte Milligan*[27] has already reached formidable proportions, we cannot pass it by without comment, for it is the only case prior to the *Steel Seizure* case in which the Court investigated an emergency exercise of domestic prerogative and found a President *ultra vires*. Milligan had been seized at his home in Indiana, and then tried and sentenced to death for disloyal activities by a military commission established under the *sole* authority of President Lincoln. Milligan claimed that his constitutional rights had been violated, and—it now being 1866—the Court leaped to the defense of constitutional rights. No procedural difficulties such as had restrained the Court's conscience in the *Vallandigham* case appeared to becloud the issue.

The outcome is well known. A unanimous Court declared that President Lincoln had been beyond his constitutional and statutory authority in creating military commissions for the trial of civilians in areas where the civil courts were functioning. The majority, bellwethered by Lincoln's intimate friend David Davis, went further and claimed that even Congress did not have the authority so to limit the constitutional rights of individuals. These rights were immutable in calm or crisis, in peace or war. If one takes *Ex parte Milligan* at constitutional face value, it is obviously not worth much as precedent—although perhaps Corwin and Rossiter have gone too far in devaluing it. However, if the majority decision is taken as a political maneuver rather than as a constitutional homily, one can possibly understand it better.

In effect, Davis and his four majority colleagues were admonishing the Radical Congress on constitutional power *without risking the danger of a face-to-face, power-to-power encounter.*[28] Such a maneuver, as it was employed by John Marshall in *Marbury* v. *Madison*, has long been enshrined in American constitutional history as a masterpiece of judicial strategy.[29] Unfortunately, the Radical Congress was not to be bluffed, and when the face-to-face encounter did result, the Court was forced to retreat to the high ground of refusing jurisdiction. One may wonder what Marshall would have done had Marbury brought his suit again to the Supreme Court through the proper channel!

But while judicial mind reading is fascinating, it is tangential to the discussion of *Ex parte Milligan* as a limit on presidential power. Here we may agree with Rossiter that it "was important, even at that late date, to announce that there were, after all, some limits to the President's power over the civilian population well behind the lines." [30] In short, a President—although deceased— was called to order by a Supreme Court, and the doctrine of domestic prerogative was—perhaps on dubious and overstated grounds—subjected to scrutiny and limitation. In a sense the fact that *Ex parte Milligan* was decided may be more important as a constitutional tradition than the actual content of the decision; the myth of presidential limitation, as it has been reinforced by generations of young Americans reading excerpts from Davis's sonorous opinion in history texts, can assume almost autonomous force and itself serve as a limitation on the actions of contemporary executives. We need cite here only the genuine wave of public opposition that developed in 1937 when President Roosevelt attempted to bridle the Supreme Court, and note that it was certainly not based on public approval of the Court's decisions in New Deal litigation. The political scientist may scoff cynically at the conception that the Supreme Court is "above politics," but this myth was strongly enough embedded in the American tradition to frustrate a President who had just won the electoral vote of forty-six of the forty-eight states. Similarly, we may confidently assert that in *Ex parte Milligan* the Court belabored a dead lion, but a concept of presidential limitation *did* emerge from the encounter. In the public mind, the President is "under the Supreme Court," and the Court keeps this myth in working order by rarely attempting to validate it.

The conception of domestic prerogative as an important strand in American constitutional law thus dates from the Presidency of Abraham Lincoln. However, in the period from the close of the Civil War to the accession of President Franklin D. Roosevelt, this tradition, probably because of a notable absence of domestic emergencies, received little exercise. One might expect that World War I would have made some substantial contribution to domestic prerogative, but President Wilson's conception of the President as a prime minister led to plenary delegations of power by Congress (for example, the Overman and Lever Acts) rather than to extensive exercises of presidential autonomy. Nevertheless, there were in this period of relative calm several presidential actions and Court decisions relevant to the discussion here.

One new aspect of domestic prerogative which is extremely significant for our purposes was the increasing intervention of the Chief Executive into industrial crises. Since Professor Rossiter has already subjected this area to painstaking scrutiny,[31] it needs no extended analysis here. Beginning with President Hayes's action in the railroad strike of 1877, Presidents have frequently utilized federal troops in suppressing industrial disorders—even, as was the case with Cleveland's action in the railroad strike of 1894, over the vigorous opposition of the governor of the state in which the disorder existed. As Professor Corwin has noted, the Presidents have in such crisis activities relied upon both delegated and inherent powers.[32] In another area of labor relations, President Wilson established in 1918, with no statutory authorization, the National War Labor Board to mediate industrial disputes; and in a famous instance when some machinists in Bridgeport, Connecticut, struck against a decision of the Board, the President initiated the tradition of "indirect sanctions" by threatening the workers with the draft. President Roosevelt perfected the technique of indirect sanctions in World War II when he, too, established machinery for industrial mediation on the basis of prerogative power.

The President's prerogative power to intervene and keep the

peace received powerful support from two Supreme Court decisions. In the first case, *In re Neagle*,[33] the Court was asked—with a certain overtone of grim humor—whether the President had the inherent power to protect a Supreme Court Justice from assassination. Certainly the President had not been explicitly endowed by either the Constitution or congressional enactment with the power to undertake this protection, but the Court held —sensibly enough—that open season on federal judges was hardly contemplated by either the Framers of the Constitution or the national legislature. This holding may have been predictable, but the Court's basis for the decision was unique: Justice Miller advanced the thesis that there is a "peace of the United States" and that the President is the keeper of the peace. Legally this is a very interesting decision, for it blew new breath into the corpse of the federal common law—a conception beloved by Marshall, Story, and Kent, but—with one major exception in the area of commercial law[34]—destroyed by the Jeffersonians. Politically, the implications of the *Neagle* case were far-reaching, for it could serve as the rationale for almost any presidential intervention into domestic disorder.

Five years later, in 1895, the Court returned to this theme. In the course of the strike of the American Railway Union against railroads using Pullman cars, violence had occurred, and President Cleveland—apparently identifying corporate with national interest—sent in federal troops to maintain "order" and see that the mails went through. In addition, the United States Attorney in Chicago obtained a blanket injunction against the strikers and, when the strike continued, had Eugene V. Debs, the union president, imprisoned for contempt of court. The validity of the injunction was appealed to the Supreme Court, for nowhere was there any specific statutory warrant for such an exercise of executive power as requesting the injunction, or of judicial power as granting it. The Supreme Court agreed unanimously that, although there was no statutory authorization for his action, the President, that is, the United States Attorney, was legitimately exercising prerogative power in seeking the injunction and that the United States Circuit Court was correct in granting it. Said Justice Brewer, "The entire strength of the nation may be used

140   AMERICAN CONSTITUTIONALISM

to enforce in any part of the land the full and free exercise of all
national powers and the security of all rights entrusted by the
Constitution to its care." [35] A more thorough repudiation of the
Jeffersonian theory that there could be no federal crime without
a specific punitive statute could not be imagined; this was federal
common law with a vengeance. As Rossiter has pointed out, "In
the light of the *Debs* and *Neagle* cases, it might easily be argued
that there are no judicial limits to the President's real or alleged
'inherent' power to protect the peace of the United States." [36]

President Theodore Roosevelt accepted the role of Protector
of the Peace as naturally as a loon takes to water. When a great
coal strike imperiled national health and safety in 1902, Roosevelt
immediately brought his moral force to bear on the situation, personally urged a settlement on the disputants, appointed a commission (including a trade unionist disguised as an "eminent sociologist"!) to investigate the matter, and even planned, as a
possible last resort, to seize the coal mines [37]—this in spite of At-
torney-General Knox's advice that seizure would be unconstitutional.[38] A settlement was reached, and the President shifted his
strenuous proclivities to other areas. Roosevelt's reminiscences on
this episode give a concise presentation of his "Stewardship Theory" of the Presidency. He observed in his *Autobiography* that
his action in the coal strike

illustrated as well as anything that I did the theory which I have
called the Jackson-Lincoln theory of the Presidency; that is, that
occasionally great national crises arise which call for immediate and
vigorous executive action, and that in such cases it is the duty of the
President to act upon the theory that he is the steward of the people,
and that the proper attitude for him to take is that he is bound to
assume that he has the legal right to do whatever the needs of the
people demand, unless the Constitution or the laws explicitly forbid
him to do it.[39]

It is interesting to note that Roosevelt's similar view of the powers
of the national government vis-à-vis the states was repudiated
by the Supreme Court in *Kansas* v. *Colorado*,[40] but his views of
presidential prerogative were not judicially challenged. In 1916
former President Taft, in his work *Our Chief Magistrate and His
Powers*,[41] denounced Roosevelt's conception in no uncertain

terms, although later as Chief Justice he seemed, in his decision in the *Myers* case,[42] to backtrack considerably. The argument between the two centered upon the very issue at stake in the *Steel Seizure* case. While Roosevelt maintained that the President had all executive powers not explicitly forbidden to him, Taft asserted that the President, like Congress, had only those powers enumerated in the Constitution. Roosevelt accepted completely the common-law responsibilities of Protector of the Peace of the United States, while Taft rejected—despite his reverence for the judiciary—the whole substance of the *Debs* and *Neagle* decisions.

Although President Wilson did establish some of the emergency agencies of World War I on the basis of his prerogative, notably the National War Labor Board, the War Industries Board, and George Creel's Committee on Public Information,[43] his whole approach to emergency power was permeated by his philosophy of unity between the executive and the legislature, rather than by the prerogative-conception of the autonomous President. Nor did his three Republican successors, all compulsive "normalists," make any lasting contribution to the tradition of domestic prerogative. We are thus able to move with great dispatch to the accession of President Franklin D. Roosevelt in March, 1933.

As Rossiter has pointed out: "In Roosevelt the voters had chosen the most crisis-minded public figure in American history, a man who thrived on crises, emergencies, dangers, perils, and panics. His long tenure of office was a continuous emergency, and not just for the Republicans." [44] In the eyes of the conservative element of the American community, Roosevelt's conception of the Presidency and his full acceptance of the assignment of Protector of the Peace brought the United States to the edge of unconstitutional presidential dictatorship. True, in the *Debs* case, a Supreme Court composed of unimpeachable conservatives had given its unanimous approval of strong, autonomous executive action, but then Debs was a dangerous radical. The utilization of emergency prerogative powers *against* corporate interests fell into a different constitutional category: "a government of men and not of laws."

While Roosevelt's actions against the economic emergency of

the thirties may have smacked of dictatorship to some elements in the community, it should be noted that the President followed the Wilsonian rather than the Lincolnian pattern; that is, he relied upon huge delegations of congressional power rather than upon inherent executive authority. Although his March 6, 1933, proclamation of a "bank holiday" was based upon a thoroughly tenuous statutory foundation—the Trading with the Enemy Act of 1917—it was nonetheless assigned legislative parentage. Similarly, in his First Inaugural Address, President Roosevelt informed the nation that he would propose certain measures to Congress, and then added that "in the event that the Congress shall fail to take one of these two courses . . . *I shall ask the Congress* for the one remaining instrument to meet the crisis—broad Executive power to wage a war against the emergency. . . ." [45]

Indeed, the pattern of strong presidential leadership exercised within a framework of delegated authority remained unchanged until the eve of World War II. Then, in the period after the outbreak of hostilities in Europe, but before the United States entered the war, Roosevelt began to supplement delegated authority with actions based on prerogative. His activities in the field of foreign affairs, notably the so-called "Destroyer Deal" of 1940 with Great Britain, should be referred to in passing, although they are not strictly relevant to the topic under discussion. In domestic affairs Roosevelt took equally strong action and made a notable contribution to the development of domestic prerogative.

The President's initial action was to proclaim, on September 8, 1939, the existence of a "limited" national emergency—a constitutional innovation which was expanded to an "unlimited" national emergency on May 27, 1940 [46]—and he then proceeded to establish a series of agencies to deal with the domestic aspects of the emergency. The first of these, the Office for Emergency Management, was founded on May 25, 1940, with statutory authorization but no statutory powers.[47] Thirty-five other agencies were subsequently created purely on executive authority, including the Board of Economic Warfare, the National Housing Agency, the Office of Civilian Defense, and the National War Labor Board.[48] Corwin suggests that Roosevelt was well aware of the lack of constitutional precedent for the creation of these many agencies, and attempted to circumvent the constitutional issue "through the device of grouping [the] various creations under the rooftree of the oldest of them, the Office of [*sic*] Emergency Management, which was in turn installed in the 'Executive Office of the President.' " [49] Corwin adds, somewhat acidly, that this process was "one that might have been dragged out to even greater length without impairing the force of the axiom that zero plus zero is zero still." [50]

There has been extensive treatment of Roosevelt's wartime actions,[51] most of which automatically fall beyond the purview of this discussion, as they were grounded on extensive delegations of congressional authority, such as the War Labor Disputes Act of 1943 or the Emergency Price Control Act of 1942. Here it will suffice to make a brief examination of three areas in which the President either exercised or threatened to exercise domestic prerogative: seizure of industrial facilities, employment of "indirect sanctions," and the famous threat to overrule a provision of the Price Control Act of 1942.

The seizure of industrial facilities for noncompliance with emergency needs was not an innovation of World War II. President Lincoln seized the railroads; President Wilson also ordered the railroads into national direction, and seized several munitions plants as well.[52] Nor were Roosevelt's claims of inherent executive seizure power new; Lincoln took over at least one railroad before the passage of the Railroad and Telegraph Act of 1862, and there seems to be some doubt as to Wilson's statutory justification for seizing the Smith & Wesson Company in World War I.[53] However, Franklin D. Roosevelt utilized the seizure power, both on statutory and on "inherent" authority, to an unprecedented degree. In the period from the outbreak of war in Europe to the passage of the War Labor Disputes Act on June 25, 1943, the President seized eleven industrial facilities, ranging from one plant of the North American Aviation Company to the whole soft-coal industry.[54] In no case did Roosevelt list any statutory authority for his action; he merely noted the "Constitution and laws" as the basis of seizure.[55] Eight of these seizures were occasioned by labor disputes, while three were based on inefficient management. In one instance, after the passage of the War Labor Disputes Act, the semicomic seizure of Montgomery Ward & Company in 1944 which featured Mr. Avery being dragged before *Life*'s camera by United States troops, the President apparently acted on the basis of inherent authority.[56] While there was some litigation on the consequences of seizure, and at least one district court judge stood up bravely against Leviathan and ruled seizure unconstitutional, in no instance was such a ruling upheld on appeal. The Supreme Court took no judicial cognizance of the *legality* of seizure, whether the latter was based on law or on presidential authority alone.[57]

Since in a discussion of constitutional theory one cannot assume that silence gives consent—although in practice it most certainly does—the issue of the constitutionality of these prerogative actions is still an open one. However, Koenig in his study of *The Presidency and the Crisis* suggests that seizure is merely an extension of the power of a military commander to requisition supplies for his troops in an emergency—an authority which has the sanction of long judicial approval.[58] The principal issue then becomes the existence or nonexistence of an emergency and the concomitant problem of who is to decide this ticklish question. Legally speaking, the precedents here are unclear, but in practical terms an answer seems apparent: when there is consensus on the existence of an emergency; that is, when public and congressional agreement on presidential action are apparent, an emergency exists. Or an emergency may be said *really* to be an emergency when the Supreme Court refuses to question its existence but rather observes, as it did in the *Korematsu* case, that it cannot question an exercise of discretion by the Executive. In the *Korematsu* case the Court refused an opportunity to replace the military general staff, but in the *Steel Seizure* case the Court intrepidly displaced the President's economic advisers and substituted its judgment for theirs on the reality of the emergency. Thus a conclusion, which will hardly satisfy the constitutional perfectionists, seems to emerge on the legality of prerogative seizure: The President can on the basis of his inherent power seize an industry if an emergency exists, and an emergency exists if the President is successful in his exercise of his prerogative.

The real job of the Supreme Court, viewed from this standpoint, is to enforce government by discussion, to prevent the President from breaching the contract of consensus. In a political system where executive action is not necessarily an outgrowth of party decision or legislative discussion, but where the President can claim potentially dangerous authority as the elected spokesman of a presumed "national will," this function of the Court can be of great value to the democratic tradition. But, as the thirties demonstrate, this calls for justices with a high degree of sensitivity to the national climate of opinion.[59]

President Roosevelt's employment of "indirect sanctions" has been well described by Professor Corwin,[60] and needs little elaboration here. The most famous instance of such presidential blackmail was the withdrawal of Post Office employees from Montgomery Ward's special post office, but "government by press release" also closed down the nation's racetracks and enforced a nationwide "dim-out." In effect, the administrators of various wartime programs employed every possible technique to enforce compliance with their "advice." The reason for this is not hard to find: most of these agencies had been established by presidential fiat without statutory *vires*, and they had to make their own way in the world largely unaided by penal legislation. Indeed, rather than cooperating with these agencies, congressmen often went out of their way to make life difficult for them, usually stopping just short of open nullification of their decisions. Nevertheless, however motivated, such blackmail tactics are hardly in the tradition of constitutional government, and should be replaced by regular criminal legislation in the event of future need.[61] In one case the Supreme Court came to grips with "indirect sanctions," and upheld an OPA order prohibiting future fuel oil allocations to a company which had violated a rationing order.[62] The Court held, in Corwin's words, that "indirect sanctions were constitutional when the deprivations they wrought were a reasonably implied amplification of the substantive power that they supported and were directly conservative of the interests that this power was created to protect and advance." [63]

President Roosevelt's famous threat to nullify a congressional enactment, a farm parity provision of the Emergency Price

Control Act of 1942, brought the *claim* of presidential prerogative to its all-time apotheosis. Speaking to the Congress on September 7, 1942, the President informed it that unless the objectionable section of the Act were repealed by the first of October, he would repeal it! He continued: "The President has the powers, under the Constitution and under Congressional acts, to take measures necessary to avert a disaster which would interfere with the winning of the war. . . . When the war is won, the powers under which I act automatically revert to the people —to whom they belong." [64] This assertion goes far beyond Theodore Roosevelt's claim, and reverts to John Locke's definition of prerogative "as the power to act according to discretion for the public good, without the prescription of the law and sometimes even against it." [65] To a mind steeped in Continental logic the next step was obvious: a guillotine in the shadow of the Washington Monument.

But Congress repealed the parity provision, not merely because of the President's threat, but rather because the President's statement echoed public sentiment. Instead of marking the end of constitutional government in the United States, this declaration merely emphasized Roosevelt's superb ability to lead from political strength. From a constitutional point of view, it may be unfortunate that Congress bowed humbly before the President, but from the viewpoint of practical politics one can be almost certain that Roosevelt knew before he issued his manifesto that he would not have to put his claims to the test. Unlike his successor, Franklin D. Roosevelt scrupulously avoided bridges that he didn't want to cross. It should be noted that he never allowed his interest in civil rights to hinder unity in the Democratic party. Instead of recalling General MacArthur, he would probably have reassigned him as Military Governor of Samoa.

The President undoubtedly has inherent powers, but to assert that they can be exercised against the will of Congress is in realistic political terms nonsense.[66] One can, for instance, build an elaborate case to demonstrate in abstract terms the extent of the President's authority in foreign affairs, but, as Daniel S. Cheever and H. Field Haviland, Jr., have recently pointed out in their excellent *American Foreign Policy and the Separation of*

Powers,[67] in practice the President must work closely with Congress if his authority is to be implemented. To make a claim is one thing: to implement it is something quite different. Thus it appears that Roosevelt's assertion that he could overrule Congress on a statute is an example of political poker-playing rather than a constitutional precedent. In domestic even more than in foreign affairs everything has a price tag, and the President must maintain close liaison with Congress if his policies are to achieve concrete fulfillment.

This highly abridged summary of a century of domestic prerogative brings us to the instant situation: the seizure by President Truman of the steel industry. What conclusions can be drawn from past experience to aid us in examining the steel seizure and the litigation that grew out of it? First, in the realm of constitutional theory, it appears that the President's prerogative power in domestic emergencies has been and will continue to be shaped by the extent and intensity of the emergency. If a real emergency exists, it seems unlikely that the Supreme Court will declare a presidential action unconstitutional. Although this runs contrary to the Court's view of its own activities, the refusal of jurisdiction in cases questioning presidential power is equivalent to a statement of *nihil obstat*, and it is this technique that lends itself most readily to avoiding pitfalls. Justice Jackson has, indeed, urged the Supreme Court to avoid litigation in which it may establish unfortunate constitutional precedents under the pressure of emergencies.[68]

Second, the danger of unconstitutional presidential dictatorship, based on vigorous exercise of domestic prerogative, seems virtually nonexistent. In real terms, Congress and the public must agree with presidential emergency actions if they are to be effective. The silences of American constitutional history lend strong support to this proposition, for, *with the exception of the seizure of the steel industry*, there has not been one single instance of a President actually taking prerogative action in a domestic crisis against the wishes of Congress.[69] While the nature of the presidential office ensures that the President will take the leadership in the exercise of emergency powers, the Congress and the President are the Siamese twins of American "constitutional dictator-

ship." The real unity of powers in the United States, the degree
to which, for example, congressional committees effectively control various branches of the administration (the Passport Division
of the State Department is virtually a bailiwick of Senator Mc-
Carran's Senate Judiciary Committee, and other examples could
be cited at length), as well as the party screening process which
makes it almost impossible for an extremist to be nominated for
the Presidency, impel the conclusion that a President could not
become a dictator on the strength of his inherent powers. Conceivably, Congress could create a *Duce*, but it is inconceivable
that the President could go it alone.[70]

The Supreme Court and the Steel Crisis

With this background in mind, we can now turn our attention
to the Supreme Court's decision in the *Steel Seizure* case. The
immediate history of this litigation might briefly be recalled. On
April 8, 1952, President Truman announced that the impending
industry-wide strike of the United Steelworkers of America,
C.I.O., would imperil the national defense. To avert this crisis,
the President issued Executive Order 10340,[71] which vested title
to the major steel companies in the United States and appointed
Secretary of Commerce Charles Sawyer as government administrator. The President, as he clearly indicated in a nationwide
radio address, took this action in lieu of utilizing the injunctive
provisions of the Taft-Hartley Act because he felt that the steel
masters were at fault in the breakdown of collective bargaining.
He asserted that to employ an injunction would unjustly penalize
the steelworkers, who had earlier postponed their strike at presidential request. The next day, April 9, 1952, President Truman
informed Congress of his action, and, in effect, asked the legislature to approve his seizure order.[72] On April 21st the President
again communicated with Congress on the matter, justifying his
action to the President of the Senate but adding that "Congress
can, if it wishes, reject the course of action that I have followed
in this matter." [73] While there was considerable objection by individual congressmen to the seizure, and the customary desultory

threats of impeachment were vented, Congress as a body took no official action.

Meanwhile, the steel companies had gone to Court, having requested Judge Holtzoff of the District Court, District of Columbia, to issue a temporary restraining order on April 9, 1952. This judge held that the equitable remedy was not applicable as there was no evidence that the seizure would do irreparable injury to the companies, and added that "to issue a restraining order against Mr. Sawyer, and in effect nullify an order of the President of the United States, promulgated by him to meet a nationwide emergency problem, is something that the Court should not do, unless there is some very vital reason for the Court stepping in." [74] In late April, 1952, the steel companies tried again, requesting Judge Pine of the District Court, District of Columbia, to issue a preliminary injunction restraining the continued seizure and possession of the steel properties. The qualms which troubled Judge Holtzoff had no impact on Judge Pine—on April 29th he issued the injunction, and accompanied it with a vigorous denunciation of the President's unconstitutional action. This opinion reads more like a Liberty League tract than a realistic appraisal of the duties and responsibilities of the President of the United States in an era of permanent crisis. Its flavor can be appreciated only by a full reading, but one extract may supply the essence: The government's contention, observed the judge, "requires a discussion of the fundamental principles of constitutional government, which I have always understood are immutable, absent a change in the framework of the Constitution itself in the manner provided therein." [75]

The District of Columbia Court of Appeals by a 5–4 decision, immediately restrained the issuance of the injunction until the Supreme Court could have an opportunity to rule on the matter. Four members of the Court felt that Pine's injunction should have been sustained, but the majority held that the matter was so delicate and of such constitutional significance that the Supreme Court itself should make the substantive determination.[76] The Supreme Court granted certiorari on May 3, 1952, and handed down its decision on June 2, 1952.[77] It should be noted that almost two months intervened between the seizure and the final determination of its legality, and in this interim it had become clear that Congress disapproved of the President's action, and the nation's leading newspapers [78] had editorially announced strong opposition to the move. This is conjecture, but it seems that congressional confidence that the High Court would interdict the seizure inhibited legislative action on the matter.

Before subjecting the views of the Justices on the legality of seizure to internal analysis, it would be worthwhile to make some generalizations about the overall picture. First, nine Justices filed seven opinions: six of these were to the point that President Truman's action was unconstitutional, while the three dissenters united on a common opinion. Justice Black's "opinion of the Court" was accepted as a common denominator by Justices Jackson, Frankfurter, Burton, and Douglas, and Justice Clark accepted the judgment but apparently not the opinion of the Court. Justice Black's opinion was a sufficiently low common denominator that all those who concurred in it felt impelled to elaborate their differences in separate opinions. Professor John Frank has suggested that only by saying very little and avoiding many issues could Justice Black persuade any of his brethren to join him in an "opinion of the Court." [79] Needless to say, a decision advanced with so many well-aired and significant differences of opinion among the majority justices can hardly be a firm precedent.

Second, and in a sense implicit in the above, it should be noted that the Court did not share Judge Pine's naïve Manichaean approach to constitutional problems. One of the notable aspects of the majority opinions is the humility with which they were rendered. The Justices were obviously aware of the thinness of the ice on which they were treading, and spoke with muffled vehemence and, in most cases, with a sensible appreciation of the role and responsibilities of the President in emergencies. This decision certainly bore very little resemblance to the ex cathedra thunderings of the 1932–1936 Court. One of the reasons for the fragmentation of the majority appears to have been the desire of each majority Justice to make perfectly clear his reasons for rejecting the President's claim and to demonstrate that he was no constitutional ingénue who would simply accept the doctrine of the separation of powers at face value. It would indeed be difficult to find a more sophisticated distillation of constitutional wisdom with regard to presidential power than is contained in the brilliant concurring opinion of Justice Jackson.[80]

Third, as Professor Frank has noted,[81] the decision was implicitly an exhortation of Congress to take action in the area of industrial emergencies. To Justices Clark, Frankfurter, and Jackson, the President's refusal to employ the provisions of the Taft-Hartley Act brought him into Court with dirty hands. But supposing the President *had* exhausted his legislative remedies by invoking the Taft-Hartley Act, and *then* the strike had been called? Would seizure have been justified in such a situation? Naturally, the Court would not deal with hypothetical situations, but one has the distinct feeling that to at least the three Justices enumerated above this fact might justify a change of position. If only two of them changed positions, a different majority would be created. To put this query another way: If a real emergency existed for the solution of which Congress had supplied no instructions, would seizure then be unconstitutional? Again, the Court gave no answer to this question, but to an analyst of domestic prerogative it is a question of vital significance. This points up a conclusion about the *Steel Seizure* case which might serve as the conclusion of this whole overall analysis: it was a highly tentative decision. To use a somewhat illogical metaphor, it was only a partial decapitation.

Justice Black's opinion of the Court [82] was notable mainly for what it didn't say. The Justice tersely examined the President's action, found it without statutory foundation, dismissed the argument that it was based on a legitimate exercise of inherent power, and ruled it violative of the separation of powers as an usurpation of the functions of Congress. This opinion was a straightforward and unadorned exposition of the doctrine of the separation of powers which avoided the basic questions created by emergencies. Justice Black concluded simply: "The Founders of this Nation entrusted the law-making power to the Congress alone in both good and bad times." [83] This may be of interest to antiquarians, but it was hardly a realistic analysis of the activities of the American President since 1789—to say nothing of the legislative role of the Supreme Court!

Justice Jackson wrote a superb concurring opinion [84] which, it is to be regretted, was not the "opinion of the Court." Cutting through the legalistic arguments of both parties, the Justice suggested that presidential actions might be placed in one of three categories: first, where the President acts on the basis of delegated congressional authority; second, where the President takes unauthorized action which does not run counter to the wishes of Congress; and, third, where the President "takes measures incompatible with the expressed or implied will of Congress." Actions in the first category would have a very strong presumption of legitimacy; actions in the second would have to be judged "on the imperatives of events and contemporary imponderables rather than abstract theories of law"; while actions in the third must be subjected to strong judicial scrutiny, for there the President's "power is at its lowest ebb" and "what is at stake is the equilibrium established by our constitutional system." [85] It is submitted that what Justice Jackson has here suggested is the replacement of the mechanistic approach to the separation of powers—which inspired several of his brethren—with the conception that it is the responsibility of the Court to maintain the "ground rules" of government by discussion. Jackson then examined the President's action in detail, relegated it to the third of his categories, and agreed that it should be held an unconstitutional exercise of power. The Justice concluded by observing that "with all its defects, delays and inconveniences, men have discovered no technique for long preserving free government except that the Executive be under the law, and that the law be made by parliamentary deliberations. Such institutions may be destined to pass away. But it is the duty of the Court to be last, not first, to give them up." [86] Thus, in Jackson's opinion, the critical point was not that presidential autonomy violated the principle of the separation of powers, but that *irresponsible* presidential autonomy, prerogative exercise which did not have its foundation in the democratic process, did breach a basic principle of American constitutionalism: that the actions of the executive must be based on community consensus.

There is little point to a seriatim examination of the opinions of the other majority justices. Three of them, Justices Frankfurter,[87] Burton,[88] and Clark,[89] devoted their opinions largely to statutory analysis. Justices Frankfurter and Burton emphasized the President's refusal to invoke the national emergency provisions of the Taft-Hartley Act, and concluded, in their separate fashions, that this rejection of a solution recommended by Congress militated against the legality of seizure. Justice Clark devoted his brief opinion to demonstrating that, in addition to eschewing the Taft-Hartley remedy, the President had not fulfilled the requirements of any statute authorizing seizure of industry. In relying heavily on the President's nonemployment of the Taft-Hartley Act as a justification for interdicting seizure, these Justices seem to have seriously questioned the tradition, clearly enunciated in *Mississippi* v. *Johnson*,[90] that the President's actions are wholly discretionary. Their interpretation appears to have been that the President's activities are ministerial to the extent that he cannot attempt an unauthorized remedy for a crisis until he has exhausted the powers delegated to him by Congress. While the Chief Executive cannot be forced by mandamus to employ a congressional remedy, he can be punished for trying one of his own in its stead. It was this view that the dissenting opinion characterized, with some justice, as a "messenger-boy concept" [91] of the Presidency. Justice Douglas,[92] the other member of the majority, wrote a brief, general, and somewhat didactic essay on the nature of constitutional government. He concluded by noting: "Today a kindly President uses the seizure power to effect a wage increase and to keep the steel furnaces in production. Yet tomorrow another President might use the same power to prevent a wage increase, to curb trade unionists, to regiment labor as oppressively as industry thinks it has been regimented by this seizure." [93] This may be true, but it is interesting to recall that when President Cleveland employed domestic prerogative against the American Railway Union, both Houses of Congress applauded his action,[94] and it was sustained by the Supreme

Court.[95] Yet the precedent of *In re Debs* carried very little weight in the decision of the *Steel Seizure* case, and it is doubtful whether the holding in the latter case would inhibit a President *with public and congressional sentiment behind him* from employing inherent seizure power against a union in future. Precedent undoubtedly has considerable value, but its worth can be overly inflated.

The vigorous dissenting opinion, written by the Chief Justice,[96] denounced the frivolity of the majority in no uncertain terms. The blindness of the majority, insisted the minority, did not for one minute alter the fact that there was an acute national emergency, that the President was the Chief Executive of the United States and not an agent of Congress, and that the action he had taken to cope with the emergency was within his constitutional *vires* as President and commander in chief of the Armed Forces. In short, the dissenters asserted that this was a *real* emergency, and took the traditional judicial attitude toward executive action in *real* emergencies. The legal arguments between the two divisions of the Court were consequently of little significance; the vital disagreement was over premises. Granted the assumption that no emergency existed, the majority view fell into the tradition of limitation. Granted the assumption that an emergency existed, the minority opinion fell into an equally well-defined tradition of judicial restraint.[97] It is submitted that this argument over premises is not one that can be solved by the process of legal ratiocination; rather, it must be determined through judicial insight into the attitudes and opinions of the American community —particularly as reflected in the views of congressmen. It is essentially a problem in social psychology, not in law. An emergency is—like the middle class—more a state of mind than an objective sociopolitical phenomenon.

Conclusions

Since conclusions have been liberally sprinkled throughout the body of this paper, this section can best serve to highlight two major points that seem to emerge from a study of the impact of the decision in the *Steel Seizure* case on inherent presidential power in the field of domestic emergencies.

First, the Court accepted the view—which is characteristic of the American people and the Congress today—that the Korean crisis and the "Cold War" are not full-scale emergencies justifying the full invocation and exercise of presidential war powers. In time of "all-out" crisis, the boundary between domestic and foreign emergencies disappears, but in the *Steel Seizure* case, the Court—over the vigorous protests of the minority—insisted on maintaining the line of division between the two. Whether this interpretation of the reality of the emergency is correct or not only time will reveal, but in the contemporary context the Court insisted that the view of the American community prevail over the views of government experts. In so doing, the Court insisted on the primacy of discussion, of pragmatic blunderings and successes, over expertise and autonomous insight.

Second, by doing this, the Supreme Court struck a blow for constitutional government for which we should all be grateful. As in the *Milligan* case, the content of the decision is less significant than the fact that it *was rendered*. While all students of government appreciate the complexities of presidential existence in the United States, and most will admit that the President requires a high degree of discretion and autonomy for the proper exercise of his function, it is also important that a line be drawn between responsible autonomy and irresponsible autonomy. While it is no easy task to draw this line, its general outline should follow the boundary between community consensus and elitist conviction. One is always faced by the dilemma that the elitists may be right and the community may be wrong, but the history of democratic government seems to support the conclusion that if the views of an elite are correct, the people will adopt them before it is too late. While historical graveyards are littered with the bones of nations that tried to shortcut consensus, democratic governments have survived. And this—while it is not conclusive proof of the validity of democratic principles —is a significant validation of the viability of government by discussion, of the view that for better or for worse democratic executives must accept, or be compelled to accept, restraint of their insights and prerogatives.

NOTES

1. *Youngstown Sheet & Tube Co.* v. *Sawyer*, 72 Sup. Ct. 863 (1952).

2. 293 U.S. 388 (1934).

3. 295 U.S. 495 (1935).

4. 295 U.S. 602 (1935). See the similar early case of *Little* v. *Barreme*, 2 Cranch 170 (1804).

5. Lincoln's Proclamation of Sept. 24, 1862, suspended habeas corpus and ordered military trials for disloyal civilians. A year later Lincoln again suspended habeas corpus for such disloyal persons, but this time his action was based on the Habeas Corpus Act of 1863. However, this statute did not authorize trial by military commission. See Clinton L. Rossiter, *The Supreme Court and the Commander in Chief* (Ithaca, N.Y., 1951), pp. 26-28.

6. Edward S. Corwin, *The President: Office and Powers* (New York, 1948). This is a definitive study of the American Presidency, and where Corwin has gone into some matter exhaustively, I have contented myself with citing his research rather than engaging in the conspicuous scholarship of citing each source, statute, or executive order separately. The historical section of this paper does not pretend to be more than a synthesis of the work that has been done on one facet of the Presidency, although certainly the scholars who did the original investigation should not be held responsible for any interpretations advanced herein! For a different approach, see Albert L. Sturm, "Emergencies and the Presidency," in *The Presidency in Transition*, ed. Robert S. Rankin (Gainesville, Fla., reprinted from *Journal of Politics*, University of Florida, 1949), pp. 121-144.

7. Wilfred E. Binkley, *President and Congress* (New York, 1947).

8. James K. Hart, *The American Presidency in Action: 1789* (New York, 1949).

9. Clinton L. Rossiter, *Constitutional Dictatorship* (Princeton, 1948), Chap. 14.

10. Edward S. Corwin, *op. cit.*, pp. 15-16. Corwin's italics have been deleted. See the same author's concise analysis of this early period in *The Twilight of the Supreme Court* (New Haven, 1934), pp. 123-130.

11. See the interesting dispute on this point between Chief Justice Hughes and Justice Sutherland in *Home Bldg. & Loan* v. *Blaisdell*, 290 U.S. 398 (1934). A cynical insight into the degree to which a "Framer" felt himself bound by the intent of the "Framers" can be found in the Circuit Court's opinion in *Collet* v. *Collet*, 2 Dallas 294 (1792). I have suggested, on the basis of internal evidence, that Justice James Wilson wrote this decision, but in any event he concurred in it. The decision purports to explain exactly what the Framers intended by the naturalization clause of Article I, Section 8, of the Constitution, and could not have been further from the truth. See John P. Roche, *The Early Development of United States Citizenship* (Ithaca, 1949), pp. 14-15.

12. Actually, the President's action in issuing Executive Order 9066 on Feb. 19, 1942, antedated congressional action on the matter by a

month. On March 21, 1942, Congress ratified the President's action, and provided penalties for violating orders issued under the authority of Executive Order 9066. However, these two actions were treated as a unit by the Supreme Court, and we shall so consider them. See *Korematsu* v. *United States*, 323 U.S. 214 (1944); Rossiter, *The Supreme Court and the Commander in Chief*, pp. 42–54.

13. 323 U.S. 214 (1944).

14. The theory that the Supreme Court was intimidated by Roosevelt's "Court-packing" scheme seems supported by chronology: no sooner did the President propose reform to Congress than the Court radically revised its views on state wage and hour legislation, *West Coast Hotel* v. *Parrish*, 300 U.S. 379 (1937), and shortly thereafter in *Jones & Laughlin Steel Co.* v. *N.L.R.B.*, 301 U.S. 1 (1937), sustained the Wagner Act. Professor Corwin was one of the first to question this *post hoc ergo propter hoc* logic, so beloved by primitive tribes and historians, and to suggest that the 1936 election, as well as the inability of the states to deal with labor disturbances, was a far more potent factor. See his *Constitutional Revolution, Ltd.* (Pomona, Calif., 1941), pp. 73 ff. Recent research has revealed that the Court had reached its decision in the *West Coast Hotel* case *before* Roosevelt presented his project of judicial reform to Congress. See Merlo J. Pusey, *Charles Evans Hughes* (New York, 1951), II, 757. Of course, this does not prove that the election induced the judicial change of heart, but this theory—although it too is suffused with "posthocianism"—seems to fit the facts somewhat better.

15. See *Mississippi* v. *Johnson*, 4 Wall. 475 (1866), and *Georgia* v. *Stanton*, 6 Wall. 50 (1867).

16. For the classic exposition of this formula, see the Court's decision in *Home Bldg. & Loan* v. *Blaisdell*, 290 U.S. 398 (1934).

17. See the admirable treatment of this problem in Fred V. Cahill, *Judicial Legislation* (New York, 1952).

18. 299 U.S. 304 (1936).

19. Cited by Corwin, *The President*, p. 25.

20. Details on Lincoln's activities may be found in Randall's definitive *Constitutional Problems Under Lincoln*. A brief, cogent insight into the President's eleven-week dictatorship is contained in Rossiter's *Constitutional Dictatorship*. See James G. Randall, *Constitutional Problems Under Lincoln* (Urbana, Ill. 1951), and Rossiter, *Constitutional Dictatorship*, Chap. 15.

21. This seizure is noted by Justice Frankfurter in Appendix II to his opinion in *Youngstown Sheet & Tube Co.* v. *Sawyer*, 72 Sup. Ct. 863, 909 (1952).

22. See Corwin, *The President*, p. 276.

23. 17 Fed. Cas. 144 (Circuit Court, 1861).

24. I Wall, 243 (1864). See Rossiter, *The Supreme Court and the Commander in Chief*, pp. 28–30, for a discussion of this decision.

25. 2 Black 635 (1863).

26. Rossiter, *The Supreme Court and the Commander in Chief*, p. 75.

27. 4 Wall. 2 (1866).

28. This hypothesis requires some further justification. Rossiter refers to the majority opinion as an "exhibition of judicial self-hypnosis," in *The Supreme Court and the Commander in Chief*, p. 37, and Corwin has described it as "sheer fustian," *Total War and the Constitution* (New York, 1947), p. 79. If one looks at Davis's opinion in a legal vacuum, these judgments have some merit, but if one puts the majority

opinion in its historical framework, these harsh views appear somewhat naïve. In the first place, Davis was no political acolyte uncontaminated by an understanding of the political process; he was, on the contrary, Lincoln's former campaign manager and a notoriously shrewd politician. Consequently, while Davis may have been attempting to hypnotize someone, we can rest assured that he and his judicial brethren were not the proposed subjects. Furthermore, there was absolutely no need to discuss congressional power in deciding the case, for Congress had not authorized the military commission that tried Milligan. In sum, this was a wholly gratuitous judicial safari, and the conclusion emerges that Davis was using the *Milligan* case as a vehicle for lecturing the Radicals, who were destroying all that Lincoln and David Davis held dear—the "Union" and the spirit of compromise.

29. Chief Justice Marshall delivered his homily to President Jefferson rather than to the Congress, but the technique was identical.

30. *The Supreme Court and the Commander in Chief*, p. 36.

31. See "The President and Labor Disputes," in *The Presidency in Transition*, pp. 93–120.

32. *The President*, p. 164.

33. 135 U.S. 1 (1890).

34. The Jeffersonians objected to federal common law as violative of both the separation of powers within the national government and the division of powers between the national government and the states. The Federalists consistently favored it as an instrument of national power. In addition, great legal scholars like Story and Kent were disgusted by a legal system which permitted each state to establish its own rules of procedure and substantive law, and

felt that only a system of federal common law could bring order to this judicial chaos. After an interval in which federal judges assumed the existence of a federal common law (see John C. Miller, *Crisis in Freedom* [Boston, 1951], *passim*, for one example), the Court ruled in *United States* v. *Hudson*, 7 Cranch 32 (1812), that there was no federal common criminal law. Oddly enough, it was the Taney Court, normally dominated by Jeffersonianism, that authorized the federal common commercial law, *Swift* v. *Tyson*, 16 Pet. 1 (1842), which continued in effect until the Supreme Court in 1938 belatedly declared it to have been unconstitutional all along, *Erie R.R. Co.* v. *Tompkins*, 304 U.S. 64 (1938).

35. *In re Debs*, 158 U.S. 564, 582 (1895).

36. *The Supreme Court and the Commander in Chief*, p. 41.

37. See Rossiter, "The President and Labor Disputes," *op. cit.*, pp. 106–107.

38. Opinion cited by Justice Frankfurter in his concurring opinion in *Youngstown Sheet & Tube Co.* v. *Sawyer*, 72 Sup. Ct. 863, 898, fn. 20 (1952).

39. Theodore Roosevelt, *An Autobiography* (New York, 1913), p. 504.

40. *Kansas* v. *Colorado*, 206 U.S. 46 (1907). It had been urged upon the Court that the federal government had the power to intervene in areas where the states were incompetent to act, even when there was no specific constitutional basis for such intervention. This was a view originally fathered by James Wilson. The Court held it to be repugnant to the Tenth Amendment.

41. New York, 1916, pp. 139 ff.

42. *Myers* v. *United States*, 272 U.S. 52 (1926).

43. See Corwin, *The President*, p. 287.

44. *Constitutional Dictatorship*, p. 256.

45. *Public Papers and Addresses Of Franklin D. Roosevelt* (New York, 1938), II, 15. Italics added.

46. See Corwin, *Total War and the Constitution*, p. 23.

47. The creation of the OEM was statutorily blessed, but it was not legislatively endowed with any substantive powers. For a thorough discussion of this and other problems of the period 1939–1941, see Louis W. Koenig, *The Presidency and the Crisis* (New York, 1944), pp. 67–96.

48. *Total War and the Constitution*, p. 51.

49. *The President*, p. 295.

50. *Ibid*.

51. See Herman M. Somers, *Presidential Agency* (Cambridge, 1950), and Eliot Janeway, *The Struggle for Survival* (New Haven, 1951), and sources cited therein.

52. See Appendix II to Justice Frankfurter's concurring opinion in *Youngstown Sheet & Tube Co.* v. *Sawyer*, 72 Sup. Ct. 863, 910–911 (1952), for a complete list of seizures during World War I.

53. See Frankfurter's opinion, *op. cit.*, p. 898, fn. 20.

54. See Frankfurter's Appendix II, *op. cit.*, pp. 912–914, 927.

55. See, for example, Executive Order 8773, 6 *Fed. Reg.* 2777 (June 9, 1941), which ordered the seizure of the Inglewood, Calif., plant of North American Aviation Co.

56. See Rossiter, *The Supreme Court and the Commander in Chief*, pp. 61–62.

57. As an example of the litigation on the consequences of seizure, see *United States* v. *Pewee Coal Co.*, 341 U.S. 114 (1950). The outstanding case in which a district judge held seizure to be unconstitutional was *United States* v. *Montgomery Ward & Co.*, 58 F. Supp. 408 (N.D. Ill., 1945).

58. Koenig, *op. cit.*, p. 79.

59. Percentagewise, very few Court decisions fall into this category—judicial review of state and national legislation or executive activities is nowhere near so continuous as popular mythology would have it. In effect, it is suggested here that the purpose of judicial review is to enforce a cooling-off period on a nation whose political system does not otherwise inhibit popular passions. The British party system acts as a formidable institutional block against sudden change and, because of the tight party organization of the House of Commons, the chances of public passion being enacted into law are slight. Here the operation of the judiciary under the separation of powers supplies an institutional chaperon. But—and this is the lesson of the thirties—the judiciary must never allow the defense against passion to become a prohibition of marriage. Once a measure has received genuine public acceptance, the Court must retreat. Thus, one might say that the political function of the Court is to maintain a certain *process of government* rather than any body of substantive governmental principles.

60. See *Total War and the Constitution*, pp. 50–70. Those in search of an "inside view" of some of these sanctions should see Somers, *Presidential Agency*, pp. 165 ff.

61. See Rossiter, "War, Depression, and the Presidency," *Social Research*, Vol. 17 (1950), pp. 417, 424–425. The homiletic overtones of this statement should not be allowed to obscure the fact that in a future emergency "indirect sanctions" will unquestionably again be employed

if Congress refuses to create normal statutory sanctions to deal with such situations.

62. *Stewart & Bro., Inc.,* v. *Bowles,* 322 U.S. 598 (1944).

63. Corwin, *Total War and the Constitution,* p. 61.

64. Cited in *ibid.,* p. 63.

65. *Ibid.,* p. 64.

66. It should be noted that Congress had its revenge on Roosevelt for the message threatening to disregard the parity provisions. The price F.D.R. paid for his moment of glory was the failure of the "Third War Powers Act." See Corwin, *The President,* p. 495, for further details.

67. Cambridge: Harvard University Press, 1952. The authors state that "both the Constitution and actual practice make it clear that the President does not have sufficient authority to control foreign policy without regard to the wishes of the legislative branch" (p. 11).

68. Dissenting in *Korematsu* v. *United States,* 323 U.S. 214 (1944).

69. Truman's defiance was *de facto,* if not *de jure;* both houses of Congress informed the President that he should invoke Taft-Hartley, and refused to supply him with the seizure powers he requested after the Court ruled the original seizure *ultra vires* the Constitution.

70. Those critics of bureaucracy who feel that the President and his "vast, centralized apparatus of tyranny" are fast usurping American freedom would do well to read Senator McCarran's reaction to President Truman's veto of the McCarran-Walter immigration bill. The senator noted with great indignation that every branch of the administration concerned with immigration and naturalization had thoroughly approved his bill! It should be noted, in fairness to the bureaucrats concerned, that Senator McCarran is a far greater threat to their livelihood

than is the President, their nominal boss, because Senator McCarran will be there next January and President Truman will not. The close connections that exist between congressional committees and various branches of the administration—while common knowledge in Washington—have not received adequate scholarly investigation. The implications of this functional nexus on the so-called "separation of powers" are far-reaching. Among the few scholars who have come to grips with this problem are Herman Somers (see "The President as Administrator," *Annals of the American Academy of Political and Social Science,* Vol. 283 [Sept., 1952], pp. 105 ff.) and Don K. Price (see *The New Dimension of Diplomacy* [New York, 1951]). Other writers have dealt with specific aspects of this clandestine administrative-legislative relationship; see James M. Burns, *Congress on Trial* (New York, 1949), pp. 89, 96, and Arthur Maass, *Muddy Waters* (Cambridge, 1951), *passim.* For Senator McCarran's comments see *New York Times,* June 26, 1952, p. 14, and for the similar views of Representative Walter, cosponsor of the bill, see *New York Times,* June 27, 1952, p. 1.

71. Included as appendix to Justice Black's opinion in *Youngstown Sheet & Tube Co.* v. *Sawyer,* 72 Sup. Ct., 863, 868–69 (1952).

72. See 98 *Cong. Rec.* No. 60, 3962–3963 (April 9, 1952).

73. See 98 *Cong. Rec.* No. 66, 4192 (April 21, 1952).

74. *Youngstown Sheet & Tube Co.* v. *Sawyer,* 103 F. Supp. 978 (D.C.-D.C., 1952).

75. *Youngstown Sheet & Tube Co.* v. *Sawyer,* 103 F. Supp. 569 (D.C.-D.C., 1952).

76. *Sawyer* v. *Youngstown Sheet & Tube Co.,* 197 F. 2d 582 (C.A.-D.C., 1952).

77. *Youngstown Sheet & Tube Co.* v. *Sawyer*, 72 Sup. Ct. 863 (1952).

78. A check of leading newspaper editorial opinion, which does not pretend to be exhaustive, reveals the following journals strongly opposing the President's seizure: *Atlanta Constitution, Boston Herald, Chicago Daily News, Chicago Tribune, Chicago Sun-Times, Cleveland Plain Dealer, Christian Science Monitor, Des Moines Register, New York Times, New York Herald Tribune, New York Journal-American, New York World-Telegram and Sun, Philadelphia Inquirer, Pittsburgh Post-Gazette, San Francisco Chronicle, St. Louis Post-Dispatch, St. Louis Globe-Democrat, Washington Post.* Where one of the above papers is a member of a large chain; e.g., *New York World-Telegram and Sun*—Scripps-Howard; *New York Journal-American*—Hearst; the views of this paper may be taken as reflecting the outlook of the other journals in the chain. No paper was found giving editorial support to the seizure.

79. John Frank, "The Future of Presidential Seizure," in *Fortune*, July, 1952, pp. 70 ff. I am deeply indebted to this incisive analysis.

80. 72 Sup. Ct. 863, 869–80.

81. Frank, *op. cit.*, p. 70.

82. 72 Sup. Ct. 863–867.

83. 72 Sup. Ct. 867.

84. 72 Sup. Ct. 869–880.

85. 72 Sup. Ct. 871.

86. 72 Sup. Ct. 880.

87. 72 Sup. Ct. 888–899.

88. 72 Sup. Ct. 880–882.

89. 72 Sup. Ct. 882–886.

90. 4 Wall. 475 (1866).

91. 72 Sup. Ct. 949.

92. 72 Sup. Ct. 886–888.

93. 72 Sup. Ct. 888.

94. 26 *Cong. Rec.* 7281–7284, 7544–7546 (1894).

95. See *In re Debs*, 158 U.S. 564 (1895).

96. 72 Sup. Ct. 929–949.

97. See Rossiter, *The Supreme Court and the Commander in Chief*, pp. 128–129.

The Utopian Pilgrimage of
Mr. Justice Murphy

On July 19, 1949, Frank Murphy, Associate Justice of the Supreme Court of the United States, died in Detroit. The liberal press mourned the passing of a mighty warrior for civil liberty. Other journals observed the protocol of the occasion by politely deploring his death; the University of Michigan Law School prepared a memorial issue of the *Michigan Law Review*[1] in honor of its distinguished alumnus; a few encomiums appeared in the law journals;[2] then silence set in. A silence which has been broken only by occasional slighting references to Murphy's talents, and by a word-of-mouth tradition in law-school circles that the Justice was a legal illiterate, a New Deal political hack who approached the sacred arcana of the law with a disrespect that verged on blasphemy, who looked upon hallowed juridical traditions as a drunk views a lamppost: as a means of support rather than a source of light.

Murphy was indeed a strange phenomenon and, given the political developments of the past generation, it seems probable that we shall not see his likes again. An Irish-American, Roman Catholic, Frank Murphy was also a militant, dedicated liberal. Probably one of the best-hated figures of the New Deal period for his uncompromising refusal to employ martial law against the sit-down strikers, he also collected enemies among the followers of President Roosevelt for his unswerving defense of civil liberties against even the "enlightened" administration. In addition,

Reprinted, with permission, from *Vanderbilt Law Review*, Volume X, 1957, pages 369–394.

because of his thoroughly instrumental approach to law and to legal traditions, he incurred the enmity of all legal scholars in the apostolic succession from Justice Felix Frankfurter. An ideological, even ritualistic liberal, he brought upon himself the scorn of the tough-minded "realists" such as Justice Robert Jackson. While Jackson fulfilled Holmes's dictum that a judge must have in him something of Mephistopheles—in fact, sometimes making Holmes himself, by comparison, appear angelic—Murphy lacked this quality completely. In a real sense, I suggest, Justice Frank Murphy was a utopian pilgrim in this vale of tears, a man with a deep-rooted, religious commitment to the building of a new society in which men would be both free and prosperous. Thus when Murphy died, the Court lost more than its leading civil libertarian; it lost a Justice who was the living incarnation of the militant liberal myth of the New Deal.

[1]

The criticisms of Justice Murphy are themselves interesting for the light they throw on his symbolic stature. The mildest critics, such as Herman Pritchett, suggest that the Justice's "hyperactive concern for individual rights" led him "into ventures little short of quixotic." [3] This is gentle, indeed, when compared with the strictures of Philip Kurland. Comparing Murphy to Chief Justice Vinson, Kurland observed:

Neither had any great intellectual capacity. Both were absolutely dependent upon their law clerks for the production of their opinions. Both were very much concerned with their place in history, though neither had any feeling for the history of the Court as an institution. . . . Neither dealt with the cases presented as complex problems: for each there was one issue which forced decision. Each felt a very special loyalty to the President who had appointed him.[4]

Chief Justice Stone apparently shared this view. From Alpheus Mason's recent biography of the Chief Justice we learn that Stone considered Murphy, along with Rutledge, a "weak sister." Consequently Stone refused to give Murphy important decisions:

"The job of the Court," [Stone] said of one of [Murphy's] opinions "is to resolve doubts, not create them." The Chief Justice was well aware that he slighted Murphy; he often agreed to give him a "break," but in the end Murphy would be nosed out partly because Stone disliked leaving a fine case to the rumination of a law clerk.[5]

The essential difference between Murphy's judicial attitude and that of his more conservative brethren was brought out in 1944 by an exchange of compliments between Murphy and Roberts. Writing for the Court in *Tennessee Coal, Iron & R.R. Co.* v. *Muscoda Local 123*,[6] the Justice observed in passing:

Such an issue [portal-to-portal pay] can be resolved only by discarding formalities and adopting a realistic attitude, recognizing that we are dealing with human beings and with a statute that is intended to secure to them the fruits of their toil and exertion.[7]

Dissenting, Mr. Justice Roberts crystallized in the following terms his opposition to Murphy's approach:

The question for decision in this case should be approached not on the basis of any broad humanitarian prepossessions we may all entertain, not with desire to construe legislation so as to accomplish what we deem worthy objects, but in the traditional and, if we are to have a government of laws, the essential attitude of ascertaining what Congress has enacted rather than what we wish it had enacted.[8]

We shall subsequently examine Murphy's judicial attitude and technique in detail; suffice it here to note the standard counts of the indictment that has been drawn up against him, and examine it briefly. Murphy, it is alleged, was a New Deal politician disguised as a Justice of the Court, and not a very bright politician at that. He was legally a creature of his law clerks, excessively loyal to President Roosevelt, simplistic in his approach to complex legal problems, and bereft of any historical appreciation of the role of the Supreme Court.

Now, as will appear later, I do not look upon my function in this essay as one of glorification, or even rehabilitation—I come neither to praise nor to bury. However, I do feel compelled to demur at the outset to the terms of this indictment. In the first place, since the days when John Marshall filled the office of Secretary of State in the morning and Chief Justice of the United States in the afternoon, we have had a high incidence of politicians concealed beneath the judicial robes of the High Court.

Indeed, I have suggested elsewhere [9] that, given the policy functions of the Supreme Court, this is both inevitable and wise: to paraphrase Clemenceau, the meaning of the Constitution is far too important to be left in the hands of legal experts. Thus the complaint against Murphy, to stand up, must be reformulated to assert that he was a "bad" political Justice, and this accusation must rest upon more than a subjective dislike of the politics with which he suffused his opinions. This charge must, in other words, rest upon some empirical evidence that his decisions were technically incompetent, and none of his critics have appeared with any documentation of this point, or even with any criteria by which an evaluation can be made.

So here the argument shifts: *Enter* the ubiquitous law clerks who seemingly saved Murphy from his stupidity. Without the kind of information which could supply substance to this accusation one way or the other, I can enter no judgment on the merits as to Murphy's legal knowledge and intelligence. However, I suggest that the law-clerk gambit is one best left unexplored, since who can tell how many judicial reputations may be destroyed by candid revelation of what occurs in the chambers? Justice Frankfurter seems to have implied to Professor Mason that Chief Justice Stone's dissent in the *Gobitis* case [10] was a consequence of fervent advocacy of the Jehovah's Witness position by his clerk, Allison Dunham.[11] Elsewhere in the biography of the Chief Justice it appears that his famous Footnote 4 in the *Carolene Products* case was the handiwork of his clerk, Louis Lusky,[12] as was the rationale of the *Gerhardt* case.[13] Obviously, we are here in dangerous territory. Yet in a fundamental casting up of accounts, is this law-clerk proposition relevant? Why should a Justice not have the right to assimilate the talents of his apprentices? And, if he takes on brilliant young men and gives them leeway, is it not evidence of his own judgment and intellectual capacity? [14]

The other points in the indictment seem to rest on equally flimsy factual assumptions. The charge that Murphy was overly loyal to President Roosevelt flies in the face of the facts: what Justice asserted more vigorously the rights of the individual, even of individuals who happened to be Nazis, Communists, or Japa-

nese generals, against the executive arm of the government? A
reading of Murphy's flaming dissent in *Korematsu* v. *United
States*,[15] which could have been designated more accurately
Korematsu v. *Franklin D. Roosevelt, Commander in Chief*, should
demonstrate the patent inaccuracy of this accusation. Undoubtedly Murphy was simplistic in his approach to legal problems,
but, as a reading of John Marshall's dispositions of Virginia's case
against the Cohen brothers should suggest,[16] this alone does not
constitute high treason against the traditions of the Court.

To conclude this evaluation of the criticism of Murphy, I
would submit that a directed verdict of not proven, if we may
borrow it from the Scottish jurisdiction, is in order. The nub of
the case against Frank Murphy appears to be the content of his
opinions rather than their form. That is, he was simplistic and
untraditional to the "wrong" ends. In fact, I believe it was
Murphy's symbolic stature rather than his personal qualities that
has drawn the attacks, and it is to his symbolic function that we
now turn.

[2]

To understand Justice Murphy's symbolic role, it is necessary
to examine briefly the New Deal tradition from which he sprang.
The New Deal was a many-faceted phenomenon and, above all,
a source of myths. Indeed, the reality—which was the masterful
expediency of Franklin D. Roosevelt moving now this way, now
that, in the effort to deal with immediate problems [17]—has long
since vanished beneath layers of myth. To American conservatives, using this elusive term in its immediate political sense, the
New Deal appeared as a wave of collectivism that, unless checked,
would end by destroying American freedom. To hopeful liberals, the New Deal seemed to present a magnificent opportunity
to remedy the economic and social defects which were brought
into sharp focus by the Depression, and armed with an essentially pragmatic philosophy of life, these worthies descended
upon Washington and set to work in piecemeal fashion amelio-
rating the abuses they found. On the far Left could be discerned small colonies of radical sectarians to whom the New Deal
represented "incipient Fascism" and "bureaucratic collectivism."

But still another mythical interpretation of the New Deal can be extracted from the public opinion of the thirties, and it is this viewpoint that is of particular concern here. For lack of a better term, I shall designate it the *militant liberal* view of the New Deal. While no specific group can be found that advanced this position in any organized fashion, it was very important nonetheless. To the militant liberal, the New Deal had an essentially millennial function: it must revolutionize American life by creating under government auspices and protection *both* an economy of abundance and an atmosphere of maximum personal freedom. Many militant liberals were close to Socialism, though repelled by the Marxist logic-chopping and sectarian feuds that were characteristic of the left-wing organizations. They were also close to the pragmatic liberals in terms of the goals to be achieved, though they differed from the latter with respect to the efficacy of pragmatic, nonideological measures of reform. In the fundamental sense, this was a temperamental difference; while the pragmatic liberals stuck close to the ground, making inch by inch inroads into economic and social problems, the militant liberals designed a full-blown American Utopia, and urged that progress toward it move at full speed.

This unorganized, amorphous *groupement*, to borrow an appropriate term from French politics where such phenomena are plentiful, had little practical impact on the Roosevelt administration. Indeed, many of its constituents detested the anti-ideological sphinx in the White House. Yet, the net impact of its message, particularly since such influential journals as *The Nation* and *The New Republic* reflected its attitude, was considerable, particularly among young people and in liberal circles abroad. In short, these were "true believers" who, rejecting insignificant left-wing factions, placed their dream of the future in the hands of Franklin D. Roosevelt and, perhaps in the hope that their attitude would become a self-fulfilling prophecy, propagandized the message that Roosevelt could be the liberal messiah. While Roosevelt made few practical, as distinguished from rhetorical, concessions to this point of view, an outstanding instance of his "fence-mending" on the Left was the New Deal career of Frank Murphy.

Since the inner life of Justice Murphy is not our concern here, biographical facts can be kept to the minimum. After a varied career at law and in the Army during World War I, Murphy was in 1923 elected a judge of the Recorder's Court in Detroit. He was then thirty-three years old. On the bench, he made a name for himself as a pioneer in the assimilation of psychiatric skills into criminal proceedings, operating on the assumption, stated a generation later in his dissent in *Fisher* v. *United States*,[18] that "only by integrating scientific advancements with our ideals of justice can law remain a part of the living fiber of our civilization." His work as the judge in a celebrated race trial—the *Sweet* case which saw Clarence Darrow defending Negroes against a murder indictment growing out of racial hostility— brought high praise on all sides for his impartiality and immunity to criticism. Reelected to the court in 1929, he resigned in 1930 to make a successful campaign for the office of Mayor of Detroit.

As mayor of a city ravaged by the Depression, he established a nationwide reputation among liberals for his statement that "not one deserving man or woman shall go hungry in Detroit because of circumstances beyond his control," thus asserting the responsibility of government for the economic welfare of the people. After a second term as mayor, he was in 1933 appointed by President Roosevelt to be Governor General of the Philippines and, in effect, leader of the movement for Philippine independence. After the Commonwealth was established in 1935, Murphy remained in Manila as United States High Commissioner. Evidence that a decade later he still felt himself *in loco parentis* to the Philippine people is revealed in his separate opinion in a case in 1945, urging that American tax laws should be construed in such a fashion as to help the struggling Islands achieve maturity and economic strength.[19]

In 1936, Murphy returned to Michigan to win the gubernatorial election, and assumed office in 1937 to find himself confronted by the famous sit-down strikes. It was his conduct at this time which really endeared the governor to the militant liberals, for, instead of declaring martial law, calling out the National Guard, and forcibly driving the workers from the factories, Murphy made every effort to avoid a violent solution, and entered into negotiations with union leaders instead of jailing them.[20] While we can now view the sit-down strikes with a certain detachment, realizing that since the workers were not prepared to launch a proletarian revolution, they would eventually get bored and go home, the conservative view of Murphy's conduct was that he was encouraging the formation of soviets. The fact that his solution worked was of course even more galling, and Governor Frank Murphy became Public Enemy Number 1 in business circles. In 1938, he was defeated for reelection and was immediately appointed United States Attorney General by President Roosevelt.

Apparently Murphy handled the usual functions of this job with competence, but his ideological convictions were not dulled by high office: within a month after he took office, on February 3, 1939, to be precise, he established a "Civil Liberties Unit" in the Criminal Division of the Department of Justice. In announcing his intention of establishing this unit, Murphy said that "where there is social unrest—as I know from having been through no little of it myself since 1930—we ought to be more anxious and vigorous in protecting the civil liberties of protesting and insecure people." [21] When the new section was set up, the Attorney General justified it in the following terms:

In a democracy, an important function of the law enforcement branch of government is the *aggressive protection* of fundamental rights inherent in a free people.

In America these guarantees are contained in express provisions of the Constitution and in acts of Congress. It is the purpose of the Department of Justice *to pursue a program of vigilant action in the prosecution* of infringement of these. [Emphasis added.] [22]

In January, 1940, Attorney General Murphy was appointed to the Supreme Court to fill the vacancy caused by the death of Pierce Butler. Like Butler, he was a middle-western Catholic, but there the resemblance ceased. In a statement made on his appointment to the Court, Murphy emphasized the need for vigorous protection of personal liberties, and added that . . . "those in government—preoccupied with grave social and economic problems—tend naturally to be less sensitive to instances of oppression and denial of constitutional rights. In this welter of confusing factors that principle which is the essence of democracy—tolerance for all sides in all questions—is the loser." [23] Two aspects of this statement are noteworthy: first, Murphy stated clearly his objection to *governmental* infringements of personal rights; and, second, his only reference is to "social and economic" problems, though war had recently broken out in Europe. Perhaps one reason that President Roosevelt elevated Murphy to the Court was his intuition that while Murphy was a fine intern for "Dr. New Deal," he would have been a first-rate nuisance to "Dr. Win-the-War."

So did Justice Murphy, on the eve of his assumption of judicial office, lay down the gage of battle to all those who would infringe on the liberties of the citizen. And this Justice was to prove himself unique among the New Deal justices in his sensitivity to injustice. His uniqueness in this regard, I suggest, can be understood by the fact that alone among the Roosevelt appointees to the High Court, Murphy was a militant liberal by background and conviction. Every judge is dominated by a *telos*, by a built-in purpose that suffuses his assumptions about law, so in asserting that he was teleological we cannot distinguish him from Black, Reed, Frankfurter, Douglas, Jackson, or Rutledge. Where he differed from his New Deal brethren was in the content of his *telos*. True, his views overlapped theirs at many points, but there is nonetheless a discrete corpus of ideals which supplied Frank Murphy with his bearings, his conviction, and his utter ruthlessness when confronted by procedural niceties that seemingly masked substantive evils.

I am not asserting that Frank Murphy was a "great" judge; my analysis and evaluation is directed to a different level where this question is irrelevant. I am concerned with Murphy's symbolic position, both in the minds of his enemies and in those of his friends, and my contention is that he was the judicial incarnation of the militant liberal myth of the New Deal, of the body of aspirations which the militant liberals hoped the New Deal would incorporate into American life. Let us examine briefly the components of this myth. [24] A rough summary might read as follows:

First, the militant liberals were dedicated exponents of the rights of minorities, automatic defenders of the persecuted without regard to the opinions which brought down the wrath of the majority.

Second, in their approach to business, the militant liberals were sentimental Populists—opponents of "bigness," of trusts, of power concentrations of any sort. This was combined with sympathy for the small farmer, particularly the farmer-debtor in the squeeze of the capitalist octopus—John Steinbeck's *The Grapes of Wrath* was required reading.

Third, the militant liberals believed that the federal government had a positive responsibility to create economic security for all Americans. They supported overall planning rather than pragmatic meliorism.

Fourth, the militant liberals believed firmly in the divine mission of trade unions, frequently shocking prosaic trade-union leaders by the fervence of their convictions, since the latter were generally under the illusion that they were committed to raising wages, not saving the world.

Fifth, though usually not pacifists in the normal usage of the word, the militant liberals were vigorous antimilitarists, asserting that civil rights were constitutional absolutes which could not be tampered with even in wartime.

This is, of course, an oversimplification, but it should suffice to identify Frank Murphy's ideological pedigree and to distinguish him from the other New Deal Justices. In the course of this comparison, it should be recalled that I am not denouncing these other Justices or excommunicating them from the liberal camp. While I would be a dissembler if I did not admit at the outset that I shared, and still share to some degree, the militant liberal *Weltanschauung*, this analysis is wholly concerned with their deficiencies *from Murphy's vantage point*. The inherent wisdom or folly of his philosophy of life is a subject for separate analysis. The clue to an understanding of Murphy's divergence from his liberal brethren lies, I think, in the hypothesis that, while by all accounts a man of considerable practical talent, the Justice was quintessentially a pilgrim in this world. A person who, like the good Christian in the theology of St. Augustine, bears witness in this *civitas* to the values of a transcendent Utopia in which he spiritually resides. To Murphy, personal liberty in a society which cherishes man's personality were the necessary preconditions for the achievement of God-given potentialities, and he would lash out with prophetic fervor against any who frustrated the achievement of this democratic Utopia in the United States. From this angle, law, indeed, all human institutions, are purely instrumental, and traditions maintain their validity only so long as their substance contributes to the fulfillment of the democratic goal. Murphy's antitraditionalism thus itself stemmed from a tradition, traceable through St. Thomas Aquinas to Aristotle, that instruments retain their legitimacy only as long as they fulfill their proper functions.

Let us now turn to the delineation of this democratic *telos* as Justice Murphy set it forth in the *United States Reports*.

[3]

The various components of the militant liberal tradition were set out above. Retaining the same categories, and adding a few minor ones to fill out the picture, let us examine the opinions of Justice Murphy.

Rights of Minorities

Someone once observed that if Frank Murphy were ever to be canonized, it would be by the Jehovah's Witnesses. Though a member of a faith which has received the full force of Witness vituperation, Murphy, after the impact of the *Gobitis* case made itself felt, consistently supported the claims of the sect. From *Jones* v. *Opelika* [25] in 1942 to *Kovacs* v. *Cooper* [26] in 1949, he accepted and endorsed the pleas of the Witnesses in every case they brought to the High Court. In *Prince* v. *Massachusetts*,[27] which was about as marginal as a religious-freedom case can get, he dissented from the opinion of the Court, written by Rutledge, that the Massachusetts child-labor laws legitimately prohibited Jehovah's Witness children from selling literature. He took this opportunity to express his views on the general problem:

The sidewalk, no less than the cathedral or the evangelist's tent, is a proper place, under the Constitution, for the orderly worship of God.

No chapter in human history has been so largely written in terms of persecution and intolerance as the one dealing with religious freedom. From ancient times to the present day, the ingenuity of man has known no limits in its ability to forge weapons of oppression for use against those who dare to express or practice unorthodox religious beliefs. And the Jehovah's Witnesses are living proof of the fact that even in this nation, conceived as it was in the ideals of freedom, the right to practice religion in unconventional ways is still far from secure.[28]

Other religious minorities uniformly received his support. A religious pacifist barred from the practice of law in Illinois [29] lost his appeal to the Court with Murphy joining in Black's dissenting opinion. Three times Murphy gave judicial comfort to the Mormon schismatics who retained the custom of plural marriage. Once he wrote the opinion of the Court condemning the employment of the Anti-Kidnapping statute against these polygamists,[30] and in two cases he was in dissent when various other legal restraints were invoked against the practice.[31]

Racial minorities could count on Justice Murphy to advance their claims for full equality. One of his best expressions of his philosophy of law arose from the Court's intricate disposal of *Steele* v. *Louisvville & N.R.R.*[32] Concurring with the judgment of the Court, Murphy insisted that the racially restrictive practices of the union local, which was attempting to utilize government authority to impose upon the employer conditions discriminatory to Negroes, should have been declared unconstitutional.

The utter disregard for the dignity and the well-being of colored citizens shown by this record is so pronounced as to demand the invocation of constitutional condemnation. To decide the case and to analyze the statute solely upon the basis of legal niceties, while remaining mute and placid as to the obvious and oppressive deprivation of constitutional guarantees, is to make the judicial function something less than it should be. . . . Racism is far too virulent today to permit the slightest refusal, in the light of a Constitution that abhors it, to expose and condemn it wherever it appears in the course of a statutory interpretation.[33]

His dissent in the *Screws* case [34] was in a similar, though more infuriated, vein.

The Japanese aliens in California, who were unable under the immigration statute of that day to become citizens of the United States, received extended sympathy from Murphy in a lengthy concurrence in the case of *Oyama* v. *California*.[35] Technically at issue in the case was the validity of an amendment to the state's alien land law which by welding escheat provisions to a broad presumption was designed to end Japanese evasions of the ban on landownership. The Court dealt with the statute on a very narrow basis, interdicting the presumption without touching on the legitimacy of the land law itself, and Murphy came out fighting. The land law, he asserted, was on its face unconstitutional as an infringement of the Fourteenth Amendment: it could only be described as a legislative implementation of racism, and the Court betrayed its responsibility to the Constitution when it refused to confront this fact. He filed a similar objection to a California law forbidding the issuance of fishing licenses to aliens ineligible for citizenship which was also disposed of by the Court on other, less ideological, grounds.[36] He consistently defended the claims of the American Indians.[37]

Murphy did not limit his concern to racial or religious minorities. Urban voters, discriminated against by an antiquated system of congressional districting,[38] and by the procedures necessary to get a minor party on the ballot;[39] members of unpopular political minorities such as the quasi-fascist Terminiello [40] and the Communist Gerhard Eisler;[41] aliens subjected to deportation orders seemingly for their political activities;[42] all these found in Justice Murphy a strong defender. He was completely undiscriminating; if his opinion holding the Communist Schneiderman illegally denaturalized was in part a ritualistically liberal approach to the nature of international Communism (he stated at one point that "we should not hold that petitioner is not attached to the Constitution by reason of his possible belief in the creation of some form of world union of soviet republics unless we are willing so to hold with regard to those who believe in Pan-Americanism, the League of Nations, Union Now. . . ."),[43] he also vigorously asserted the immunity from denaturalization proceedings of admitted Nazis.[44]

One last minority group to which Murphy extended his judicial support was a thoroughly marginal one indeed—operators of houses of prostitution caught in the dragnet of the Mann Act. Murphy insisted that the sole purpose of the Mann Act was to eliminate and punish white slavery; that the government had no right to stretch it to convict a genial proprietor who took two of his employees on a Florida vacation. Writing for the Court, he stated that "the sole purpose of the journey from beginning to end was to provide innocent recreation and a holiday," [45] and elsewhere he dissented from a decision in the *Caminetti* tradition which employed the Mann Act against private, noncommercial debauchery.[46] Reading these cases, one gets the distinct feeling that Murphy was repelled by the employment of the majestic sanctions of government against these pathetic, wayward individuals.

No other New Deal Justice approached his record in this area. Without attempting any mathematic computations, certain things are immediately apparent from reading the opinions. Black, for example, wrote most of the Indian opinions that Murphy dissented from, and at no point did Rutledge join Murphy in these dissents. Of the other Justices, Rutledge came nearest to equaling Murphy's score.

The Judicial Process

Under this heading I have grouped those decisions which related in one way or another to the conduct of the judicial process: fair trial, search and seizure, confessions, contempt of court, and the like. Here Murphy's position was forthright, ruthless, and enormously irritating to those who look upon the procedural aspects of law as meaningful. As he put it, dissenting in *Carter v. Illinois* [47] from an opinion of Justice Frankfurter holding that petitioner had not been denied the elements of due process:

Legal technicalities doubtless afford justification of our pretense of ignoring plain facts before us, facts upon which a man's very life or liberty conceivably could depend. . . . The result certainly does not enhance the high traditions of the judicial process.[48]

In another case, dissenting all alone from an opinion by Justice Black, Murphy savagely asserted, "The complete travesty of justice revealed by the record in this case forces me to dissent." [49]

Now the implication of these remarks, and others in a similar genre scattered throughout his opinions, is clear. It is a self-righteous, even smug, claim to a higher moral perspective than his brethren. So spoke Savonarola to the Florentines, and doubtless some of the Justices on the Court wished on occasion that they could deal with their conspicuously moral brother as Florence dealt with its scorpion.

Two cases bring out the strength and weakness of Murphy's approach to due process of law. First, in 1942, Murphy for the Court held that one Glasser had been denied a fair trial in federal court because he had not received adequate protection by counsel. Now, Glasser, as Justice Frankfurter pointed out in a powerful dissent, was a former United States Attorney who should have been well aware of his legal rights and seen to it that they were asserted. But Murphy acted as though an ignorant Negro farmhand, or an illiterate youth, denied counsel, were sufficient precedents for holding an educated and experienced lawyer to be in the same maltreated category.[50] And Murphy did approach such problems in an absolutist mood, and, one suspects, with an inarticulate assumption that petitioner was always in the right.

Second, in 1947, Murphy for the Court held a Texas judge's contempt proceedings against a local newspaper to be a violation of the First Amendment. His opinion was a restatement of his concurrence in *Pennekamp* v. *Florida* [51] in which he had declared that criticism of the courts is a legitimate form of behavior:

[E]ven though the terms be vitriolic, scurrilous or erroneous . . . Judges should be foremost in their vigilance to protect the freedom of others to rebuke and castigate the bench and in their refusal to be influenced by unfair or misinformed censure.[52]

In one of his brilliant opinions, Justice Jackson dissented lock, stock, and barrel from what he considered Murphy's ritualistic liberalism. Cutting to the heart of the matter, Jackson asked one of those disconcerting questions for which his opinions were notable: Supposing the nation's press were controlled by one organization, would we be so lofty? The Court's opinion, he felt, had completely lost touch with the coercive potentialities of a monopoly press, particularly upon an elected judge.[53] Murphy was, however, unimpressed; he never supported a conviction for contempt on appeal, and one has the suspicion that he could not conceivably have found a situation in which contempt action was justified against a newspaper.[54]

There is no need to go further with chapter-and-verse citation. Whether the issue was the legality of a confession,[55] self-incrimination,[56] search and seizure,[57] jury selection,[58] or the right to a writ of habeas corpus,[59] Justice Murphy could be counted on to vote for the aggrieved party. Many Justices joined him at various points, but there was one additional hobby of Murphy's that got him little companionship from his liberal brethren—his suspicion of certain aspects of administrative procedure, notably the employment by administrative officials of the subpoena power. Thus, in 1942, he joined Chief Justice Stone's opinion of the Court in *Cudahy Packing Co.* v. *Holland*[60] limiting the use of subpoenas in administrative investigations. Douglas, Black, Byrnes, and Jackson dissented vigorously.

This decision was not just a sport: the following year Murphy wrote a dissent, joined by Justice Roberts, objecting to the conference upon Secretary of Labor Perkins of broad inquisitorial jurisdiction and the subpoena weapon. He pointed out to his former Cabinet colleague that "under the direction of well-meaning but over-zealous officials they [subpoenas] may at times become instruments of intolerable oppression and injustice."[61] Three years later he returned to the assault again in a lone dissent, asserting that the subpoena power should be confined "exclusively to the judiciary."[62] One of his few significant inconsistencies occurred in this area: in *Fleming* v. *Mohawk Wrecking & Lumber Co.*,[63] in which the Court sustained the authority of the Price Administrator to delegate his subpoena power to subordinates, Murphy silently joined the majority.

Related to Murphy's distrust of bureaucratic inquisitors was his concern about vague statutes and administrative regulations. The Constitution required, as he saw it, that crimes be narrowly defined in order that the individual could have reasonable security, that he might have clear advance knowledge of what the law forbids and what it permits. Thus a vague statute, or the application of an elastic statute to an individual's action, or the formulation of an ambiguous administrative rule called for judicial intervention. Beginning in 1941, when he joined Douglas's dissent in the *Classic* case,[64] and continuing with his dissent in *United States* v. *Dotterweich* [65] in 1943, there are a series of opinions which he either wrote or joined to this effect.[66] It should be noted that in many cases where a statute or regulation was allegedly too vague to stand up, notably in connection with the activities of the National Labor Relations Board, Murphy did not agree. But it seems significant that he alone of the New Deal Justices persistently reiterated this point over the years.

Freedom of the Press and Airways

Closely connected with his deep dedication to individual freedom of speech was his special interest in freedom of communication. And here he really parted company with his New Deal colleagues. It was probably his dissents in the network cases [67] and the *Associated Press* case [68] which motivated John P. Frank's suggestive comment that Murphy on occasion allowed "activities he opposed [to] hide behind symbols he cherished." [69] In the network cases, which involved action by the Federal Communications Commission to eliminate certain monopolistic characteristics of the National and the Columbia Broadcasting systems, Murphy wrote a vigorous dissent, joined only by Roberts, asserting that the FCC had arrogated to itself this power without congressional authorization. Only Congress, he claimed, could legitimately undertake such action. Exposing his real motive, he said:

[B]ecause of its vast potentialities as a medium of communication, discussion and propaganda, the character and extent of control that should be exercised over it [radio] is a matter of deep and vital concern.[70]

In 1945, dissenting in the *Associated Press* case, Murphy returned to this theme. "Today is . . . the first time that the Sherman Act has been used as a vehicle for affirmative intervention by the Government in the realm of dissemination of information." [71] Incidentally, Murphy's dissent in this case—an opinion separate from that of the other two dissenters, Roberts and Stone—did not say that the antitrust laws could never be used against the press. What he objected to was the government's procedure in the case, which was by injunction and summary judgment, and what seemed to him a lowering of the standards of proof required in an antitrust case. The evidence, he felt,

falls far short of proving such a program [of restrictive practices] and *hence* the decision has grave implications relative to governmental restraints on a free press. . . . [S]uch a failure has unusually dangerous implications when it appears with reference to an alleged violation of the [Sherman] Act by those who collect and distribute information.[72]

Other opinions of his in this area, dealing with the power of courts to punish newspapers for contempt, have already been discussed above. Another opinion in this area which he endorsed was Justice Rutledge's concurrence in *United States* v. *CIO*.[73] Here Rutledge and Murphy, rejecting the course of the Court though sharing in its judgment, insisted that the Taft-Hartley provision forbidding trade unions to support political candidates was unconstitutional on its face.

Governmental Responsibility
for the "Good Life"

Under this rubric, I have placed those opinions of Justice Murphy in which he asserted the responsibility of the federal government over the economic life of the nation, for the fostering of a strong trade-union movement, and for destroying irresponsible private centers of economic power.

The great battles over the meaning of the commerce clause

were won when Murphy arrived on the bench. The main problems that remained were those of delineating the activities that Congress intended to regulate, and determining the degree to which Congress desired to preempt the regulation of interstate commerce and eliminate state regulation. It seems hardly necessary to note that Murphy took an extremely comprehensive view of the commerce power,[74] though from 1946 on, he tended to affiliate with the "states'-rights" position of Justices Black and Douglas, that is, to accept the wide latitude these Justices were prepared to give to state taxes and regulations affecting interstate commerce.[75]

Murphy's opinions in this area can conveniently be subdivided into four groups: those which interpret the scope of the commerce power under the Fair Labor Standards Act and the Public Utilities Holding Company Act; those examining the rights of labor; those dealing with the operating procedures of administrative agencies; and those adumbrating the prerogatives of state governments over interstate commerce. Obviously there is some overlap, but if not definitive, this division is accurate enough for our purposes here.

In a series of opinions, both majority and dissenting, Justice Murphy gave a broad interpretation of the FLSA.[76] One case in particular is worth singling out—the *Jewel Ridge* case [77] in which Murphy for the Court overruled the Administrator and held portal-to-portal travel time part of the miner's workweek. Justice Jackson, in dissent, denounced the holding as an extreme instance of judicial lawmaking, one demonstrably against the wishes of Congress. Similarly, Justice Murphy for the Court sustained the "death sentence" provisions of the Public Utilities Holding Company Act of 1935 when, after lurking for years in constitutional limbo,[78] this provision finally came under judicial appraisal.[79]

Murphy's record as a defender of the rights of labor is somewhat more ambiguous than is often realized. Although he was responsible for the key decisions in *Thornhill* v. *Alabama* [80] and *Carlson* v. *California*,[81] which held that peaceful picketing was a manifestation of freedom of speech and thus protected against state infringement by the due-process clause of the Fourteenth Amendment, Murphy did not join the dissent of Justices Black, Douglas, and Reed in the *Meadowmoor* case.[82] This in spite of the fact that Black went to great pains to point out in his dissent, perhaps with an eye on Murphy, that the injunction in the instant case was almost identical in wording with the statutes held void on their face in the two earlier cases.[83] Moreover, while he joined Black's dissent in *Carpenters & Joiners Union, Local 213* v. *Ritter's Cafe*,[84] alleging that the employment of the Texas antitrust law against a secondary boycott was a violation of the union's freedom of speech, and seemed in *AFL* v. *Watson* [85] to be eager to strike down the Florida "right to work" law as unconstitutional, he equivocated without opinions when state "right to work" statutes finally arrived for substantive evaluation.[86]

However, as a defender of the National Labor Relations Board, he was without peer on the Court. Once it was established to his satisfaction that the Board was operating within its statutory *vires,* and providing no civil-liberties issue was apparent on the face of the record,[87] he felt that the task and proper function of the court was done. As he put it in the *Phelps-Dodge* case,[88] partially dissenting:

Our only office is to determine whether the rule chosen, tested in the light of statutory standards, was within the permissible range of the Board's discretion.[89]

He followed the same track in discussing the actions of other administrative agencies, notably the Securities and Exchange Commission,[90] and the Federal Power Commission.[91] He was never particularly happy about the price-control system, probably because of what he felt to be certain unconstitutional procedures that were established for handling violations [92]—and perhaps fundamentally because of his allergy to the war powers and all their legal ramifications which will be discussed later—but he did join with Douglas in a dissent against a judicial weakening of the price-control mechanism.[93] However, the Interstate Commerce Commission, often considered in liberal circles as a feudal vassal of the railroad interests, got little aid and comfort from Murphy.[94] In the *Inland Waterways* case, for example, there was no discussion by the dissenters of the finality of administrative determinations. On the contrary, Justice Black, speaking for Douglas and Murphy, asserted that:

The issue in this case is whether the farmers and shippers of the middle west can be compelled by the Interstate Commerce Commission and the railroads to use high-priced rail instead of low-priced barge transportation for the shipment of grain to the east.[95]

This quotation, though from an opinion by Justice Black, brings out a characteristic that Murphy shared with that Justice and Douglas, a quality which I have designated "Populism." There is a sentimental anticapitalism, or more correctly, a sentimental attachment to a world of small businessmen and independent farmers, which comes out clearly in a series of opinions dealing with various aspects of the administrative process. In his concurring opinion in *United States* v. *Bethlehem Steel Corp.*,[96] Murphy, irritated by the profits claimed by the steel company in some World War I contracts, went out of his way to declare:

In voting for affirmance of the judgment, I do not wish to be understood as expressing approval of an arrangement like the one now under review, by which a company engaged in doing work for the government in time of grave national peril—or any other time—is entitled to a profit of 22 per cent under contracts involving little or no risk and grossing many millions of dollars. Such an arrangement not only is incompatable with sound principles of public management, but is injurious to public confidence and public morale.[97]

In this same "Populist" tradition, we find him dissenting in behalf of the farmer-debtor burdened by a "narrow formalistic" interpretation of Section 75 of the Bankruptcy Act,[98] and, in particular, advancing an antimonopolistic interpretation of patent rights.[99] As might have been expected, he joined the Douglas dissent in *United States* v. *Columbia Steel Co.*,[100] which is as vigorous and well reasoned an antimonopoly tract as any Populist could hope for. Perhaps the full flavor of this viewpoint is best set forth by an excerpt from a dissent by Justice Black in an enormously intricate case:

Hereafter [said Black, in view of the interpretation of the full faith and credit clause expounded by the Court], . . . the state in which the most powerful corporations are concentrated, *or those corporations themselves*, might well be able to pass laws which would govern contracts made by the people in all of the other states. [Emphasis added.] [101]

Murphy joined Black in this opinion, which surely states in its essence the Populist assumptions about the extent of corporate power over the political process.

In the general area of "states'-rights" over interstate commerce, Murphy apparently had no strong views of his own. The evidence suggests that he accepted Chief Justice Stone's leadership in this tricky field until the latter died; then Murphy moved over to the Black-Douglas camp. His one opinion of the Court in this connection dealt with a conflict between the ICC and the state of California.[102]

The Constitution and the War

While Murphy differed in degree from his New Deal colleagues on many of the problems we have examined, it was in connection with the war powers that he demonstrated his uniqueness. While for all the other Justices, to a greater or lesser degree, the Constitution went into judicious hibernation during World War II, to Frank Murphy it stood in its pristine form as a guardian of the rights of the individual and the ideals of American society.

True, he got off to a slow start by disqualifying himself in *Ex parte Quirin*,[103] the case of the Nazi saboteurs, presumably because he was temporarily a lieutenant colonel in the Army on active service,[104] and in the first draft case involving the rights of conscientious objectors, he joined the majority opinion, sustaining the government, rather than Jackson's dissent.[105] But from the *Hirabayashi* case on,[106] he was a consistent, even doctrinaire, opponent of the view that the Constitution had gone to war.

And here he violently parted company with his liberal brethren. Black and Douglas, in particular, became vigorous war hawks;[107] Jackson retired to a private universe of *Realpolitik*, suggesting that the Court should avoid ruling on nasty wartime problems since it was bound, given the power situation of the moment, to make bad decisions;[108] and even Rutledge, who had stood shoulder to shoulder with Murphy in many a lost cause, defected. In short, Justice Murphy found himself isolated on an extreme promontory, standing in lonely, and perhaps visionary, grandeur, and with the fiery virulence of a religious prophet he castigated his friends and erstwhile associates for their betrayal of the democratic faith. Indeed, one suspects that he became a bit obsessed about the matter: if one reads carefully the first two or three hundred pages of Volume 327 of the *United States Reports*, beginning with the *Yamashita* case,[109] he gets the feeling that Murphy has become literally frenzied, striking about him at his colleagues in all types of cases with the angry passion of a betrayed lover.

We have it on the testimony of his law clerk, Eugene Gressman, that Murphy almost immediately regretted his concurrence in the *Hirabayashi* case,[110] feeling that the real motive for the detention and expulsion of the nisei from the West Coast to concentration camps in the hinterland was not military, but racial. Only hesitantly had he given his approval to the judgment of the Court, and he insisted on writing a separate opinion to make clear his reasons. In this he stated:

In voting for the affirmance of this judgment I do not wish to be understood as intimating that the military authorities in time of war are subject to no restraints whatsoever, or that they are free to impose any restrictions they may choose on the rights and liberties of individual citizens or groups of citizens in those places which may be designated as "military areas." While this Court sits, it has the inescapable duty of seeing that the mandates of the Constitution are obeyed. That duty exists in time of war as well as in time of peace, and in its performance we must not forget that few indeed have been the invasions upon essential liberties which have not been accompanied by pleas of urgent necessity advanced in good faith by responsible men.[111]

When the plight of the American-Japanese came again to the Court in 1944, Justice Murphy drew the sword of duty and wrote one of the most passionate dissents in the history of the Supreme Court. He denied utterly that the decision had been founded on military criteria, and declared flatly that the evacuation and detention—for he refused to join the sophistry of the Court that these were separate, discrete actions—fell into "the ugly abyss of racism." [112] At the heart of his dissent is the point, ignored by Justice Black's majority opinion, that a "military judgment" cannot be simply, and circularly, defined as a judgment by a military officer. Thus the Court, while not having the right to supersede the Chiefs of Staff as military experts, has the duty to see that military judgments are *in fact* founded upon military considerations and not upon views on social policy temporarily in uniform.

With regard to the enforcement of the Selective Service Act, particularly with reference to conscientious objectors, Murphy consistently insisted that "all of the mobilization and all of the war effort will have been in vain if, when all is finished, we discover that in the process we have destroyed the very freedoms for which we fought." [113] Dissenting alone from Black's opinion of the Court in *Falbo* v. *United States*—a case involving the rights of conscientious objectors—Murphy uttered what is probably the clearest and most forceful statement of his *telos:*

The law knows no finer hour than when it cuts through formal concepts and transitory emotions to protect unpopular citizens against discrimination and persecution.[114]

During the war, various sorts of legal action were brought against Nazi sympathizers and alleged enemy agents. When the convictions resulting from these actions came before the Supreme Court on appeal, Murphy without exception voted against affirmation, and was the only Justice with this record. It was his view that, if anything, the existence of a state of war required an increase in constitutional sensitivity, and militantly flung his influence against the passions of the moment.[115]

Probably his most notable effort to view the tumults of the hour *sub specie aeternitatis* occurred when counsel for General Yamashita attempted to obtain a writ of habeas corpus from the High Court, claiming that the military commission established to try Japanese "war criminals" was unconstitutional and without jurisdiction. The Court held itself without jurisdiction—at least this seems to be what the Court held: the opinion is in John P. Frank's words, "sufficiently opaque to defy brief statement" [116] —with Rutledge writing a dissent joined by Murphy, and Murphy writing a separate solitary dissent.[117] Murphy's dissent was a blistering attack on the whole war-crimes procedure in the Far East as "unworthy of the traditions of our people." [118] Noting that the real lesson of the trials was *Don't Ever Lose a*

War, he asserted that even the admitted Japanese atrocities "do not justify our abandonment of our devotion to justice in dealing with a fallen enemy commander. To conclude otherwise is to admit that the enemy has lost the battle but has destroyed our ideals." [119]

Murphy's antimilitarism was more dogged than fruitful, but it can be found in a whole series of opinions, the most noteworthy of which is his lengthy concurring opinion in *Duncan* v. *Kahanamoku* [120] reasserting the vitality of David Davis's sonorous holding in *Ex parte Milligan* [121] that "the Constitution of the United States is a law for rulers and people, equally in war and peace, and covers with the shield of its protection all classes of men, at all times, and under all circumstances." [122] And who but Murphy could have achieved the combination of antimilitarism and Populism attained by the following statement?

> In my opinion it is of greater importance to the nation at war and to its military establishment that high standards of public health be maintained than that the military procurement authorities have the benefit of unrestrained competitive bidding and lower prices in the purchase of needed milk supplies.[123]

In regard to Murphy's attitude toward the war powers, there is one point that remains for brief treatment: his attitude toward the limitations on the right of appeal incorporated in the price-control legislation. It will be recalled that an Emergency Court of Appeals was established to handle cases arising under the statute, and elaborate procedures were set up governing the legal aspects of appeal. When, in 1944, the constitutionality of this structure was challenged, Roberts, Rutledge, and Murphy dissented from Stone's holding that it was a valid exercise of the war powers.[124] That this was not just constitutional windmill tilting is suggested by the fact that the Rutledge dissent, which Murphy joined, has impressed even such a hard-boiled realist as Edward S. Corwin.[125]

This examination of the judicial record of Justice Murphy has, I suspect, been a tedious trip for the reader. However, it seems important to get the data on the record before moving on to the final section of this essay in which I shall summarize what seems to me the judicial essence of Frank Murphy.

[4]

It was suggested earlier that Justice Frank Murphy was the judicial incarnation of the militant liberal myth of the New Deal, and while at some points, for example, his view of trade unions, he fell a bit short of the archetypical aspiration, it is nonetheless true that he fitted the pattern far more closely than did any of his New Deal colleagues on the Court. While each of the other Justices went partway down the road with him, each turned off somewhere short of Murphy's destination.

But this still leaves open the persistent question: Was he a "good" judge? To the extent that this means Was he a good legal craftsman? I would venture the opinion, based on a careful reading of every opinion he wrote (including a mass of technical tax opinions which have not been discussed here: of the 132 opinions he wrote for the Court in his nine years of service, almost a third were in this category, and they were mostly for a unanimous Court), and disregarding as irrelevant the question of authorship on grounds explained earlier, that while Justice Murphy surely did not have the technical competence of a Frankfurter or a Stone, he was certainly not below par for the Court. The basic proposition that has to be understood in dealing with Murphy, I think, was that he *chose* not to immerse himself in the mysteries of the guild.

This choice was based on both temperamental and intellectual reasons: by temperament he was a fighter who was aroused by seeming injustice, and did not want to check the rule book before he went into action; by intellect he was an instrumentalist, not in the Deweyan sense of being a pragmatist, but in the natural-law tradition of viewing all the phenomena of the world about us in terms of a higher purpose, as instruments for the fulfillment of the *telos*. In other words, Murphy mounted the wild horse of natural law and mercilessly rode down those institutions, traditions, and legal precedents which stood between him and his destination—a democratic Utopia.

Therefore it is perhaps not unfair to his memory to suggest that he was the McReynolds of the Left, though I hasten to add that he did not share the latter's misanthropic disposition. Like McReynolds, he was a vigorous, even belligerent, fighter for the things he believed in, and like McReynolds, he called a spade a spade. He was also a judicial activist, who had no time for philosophies of "self-restraint"—except, of course, when judicial self-restraint contributed to his substantive goal. But here he is in good company. Even the Court's leading advocate of self-restraint, Justice Frankfurter, has been known to rise above principle—a dissent in *Brown* v. *Board of Education* would surely have followed logically from the author of the *Gobitis* opinion.[126]

Yet, given these qualities, there was a quality about Murphy which made him an asset to the Court. No one, and certainly no student of constitutional law, would want a Supreme Court composed entirely of Murphys—or of Jacksons or Frankfurters, for that matter—but is it not valuable to sprinkle the high tribunal from time to time with men who, disdaining the tortuous paths of the law, assert in a clarion peal the basic truth, so often forgotten by those with their nose close to the earth of precedent, that law is at root an instrument for the achievement of social goals? And that in a democracy, there are no more priceless goals than individual liberty and collective prosperity? If this is so, then the utopian pilgrimage of Mr. Justice Murphy was not made in vain.

NOTES

1. *Mich. L. Rev.*, Vol. 48 (1950), pp. 737–810.

2. *Ibid*. See also John P. Frank, "Justice Murphy: The Goals Attempted," *Yale Law Journal*, Vol. 59 (1949), p. 1; Eugene Gressman, "Mr. Justice Murphy: A Preliminary Appraisal, *Columbia Law Review*, Vol. 50 (1950), p. 29; Comment, "Mr. Justice Murphy," *Harvard Law Review*, Vol. 63 (1949), p. 289.

3. Pritchett, *The Roosevelt Court* (1948), p. 285.

4. Kurland, "Review of Pritchett, Civil Liberties and the Vinson Court, *University of Chicago Law Review*, Vol. 22 (1954), pp. 297, 299.

5. Mason, *Harlan Fiske Stone: Pillar of the Law* (1956), p. 793.

6. 321 U.S. 590 (1944).

7. *Ibid*. at 592.

8. *Ibid*. at 606.

9. See Roche, "*Plessy* v. *Ferguson*: Requiescat in Pace?", *University of Pennsylvania Law Review*, Vol. 99 (1954), pp. 44, 52.

10. *Minersville School District* v. *Gobitis*, 310 U.S. 586, 601 (1940).

11. Interview cited in Mason, *op. cit. supra*, Note 5, at 528.

12. *Ibid*. at 513.

13. *Ibid*. at 505.

14. Murphy had only four clerks in nine years.

15. 323 U.S. 214, 233 (1944).

16. *Cohens* v. *Virginia*, 19 U.S. (6 *Wheat.*) 264 (1821). In Henry Adams's phrase, Marshall was "the

despair of bench and bar for the unswerving certainty of his legal method." *The Formative Years* (Agar ed. 1948), I, 104.

17. For a superb analysis, see J. M. Burns, *Roosevelt: The Lion and the Fox* (1956).

18. 328 U.S. 463, 494 (1946).

19. *Hooven & Allison Co.* v. *Evatt*, 324 U.S. 652 (1945).

20. Governor Murphy was apparently quite close to the Catholic worker movement which was, and is, strongly prolabor.

21. Cited by R. Carr, *Federal Protection of Civil Rights* (1947), p. 25.

22. Cited, *ibid.* at p. 1.

23. Cited, *ibid.* at p. 26, Note 37.

24. For a good discussion of the various strands of New Deal liberalism, see Eric F. Goldman, *Rendezvous with Destiny* (Rev. Ed., 1956). The treatment of Roosevelt's relations with the Left by Hofstadter, *The American Political Tradition* (1948), p. 331, is very insightful. I should note that much of this composite of the militant liberal I have gained from intensive reading of the liberal and radical literature of the thirties and forties in connection with a Fund for the Republic project. The files of *The Nation* and *The New Republic* are indispensable, and for a somewhat more jaundiced view of the New Deal that yet remains within the militant liberal tradition, *Common Sense* is most revealing.

25. 316 U.S. 584, 611 (1942). Murphy here joined the penitential concurring dissent of Justices Black and Douglas in which the trio apologized for joining the majority in *Gobitis*. 316 U.S. at 623.

26. 336 U.S. 77, 89 (1949).

27. 321 U.S. 158, 171 (1944).

28. *Ibid.* at 174–176.

29. *In re* Summers, 325 U.S. 561, 573 (1945).

30. *Chatwin* v. *United States*, 326 U.S. 455 (1946).

31. A state law prohibiting the advocacy, encouragement, etc., of polygamy: *Musser* v. *Utah*, 333 U.S. 95, 98 (1948); the employment of the Mann Act: *Cleveland* v. *United States*, 329 U.S. 14, 24 (1946). In the latter case, he observed in dissent: "[M]arriage, even when it occurs in a form of which we disapprove, is not to be compared with prostitution or debauchery. . . ." 329 U.S. at 26.

32. 323 U.S. 192 (1944).

33. *Ibid.* at 208–209.

34. *Screws* v. *United States*, 325 U.S. 91, 134 (1945).

35. 332 U.S. 633, 650 (1948).

36. *Takahashi* v. *Fish & Game Comm'n*, 334 U.S. 410, 422 (1948).

37. See *Confederated Bands of Ute Indians* v. *United States*, 330 U.S. 169, 180 (1947); *Northwestern Bands of Shoshone Indians* v. *United States*, 324 U.S. 335, 362 (1945); *Mahnomen County* v. *United States*, 319 U.S. 474, 480 (1943); *Oklahoma Tax Comm'n* v. *United States*, 319 U.S. 598, 612 (1943); *Creek Nation* v. *United States*, 318 U.S. 629, 641 (1943). In each of these cases he dissented. In this area, he wrote two opinions of the Court: *Choctaw Nation of Indians* v. *United States*, 318 U.S. 423 (1943); *Seminole Nation* v. *United States*, 316 U.S. 286 (1942).

38. Joining Black's dissent in *Colegrove* v. *Green*, 328 U.S. 549, 566 (1946).

39. Joining Douglas's dissent in *MacDougall* v. *Green*, 335 U.S. 281, 287 (1948).

40. Joining Douglas's opinion of the Court in *Terminiello* v. *Chicago*, 337 U.S. 1 (1949).

41. Dissenting in *Eisler* v. *United States*, 338 U.S. 189, 193 (1949).

42. Concurring opinion in *Bridges* v. *Wixon*, 326 U.S. 135, 157 (1945). In general, see this opinion for his views on deportation procedure. He

also joined the dissenting opinions in *Ahrens* v. *Clark*, 335 U.S. 188, 193 (1948); *Ludecke* v. *Watkins*, 335 U.S. 160, 173 (1948).

43. *Schneiderman* v. *United States*, 320 U.S. 118, 145 (1943). Wendell Willkie was Schneiderman's counsel. This opinion, when circulated among his brethren for their comments, brought the following rejoinder from an unidentified Justice: "I think it is only fair to state in view of your general argument that Uncle Joe Stalin is at least a spiritual co-author with Jefferson of the Virginia statute for religious freedom." Cited by Mason, *op. cit., supra*, Note 5, at 795.

44. Murphy concurred in *Baumgartner* v. *United States*, 322 U.S. 665, 678 (1944), objecting to Frankfurter's watering down of his *Schniederman* rationale; and joined Rutledge's dissent in *Knauer* v. *United States*, 328 U.S. 654, 675 (1946), and the latter's concurrence in *Klapprott* v. *United States*, 335 U.S. 601, 616 (1949).

45. *Mortensen* v. *United States*, 322 U.S. 369, 375 (1944).

46. *United States* v. *Beach*, 324 U.S. 193, 197 (1945).

47. 329 U.S. 173, 182 (1946).

48. *Ibid.* at 183.

49. *Canizio* v. *New York*, 327 U.S. 82, 87 (1946).

50. *Glasser* v. *United States*, 315 U.S. 60 (1942).

51. 328 U.S. 331 (1946).

52. *Ibid.* at 370.

53. *Craig* v. *Harney*, 331 U.S. 367, 394 (1947).

54. See his dissents in *Fisher* v. *Pace*, 336 U.S. 155, 166 (1949); *United States* v. *United Mine Workers*, 330 U.S. 258, 335 (1947).

55. See, e.g., *Taylor* v. *Alabama*, 335 U.S. 252 (1948); *Lee* v. *Mississippi*, 332 U.S. 742 (1948); *Lyons* v. *Oklahoma*, 322 U.S. 596 (1944).

56. See, e.g., *Shapiro* v. *United States*, 335 U.S. 1 (1948); *Adamson*

v. *California*, 332 U.S. 46 (1947); *Goldman* v. *United States*, 316 U.S. 129 (1942); *Goldstein* v. *United States*, 316 U.S. 114 (1942).

57. See *Wolf* v. *Colorado*, 338 U.S. 25 (1949); *Trupiano* v. *United States*, 334 U.S. 699 (1948); *Johnson* v. *United States*, 333 U.S. 10 (1948); *Harris* v. *United States*, 331 U.S. 145 (1947); *Zap* v. *United States*, 328 U.S. 624 (1946); *Davis* v. *United States*, 328 U.S. 582 (1946).

58. See *Frazier* v. *United States*, 335 U.S. 497 (1948); *Moore* v. *New York*, 333 U.S. 565 (1948); *Fay* v. *New York*, 332 U.S. 261 (1947); *Thiel* v. *Southern Pacific Co.*, 328 U.S. 217 (1946); *Akins* v. *Texas*, 325 U.S. 398 (1945).

59. See *Wade* v. *Mayo*, 334 U.S. 672 (1948); *Price* v. *Johnston*, 334 U.S. 266 (1948); *Parker* v. *Illinois*, 333 U.S. 571 (1948); *Marino* v. *Ragen*, 332 U.S. 561 (1947); *Ex parte Hull*, 312 U.S. 546 (1941).

60. 315 U.S. 357 (1942).

61. *Endicott Johnson Corp.* v. *Perkins*, 317 U.S. 501, 510 (1943).

62. *Oklahoma Press Co.* v. *Walling*, 327 U.S. 186, 219 (1946).

63. 331 U.S. 111 (1947).

64. *United States* v. *Classic*, 313 U.S. 299, 329 (1941).

65. 320 U.S. 277, 285 (1943).

66. See his dissent in *National Broadcasting Co.* v. *United States*, 319 U.S. 190, 227 (1943), which will be discussed later in this analysis; his agreement with Roberts's dissent in *California* v. *United States*, 320 U.S. 577, 586 (1944); his opinion for the Court in *Kraus & Bros. Inc.* v. *United States*, 327 U.S. 614 (1946).

67. *National Broadcasting Co.* v. *United States*, 319 U.S. 190, 227 (1943).

68. *Associated Press* v. *United States*, 326 U.S. 1, 49 (1945).

69. Frank, *supra*, Note 2, at p. 3.

70. *National Broadcasting Co.* v. *United States*, 319 U.S. 190, 228 (1943).

71. *Associated Press* v. *United States*, 326 U.S. 1, 51 (1945).

72. *Ibid.* at 50, 52.

73. *United States* v. *CIO*, 335 U.S. 106, 129 (1948).

74. See, e.g., his opinions of the Court in *United States* v. *Yellow Cab Co.*, 332 U.S. 218 (1947); *United States* v. *Walsh*, 331 U.S. 432 (1947).

75. He also in a sense defended "states' rights" in the area of divorce. Some have suggested that this was his Catholic conviction surfacing in a sphere where the Church holds strong views, but the logic of this contention escapes me. After all, he was not denying the right of a state to grant a divorce to bona fide residents, but rather disagreeing with the conditions under which "full faith and credit" shall be given to a divorce consummated in another state. In what were probably the most important cases—*Coe* v. *Coe*, 334 U.S. 378, 386 (1948); *Sherrer* v. *Sherrer*, 334 U.S. 343, 365 (1948)—he joined Justice Frankfurter's learned and masterful dissents. See also his concurring opinion in *Williams* v. *North Carolina*, 325 U.S. 226, 239 (1945), and his dissent in *Williams* v. *North Carolina*, 317 U.S. 287, 308 (1942). In another area where his religion might have been expected to influence his judgment, if anywhere, there is no apparent correlation. In the "Church and State" cases, he rode silently with the majority first one way and then the other. See *Illinois ex rel. McCollum* v. *Board of Education*, 333 U.S. 203 (1948); *Everson* v. *Board of Education*, 330 U.S. 1 (1947). Murphy's religious convictions gave him a deep set of natural-law premises which penetrated every aspect of his legal thought, but did not result in any immediately "religious" opinions.

76. See his opinions of the Court in *Borden Co.* v. *Borella*, 325 U.S. 679 (1945); *Jewel Ridge Coal Corp.* v. *United Mine Workers*, 325 U.S. 161 (1945); *Phillips Inc.* v. *Walling*, 324 U.S. 490 (1945); *United States* v. *Rosenwasser*, 323 U.S. 360 (1945); *Overstreet* v. *North Shore Corp.*, 318 U.S. 125 (1943); *Warren-Bradshaw Drilling Co.* v. *Hall*, 317 U.S. 88 (1942). See also his dissents in *10 East 40th Street Building, Inc.* v. *Callus*, 325 U.S. 578, 585 (1945); *Western Union Tel. Co.* v. *Lenroot*, 323 U.S. 490, 509 (1945); *McLeod* v. *Threlkeld*, 319 U.S. 491, 498 (1943). His one rejection of the claims for broad coverage may have been motivated by his special concern for the press, or by simple common sense. In 1946, he dissented from the Court's holding that a newspaper that shipped 45 of 10,000 newspapers into interstate commerce was subject to coverage under the FLSA. *Mabee* v. *White Plains Publishing Co.*, 327 U.S. 178, 185 (1946).

77. *Jewel Ridge Coal Corp.* v. *United Mine Workers*, 325 U.S. 161 (1945).

78. See, for a discussion of the difficulties involved in getting a judicial evaluation of the "death sentence" provision of the Public Utilities Holding Company Act, Stern, "The Commerce Clause and the National Economy, 1933–1946," Part II, *Harv. L. Rev.*, Vol. 59 (1946), pp. 883, 940–942.

79. *American Power & Light Co.* v. *SEC*, 329 U.S. 90 (1946); *North American Co.* v. *SEC*, 327 U.S. 686 (1946).

80. 310 U.S. 88 (1940).

81. 310 U.S. 106 (1940).

82. *Milk Wagon Drivers Union* v. *Meadowmoor Dairies*, 312 U.S. 287 (1941).

83. *Ibid.* at 308–309.

84. 315 U.S. 722, 729 (1942).

85. 327 U.S. 582 (1946).

86. *AFL* v. *American Sash & Door Co.*, 335 U.S. 538 (1949); *Lin-*

coln *Federal Labor Union, AFL* v.
Northwestern Iron & Metal Co., 335
U.S. 525 (1949). In the former case,
he dissented without opinion; in the
two grouped together under *Lincoln
Federal Labor Union, AFL* v.
Northwestern Iron & Metal Co.,
supra, he concurred with Rutledge's
opinion which accepted the judgment, but not the rationale, of the
Court.

87. This respect for what the
British term the "principles of natural justice" appears clearly in two
cases: In 1941, Murphy for the Court
remanded to the NLRB the *Virginia
Power Co.* case for evidence that
defendants in encouraging a company union had not merely been exercising their right of freedom of
speech. *NLRB* v. *Virginia Elec. &
Power Co.*, 314 U.S. 469 (1941). The
NLRB adduced further evidence
that coercion beyond mere verbal
encouragement had been involved,
and on the basis of the new record
the Court through Murphy sustained
the Board's disestablishment of the
company union. *Virginia Elec. &
Power Co.* v. *NLRB*, 319 U.S. 533
(1943). In 1949, he employed the
same technique in *NLRB* v. *Stowe
Spinning Co.*, 336 U.S. 226 (1949),
supporting the Board up to the point
where an employer was handed a
broad, vague injunction to desist
from frustrating certain union activities. The latter technique, he maintained, was bad, and the injunction
must be reformulated in specific,
equitable terms.

88. *Phelps Dodge Corp.* v. *NLRB*,
313 U.S. 177, 200 (1941).

89. *Ibid.* at 206. See also his dissent
for the Board in *International Union
of Mine Workers* v. *Eagle-Picher
Mining & Smelting Co.*, 325 U.S.
335, 344 (1945), and his agreement
with Reed's dissent in *Southern
S.S. Co.* v. *NLRB*, 316 U.S. 31, 49
(1942).

90. See his opinions for the Court

in *SEC* v. *Howey Co.*, 328 U.S. 293
(1946), and *American Power &
Light Co.* v. *SEC*, 325 U.S. 385
(1945); and his agreement with
Black's dissent in *SEC* v. *Chenery
Corp.*, 318 U.S. 80, 95 (1943).

91. See his dissent in *Connecticut
Light & Power Co.* v. *FPC*, 324 U.S.
515, 536 (1945), and his agreement
with Black's dissent in *FPC* v. *Natural Gas Pipeline Co.*, 315 U.S. 575,
599 (1942).

92. Joining the Rutledge dissent in
Yakus v. *United States*, 321 U.S.
414, 448 (1944), in which the two
Justices asserted that the procedures
for handling violations impaired
constitutional liberties.

93. *Davis Warehouse Co.* v.
Bowles, 321 U.S. 144, 156 (1944).
But see the *Kraus Bros.* case, 327
U.S. 614 (1946), in which he con-
demned for the Court the creation
of ambiguous offenses by the Price
Control Administration.

94. See his agreement with Roberts's dissent in *California* v. *United
States*, 320 U.S. 577 (1944), and his
agreement with Black's dissent in
California v. *United States Waterways Corp.*, 319 U.S. 671, 692 (1943).

95. 319 U.S. 671, 692 (1943).

96. 315 U.S. 289, 310 (1942).

97. *Ibid.*

98. *State Bank* v. *Brown*, 317 U.S.
135, 142 (1942). See also his opinion
of the Court in *Carter* v. *Kubler*,
320 U.S. 243 (1943).

99. See his position in *Bruce's
Juices, Inc.* v. *American Can Co.*,
330 U.S. 743 (1947); *Transparent-
Wrap Mach. Corp.* v. *Stokes &
Smith Co.*, 329 U.S. 637 (1947);
Precision Instrument Mfg. Co. v.
Automotive Maintenance Co., 324
U.S. 806 (1945); *Special Equipment
Co.* v. *Coe*, 324 U.S. 370 (1945);
Central States Elec. Co. v. *City of
Muscatine*, 324 U.S. 138 (1945);
Goodyear Tire & Rubber Co. v.
RAY-O-VAC Co., 321 U.S. 275, 279
(1944).

100. 334 U.S. 495, 534 (1948).

101. *Order of United Commercial Travelers* v. *Wolfe*, 331 U.S. 586, 642 (1947).

102. He joined Stone's dissent in *Cloverleaf Butter Co.* v. *Patterson*, 315 U.S. 148, 177 (1942); Stone's opinion of the Court in *Southern Pacific Co.* v. *Arizona*, 324 U.S. 761 (1945); Stone's concurrence in *New York and Saratoga Springs Comm'n* v. *United States*, 326 U.S. 572, 586 (1946). He joined Black and Douglas only once before Stone's death, dissenting in *Nipper* v. *Richmond*, 327 U.S. 416, 435 (1946). However, from that time on he was generally with Black and Douglas. See *Interstate Oil Pipe-line Co.* v. *Stone*, 337 U.S. 662 (1949); *H. P. Hood & Sons, Inc.* v. *Du Mond*, 336 U.S. 525 (1949); *Central Greyhound Lines, Inc.* v. *Mealey*, 334 U.S. 653 (1948). The case in which he wrote the opinion of the Court sustaining the California motor-vehicle regulations was *California* v. *Zook*, 336 U.S. 725 (1949).

103. 317 U.S. 1 (1942).

104. *Mason, op. cit., supra*, Note 5, at p. 655.

105. *Bowles* v. *United States*, 319 U.S. 33, 36 (1943).

106. *Hirabayashi* v. *United States*, 320 U.S. 81 (1943).

107. See, e.g., their dissents in *Viereck* v. *United States*, 318 U.S. 236, 249 (1943), and *Cramer* v. *United States*, 325 U.S. 1 (1945); Black's opinions of the Court in *Korematsu* v. *United States*, 323 U.S. 214 (1944), and *Falbo* v. *United States*, 320 U.S. 549 (1944); Douglas's opinion of the Court in *Singer* v. *United States*, 323 U.S. 338 (1945), for their general approach to the interpretation of war powers.

108. See his amazing dissent in *Korematsu* v. *United States, supra*, Note 106, at 233, for a full statement of his views.

109. *Yamashita* v. *Styler*, 327 U.S. 1 (1946).

110. *Gressman, supra*, Note 2, at p. 36.

111. *Hirabayashi* v. *United States*, 320 U.S. 81, 113 (1943).

112. *Korematsu* v. *United States*, 323 U.S. 214, 233 (1944).

113. Concurring separately in *Estep* v. *United States*, 327 U.S. 114, 132 (1946). See also his dissents in *Sunal* v. *Large*, 332 U.S. 174, 193 (1947), and *Cox* v. *United States*, 332 U.S. 442, 457 (1947); and his agreement with Frankfurter's dissent in *Singer* v. *United States*, 323 U.S. 338, 346 (1945).

114. 320 U.S. 549, 561 (1944).

115. See *Von Moltke* v. *Gillies*, 332 U.S. 708 (1948); *Haupt* v. *United States*, 330 U.S. 631 (1947); *Keegan* v. *United States*, 325 U.S. 478 (1945); *Cramer* v. *United States*, 325 U.S. 1 (1945); *Hartzel* v. *United States*, 322 U.S. 680 (1944); *Viereck* v. *United States*, 318 U.S. 236 (1943).

116. J. P. Frank, *Cases on Constitutional Law* (1950), p. 797.

117. *Yamashita* v. *Styler*, 327 U.S. 1, 26 (1946).

118. *Ibid.* at 28.

119. *Ibid.* at 29.

120. 327 U.S. 304, 324 (1946). See also *Humphrey* v. *Smith*, 336 U.S. 695 (1949); *Wade* v. *Hunter*, 336 U.S. 684 (1949); *Hirota* v. *MacArthur*, 338 U.S. 197 (1948).

121. 71 U.S. (4 Wall.) 2 (1866).

122. 327 U.S. at 335.

123. Concurring opinion in *Penn Dairies, Inc.* v. *Milk Control Comm'n*, 318 U.S. 261, 280 (1943).

124. *Yakus* v. *United States*, 321 U.S. 414, 460 (1944).

125. Corwin, *Total War and the Constitution* (1947), p. 131.

126. See my discussion of this point in Roche, "Judicial Self-Restraint," *American Political Science Review*, Vol. 49 (1955), p. 762. (Reprinted on pp. 194–208 of this book.)

Judicial Self-Restraint

Every society, sociological research suggests, has its set of myths which incorporate and symbolize its political, economic, and social aspirations. Thus, as medieval society had the Quest for the Holy Grail and the cult of numerology, we, in our enlightened epoch, have as significant manifestations of our collective hopes the dream of impartial decision-making and the cult of "behavioral science." While in my view these latter two are but different facets of the same fundamental drive, namely, the age-old effort to exorcise human variables from human action, our concern here is with the first of them, the pervasive tendency in the American political and constitutional tradition directed toward taking the politics out of politics, and substituting some set of Platonic guardians for fallible politicians.

While this dream of objectivizing political Truth is in no sense a unique American phenomenon, it is surely true to say that in no other democratic nation has the effort been carried so far and with such persistence.[1] Everywhere one turns in the United States, he finds institutionalized attempts to narrow the political sector and to substitute allegedly "independent" and "impartial" bodies for elected decision-makers.[2] The so-called "independent regulatory commissions" are a classic example of this tendency in the area of administration, but unquestionably the greatest hopes for injecting pure Truth-serum into the body politic have been traditionally reserved for the federal judiciary,

Reprinted, with permission, from *The American Political Science Review*, Volume XLIX, Number 3, September, 1955, pages 762–772.

and particularly for the Supreme Court. The rationale for this viewpoint is simple: "The people must be protected from themselves, and no institution is better fitted for the role of chaperon than the federal judiciary, dedicated as it is to the supremacy of the rule of law."

Patently central to this function of social chaperonage is the right of the judiciary to review legislative and executive actions and nullify those measures which derogate from eternal principles of truth and justice as incarnated in the Constitution. Some authorities, enraged at what the Supreme Court has found the Constitution to mean, have essayed to demonstrate that the Framers did not intend the Court to exercise this function, to have, as they put it, "the last word." [3] I find no merit in this contention; indeed, it seems to me undeniable not only that the authors of the Constitution intended to create a federal government but also that they assumed *sub silentio* that the Supreme Court would have the power to review both national and state legislation.[4]

However, since the intention of the Framers is essentially irrelevant except to antiquarians and polemicists, it is unnecessary to examine further the matter of origins. The fact is that the United States Supreme Court, and the inferior federal courts under the oversight of the High Court, have enormous policy-making functions. Unlike their British and French counterparts, federal judges are not merely technicians who live in the shadow of a supreme legislature, but are fully equipped to intervene in the process of political decision-making. In theory, they are limited by the Constitution and the jurisdiction it confers, but, in practice, it would be a clumsy judge indeed who could not, by a little skillful exegesis, adapt the Constitution to a necessary end.[5] This statement is in no sense intended as a condemnation; on the contrary, it has been this perpetual reinvigoration by reinterpretation, in which the legislature and the executive as well as the courts play a part, that has given the Constitution its survival power. Applying a Constitution which contains at key points inspired ambiguity, the courts have been able to pour the new wine in the old bottle. Note that the point at issue is not the legitimacy or wisdom of judicial legislation; it is simply the enormous scope that this prerogative gives to judges to substitute their views for those of past generations, or, more controversially, for those of a contemporary Congress and President.

Thus it is naïve to assert that the Supreme Court is limited by the Constitution, and we must turn elsewhere for the sources of judicial restraint. The great power exercised by the Court has carried with it great risks, so it is not surprising that American political history has been sprinkled with demands that the judiciary be emasculated.[6] The really startling thing is that, with the notable exception of the McCardle incident in 1869,[7] the Supreme Court has emerged intact from each of these encounters. Despite the plenary power that Congress, under Article III of the Constitution, can exercise over the appellate jurisdiction of the High Court, the National Legislature has never taken sustained and effective action against its House of Lords.[8] It is beyond the purview of this analysis to examine the reasons for congressional inaction; [9] suffice it here to say that the most significant form of judicial limitation has remained self-limitation. This is not to suggest that such a development as statutory codification has not cut down the area of interpretative discretion, for it obviously has. It is rather to maintain that when the Justices have held back from assaults on legislative or executive actions, they have done so on the basis of self-established rationalizations such as Justice Brandeis's famous "Ashwander rules." [10]

The remainder of this paper is therefore concerned with two aspects of this auto-limitation: first, the techniques by which it is put into practice; and, second, the conditions under which it is exercised. It might be noted that no judgment will be entered on the merits of judicial action: the American people, however wisely or foolishly, have incorporated the notion of judicial supremacy in their social myths; I accept that fact as a constant in the equation. Furthermore, there seems to be little question of principle in the long-standing argument over the legitimacy of judicial legislation. On the contrary, it appears that all hands have been in favor of judicial restraint when it operates on their behalf, and in favor of judicial intervention when such action forwards their objectives. From the Jeffersonians, who maintained that the judiciary should declare the Sedition Act of 1798 unconstitutional,[11] to President Franklin D. Roosevelt, who kept to himself his view that a section of the Lend-Lease Act was unconstitutional to avoid embarrassing his congressional lieutenants,[12] American politics have demonstrated little abiding concern with "principles of jurisprudence." An analyst may be devoted to such principles, but he should not permit his ideological "a prioris" to dominate his presentation of descriptive data.[13]

Techniques of Judicial Self-Restraint

The major techniques of judicial self-restraint appear to fall under two familiar rubrics: procedural and substantive. Under the former fall the various techniques by which the Court can avoid coming to grips with substantive issues, while under the latter would fall those methods by which the Court, in a substantive holding, finds that the matter at issue in the litigation is not properly one for judicial settlement. Let us examine these two categories in some detail.

Procedural Self-Restraint. Since the passage of the Judiciary Act of 1925,[14] the Supreme Court has had almost complete control over its business. United States Supreme Court *Rule 38,* which governs the certiorari policy, states (Section 5) that discretionary review will be granted only "where there are special and important reasons therefor." Professor Fowler Harper has suggested in a series of detailed and persuasive articles on the application of this discretion [15] that the Court has used it in such a fashion as to duck certain significant but controversial problems. While one must be extremely careful about generalizing in this area, since the reasons for denying certiorari are many and complex,[16] Harper's evidence does suggest that the Court in the period since 1949 has refused to review cases involving important civil-liberties problems which on their merits appeared to warrant adjudication.[17] As he states at one point: "It is disconcerting when the Court will review a controversy over a patent on a pin ball machine while one man is deprived of his citizenship and another of his liberty without Supreme Court review of a plausible challenge to the validity of government action." [18] That this restraint is not wholly accidental is suggested by Professor Pritchett's recent study of the general attitude of the Vinson Court toward civil-liberty issues.[19]

Furthermore, the Supreme Court can issue certiorari on its own terms. Thus in *Dennis* v. *United States*,[20] appealing the Smith Act convictions of the American Communist leadership, the Court accepted the evidential findings of the Second Circuit as final, and limited its review to two narrow constitutional issues.[21] This, in effect, burked the basic problem: whether the evidence was sufficient to demonstrate that the Communist Party, U.S.A., was *in fact* a clear and present danger to the security of the nation, or whether the Communists were merely shouting "Fire!" in an empty theatre.

Other related procedural techniques are applicable in some situations. Simple delay can be employed, perhaps in the spirit of the Croatian proverb that "Delay is the handmaiden of justice." The case of *Duncan* v. *Kahanamoku*,[22] contesting the validity of military trials of civilians in Hawaii during the war, is a good instance of the judicial stall: Duncan was locked up in August, 1942, and succeeded in bringing habeas corpus action in the District Court only in April, 1944. In November, 1944, the Ninth Circuit affirmed the denial of the writ,[23] and Duncan immediately applied to the Supreme Court for certiorari—which was granted in February, 1945. The Supreme Court studied the case carefully while the war ended, then in February, 1946, determined that Duncan had been improperly convicted. The Japanese-Americans, attempting to get a judicial ruling on the validity of their detainment in relocation centers, met with the same Kafkaesque treatment.[24] However, the technique of procedural self-restraint is founded on the essentially simple gadget of refusing jurisdiction, or of procrastinating the acceptance of jurisdiction, and need not concern us further here.

Substantive Self-Restraint.   Once a case has come before the Court on its merits, the Justices are forced to give some explanation for whatever action they may take. Here self-restraint can take many forms, notably, the doctrine of political questions, the operation of judicial parsimony, and—particularly with respect to the actions of administrative officers or agencies—the theory of judicial inexpertise.

The doctrine of political questions is too familiar to require much elaboration here. Suffice it to say that if the Court feels that a question before it, for example, the legitimacy of a state government,[25] the validity of a legislative apportionment,[26] or the correctness of executive action in the field of foreign relations,[27] is one that is not properly amenable to judicial settlement, it will refer the plaintiff to the "political" organs of government for any possible relief. The extent to which this doctrine is applied seems to be a direct coefficient of judicial egotism, for the definition of a political question can be expanded or contracted in accordion-like fashion to meet the exigencies of the times.[28] A juridical definition of the term is impossible, for at root the logic that supports it is circular: political questions are matters not soluble by the judicial process; matters not soluble by the judicial process are political questions. As an early dictionary explained, a violin is a small cello, and a cello is a large violin.

Nor do examples help much in definition. While it is certainly true that the Court cannot mandamus a legislature to apportion a state in equitable fashion, it seems equally true that the Court is without the authority to force state legislators to implement unsegregated public education. Yet in the former instance the Court genuflected to the "political" organs and took no action, while in the latter it struck down segregation as violative of the Constitution.

Judicial parsimony is another major technique of substantive self-restraint. In what is essentially a legal application of Ockham's razor, the Court has held that it will not apply any more principles to the settlement of a case than are absolutely necessary; for example, it will not discuss the constitutionality of a law if it can settle the instant case by statutory construction. Furthermore, if an action is found to rest on erroneous statutory construction, the review terminates at that point: the Court will not go on to discuss whether the statute, properly construed, would be constitutional. A variant form of this doctrine, and a most important one, employs the "case or controversy" approach; to wit, the Court, admitting the importance of the issue, inquires as to whether the litigant actually has standing to bring the matter up.

But while on the surface this technique of limitation appears to be quasi-automatic in operation, such is not always the case. For example, the Court held in the *United Public Workers* [29] and the *Alaskan cannery workers* [30] cases that the plaintiffs could not get adjudication until the laws they challenged had been employed against them; it also agreed to review the constitutionality of the New York Teacher Loyalty statute *before* anyone had been injured by its operation.[31] Similarly, the Court for years held that a state government had no standing to intervene *parens patriae* on behalf of the interests of its citizens,[32] but changed its mind in 1945 to permit Georgia to bring action under the antitrust laws against twenty railroads.[33]

A classic use of parsimony to escape from a dangerous situation occurred in connection with the evacuation of the Nisei from the West Coast in 1942. Gordon Hirabayashi, in an attempt to test the validity of the regulations clamped on the American-Japanese by the military, violated the curfew and refused to report to an evacuation center. He was convicted on both counts by the district court and sentenced to three months for each offense, the sentences to run *concurrently*. When the case came before the Supreme Court, the Justices sustained his conviction for violating the *curfew*, but refused to examine the validity of the evacuation order on the ground that it would not make any difference to Harabayashi anyway; he was in for ninety days no matter what the Court did with evacuation.[34]

A third method of utilizing substantive self-restraint is particularly useful in connection with the activities of executive departments or regulatory agencies, both state and federal. I have entitled it the doctrine of judicial inexpertise, for it is founded on the unwillingness of the Court to revise the findings of experts. The earmarks of this form of restraint are great deference to the holdings of the expert agency usually coupled with such a statement as "It is not for the federal courts to supplant the [Texas

Railroad] Commission's judgment even in the face of convincing proof that a different result would have been better." [35] In this tradition, the Court has refused to question *some* exercises of discretion by the National Labor Relations Board,[36] the Federal Trade Commission,[37] and other federal and state agencies. But the emphasis on *some* gives the point away: in other cases, apparently on all fours with those in which it pleads its technical inexpertise, the Court feels free to assess evidence *de novo* and reach independent judgment on the technical issues involved. Without getting involved in the complexities of the *Ben Avon* case,[38] *Crowell* v. *Benson*,[39] or *FPC* v. *Hope Natural Gas Co.*,[40] we need only cite the instance of *N.L.R.B.* v. *Highland Park Manufacturing Co.*, in which the Court overruled the N.L.R.B.[41] The Board had held that the C.I.O. was not a "national union" within the meaning of the Taft-Hartley Act, but was rather a confederation of labor unions; but Justice Jackson announced for the Court that "the C.I.O. . . . is certainly in the speech of people a national union, whatever its internal composition." [42] Justices Frankfurter and Douglas dissented, suggesting that the Supreme Court was not qualified to replace the Board.[43]

In short, with respect to expert agencies, the Court is equipped with both offensive and defensive gambits. If it chooses to intervene, one set of precedents is brought out; while if it decides to hold back, another set of equal validity is invoked. Perhaps the best summary of this point was made by Justice Harlan in 1910, when he stated bluntly that "the Courts have rarely, if ever, felt themselves so restrained by technical rules that they could not find some remedy, consistent with the law, for acts . . . that violated natural justice or were hostile to the fundamental principles devised for the protection of the essential rights of property." [44]

This does not pretend to be an exhaustive analysis of the techniques of judicial self-restraint; [45] on the contrary, others will probably find many which are not given adequate discussion here. The remainder of this paper, however, is devoted to the second area of concern: the conditions under which the Court refrains from acting.

The Conditions of Judicial Self-Restraint

The conditions which lead the Supreme Court to exercise auto-limitation are many and varied. In the great bulk of cases, this restraint is an outgrowth of sound and quasi-automatic legal maxims which defy teleological interpretation. It would take a master of the conspiracy theory of history to assign meaning, for example, to the great majority of certiorari denials; the simple fact is that these cases do not merit review. However, in a small proportion of cases, purpose does appear to enter the picture, sometimes with a vengeance. It is perhaps unjust to the Court to center our attention on this small proportion, but it should be said in extenuation that these cases often involve extremely significant political and social issues. In the broad picture, the refusal to grant certiorari in 1943 to the Minneapolis Trotskyites convicted under the Smith Act is far more meaningful than the similar refusal to grant five hundred petitions to prison "lawyers" who have suddenly discovered the writ of habeas corpus. Likewise, the holding that the legality of congressional apportionment is a "political question" vitally affects the operation of the whole democratic process.

What we must therefore seek are the conditions under which the Court holds back *in this designated category of cases*. Furthermore, it is important to realize that there are positive consequences of negative action: as Charles Warren has implied,[46] the post–Civil War Court's emphasis on self-restraint was a judicial concomitant of the resurgence of states' rights. Thus self-restraint may, as in wartime, be an outgrowth of judicial caution, or it may be part of a purposeful pattern of abdicating national power to the states.

Ever since the first political scientist discovered Mr. Dooley, the changes have been rung on the aphorism that the Supreme Court "follows the election returns," and I see no particular point in ringing my variation on this theme through again.[47] Therefore, referring those who would like a more detailed explanation to earlier analyses,[48] the discussion here will be confined to the bare bones of my hypothesis.

The power of the Supreme Court to invade the decision-making arena, I submit, is a consequence of that fragmentation of political power which is normal in the United States. No cohesive majority, such as normally exists in Britain, would permit a politically irresponsible judiciary to usurp decision-making functions, but, for complex social and institutional reasons, there are few issues in the United States on which cohesive majorities exist. The guerrilla warfare which usually rages between Congress and the President, as well as the internal civil wars which are endemic in both the legislature and the administration, give the judiciary considerable room for maneuver. If, for example, the Court strikes down a controversial decision of the Federal Power Commission, it will be supported by a substantial bloc of congressmen; if it supports the FPC's decision, it will also receive considerable congressional support. But the important point is that *either* way it decides the case, there is no possibility that Congress will exact any vengeance on the Court for its action. A disciplined majority would be necessary to clip the judicial wings, and such a majority does not exist on this issue.

On the other hand, when monolithic majorities do exist on issues, the Court is likely to resort to judicial self-restraint. A good case here is the current tidal wave of anti-Communist legislation and administrative action, the latter particularly with regard to aliens, which the Court has treated most gingerly. About the only issues on which there can be found cohesive majorities are those relating to national defense, and the Court has, as Clinton Rossiter demonstrated in an incisive analysis,[49] traditionally avoided problems arising in this area irrespective of their constitutional merits. Like the slave who accompanied a Roman consul on his triumph, whispering, "You too are mortal," the shade of Thad Stevens haunts the Supreme Court chamber to remind the Justices what an angry Congress can do.

To state the proposition in this brief compass is to oversimplify it considerably. I have, for instance, ignored the crucial question of how the Court knows when a majority *does* exist, and I recognize that certain aspects of judicial behavior cannot be jammed into my hypothesis without creating essentially spurious epicycles. However, I am not trying to establish a monistic theory of judicial action; group action, like that of individuals, is motivated by many factors, some often contradictory, and my objective is to elucidate what seems to be one tradition of judicial motivation. In short, judicial self-restraint and judicial power seem to be opposite sides of the same coin: it has been by judicious application of the former that the latter has been maintained. A tradition beginning with Marshall's *coup* in *Marbury* v. *Madison* and running through *Mississippi* v. *Johnson* and *Ex Parte Vallandigham* to *Dennis* v. *United States* suggests that the Court's power has been maintained by a wise refusal to employ it in unequal combat.[50]

NOTES

1. See Kenneth C. Wheare, *Federal Government*, 3rd ed. (New York, 1953), pp. 60–68, for a discussion of the application of judicial review in other nations. The British formerly utilized "impartial" bodies extensively in administration, but in recent years there has been a trend toward subsuming all administrative agencies under the direction of politically responsible ministers; see William A. Robson, "The Public Corporation in Britain Today," *Harvard Law Review*, Vol. 63 (June, 1950), pp. 1321–1348. The French, in their postwar nationalization acts, tried to excise politics from the operation of the state industries by establishing functional boards composed on the basis of interest representation; see Mario Einaudi, "Nationalization in France and Italy," *Social Research*, Vol. 15 (March, 1948), pp. 22–43, but apparently Truth was as elusive as ever; see Adolf Sturmthal, "The Structure of Nationalized Industries in France," *Political Science Quarterly*, Vol. 67, (Sept., 1952), pp. 357–377. The failure of a classic effort to take economics out of politics was chronicled by Lindsay Rogers and W. R.

Dittmar, "The Reichswirtschaftsrat: De Mortuis," *Political Science Quarterly*, Vol. 50 (Dec., 1935), pp. 481–501.

2. See Avery Leiserson, *Administrative Regulation: A Study in Representation of Interests* (Chicago, 1942); E. Pendleton Herring, *Public Administration and the Public Interest* (New York, 1936); John P. Roche and Murray S. Stedman, Jr., *The Dynamics of Democratic Government* (New York, 1954), Chap. 12.

3. The classic statement of this position was Charles G. Haines's *The Role of the Supreme Court in American Government and Politics, 1789–1835* (Berkeley, 1944). William W. Crosskey has recently thrown some semantic fagots on this dying fire, *Politics and the Constitution*, 2 vols. (Chicago, 1953). It might be useful to point out that under the American system of checks and balances, the Supreme Court does *not* have the last word. If the Court abuses its prerogatives, as it did in the income-tax case, the power to amend the Constitution serves as an antidote. This was particularly true in the formative years of the Re-

public when the Court's decision in *Chisholm* v. *Georgia*, 2 Dallas 419 (1793), was immediately countered by the Eleventh Amendment; see *Hollingsworth* v. *Virginia*, 3 Dallas 378 (1798), for a discussion of the impact of this amendment on judicial procedure. Today the amending power has become quite difficult to implement (but see the exceptionally rapid passage of the Twenty-second Amendment); however, at a time when senators were chosen by state legislatures it was highly probable that an amendment receiving two-thirds of the votes in the Senate would reflect directly the sentiments of the sovereign states.

4. See the recent statement by Professors Hart and Wechsler that "the grant of judicial power was to include the power, where necessary in the decision of cases, to disregard state or federal statutes found to be unconstitutional. Despite the curiously persisting myth of usurpation, the Convention's understanding on this point emerges from its records with singular clarity." Henry M. Hart, Jr., and Herbert Wechsler, *The Federal Courts and the Federal System* (Brooklyn, 1953), p. 14.

5. See the fine study by Benjamin Twiss, *Lawyers and the Constitution* (Princeton, 1942).

6. The first major effort was made by the Jeffersonians when they impeached Justice Samuel Chase for his bitter displays of anti-Jeffersonianism on the bench. Although the attempt failed to gather the necessary two-thirds vote in the Senate required for conviction—and a constitutional amendment which would have made federal judges removable by the President upon joint address by Congress also died aborning—the Supreme Court went into judicious hibernation; see Haines, pp. 264–265. The Dred Scott decision brought from Republicans demands that the

Court be curbed, including the famous statement by Lincoln to the effect that while the Court's views were interesting, they were not necessarily binding upon the coordinate branches of government; see Charles Warren, *The Supreme Court in United States History*, 2 vols. (Boston, 1947), II, 331. In the post–Civil War period, the demand was taken up by the agrarian radicals and later by the Socialists, and the Progressive platform in the 1912 election contained an endorsement of recall of Supreme Court decisions by referendum. The most recent struggle, that between President Franklin D. Roosevelt and the "Nine Old Men," concerned the right to add personnel to the Court rather than to impeach the content of judicial decisions *qua* decisions. Since the segregation decision of June, 1954, some new precincts have reported: southern statesmen, allegedly pillars of conservatism and the rule of law, have been denouncing what they call the Court's "political decision," and one of the candidates for nomination in the 1954 Democratic gubernatorial primary in Georgia ran on the slogan: "Abolish the Supreme Court!" He lost, but before too much consolation is drawn from this defeat, it should be added that the winner seemingly favored the abolition of the *whole* national government if necessary to prevent desegregation.

7. *Ex parte McCardle*, 7 Wall. 506 (1869). See Warren, II, 473–489, for a discussion of this famous judicial emasculation.

8. For this expressive phrase, I am indebted to the analysis of Maurice Finkelstein, "Judicial Self-Limitation," *Harvard Law Review*, Vol. 37 (Jan., 1924), pp. 338–364.

9. See Roche and Stedman, Chap. 10, for a brief attempt to explain

why the United States courts have remained so autonomous.

10. Promulgated by Justice Brandeis in his concurring opinion in *Ashwander* v. *T.V.A.*, 297 U.S. 288, at 345–348 (1936).

11. Most notably in the trial of Callander for sedition in the Virginia Circuit Court. Haines, pp. 163–165, distinguishes this case on the ground that the Jeffersonian lawyers asked the *jury* to declare the Sedition Act unconstitutional, but fails to point out that they used as precedent two Virginia cases in which *judges* had declared Virginia statutes violative of the state constitution. Tactics in this case, with Samuel Chase on the bench, obviously precluded asking the judge to hold the law null and void; see Francis Wharton, *State Trials of the United States During the Administrations of Washington and Adams* (Philadelphia, 1849), pp. 709 ff. Chase declared the Sedition Act to be constitutional, and further asserted his jurisdiction to make this finding. He made the same assertion in *Cooper* v. *Telfair*, 4 Dallas 14, at 19 (1800). The abolitionists later made a name for themselves by urging the Court to hold the Fugitive Slave Act unconstitutional while simultaneously maintaining that states' rights forbade judicial enforcement of the statute; see Jacobus ten Broek, *The Anti-Slavery Origins of the Fourteenth Amendment* (Berkeley, 1951), Chap. 2.

12. Robert H. Jackson, "A Presidential Legal Opinion," *Harvard Law Review*, Vol. 66 (June, 1953), pp. 1353–1361, in which the late Justice Jackson recorded F.D.R.'s conviction and privately recorded opinion that the termination-by-concurrent-resolution section of the Lend-Lease Act was unconstitutional. The President refused to make his views public because several isola-

tionist senators had made the same point in attacking the measure, and the administration's leaders in the Senate had gone firmly on record as to its constitutionality.

13. The purpose of this statement is to make it clear that I am not an advocate of oligarchy or judicial irresponsibility, although I do not take time out in the course of this analysis to engage in missionary activities.

14. 43 *Stat.* 936.

15. Fowler Harper and Alan S. Rosenthal, "What the Supreme Court Did Not Do in the 1949 Term," *University of Pennsylvania Law Review*, Vol. 99 (Dec., 1950), pp. 293–325; Harper and Edwin D. Ethrington, "What the Supreme Court Did Not Do in the 1950 Term," *University of Pennsylvania Law Review*, Vol. 100 (Dec., 1951), pp. 354–409; Harper and George C. Pratt, "What the Supreme Court Did Not Do During the 1951 Term," *University of Pennsylvania Law Review*, Vol. 101 (Jan., 1953), pp. 439–479; and Harper and George Leibowitz, "What the Supreme Court Did Not Do During the 1952 Term," *University of Pennsylvania Law Review*, Vol. 103 (Feb., 1954), pp. 427–463.

16. As Justice Frankfurter pointed out in *Maryland* v. *Baltimore Radio Show*, 338 U.S. 912 (1950).

17. Among them: *Lapides* v. *Clark*, 176 F.2d 619 (D.C. Cir. 1949) [loss of citizenship]; cert. denied, 338 U.S. 861 (1949); *Trumbo* v. *U.S.* 176 F.2d 49 (D.C. Cir. 1949) [attack on *vires* of House Committee on Un-American Activities]; cert. denied, 339 U.S. 434 (1950); *Dorsey* v. *Stuyvesant Town Corp.*, 299 N.Y. 512 (1949) [legality of segregation in housing built with state aid]; cert. denied, 339 U.S. 981 (1950); *Mastrapasqua* v. *Shaughnessy*, 186 F.2d 717 (2d Cir. 1950) [judicial review of

Judicial Self-Restraint

deportation order]; cert. denied, 341
U.S. 930 (1951); *Taylor* v. *Birmingham*, 253 Ala. 369 (1949) [segregation enforced by breach of the peace warrants]; cert. denied, 340 U.S. 832 (1950).

18. *University of Pennsylvania Law Review*, Vol. 99 (Dec., 1950), p. 323.

19. See C. Herman Pritchett, *Civil Liberties and the Vinson Court* (Chicago, 1954).

20. 341 U.S. 494 (1951). It might be noted here that by refusing to grant certiorari, the Court avoided ruling on the Smith Act in 1943; see *Dunne* v. *U.S.*, 138 F.2d 137 (8th Cir. 1943) [conviction of Minneapolis Trotskyites under Smith Act]; cert. denied, 320 U.S. 790 (1943); rehearing denied, 320 U.S. 814 (1943).

21. *First*, whether the Smith Act violated the First Amendment guarantee of free speech, and, *second*, whether the Act was so indefinite as to constitute a violation of the Fifth Amendment guarantee of due process of law.

22. 327 U.S. 304 (1946).

23. *Ex parte Duncan*, 146 F.2d 576 (9th Cir. 1944); cert. granted, 324 U.S. 833 (1945).

24. The Court, by an ingenious maneuver, avoided ruling on the legality of evacuation until December, 1944, almost two years after the policy was initiated, although it had an opportunity to do so in *Hirabayashi* v. *U.S.*, 320 U.S. 93 (1943). The technique utilized in the *Hirabayashi* case to avoid the evacuation issue is discussed later in this article.

25. *Luther* v. *Borden*, 7 Howard 1 (1849); *Pacific States Telephone & Telegraph Co.* v. *Oregon*, 223 U.S. 118 (1912).

26. *Colegrove* v. *Green*, 328 U.S. 549 (1946); *South* v. *Peters*, 339 U.S. 276 (1950).

27. *Oetjen* v. *Central Leather Co.*, 246 U.S. 297 (1918).

28. See the excellent discussion by John P. Frank in *Supreme Court and Supreme Law*, ed. Edmond Cahn (Bloomington, 1954), pp. 36–47.

29. *United Public Workers* v. *Mitchell*, 330 U.S. 75 (1947) [federal loyalty program].

30. *Int'l Longshoremen's & Warehousemen's Union, Local 37* v. *Boyd*, 347 U.S. 222 (1954) [reentry provisions of McCarran Act].

31. *Adler* v. *Board of Education*, 342 U.S. 485 (1952). See the discussion of standing by Ralph E. Bischoff in Cahn, ed., *op. cit.*, pp. 26–36.

32. *Massachusetts* v. *Mellon*, 262 U.S. 447 (1923); *Jones ex rel. Louisiana* v. *Bowles*, 322 U.S. 707 (1944).

33. *Georgia* v. *Pennsylvania Railroad*, 324 U.S. 439 (1945).

34. *Hirabayashi* v. *U.S.*, 320 U.S. 93 (1943).

35. *Railroad Commission of Texas* v. *Rowan & Nichols Oil Co.*, 310 U.S. 573 (1940).

36. *NLRB* v. *Hearst Publications*, 322 U.S. 111 (1944).

37. *FTC* v. *Ruberoid Co.*, 343 U.S. 470 (1952).

38. *Ohio Valley Water Co.* v. *Ben Avon Borough*, 253 U.S. 287 (1920) [independent judicial reëvaluation of administrative holding].

39. *Crowell* v. *Benson*, 285 U.S. 22 (1932) [use of doctrine of jurisdictional fact to justify *de novo* trial of administrative adjudication].

40. *FPC* v. *Hope Natural Gas Co.*, 320 U.S. 591 (1944) [presumptive validity of rate determination if the result is "just and reasonable"].

41. 341 U.S. 322 (1951).

42. *Ibid.*, at 324.

43. "The best source for us in determining whether a term used in the field of industrial relations has a technical connotation is the body

to which Congress has committed the administration of the statute." *Ibid.*, at 327.

44. *Monongahela Bridge Co.* v. *U.S.*, 216 U.S. 177 at 195 (1910).

45. The "presumption of constitutionality" might be considered as a separate technique of judicial self-restraint, but I consider it as a variant of judicial parsimony, a point of departure for applying Ockham's razor.

46. *The Supreme Court in United States History*, II, 533–561.

47. See the treatment of this problem by Professor Pritchett, *op. cit.*, Chap. 13.

48. See "Executive Power and Domestic Emergency: The Quest for Prerogative," *Western Political Quarterly*, Vol. 5 (Dec., 1952), pp. 592–618. (Reprinted on pp. 127–161 of this book.) "Education, Segregation and the Supreme Court—a Political Analysis," *University of Pennsylvania Law Review*, Vol. 99 (May, 1951), pp. 949–59; "Plessy v. Ferguson: *Requiescat in Pace?*" *University of Pennsylvania Law Review*, Vol. 103 (Oct., 1954), pp. 46–58; and Roche and Stedman, Chap. 10.

49. *The Supreme Court and the Commander in Chief* (Ithaca, 1951).

50. While this article was wending its leisurely way toward publication, the federal courts have begun to emphasize an interesting variant of judicial self-restraint in civil rights cases. Without ruling on the merits of cases at bar, judges in several key cases have utilized procedural grounds to frustrate government ac-

tion. In San Francisco a district judge ruled that the United States had not adequately sustained its evidential burden against Harry Bridges, thus saving the latter from denaturalization. In New York the contempt-of-Congress indictments of Corliss Lamont and others similarly situated were quashed on the ground that the true bill did not proclaim the *vires* of the subcommittee before which the contempts were allegedly committed. After a long and complicated legal battle, the Court of Appeals, District of Columbia, quashed the key charge in the perjury indictment of Owen Lattimore, and the same Court undermined the plenary jurisdiction of the Passport Division of the State Department by requiring an adherence to due process in passport denials. Finally, in *Peters* v. *Hobby*, 349 U.S. 341 (1955), the Supreme Court—on a basis so narrow as to be virtually invisible (*i.e.*, that the Loyalty Review Board was *ultra vires* in reopening, by its own action, the case of Dr. Peters) —overruled Peters's dismissal. Perhaps henceforth the protection of civil liberties will be effected by procedural meticulousness! This is not a new technique: in the seventeenth century it was applied by the British courts to mitigate the substantive injustices of outlawry. Even misspellings in the writ of exigent were employed to invalidate the proceedings, as, for instance, in *Griffith* v. *Thomas*, Style 334 (1652), where the error of spelling *praecipimus* "praecipipimus" was held to be fatal.

Political Science and Science Fiction

I want to dissent initially from the rather constricting frame of reference that Glendon Schubert has established in his paper "The Study of Judicial Decision-Making as an Aspect of Political Behavior." He has every right in the world to set rhetorical snares, but I have no intention of walking into them. If I may summarize, Schubert asserts that he is a spokesman for a radical new direction in the study of public law, claiming that the old ways are moribund. He further urges that we should look with envy at the creative function of the social psychologists who supplied the Supreme Court with the banners it carried in *Brown* v. *Board of Education* while we were bumbling around with historical and philosophical trivia. He concludes that instead of wasting our time with talmudic disputations on whether the Supreme Court reached the "right" or "wrong" decisions in specific cases, we should settle down to build a firm "scientific" foundation for our discipline.

Not the least amusing aspect of this indictment is that I find myself billed as the defender of the *ancien regime*, as the De Maistre of public law. Therefore, for the benefit of the young and impressionistic, let me break loose from Schubert's rhetorical trap: I too think that much of the research done in public law —and, for that matter, in political science generally—has been trivial. But I insist that this triviality has been due to the lack of ideas, not "scientific method." It is admittedly more difficult to

Reprinted, with permission, from *The American Political Science Review*, Volume LII, Number 4, December, 1958, pages 1026–1029.

unmask banality when it is draped in algebraic disguise than when
it is set forth in English or sociologese, but excoriating banality
in whatever guise it may appear is the task we must undertake if
political science is to fulfill its creative function. It was formerly
alleged that when a scholar came to a weak point in his argument, he threw in a Greek quotation; now it often appears to
me that he breaks out into calculus.

But before going into the science-fiction quality of much
current work in political behavior, I should like to deal briefly
with the Supreme Court and the social psychologists. "Social
scientists" have been cheering the Court because in the segregation cases the Justices seemingly abandoned the unscientific tradition in jurisprudence and rested their decision on the firm bedrock of "science." The shades of Bentham and Comte have no
doubt joined in this claque.

But with all due regard for "the vanguard of the public law
proletariat," I would insist that this was not the first time the
Justices based an opinion on the latest insights of contemporary
social science (allowing only for purposes of argument that this
was indeed the rationale of their decision). On the contrary,
Plessy v. *Ferguson* was suffused with the racist principles of
the social scientists of the 1890's.[1] This, by our present-day
standards, was "bad" social science, accepting as it did the doctrine of innate racial differences; but it was social science nonetheless. Viewed in this light, the great merit of Justice Harlan's
dissent in *Plessy* was that, despite his acceptance of innate racial
differences, he refused to write that "science" into law. In effect,
he stated that even if the Negro belonged to a different (and the
implication was always inferior) species from the white, he was
entitled to the same constitutional rights.

I think that the Supreme Court in *Brown* v. *Board of Education* could have profited from Harlan's example by making it
clear that the ground on which segregation was condemned was
moral, not utilitarian. Segregation was banned because it was
incompatible with the moral precepts of a democratic society,
not because it led to inefficient education. Even if psychologists
conclusively "proved"—as some are now doing—that segregation
led to *efficient* education, the real gravamen of the indictment

would have been the same: the practice violated personal rights guaranteed by the Fourteenth Amendment. But the Court, by invoking the imprimatur of science for its holding, seriously compromised its moral posture.

And what about the "science" that was utilized? What was the nature of the social psychological evidence that the Court listed in its famous footnote? Here I am afraid the "scientific method" was conspicuous by its absence. Disregarding Myrdal's sprawling *corpus* of undigested data, which is about as scientific as the *Columbia Encyclopedia*, the studies cited were prepared by men who must be considered advocates rather than disinterested analysts. Professor Isidor Chein, for example, later stated:

I can here testify on behalf of the expert witnesses in the segregation cases that nobody asked us for the base on which we reached our conclusions. I might add that, in another case, I pointed out . . . that whereas I had an opinion on a certain matter I did not know whether I could marshal sufficient scientific evidence to support that opinion. I was told in reply that this was all that the court was interested in, my opinion—that the presumption is that, if I qualify as an expert, my *opinion* carries weight that is not carried by ordinary opinion.[2]

Professor Edmond Cahn has discussed this matter persuasively in two trenchant articles; I therefore see no point in elaborating it further except to note my suspicion that had not the "empirical" tests employed by Professor Kenneth Clark demonstrated the inherent inequality of segregated education, he would have changed the tests.[3] Professor Clark was social-science consultant to the NAACP, and a dedicated opponent of segregation.

Note that I am not condemning these men or their objectives. I am merely suggesting that the scientific method is not autonomous but depends on the value structure of its employers. Indeed, no scientist dealing with "race" in his scientific capacity could go any further by way of generalization than to state that no evidence to date supports the doctrine of innate racial characteristics. The conviction that racial equality is sound public policy is moral, not scientific.

Finally, to wind up this discussion of the wonder-working providences of social science in the school desegregation litigation, only a naïf—or perhaps a southern politician—could believe that the Supreme Court ruled the way it did in *Brown* v. *Board of Education* because the Justices had absorbed some social psychological reprints. Surely we know enough by now, even though our information is based on hopelessly traditional scholarship, to recognize the *a posteriori* function of footnotes in Supreme Court decisions.

Now, with respect to the broader questions raised by Schubert's paper, I must confess that "The Study of Judicial Decision-Making as an Aspect of Political Behavior" is superior to most efforts in this genre that have appeared in recent years. Not only is it clear that Schubert is acquainted with the traditional virtues, or vices, of public law; he has also spared us the full explication of the "Shapely-Shubik empirical power index" and the "coefficient of reproducibility." Moreover, he has not added a veneer of sociological argot to his presentation.

My remarks here are therefore not so much aimed at Schubert's paper as at the "new look" in political science of which this analysis is a relatively moderate example. I object to the spell of numerology which seems to have fallen over the study of politics, and my objections do not run against the techniques but against the basic assumptions of the new Establishment. I am not by any means antiempirical. The study of data, their classification and measurement whenever possible in as precise a fashion as is feasible, is patently crucial to the examination of political behavior. I have nothing but admiration for the quantitative skill of, *inter alios*, David Butler, V. O. Key, Angus Campbell, and Leon Epstein. What I object to is not quantification, but bogus quantification, the assumption that one can create a measurable thing merely by assigning it a numerical symbol. No one in his sense doubts that we can tabulate Republican votes, but does it follow that we can count Oedipus complexes on the same easy basis? The first calculation involves counting heads; the second, measuring their content. Logically any analyst is within his rights to postulate that voting Republican is proof of Oedipal tendencies, but no one need take him seriously. If he proceeds on the basis of his premise to announce that there were in November, 1956, at least 35,585,316 Americans with Oedipus complexes, he is on secure ground in terms of formal logic, but in real terms he has engaged in pseudoempiricism. In short, the absurdity of logical premises, providing they are not internally inconsistent, in no way impairs the validity of the logical proof.

There is nothing wicked about proving absurd propositions, nor in building elaborate methodological superstructures on self-validating foundations, but there is no reason these exercises should be considered relevant to the study of politics. Method is indeed important to the political scientist, but we must beware of the mad dream—worthy of H. G. Wells—of the autonomous "methodology" which will clank along forever in a value-free vacuum and eliminate once for all the knotty problems of belief and subjective insight. Our major concern, I submit, is with premises, and particularly with the premises about human nature on which systems are constructed.

Take the study of the Supreme Court and right to counsel cases in which the ingenious Kort fulfilled the alchemist's dream by converting legal dross into scientific gold.[4] From the objective voting behavior of Supreme Court Justices, he has drawn certain uniformities of a mathematical character, and posited certain mathematical principles which enable prediction of their future action in similar cases. Schubert endorses Kort's work, and utilizes the same general method with respect to search and seizure cases. What interests me here is the misuse of what I understand to be the canon of contemporary science, and the self-validating character of the fundamental assumptions about the nature of the judicial process.

Briefly, Schubert and Kort seem to have confused the scientist with the bookmaker. The scientist deals in prediction only in statistical terms, that is, on the basis of adequate samples, and never engages in the hubris of trying to predict the behavior of individual units. A careful student of voting behavior may talk cautiously of predispositions which emerge statistically in the cases of, say, white Protestants who live in Bronxville, New York. He would, however, blench at the thought of predicting the vote of any one individual in this category. Thus when Schubert, Kort, *et al.* invoke the authority of science for predicting the actions of a few judges on the basis of statistically trivial samples, they are in a tradition that owes more to the racing form than to the work of Fermi, Heisenberg, or Einstein. This interpretation of science seems to be founded on an epistemological lag, on a belated dedication to a mechanistic science which has long been transcended by the physical sciences. At a time when pioneers in the physical sciences sound more like poets and metaphysicians than like hard-boiled empiricists, the "social scientists" have taken to worshiping at the tomb of Isaac Newton.

Moreover, when Kort and Schubert set up their analytical propositions, it appears to me that they egregiously perpetrate the fallacy of *petitio principii*, that is, they assume the validity of the premise that must be proved if their statements are to be more than exercises in formal logic. Again let it be understood that they have every right to set up abstract analytical models, but it is equally the right of the reader to demand that these paradigms be relevant to the analysis of real judges engaged in real litigation. To be precise, the use of content analysis to set up a scale of mathematical determinants of judicial action is predicated on the assumption that judicial decision-making is at root a process that proceeds mathematically. Similarly, the use of game theory for analytical purposes takes for granted what in reality must be demonstrated: that judges are gamesmen.

Indeed, it is possible that the judicial process is a dignified variation of blackjack, but until some substantive evidence is adduced to demonstrate that judges do think this way, I can not take the proposition seriously. And until our behaviorist colleagues concern themselves with this level of analysis, instead of spinning out their methodological webs on the insecure mooring of "as if" propositions, their labors are essentially marginal to the concerns of political science.

NOTES

1. See John P. Roche, "The Future of Separate but Equal," *Phylon*, Vol. 12 (1951), p. 219.

2. Cited by Edmond Cahn, "The Lawyer, the Social Psychologist, and the Truth," *New York University Law Review*, Vol. 31 (1956), pp. 182, 186.

3. Professor Clark's "empirical" evidence is discussed in Cahn, "A Dangerous Myth in the School Segregation Cases," *New York University Law Review*, Vol. 30 (1955), pp. 150, 161–165.

4. Fred Kort, "Predicting Supreme Court Decisions Mathematically," *American Political Science Review*, Vol. 51 (1957), p. 1.

A Review of
Nine Men by Fred Rodell,
and of *The Supreme Court*
in the American System of Government
by Robert H. Jackson

At a time when the Supreme Court is undergoing the most serious attack that has threatened it since 1937, if not 1867, it is useful to stop and examine the function that today's Court exercises in the government of the United States. Both Professor Rodell's *Nine Men* and the late Justice Jackson's *The Supreme Court in the American System of Government* are directed toward this examination, and present the reader with a striking study in contrasts. Rodell is what Jackson refers to slightingly as a "libertarian judicial activist," while Rodell bluntly describes Jackson as a "turncoat-to-conservatism." While neither book is particularly valuable, the two combined throw considerable light on the difficulties one faces in trying to evaluate the proper role of the Court in the political process.

[1]

One has the same feeling in reading *Nine Men* that he would have today on finding a militant suffragette pounding the sidewalks demanding votes for women. Indeed, Professor Rodell's book strikes me as a tract from the past, one perhaps written to justify F.D.R.'s Court-packing plan, rather than a study of the Supreme Court presumably written in 1955 for a contemporary audience. All the old horses turn up—clever John Marshall, slavocrat Roger Taney, reactionary Stephen Field, magnificent Holmes, noble Brandeis—and they are duly beaten. Moreover,

Reprinted, with permission, from the *Cornell Law Quarterly*, Volume 41, 1956, pages 538–543.

perhaps to attract the semiliterate layman in whose judgment, if not literary taste, Rodell puts so much trust, *Nine Men* is written in a style I find obnoxious. His reliance is mainly on two literary gambits: first, the cozy sit-down-by-the-fireside pitch— "Now, folks, no big words"; and, second, the inside-dopester ploy—"Folks, no matter how they try to fool you, judges are just people." There must be an alternative to dull legal writing, but surely this is not it.[1]

Rodell's case against the Supreme Court is founded on two complaints. On the one hand, he thunders against judicial review of legislation as an undemocratic, oligarchic practice, one which gives nine unrepresentative and politically irresponsible men the power to override decisions of the popularly elected organs of government. On the other hand, he objects to the Court's refusal to employ the weapon of judicial review on behalf of civil liberties. Logically, there seems to be a contradiction here, but since Rodell avoids abstraction like the plague, he never comes to grip with it. Indeed, his tirades against such Justices as Frankfurter and Jackson, who have at least *tried* to evolve a consistent theory of the judicial function, are largely based on their refusal to vote "right" in civil-liberty issues where he feels the Court should have intervened.

In any case, whether consistent or not with the remainder of his book, one of Rodell's main themes is that judicial review is a dirty trick that the Court has imposed upon an unthinking nation. While I have in my own mind serious reservations about the democratic character of judicial review, it seems to me that this assault is misconceived. I think that American political experience demonstrates that the Court has exercised this function within a framework of popular consent. For better or worse, the concept that the Supreme Court "has the last word" has been enshrined among the vital myths of American society. Disaffected segments of the population—the Populists, the Socialists, the New Dealers, and now the southern pillars of conservatism—have raged against this or that body of precedent, but all serious attempts to deprive the Court of its policy functions have come to naught.

Rodell's book can, I suppose, be considered as an effort to reverse this popular tradition, but here he neutralizes his force considerably by his inconsistency. When it comes to civil rights problems, Rodell cheers on the invading Justices as they strike down school boards, city police, and state legislatures, and engages in bitter criticism, and often cheap personal attacks, when his team loses. This I could call the "Western movie approach" to judicial review, and while it is sometimes fun, it does not seem to me to add much to our understanding of the problem.

As a footnote-loving-specialist (to borrow his favorite implement, the hyphen, from the civil-rights-loving-professor), I would disagree with many of Rodell's judgments on the history of the Court. In the first place, in order to write the book at all, he had to assign to the Court far more policy control over the operation of government that I think the facts justify. Although the Court has much power, it is patent exaggeration to say that the Justices wield "top political power," [2] or that *Marbury* v. *Madison* [3] "nailed down Supreme Court dominance of the national government." [4] His treatment of John Marshall—a treatment that is necessary to sustain the extreme argument just cited—turns that worthy into a Superman: "Thus the great Chief Justice, by dominating the Supreme Court which dominated the judiciary which dominated the federal government which dominated the states [*sic*]—and with each of these steps substantially his own indomitable doing—himself effectively dominated the nation for a third of a century." [5]

Now, Marshall was a great judge, but this is too much. This ancient myth of Marshall's omnicompetence rests fundamentally on a lack of understanding of the period 1800–1830, a period of strong nationalism in the central government, though the latter was ostensibly under Jeffersonian auspices. True, Marshall's major consolidating opinions did fulfill Federalist dreams, but the key factor was that public policy, particularly after the War of 1812, can best be described as Federalism without Federalists. The nationalizing impact of the war, in which it must be recalled the Federalists were associated with states' rights, and of the western lands, which turned the nation's face toward the interior and led to an increasing reliance on the central government, must not be underestimated. Consequently, Marshall was not just speaking for himself or the defunct Federalists when he asserted the supremacy of the nation; he was a spokesman for the *Zeitgeist*. The states'-rights movement and the national disintegration that accompanied it were later manifestations which grew up in the 1830's, 1840's, and 1850's, with slavery as their fulcrum.

I have other complaints, but space permits discussion of only one: Rodell's worship of Oliver Wendell Holmes. Holmes's dissents stand as major contributions to judicial thinking and legal literature, but—perhaps because he shares Holmes's contempt for abstract thinking—Rodell assigns the Justice far too significant a role as a defender of civil liberty. While he cites the dissent in the *Abrams* [6] case, and mildly denigrates the "clear and present danger rule" of *Schenck* [7] (one may parenthetically wonder what Rodell would have said if Justice Frankfurter or Justice Jackson had formulated this slippery rule!), he avoids Holmes's basic premise that justice is the will of the stronger. Thus when Holmes went to the defense of Abrams, it was an outgrowth not of a conceptualized belief in civil liberties, but out of a sense of outraged decency. I am not deprecating Holmes's great role in American jurisprudence, nor his greatness as a human being; what I am suggesting is that a man with his outlook, his worship of power (compare *Moyer* v. *Peabody*,[8] a case Rodell does *not* cite), can not be considered as a pillar of the civil-liberties tradition. It is interesting that Justice Jackson, who shared much of Holmes's reverence for Power, is Rodell's contemporary bête noire.

In short, though I share many of Professor Rodell's prejudices, I do not consider *Nine Men* a useful, or even a provocative, book. The political operations of the Supreme Court certainly need analysis and discussion, but if anything, this study, with its patent exaggerations and inconsistencies, plays into the hands of those whom both Rodell and I consider the Enemy: those antiseptic legalists who claim that the law is not subject to political analysis and that anything written along this line is bunk.

[2]

The late Justice Jackson, at a time when he knew the sands of his life had about run out, was invited to give the Godkin Lectures at Harvard. The three brief essays that make up *The Supreme Court in the American System of Government* were the lectures that he prepared, but never delivered. In a sense, they constitute his legal testament, although their brevity and spottiness lead one to wish that they had not been published in this form. The Jackson wit flashes occasionally, and the Justice was incapable of bad writing, but he deserves to be remembered on the basis of work far more substantial than this.

Jackson was an odd Justice. A brilliant mind coupled with extensive political and administrative experience gave him a deeper insight into the political process than any of his brethren. But if this was a great asset, it was also a liability, for Jackson knew too much, and always approached the sovereign, in the spirit of T. H. Green, in "fear and trembling." Thus his approach to the judicial function suffered from schizophrenia: in one capacity, he was a firm believer in freedom and civil rights, while in another, he was too sophisticated in the ways of power to believe that a Court could stand against the passions of a nation. More than any other Justice, with the possible exception of Frankfurter, whose motivation was quite different, he tried to stand aside from the emotional impact of a case and rule *sub specie aeternitatis*. Added to this, perhaps as a consequence of his Nuremberg experience, was a conviction that nineteenth century clichés about freedom of opinion were inadequate to the requirements of twentieth century democracy confronted by the totalitarian threat.

It was his capacity for dispassionate, disembodied analysis that led him to write such strange, yet striking, opinions as his "count me out" dissenting-concurrence in the *Korematsu* case.[9] Described somewhere by E. V. Rostow as "an essay in judicial nihilism," Jackson here asserted that the Court should have refused to take the case, for under the circumstances it could only abet injustice. Similarly, his concurrence in the *Steel Seizure* case [10] cut to the heart of the matter in most unjudicial terms: this seizure was illegal because Congress did not like it, but regarding other seizures the deponent sayeth not.

The basic thesis that emerges from this little book fits clearly into the pattern. The Supreme Court can not save the American people from themselves. Nor should it try, for such efforts are "wholly incompatible with faith in democracy, and insofar as it encourages a belief that the judges may be left to correct the result of public indifference to issues of liberty in choosing Presidents, Senators, and Representatives, it is a vicious teaching." [11] The appropriate job of the Court, then, is to strive to maintain "the great system of balances upon which our free government is based." [12] But at all points the Court must take cognizance of the realities of power, must realize that its survival as an institution depends upon a willingness to retreat from exposed positions. One may not like this fact; but, like it or not, there it is, and no responsible judge can hide his head in the sand.

As an examination of the power role of the Supreme Court, there is much to be said for this viewpoint. As I have suggested at length elsewhere, judicial power in the United States is a direct coefficient of judicial self-restraint.[13] But Jackson seems to me to go wrong at two points: first, he confuses knowledge with duty; and, second, he goes almost as far in underrating the power of the Court as Rodell goes in overrating it. Let us examine these points briefly.

When I said that Jackson confused knowledge with duty, I was referring to his unwillingness to enter even the best of probably lost causes. To take an example from a foreign context, the Judges of the South African Supreme Court must have known that to frustrate the demands of the Malan Government would lead to judicial emasculation. Yet in the name of humanity they struck down the racist moves of the government as violative of the Constitution of the Union, and have subsequently been neutralized by the vengeful Afrikaners. In such a situation, Justice Jackson would have felt, if we can extrapolate his consistently held views in this manner, that the judges were mistaken in their death wish. They should have realized that no action of theirs could stem the tide, and should have retreated into judicious hibernation. As he stated it quite clearly: "Whether in case of a clearly unconstitutional usurpation of power by one of the other branches the Court would be justified in stepping out of its judicial role and itself exercising a usurped counterbalancing power, I do not stop to consider, because I think in such an event the judicial voice would be little heeded in the chaos." [14] What this implies is that a judge's decision in a key political case becomes wholly a function of his political prescience, rather than of the merits of the issue at bar, and this may justly be termed "judicial nihilism."

Growing out of his fundamental pessimism about the power of the judiciary is Jackson's underestimation of the role the Court can play in critical areas. He seems to neglect the power that judicial decisions have merely as symbols, to say nothing of the educational function they can play in society as a whole. Much lawmaking—judicial or otherwise—operates, in the phrase of the sociologist Robert Merton, as "self-fulfilling prophecy." Public opinion is not fixed, but fluid, and in civil liberties, as in other types of litigation, a Court decision is not merely a settlement between parties, but is also an opinion-molding influence of considerable importance. Jackson wholly neglects the Court's role as an educational institution, and thus misses a vital source of its continuing power.[15]

NOTES

1. Since Professor Rodell expects such criticism from stuffy legalists writing in law reviews, I might note for what it is worth that my legal friends have long since consigned me to the inferior status of a Layman. I admit I never took Torts I and Torts II, to say nothing of Future Interests, and I suppose I might as well capitalize my assets and write as a Professional Layman. This review is written in that capacity.

2. Rodell, at 26.

3. 5 U.S. (1 Cranch) 137 (1803).

4. Rodell at 90.

5. *Ibid.* at 79.

6. *Abrams* v. *United States*, 250 U.S. 616 (1919).

7. *Schenck* v. *United States*, 249 U.S. 47 (1919).

8. 212 U.S. 78 (1909).

9. *Korematsu* v. *United States*, 323 U.S. 214 (1944).

10. *Youngstown Sheet and Tube Co.* v. *Sawyer*, 343 U.S. 579 (1952).

11. Jackson at 58. Compare this with the view of Holmes: "What proximate test of excellence [in government] can be found except correspondence to the actual equilibrium of force in the community—that is, conformity to the wishes of the dominant power? Of course, such conformity may lead to destruction, and it is desirable that the dominant power should be wise. But wise or not, the proximate test of a good government is that the dominant power has its way." Holmes, "Montesquieu," in *Collected Legal Papers* (1920), 258.

12. Jackson at 61.

13. See Roche, "Judicial Self-Restraint," *American Political Science Review*, Vol. 49 (1955), p. 762.

14. Jackson at 62.

15. For a discussion of this point, see Roche and Gordon, "Can Morality Be Legislated?" *The New York Times Magazine*, May 22, 1955.

A Review of *Prejudice, War, and the Constitution* by Jacobus ten Broek, Edward N. Barnhart, and Floyd W. Matson

In Great Britain and France, World War II is often referred to as the "easy war," because of the absence of organized, large-scale butchery which characterized the military conduct of World War I. American civil libertarians also have reason to apply this designation, for the mass hysteria, lynch rule, and asinine xenophobia of Wilson's holy crusade were largely unknown in the recent conflict. Sauerkraut did not become "liberty cabbage"; few Germans or Italians were maltreated; and even pacifists, who insisted on taking the Sermon on the Mount seriously, were generally treated with consideration. There can be no question that the Department of Justice and Attorney General Francis Biddle, who held the reins throughout these difficult years, deserve the major credit for this policy.

But there was one great exception which must live on in the memories and consciences of Americans: the evacuation and imprisonment of our American-Japanese minority, seventy thousand strong, on the revolutionary charge that they possessed enemy chromosomes. There is little need here to recapitulate the Kafkaesque nightmare that these citizens lived through; suffice it to say that by military edict they were evicted from their West Coast homes and herded into concentration camps while the President, the Congress, and the courts stood by in silence. A few courageous voices were lifted in protest: Harrop Freeman in this *Quarterly*,[1] E. V. Rostow,[2] Nanette Dembitz,[3] Norman

Reprinted, with permission, from *The Cornell Law Quarterly*, Volume 40, 1955, pages 633–636.

Thomas, and a few church groups. But by and large the evacuation and relocation were accompanied by a conspiracy of silence; when confronted with the question, all that a majority of the "liberal" Supreme Court could bring itself to observe, *in nuce*, was that war is war, and tough on everybody.[4]

How did this happen? Why did the American people permit it? Who was responsible? These are the questions which have troubled scholars for a decade. Morton Grodzins, in his study *Americans Betrayed*,[5] suggested that a combination of California politicians and self-serving pressure groups got the policy adopted. In an analysis written in 1946,[6] I tended to place the major blame on General De Witt, in whose hands the power to evacuate "military areas" was placed, and who employed this power to implement his outspoken anti-Japanese, indeed, anti-Oriental, opinions. Other analyses have played variations on these two themes, but the basic issue has remained unresolved.

Meanwhile, a group of scholars at the University in Berkeley have been collecting, organizing, and publishing a series of definitive studies of the whole evacuation problem. In two previously published studies—*The Spoilage*[7] and *The Salvage*[8]—the sociologists and statisticians have had their day; now, with the publication of *Prejudice, War, and the Constitution*, it is the turn of the Law Department, building on the work of the others, to render a final judgment on the merits. Writing with balance and objectivity, though unsparing in their criticism, Professor ten Broek and his associates have, in my view, submitted a definitive study. While the writing is uneven, the section of primary interest to lawyers—Part III: "Leviticus"—is superb legal scholarship at its best.

J. ten Broek, Barnhart, and Matson carefully examine the various theories of responsibility that have been advanced, and reject them all as inadequate. While it is convenient to blame the noisy pressure groups, with their record of anti-Orientalism, and the California politicians who have, over the years, thrived on racial bigotry, the authors demonstrate convincingly that their activities were not decisive. Furthermore, while De Witt, with his overt racial bias, provided a splendid scapegoat, responsibility cannot be laid on his doorstep. In fact, ten Broek and his colleagues suggest, the body cannot be disposed of so easily; while the military and the West Coast pressure politicians were unquestionably involved in the decision, the fundamental responsibility for evacuation and internment must be placed on the American people and their elected political leaders.

It is often forgotten that democratic government is founded upon a rigorous doctrine of responsibility: the elected official is held responsible and *must* be held responsible, if democratic political theory is to have any meaning, for all acts of his subordinates. There are no excuses: his *de facto* ignorance of the motives or consequences of subordinate action is irrelevant. (Conversely, such an official may justifiably claim credit for all the virtues of his delegates.) Consequently, it is irrelevant to discuss General De Witt's racial bias, for he was an agent merely. The finger thus points squarely at the President, for the founders of the Republic, with their pessimistic genius, assumed that by and large military men would be Neanderthalers, if not knaves, and therefore carefully excluded them from the decision-making arena. The President of the United States is by constitutional fiat the commander in chief of the Armed Forces, and it is therefore on the head of Roosevelt that we must place the sins of De Witt—as we must credit him with the virtues of Biddle.

But, while Roosevelt must bear the onus for the evacuation and relocation program, the Congress and the Supreme Court were active accomplices in the deed: the Congress for so readily agreeing to Public Law 503, which made it a crime to disobey a military evacuation order—a statute which passed both Houses without recorded dissent; and the Supreme Court for its cavalier treatment of the claims of the Nisei. The Court in particular merits censure, and receives it from ten Broek and his colleagues, for its refusal even to grant serious consideration to the claims of the American-Japanese. The various cogent pleas—that the Nisei had been denied due process, that they had been denied the equal protection of the laws—were dismissed by a unanimous Court in the *Hirabayashi* case,[9] and by a six-three majority in the *Korematsu* case,[10] as though no significant constitutional issues existed. While it is a strong statement, it seems true to say that the justices have given more consideration to the habeas corpus petition of a self-educated guardhouse lawyer than they did to an appeal on behalf of seventy thousand Americans for their rights under the Constitution.

The crucial point in the *Korematsu* case needs reexamination, for the Court's holding may live on to haunt us in the unpredictable future.[11] The essence of the holding was that the drastic actions of the military were founded on a military decision, by its nature unreviewable, that the national security required evacuation and relocation. Although the Court is composed of experts who are prepared to substitute their judgment for that of the N.L.R.B., the F.T.C., and any number of minor regulatory agencies, it seemingly draws the line this side of the Joint Chiefs of Staff. Military expertise is *sui generis*.

Now, obviously the military must, in time of emergency, have a wide discretion, and few would recommend that the Justices replace the Chiefs of Staff. However, there is in the Court's waiver of jurisdiction an extremely dangerous precedent, for—as ten Broek emphasizes—not only did the Justices accept without question the assertion that evacuation was based on military judgment, but they also condoned, *sub silentio*, a radical definition of military judgment, to wit, that a military judgment is the judgment of a military commander. In short, the military were permitted *to define their own area* of plenary jurisdiction. It is one thing to refuse to review a military decision on the ground that it is founded on unreviewable security considerations; it is quite a different proposition to accept without question the assertion that a military act is founded on unreviewable security considerations. In the first instance, the Court investigates the decision to ascertain that it is, in truth, based on military considerations; in the second, the Court simply agrees that since the decision was made by a military official, it is in substance a military decision, and unreviewable. It was the latter criterion which was applied in *Korematsu*; although substantial evidence was introduced to indicate that De Witt's action was not founded on motives military in character, the Court shut the door on any jurisdictional niceties.

In conclusion, ten Broek and his associates have presented us with an incisive case study of a failure in democratic government.

It is essential reading for all those who are striving in this time of peril for the appropriate balance between liberty and security and for the institutional techniques which will give this balance concrete meaning.

NOTES

1. Freeman, "Genesis, Exodus and Leviticus: Geneology, Evacuation and Law," *Cornell Law Quarterly*, Vol. 28 (1943), p. 414.

2. Rostow, "The Japanese American Cases—A Disaster," *Yale Law Journal*, Vol. 54 (1945), p. 496.

3. Dembitz, "Racial Discrimination and the Military Judgment: The Supreme Court's Korematsu and Endo Decisions," *Columbia Law Review*, Vol. 45 (1945), p. 175.

4. *Korematsu* v. *United States*, 323 U.S. 214 (1944). Justice Black, gave the opinion of the Court; Justices Roberts and Murphy clearly dissented, and Justice Jackson, went off on a tack of his own which Rostow

characterized as "an essay in judicial nihilism."

5. 1949.

6. Justice and Ancestry, unpublished dissertation, Cornell University Library, 1946.

7. D. Thomas and R. Nishimoto, *The Spoilage* (1946).

8. D. Thomas, *The Salvage* (1952).

9. *Hirabayashi* v. *United States*, 320 U.S. 81 (1943).

10. *Korematsu* v. *United States*, 323 U.S. 214 (1944).

11. See the cogent article by Dunbar, "Beyond Korematsu: The Emergency Detention Act of 1950," *University of Pittsburgh Law Review*, Vol. 13 (1952), p. 221.

A Review of *Render unto Caesar:*
The Flag-Salute Controversy
by David R. Manwaring

Professor David Manwaring's meticulous study of the adventures of the Jehovah's Witnesses in their campaign against the compulsory flag salute arrives at a propitious moment. Advocates of prayer and Bible reading in public schools, currently smarting under the Supreme Court's recent ban on the New York "nonsectarian" formula,[1] are demanding that such invocations of divine grace be legitimized on the ground that an appropriately nonpartisan prayer does not violate the separation of Church and State. The notion behind this seems to be that a neutral prayer (perhaps addressed "to Whom it may concern"?) is actually a secular exercise, a component in the American version of Rousseau's "civic religion." In other areas too—most notably education—the Supreme Court has been called upon to clear away the fog that conceals the location of that "impenetrable wall" separating the secular from the religious jurisdiction in American life. As Philip Kurland demonstrated in a superb essay,[2] the whole Church-State issue constitutes a logician's nightmare, and while *Render unto Caesar* is a rather inert volume—an insufficiently reformed doctoral dissertation—Manwaring has nonetheless brought home some extremely valuable lessons to those who talk glibly of "absolute rights" or, on the other side of the barricade, of "neutral principles of constitutional law."

Perhaps, since Manwaring has avoided theoretical considerations like the plague, it might be well to put the key issue of his

Reprinted, with permission, from *The University of Chicago Law Review*, Volume 30, Winter, 1963, Number 2, pages 406–415.

227

book in perspective. The core dilemma is as old as human speculation on the relationship of the individual to the community.
It was already ancient when St. Augustine excoriated the Donatists, and lay at the root of much bitter controversy in the age
of the Protestant Reformation. In a nutshell, the question is:
What does society do with the disruptive messenger from God?
As the Jehovah's Witness brief put the matter to an undoubtedly
startled Supreme Court in the *Gobitis* case: [3] "The flag salute
regulation is invalid because it may not be assumed that it was
within the intention of the [Pennsylvania] legislature to empower
school authorities to enact regulations contravening the law of
Almighty God." [4] This presentation of the "law of Almighty
God" as if it were a matter of common knowledge may have
surprised the Justices, but it was merely an echo of the historic
claim of religious enthusiasts to the right of private judgment.[5]
To put the matter differently, the issue ultimately results in the
injection of subjective matters of belief into the framework of
objective legal decision-making: An individual or group, on the
basis of unverified and by the very nature of things unverifiable
inspiration (at least by the standard canons of evidence), asserts
the right to reject the norms of the community.

Moreover, the confrontation between the enthusiasts and the
community is seldom a matter of abstract argument; the Cathari,
the Quakers, the Hasidim, the Dukhobors, or the Jehovah's Witnesses have never taken their theological case to a Church council, a Sanhedrin, or a seminar at Union Seminary for rational
adjudication. In part the antitheology of enthusiasm is directed
against the very existence and structure of religious authority—
there is a heavy dosage of anarchy and spiritual megalomania—
and in part the message itself demands stark evangelism. Thus
the chiliast, cherishing his special state of grace, will seldom let
sleeping dogmas lie. He must carry the fight into the enemy
fortress and, completely eschewing a "no-win" policy, demand
unconditional surrender. Rarely will he settle for "toleration"; indeed, the notion that evil should be tolerated is precisely the
source of his complaints against the Establishment.

The reaction of a society to such divine messengers has in
historical terms varied from indifference to savage persecution.

If a community was nurtured upon a set of religious convictions (Catholic, Presbyterian, Puritan), it generally reacted by invoking sanctions against sacrilege, blasphemy, or heresy (the ecclesiastical twin of high treason). When James Naylor rode a mule through Norwich accompanied by women distributing palms and announcing the second coming, Cromwell's judges were surprisingly lenient. Perhaps touched by the decency of a devoutly mad Christian, they bored his tongue for blasphemy and turned him loose. During the same period, the Puritan Zionists of Massachusetts Bay were cursed by a "pestilence" of Quakers.[6] In the Bay Colony, the judges tried a number of coercive techniques upon the Quaker commandos: They were put in the stocks, whipped, and exiled to Rhode Island, where a joyous state of religious anarchy prevailed. But these dogged enthusiasts were not interested in debating with Roger Williams; back they rushed to the Bible Commonwealth to witness to their truth. Finally, in a fit of bored rage, the Massachusetts judges hanged four, including a woman, Mary Dyer. In 1661 the newly restored Charles II ordered Massachusetts to send all Quakers under indictment to England for trial, and the Puritans lost their *vires* over seditious heresy.

Massachusetts has been condemned for this condign action, but, given the premise that the Commonwealth was established upon the Word of God, it is difficult to know what else the judges could have done. Later generations, which look on the whole affair as an exercise in comparative superstition, have done less than justice to both sides. The Quakers challenged the fundamental principles of ecclesiastical polity which supported the regime, and invited martyrdom—they never advanced any claim to a privilege against self-incrimination. Puritans and Quakers alike realized that this was no trifling matter of "opinion"; the attack on the theocracy jeopardized the whole structure of the community. When a society is integrated around the matrix of religious truth, it must exterminate religious opposition or abdicate its claim to legitimacy.

A society founded on secular premises handles the problem in a different fashion. The fundamental operating assumption is that religion is a "private" matter, and every effort is made to "take religion out of politics." A chiliastic troublemaker is therefore subjected to sanctions as a public nuisance (or, as in Elizabethan England, where the supremacy of the Crown was an article of faith in the Established Church, as a sedition-monger and traitor). The state, in other words, invokes no ecclesiastical authority but disposes of the disruptor as a menace to public order. As John Locke put it in his *Letter Concerning Toleration:* "[N]o opinions contrary to human society, or to those moral rules which are necessary to the preservation of civil society, are to be tolerated." [7] The first two drafts, but not the final version, of Jefferson's great Virginia Statute of Religious Freedom echoed this Lockean concern: "[B]ut this [liberty of religious opinions] shall not be held to justify any seditious preaching or conversation against the authority of the civil government." [8] Note carefully the definitional device employed here: "Seditious preaching" was put in a different *category* than religious opinion. Thus one could suppress "seditious preaching" without in any way impairing religious freedom; in logical terms, freedom of religion stopped where sedition began.

The classic American doctrine of religious freedom must, I submit, be understood in this historical context. And superadded upon this formulation, which Mr. Manwaring styles the theory of "secular regulation," are the complications of the principle of the separation of Church and State and the First Amendment guarantee of religious liberty. Let us assume for purposes of discussion what I believe to be the case, namely that the evidence available does not support a broad construction of the First Amendment provisions on religion.[9] With a minimum definition we have two limitations on congressional power: *First,* there shall be no established church or multiple establishment under the auspices of the general government; and, *second,* the United States cannot favor or penalize any one religious body, or coalition, in the enactment of public policy. Now we have the full dimensions of the quagmire into which all legal explorations of Church-State problems must penetrate.

Let us begin with some examples and examine the various facets that emerge. The United States enacts a draft law applicable to all men between the ages of eighteen and forty-five. This is clearly a "secular regulation"; indeed, it is only a national application of the ancient common-law institution of the militia. A Quaker claims that the statute is unconstitutional as a "conscription of conscience," and invokes the First Amendment as a bar to military service for those with religious scruples. A court confronted with this issue can rule in either of two fashions: First, it can announce that it is the character of the statute rather than the individual response that determines the outcome, and sustain the conscription of the pacifist on the ground that the law—although it has provoked a religious riposte—is secular and that the nature of an individual's reaction is wholly irrelevant. Second, the court could hold that the draft is an unconstitutional restriction on the religious freedom of Quakers, a holding that should bring equally loud cheers from opponents of both war *and* separation of Church and State. In effect, this holding gives a special benefit to one religious persuasion: It would be roughly analogous to a ruling that Catholics who support their own schools as a matter of faith cannot be taxed for the support of public education.

The Supreme Court found itself in precisely this sort of dilemma in a recent case where Orthodox Jewish storekeepers asserted that Massachusetts' Sunday closing legislation worked a religious discrimination against those who closed shop on Friday night and remained closed through sundown on Saturday. In objective terms the law did penalize the religious, both Jews and Seventh Day Adventists. Yet, if the Supreme Court had agreed that the plaintiffs could not be penalized for their religious convictions, it had either to declare Sunday-closing laws generically unconstitutional as a violation of the separation of Church and State, or give Orthodox Jews and Seventh Day Adventists a special dispensation which would itself amount to a violation of that principle. The opinion of the Court is, perhaps understandably, a bit obscure, but it appears that reliance was placed on the "secular regulation" rule; Sunday was miraculously transformed into a secular day of rest.[10]

There is one more thorny hedge to be surmounted involving that Forgotten Man, the secular nonbeliever. To put the problem succinctly, when statutory exemption from military service is granted to members of the historic "peace churches" (Friends, Mennonites, Brethren) because of religious scruples, why should similar exemption not be given to the freethinker who, bereft of revelation or scripture, is simply against fighting? Some years ago the Federal Communications Commission enlivened discussion of this topic by momentarily suggesting that an atheist had the right to equal time on the airwaves to counter the "opinions" of churchmen on the role and functions of the Deity.[11] The FCC's position was intrinsically sound, though it ran into heavy weather, and a logician could argue with equal soundness that exemption from military service (which Congress has ruled can be granted only to those with bona fide religious motivation) can not discriminate against the nonbeliever without violating the separation of Church and State.

Probably the classic case of the enforcement of "secular regulation" was the savage campaign mounted by the federal government in the 1870's and 1880's to extirpate polygamous Mormonism. The details of this police action have never been adequately chronicled. Congress employed the mailed fist—barring Mormons from juries, requiring from them a "disclaimer affidavit" before voting, and eventually escheating all the nonecclesiastical properties of the Mormon Church. The Mormons relied heavily on the First Amendment to protect their peculiar institution of "celestial marriage," but to no avail. Polygamy was a crime, and, said Justice Field for a unanimous Court, "crime is not the less odious because sanctioned by what any particular sect may designate as religion."[12] The same rationale was more recently employed to sustain the use of the Mann Act against polygamous Mormon remnants.[13]

To summarize, the background of the Church-State discussion is a logical shambles. If one interprets the First Amendment as *protecting* religious eccentricities from the police power, he suddenly finds himself hurdling the "impenetrable wall" between Church and State, and claiming special rights or exemptions for specified categories of citizens *on the basis of their religious views*. Moreover, can one not argue (as Justice Jackson did in the first *Russian Orthodox Church* case [14]) that when the courts begin to define religious points—for example, by deciding that polygamous Mormonism was *not* a free exercise of religion but a criminal conspiracy—their very intervention constitutes a violation of the principle of separation? If Congress has no right to interpret religious doctrine, it could hardly confer jurisdiction to do so upon the federal courts. The legitimate role of a court under this interpretation is to examine the statute or ordinance— not its impact—and determine whether it is secular in purpose. The moral fervor of those opposing it is irrelevant; they can take their problems to a different court and perhaps get suspended sentences for sincerity. Yet nothing is quite so elusive as "purpose." As Manwaring points out, "secular regulation" readily lends itself to disguised persecution—as in the Oregon system for ending Catholic parochial education by requiring all children to attend public schools, a technique highly touted by the Ku Klux Klan, which the Supreme Court blocked in 1925.[15]

In short, any road one takes leads to difficulties. In Massachusetts a year or so ago there was a textbook case of the logical bind: The Orthodox Jewish community requested the Commonwealth to appoint an Orthodox rabbi as state supervisor of kosher products, claiming that otherwise the state inspection laws worked discrimination against them. In essence, they demanded equal protection of the health laws. The Civil Liberties Union of Massachusetts, however, after a discussion worthy of a theological conclave, opposed this request as a breach in the wall of separation between Church and State.[16] Even a "neutral principle" of constitutional law could hardly provide guidance in this labyrinth.

Professor Manwaring's Witnesses marched squarely into this chaotic intersection of personal liberty and the police power. Their rejection of the flag salute was only incidental to their basic contention, namely, that the Witnesses had the right to select those aspects of the police power to which they would conform, and repudiate those which, in their view, had received divine condemnation. Now, it is obvious that an organized society cannot permit any individual or group to revise the criminal code on the basis of an alleged relationship with higher authority. But, at the same time, a democratic society must put a high valuation on the conscience of the individual (whether founded on reli-

gious or humanistic values). The characteristic democratic technique for dealing with such a conflict is to ignore it in the hope
it will go away, to apply in sensible fashion an administrative
version of *de minimus* (the teacher overlooks the nonsaluting
child; he is quietly told to come to school *after* assembly, and
so on). The truth of the matter is that democratic political theory
has never managed to reconcile its two essential but antipodal
elements: The rights of the majority and the authority of individual conscience. And, as a matter of fact, a number of sticky
problems have been "solved" over the years by the tactic of
evasion. The British are particularly adept at this.

The Witnesses, unfortunately, were on the warpath; quite literally they were preparing for Armageddon and were bristling
with resistance to the godless claims of the state, whether Pennsylvania or Hitler's Reich. Moreover, their strong language and
persistence had aroused a great deal of public resentment: Catholics were infuriated by their references to the Holy Roman and
Apostolic Church as the "whore of Babylon," and the American
Legion was panting to teach them a lesson in patriotism and respect for the flag. In this regard, Manwaring has made a particularly useful contribution by his careful analysis of Witness persecution.[17] His statistics indicate that anti-Witness mob violence
was most virulent in small-town America as distinct from the big
cities, a conclusion that tends to confirm the thesis I advanced
some years ago that there has been a direct correlation between
urbanization and the decline of mob rule.[18] In any event, the confrontation could not be avoided and, as inevitably occurs in the
United States, the courts were called upon to settle the issues in
dispute.

It would be pointless to recapitulate the history of the litigation here. Manwaring has picked his way through the material
in sharp, concise fashion and has for the first time set forth clearly
just what the Supreme Court did and did not say. Suffice it here
to note that in 1940 in *Gobitis*,[19] Justice Frankfurter upheld the
Pennsylvania flag salute as a secular ceremony within the range
of reasonable state authority, and ruled that a private religious
opinion to the contrary was irrelevant. In short, Frankfurter refused to consider the freedom of religion argument as analytically

meaningful in the situation at bar. Justice Stone, in dissent, asserted that religious freedom was an issue, went on to weigh the merits of the religious claim against the merits of the police power, and found the latter wanting. In other words, Frankfurter and his seven colleagues held there was *no conflict* in the *Gobitis* case between religious freedom and the rights of the community, while Stone believed there was a confrontation and that the rights of the Witnesses should prevail. As he put it:

If these guaranties [of civil liberty] are to have any meaning they must, I think, be deemed to withhold from the state any authority to compel belief or the expression of it where that expression violates religious convictions, whatever may be the legislative view of the desirability of such compulsion.[20]

Had the Court, when it shifted its view on the constitutionality of the mandatory flag salute, followed Stone's lead, it would patently have violated the separation of Church and State. The Justice, in effect, gave a special constitutional bonus to religious dissenters. His sympathy, I take it, would not have gone out to the child who refused to salute because he detested the colors red, white, and blue, or who rejected for rationalistic reasons the whole syndrome of flag fetishism. As Manwaring notes, his compassion had gone out to the religious pacifists of World War I, whom he distinguished from the political objectors, the "glib talkers." [21] But in the eyes of the law, in a society founded on secular principles there can be no favoritism of this sort: "glib" political objections to war can be no worse, or better, than tormented and perhaps incoherent religious views. A jury may take sincerity into consideration in its meditations; a judge can evaluate it before sentencing; and the executive can take notice of it in his employment of the pardoning power; but it has no place in the objective legal structure. It is immaterial to constitutional law, for example, whether a state official denies a Negro the equal protection of the laws because he despises him or because he interprets the Old Testament as asserting the eternal subordination of the Sons of Ham.

Stone may have got his logical categories a bit confused, but Justice Robert Jackson, who wrote the opinion of the Court in the *Barnette* case,[22] overruling *Gobitis*, kept his straight. Undoubtedly recognizing that Stone's line of reasoning led directly to a policy of special rights for the religious, that brilliant buccaneer took off on a different tack. Ignoring, except by implication, the religious issues in the case, Jackson accepted Frankfurter's earlier view that the flag salute was a "secular regulation," but held it to be a bad one, inherently unreasonable and arbitrary, which attempted to constrain freedom of thought—not religious thought, but *thought*. Thus the state, Jackson announced in the middle of World War II, had no right to demand this ritual of *anyone*. The crux of the argument between Jackson and Frankfurter was therefore not the rights of religious dissenters but the criteria the Supreme Court should employ in evaluating, in terms of the First and Fourteenth amendments, the "reasonableness" of state action.

In his treatment of the flag-salute litigation, Manwaring has given us a fine case study of the problems a court of law encounters when it attempts to arbitrate the claims of conscience. We see the whole range of positions: Frank Murphy at one extreme, who once he had become settled on the Court was *always* approving special privileges for those claiming a spiritual imprimatur (he even defended the Mormons against the Mann Act! [23]); Harlan F. Stone, prudently weighing the conflicting claims of religious inspiration and the police power; Felix Frankfurter and Robert H. Jackson agreeing that the salute is a "secular regulation," but disagreeing violently on whether the Court should exercise restraint or oversight—whether it should act as a tight-laced constitutional chaperon to the state legislatures; Black and Douglas asserting the "absolute" character of religious freedom up to the line of "clear and present danger" to the community. In addition, Manwaring has filled in a great deal of interesting background, examining, for instance, the attitudes of newspapers, journals, and law reviews at the various stages of the adjudication, and the role that various pressure groups such as the American Legion, the American Civil Liberties Union, and the Committee on the Bill of Rights of the American Bar Association played in supporting and arguing the test cases.

Finally, Manwaring has strengthened my conviction that existing legal precedents have outlived their usefulness in the religion-politics area and that before we can cope with the intricate dilemmas we confront in education, public ceremonies,[24] and the rights of religious minorities, we must get some new categories. Manwaring concludes on a pessimistic note by saying that all the rules the Court has employed have "serious drawbacks," and adds, "Which is preferable would seem almost a matter of taste." [25] Taste does play a part, but on the fundamental level a huge pluralistic society has simply refused to be constrained by eighteenth century rubrics, and has established a civic religion of a theologically nonpartisan character. As Will Herberg pointed out a decade ago,[26] being Protestant, Catholic, or Jewish is an essential part of being an American: we have an unofficial tripartite Establishment.[27] Even those who sympathize with his logic must admit that Justice Douglas's concurring opinion in the *Regent's Prayer* case [28] was distinctive for its archaic quaintness; it was rather like meeting a parade of suffragettes on the street, or hearing an oration on the economic virtues of free silver.

To state this is hardly to endorse it. I personally feel that this civic religion leads to a degeneration of spiritual values and a stultification of secular thought. However, as a student of American constitutional history, it seems clear to me that the classical theory of the relationship of politics and religion in the United States has reached dead end; it no longer has any logical nexus with social and political reality.[29] Where we go from here is anybody's guess. Perhaps to the Forum to burn incense before The God of One's Choice?

NOTES

1. *Engel* v. *Vitale*, 370 U.S. 421 (1962).

2. "Of Church and State and the Supreme Court," *University of Chicago Law Review*, Vol. 29 (1961), p. 1; *Religion and the Law* (1962). I regret that I can find no solace in Professor Kurland's prescription that the Court employ "neutral principles" of constitutional law. This phrase always puts me in mind of an event in the Irish Parliament in September, 1939. When Prime Minister De Valera announced that Eire was neutral in the war, a spokesman for the Clan na Gael opposition arose and stated that his party was in full agreement with De Valera in principle, but demanded to know whom the Irish were neutral *against*.

3. *Minersville School Dist.* v. *Gobitis*, 310 U.S. 586 (1940).

4. Manwaring, p. 110.

5. See generally, Ronald A. Knox, *Enthusiasm* (1950).

6. It should be noted that seventeenth century Friends were hardly the gentle quietists of later times. In Britain, George Fox was addicted to heckling the sermons of Puritan divines and on at least one occasion rode his horse into a hostile church. One can perhaps even sympathize with a Puritan congregation when a nude Quaker crashed its Sabbath service, announcing himself a symbol of the "Naked Truth."

7. *The Second Treatise of Civil Government and a Letter Concerning Toleration* (Gough ed., 1948), p. 154.

8. *The Papers of Thomas Jefferson* (Boyd ed., 1950), I, 344, 353.

9. Dean Leonard W. Levy, of Brandeis University, has recently argued that the First Amendment provisions on religious freedom were intended to establish an "impenetrable wall," but the evidence he advances indicates that this was James Madison's view. The others involved in the formulation and passage may have agreed with Madison—there is no basis for saying they disagreed—but I still stand by my view that without a great deal more data than appears to be available, the minimal interpretation of the reach of the amendment seems most plausible, *i.e.*, "In God We Trust" on the coinage, the Supreme Court's opening invocation, and Thanksgiving proclamations would not fall under the Amendment's interdiction. See L. W. Levy, "School Prayers and the Founding Fathers," *Commentary*, Vol. 34 (1962), p. 225; Roche, "The Founding Fathers: A Reform Caucus in Action," *Am. Pol. Sci. Rev.* Vol. 55 (1961), pp. 799, 815. Perhaps I should add that the Bill of Rights was not in my view inspired by libertarian sentiments, but by states'-rights commitments; *i.e.*, the new

general government was forbidden to dabble in religion, press, speech, etc., but the states retained the right to handle these matters as they saw fit. Only a *state* bill of rights could inhibit a member of the union from, say, establishing Catholicism and hanging Protestants for heresy or, conversely, renewing the suppression of Catholicism. "The inner life of the states, or of private organizations within the states, was thus [virtually placed] beyond constitutional jurisdiction." Roche, "American Liberty: An Analysis of the 'Tradition' of Freedom," *Aspects of Liberty* (Konvitz and Rossiter, eds., 1958), p. 145. See also the superb analysis of freedom of speech and press in early American history, L. W. Levy, *Legacy of Suppression* (1960).

10. *Gallagher* v. *Crown Kosher Super Market*, 366 U.S. 617 (1961).

11. Scott, 11 F.C.C. 372 (1946). This remarkable, if murky, ruling touched off a congressional investigation of the FCC. See H.R. Rep. No. 2461, 80th Cong., 2d Sess., 1948. The Select Committee of the House, after grilling Chairman Wayne Coy, called upon the Commission to "expunge" the decision from its records as an offense against "the moral standards of the nation." The FCC hastily realigned itself with the *Zeitgeist*. See *Journal of the Federal Communications Bar Association* (1949), pp. 245–246.

12. *Davis* v. *Beason*, 133 U.S. 333, 345 (1890). Even such a fine study as Harold Hyman's *To Try Men's Souls: Loyalty Tests in American History* (1959) omits any reference to the Mormon episode.

13. *Cleveland* v. *United States*, 329 U.S. 14 (1946).

14. *Kedroff* v. *St. Nicholas Cathedral*, 344 U.S. 94, 126 (1952) (dissenting opinion).

15. *Pierce* v. *Society of Sisters*,

268 U.S. 510 (1925). The Court did not invoke the First Amendment or deal with the issue of religious freedom in the decision; the Oregon measure was struck down as an infringement on property rights.

16. The issue apparently was never taken to the courts.

17. Manwaring, pp. 163–175.

18. Roche, "American Liberty: An Analysis of the 'Tradition' of Freedom," *Aspects of Liberty* (Konvitz and Rossiter, eds., 1958), pp. 129, 151–162.

19. *Minersville School Dist.* v. *Gobitis,* 310 U.S. 586 (1940).

20. *Ibid.,* at p. 604. Cited by Manwaring, p. 145. Presumably in this tradition the Philadelphia branch of the American Civil Liberties Union in 1962 "supported legislation to exempt members of the Amish religious sect from paying a Social Security tax on the grounds that the Amish conscientiously object to receiving benefits from anyone except God" "Freedom Through Dissent," *Ann. Rep. A.C.L.U.,* Vol. 42 (1962), p. 26. The Amish are, of course, free to reject benefits, but a statute such as this would clearly run afoul of the logic of separation of Church and State unless it exempted *anyone* with objections from the burden of taxation.

21. Manwaring, p. 143.

22. *Board of Educ.* v. *Barnette,* 319 U.S. 624 (1943).

23. See his dissents in *Cleveland* v. *United States,* 329 U.S. 14, 24, (1946), and in *Musser* v. *Utah,* 333 U.S. 95, 98 (1948), where the issue was a state law prohibiting the advocacy, encouragement, etc., of polygamy.

24. Query: When a President rolls the first Easter egg down the White House lawn, or lights the Christmas tree on the mall, is he boring into the "impenetrable wall"?

25. P. 253.

26. *Protestant, Catholic, Jew* (1955).

27. While this is hard on the nonbeliever, he too has a solution: he can become a nonbelieving Protestant, Catholic, or Jew.

28. *Engel* v. *Vitale,* 370 U.S. 421, 437 (1962).

29. See my discussion of this in "Religion et Politique aux Etats-Unis" *Laïcité* (1960).

McCloskey v. *Diamond:* A Comment

As one who has for some years been trying to establish, both in teaching and research, a *modus vivendi* with American political thought, I was immensely impressed by Professor McCloskey's "American Political Thought and the Study of Politics," in the March issue of this *Review*. He has stated clearly and without cant what seem to me to be the goals of the teacher in this somewhat neglected field of interest, and his formulation has helped me, for one, to a better appreciation of the intricate relationships between thought and action which characterize the American political tradition. What I have to say here is essentially an elaboration of his position in one specific, but to me important, area.

My one significant criticism of McCloskey's article arises from his apparent acceptance of the view that American political thought is second-rate, an acceptance which seems to me an unnecessary and unwarranted concession to our critics who assert in season and out that since we have produced no Plato or Aristotle, no Hegel or Marx, our tradition is barren of any real thought. Some of my best friends are metaphysicians, but I still insist that we have succumbed too long to their ontological bullying. To say this is not to claim that American political thought is first-rate, or to advocate the antimetaphysical nihilism of positivism and its derivative cults; it is merely to assert the inadequacy of traditional metaphysical criteria when used to

Reprinted, with permission, from *The American Political Science Review*, Volume LI, Number 2, June, 1957, pages 484–488.

evaluate American political thought—to note that it is possible for a high-level civilization to exist, and with it a significant corpus of political ideas, without producing great philosophical figures. The mere absence of a Plato or a Locke is not sufficient in itself to consign a political tradition to the limbo of mediocrity. The Byzantine Empire, that mysterious entity and great culture which existed but five hundred miles from the primitive feudal institutions to which we devote so much time, never produced a Plato or a St. Thomas—a fact which Steven Runciman suggests was a tribute to the effectiveness of its operational ideas which "worked too well for abstract discussions to be needed." [1]

Byzantium was undeniably a metaphysical failure, but the reason for this appears to be the astounding success of its day-to-day, century-to-century, political ideas, that is, the success of its political thought. Granting the danger of argument by analogy, I would yet urge that the American situation is roughly parallel to that of the Byzantine Empire, though obviously the contents of the two political traditions are radically divergent. Unquestionably we do not rate more than a gentlemanly C— in metaphysics. But the connection between this proposition and one alleging that our political thought is second-rate has nowhere been demonstrated. Only after an identity between first-rate philosophy and first-rate political thought has been established—not assumed *sub silentio*—could this proposition be sustained. One could, indeed, suggest—at least for purpose of argument—that the appearance of great philosophers in a society is an almost certain sign of a failure or crisis in political theory, of the growth of anomie—do not great philosophic owls hoot only at twilight? To quote Runciman again, "It was only in the last years of the Empire, when it was clearly dying, that the theorists arose with schemes to put the world right." [2]

Professor Martin Diamond's critique of McCloskey comes to mind at this point. Diamond, after some semantic exercise, assaults McCloskey because the latter did not keep mirrors and creators in discrete logical categories. This, while doubtless devastating from the viewpoint of formal logic, strikes me as merely irrelevant, since, as I read his piece, McCloskey was asserting precisely the difficulty, if not impossibility, of distinguishing in American political thinkers between the creative and reflective acts. Put another way, McCloskey was emphasizing the absence of alienation, which might be defined as the *separation* of creative from reflexive processes. Particularly in the eighteenth and nineteenth centuries, American political thinkers were totally immersed in the day-to-day life of the body politic, and their creativity was a merged coefficient of their reflection.

Diamond's attack wanders off down a dead-end street, I suggest, because he is approaching the American political tradition with the critical apparatus of philosophy. Note again: I am not denying the validity of these metaphysical canons in their proper sphere, but I insist that their role is supplementary at best in the evaluation of political thought. We have been abashed and uneasy in the presence of our philosophical critics to the extent that we have failed to note the trickery involved in their critique of American political thought. They have smote us, in essence, with a self-validating proposition. The syllogism might be set up as follows: (1) great political thought is founded on great metaphysics; (2) the United States has produced no great metaphysicians; *ergo* (3) American political thought is second-rate. American political thought may be second-rate, but a judgment to this effect cannot merely be founded on the foregoing tautology that it has produced no Plato.

Assuming, then, that the criteria of professional philosophy are inappropriate for evaluating American political thought, what criteria should be applied? Here Diamond has registered a serious complaint against McCloskey. If one does not judge American political thought in terms of philosophical merit, is he not forced into a descriptive nominalism? Into simply asserting that there is, or is not, an intimate connection between ideas and political action? If all we can say is that Calhoun reflected brilliantly the aspirations of the antebellum South or that John Taylor of Caroline was out of step with the emergent nationalism of his time, we might as well shut up shop and go back to teaching American national government.

But are we so circumscribed? I don't believe so, and it seems to me that McCloskey has also implicitly rejected this nominalistic stand. True, an important level of analysis is concerned precisely with the pragmatic question: How well did this idea work? The concern at this point is with the correspondence of any particular body of ideas, for example, the abolitionist interpretation of due process of law, to the substantive goals of the group holding it, for example, freedom for the slaves. Similarly, one can examine the success of the cult of Herbert Spencer in supplying a political formula to the emerging "robber barons" or—to avoid antagonizing the younger generation—"industrial statesmen."

However, above and beyond this important level of description, there is a vital area of analysis which is concerned with goals and dreams, with the role that ideals play in the development of American political thought. On this level of ulterior analysis, one of course becomes involved in the innate subjectivism of ethics. Here one asks, for example, Did the importance of ending the "Mexicanization" of American politics justify the corruption and boodling involved in the Compromise of 1877? Was there an alternative route to consensus? If one chooses to bypass such a subjective quagmire as this, he has the option of confronting the spokesmen of any given period with the precepts upon which the Republic was founded: Professor Louis Hartz dealt perceptively in this fashion with the "Reactionary Enlightenment," demonstrating that Calhoun's philosophy was vitiated and aborted by the doctrines of natural right he was incapable of rejecting and powerless to transcend.

This gets the critical observer deep into the greatest mystery of all: What has given to American political thought its architectonic design? In attempting to answer this question, I have—and I take it from McCloskey's acute remarks about federalism, particularly his quotation from Acton, that we are in the same camp—found it necessary to break radically with the standard techniques of political theory. Recognizing that this may result in a court-martial, I confess that I have deemphasized ideas, and concentrate almost wholly on institutional development. Rather than starting out with a Geiger counter in search of Thomists, liberals, conservatives, or Gnostics, I spend my time tracing the growth, power, or decline of American institutions, pressure groups among them, and examining the impact of these changes on the content of American political thought. I claim no originality in this; the technique is an old one which reached its peak in the work of Frederic Maitland and John Neville Figgis, and was used with great effectiveness by Sir Lewis Namier and his disciples to examine eighteenth century Britain. It seems particularly appropriate to the American scene.

Thus in examining the history of freedom in the United States, I do not begin with the growth of a mustard seed in the colonial period and trace the ever-widening vistas of freedom through the Declaration of Independence and on into the nineteenth century. I begin with an Americanization of Figgis's famous dictum, "Political liberty is the residuary legatee of ecclesiastical animosities"; namely, that American freedom has largely been a by-product of the practical inability of any group successfully to impose its truth on the nation. Like McCloskey, and in the spirit of Maitland's famous remark that British liberty was an outgrowth of "writs not rights," I emphasize heavily the growth of procedural traditions which act as a cushion against injustice. With one or two exceptions, notably the Pennsylvania Quakers of the colonial period, I have yet in the course of my research to discover any significant American group which was unwilling, *when it had the power*, to deny freedom to its enemies. Respect for the civil liberties of opponents has been scant: if Adams could approve the application of the Sedition Act to Jeffersonian newspapers, Jefferson could casually write Governor Claiborne of the Orleans Territory with respect to the illegal arrest and confinement of Burr and his minions:

The Feds, and a little band of Quids, in opposition, will try to make something of the infringement of liberty by the military arrest and deportation of citizens, but if it does not go much beyond [the few leaders], they [the arrests] will be supported by public approbation.[3]

This has a certain contemporary ring—at least for civil libertarians who are constantly being told with respect to violations of constitutional rights that while illegitimate, the baby is very *small*.

The "tradition of liberty" thus breaks down into a study of practice, and of the development of social traditions which drew the sting from intergroup relations. My tentative view is that the very impersonalization of urban industrial society which is so deplored by psychoanalytical and sociological commentators has been a major factor in an increase in freedom for the American nonconformist. However, my views, whether sound or fatuous, are not relevant here. What is relevant is the technique: the close exploration of the nexus between political structure and political thought. Howard Jay Graham has, for example, done a superb job of demonstrating the connection between the demands of railroads and insurance companies for protection from state regulation and the incorporation of Herbert Spencer's *Social Statics* in the Fourteenth Amendment. His research suggests that a major consideration in this process was the legal upbringing of corporation counsel, for most of the leaders of the bar were in their youth steeped in the higher law, substantive due-process tradition of the abolitionists.[4]

Similarly, a close examination of states' rights breaks down the view that there is a states'-rights "tradition" in the European sense, that is, a group which consistently clings to a body of dogma come hell or high water. We find the emphasis on states' rights as a direct coefficient of political imperatives. True, one and all look to and quote the Virginia and Kentucky Resolutions, but a tradition must be built on more than rhetorical plagiarism, and a reading of Henry Adams's magisterial *History of the United States in the Administrations of Thomas Jefferson and James Madison* should destroy once for all the illusion that the Jeffersonians were principled decentralists.

At this point a critic can legitimately inquire: "So what?" Are teachers of American political thought to abandon the realm of ideas entirely and become structural engineers? Obviously not; I am not suggesting that explorations of the sort I have described are *sufficient* for an evaluation of our political tradition, but rather that they are necessary, absolutely necessary. The achievement of "good" goals must be linked up with the creation or maintenance of effective institutional forms. One can suggest, as James M. Burns does in his fine study of Franklin D. Roosevelt, that the President failed to fulfill the potentialities of "liberal" leadership because he did not create a presidential party in Congress, but without a fight left control in the hands of the senior southern legislators. In short, one can insist on the intimate tie between instruments and goals, though recognizing that the latter are not immanent in the forms but must be arrived at by philosophical processes and imposed upon the tradition from without. He does not go looking for "great" philosophy as the proof of great political thought—he utilizes great philosophical traditions to judge the content of the thought, and, hopefully, to alter its direction. A first-rate body of political thought is not, therefore, one which shoots off great metaphysicians like alpha particles; it is one which moves toward first-rate goals.[5]

We terminate this journey staring morosely at the barrier of first principles. Our tradition is not first-rate because it has worked, nor is it second-rate because it has produced no political philosophers of genius. Whether it is good or bad can be determined only in terms of external categories, and our function as teachers and scholars in this field is to dedicate ourselves to the arduous task of refining these analytical criteria. Subjective they may be, yet without them it is impossible to evaluate in an ethically meaningful fashion the merits of American political thought. And no amount of scientific jargon or numerology can exorcise this metaphysical shade. Much as some would like to believe it possible, in ethics and metaphysics the Indian rope trick can not be managed: no one can climb up his premises and then pull them up behind him. Thus, like it or not, we find ourselves projected into the realm of moral speculation; and, while I realize what a sense of unease speculating about the moral order creates in most of us, I suggest that the sooner we confront the problem, the better. We can, of course, ignore the issue, but it will not go away. The only thing that will occur is that self-appointed prophets of Truth will continue to fill the vacuum and to usurp the function of judgment in the name of their esoteric cults.

NOTES

1. Steven Runciman, *Byzantine Civilization* (London, 1933), p. 65.
2. *Ibid.*
3. Cited by Thomas P. Abernethy, *The Burr Conspiracy* (New York, 1954), p. 196.
4. See Howard Jay Graham, "Builded Better than They Knew,"
University of Pittsburgh Law Review, Vol. 17 (1956), p. 537; and "Our Declaratory Fourteenth Amendment," *Stanford Law Review*, Vol. 7 (1954), p. 3.
5. Cf. Clinton Rossiter, *Seedtime of the Republic* (New York, 1953), pp. 438–439.

A Review of
Banks and Politics in America
by Bray Hammond

When, in 1928, Lewis Namier published his monumental *Structure of Politics at the Accession of George III*, a new verb was coined to describe the scholarly carnage the work performed: to namierize. The earmarks of namierization are a complete skepticism toward even the best-recommended theories and a stubborn insistence on the intimate and determining relationship between discrete pieces of historical data and historical generalizations. Thus, in examining the politics of the past, one exhumes the day-by-day activities of actual politicians rather than the "spirit of politics"; in analyzing economic history, one delves into the minute and often fearfully tedious workings of the actual economic mechanism rather than into the rhetoric of "agrarians" or "bourgeois" (who have in all likelihood been drafted into these historical battalions to fulfill the *a priori* commitments of the analyst).

The historian who accepts the Namier canon simultaneously brings upon himself a life of trouble. For one thing, he can never be a prophet, and the more vigorously he attacks the posturings of historical messiahs, of those like Arnold Toynbee who specialize in turning water into wine and very active crustaceans into fossils, the more he is written off as "small-minded," "petty," and obsessed with "mere facts." This attack in turn engenders even greater acerbity on the part of the critic: There is one case recorded in apocrypha of a namierite who was finally led away after he had sent several savage reviews of his own books to the editor of the London *Times Literary Supplement*.

Reprinted, with permission, from *The New Leader*, July 21–28, 1958.

Moreover, he is suspect among his own colleagues. When some great theory is launched and the world stands in awe, he gets in his submarine. Worse, he is not "clubby": where another would prepare a genial review of a book yet decry it privately, the namierite attacks in the full light of day. He takes a rapier, not a back scratcher, to scholarly seminars and panels and somehow seems oblivious to the obligations of friendship. (He makes some absurd distinction between attacking ideas and attacking the person who holds them, overlooking the fact that when he topples an intellectual edifice, its author will probably be crushed in the ruins.) In short, the namierite is dangerous and unpredictable; he takes ideas seriously and is infuriated by that corruption of the word which is the earmark of so much contemporary scholarship.

Unfortunately, in Britain Sir Lewis has sired a generation of epigones who have moved from his high skepticism about generalizations to a positivistic rejection of ideas per se which occasionally verges on blatant, cynical anti-intellectualism. While skepticism and cynicism often seem close neighbors, they are, in fact, antipodal positions. Skepticism is founded on concern; the skeptic cannot avoid being *engagé*. Cynicism, in contrast, is the ultimate betrayal of the human spirit, for it is based on contempt, and amounts in fact to a severing of the umbilical cord which unites one with his fellow human beings. Sir Lewis never has forgotten that men are creatures of belief and faith as well as of self-interest—it is a pity that his disciples have not read their master more closely.

All this is preparatory to an appraisal of the true worth of *Banks and Politics in America*, for Bray Hammond writes in the tradition and with the genius for detail that is characteristic of Namier at his best, and he has brilliantly namierized a crucial period of American economic history. In my opinion, this study of the credit structure of the United States from the Revolution to the Civil War is the most significant book to appear in American history since Vann Woodward brought out his *Origins of the New South* in 1951. By some strange coincidence, perhaps due to the fact that Senator Kennedy has not had time to write a competing volume, Hammond was awarded a Pulitzer Prize.

This public tribute to Hammond's accomplishment is fully

justified, and to it I should like to add a note of personal indebtedness. Even though I have never met Bray Hammond, I am deeply in his debt. Indeed, all unknowingly, he was instrumental in launching me on my career as a vulgar empiricist. When I was discharged from the Army and entered graduate school, I was hypnotized and captivated by Great Ideas. When someone mentioned the *Zeitgeist*, I would look abashed, not realizing that this was only a Hegelian way of begging causal questions. History I viewed as the ebb and flow of great ideological tides on which men were carried, willy-nilly, and thrown onto predestined beachheads. Following in the footsteps of A. M. Simons, Parrington and Co., I looked upon the history of the United States as an area in which the good progressive forces were locked in never-ceasing combat with the bad reactionary forces. It was so delightfully simple.

Then the snake appeared in the Garden of Eden; at the suggestion of a friend, in rapid succession I read Arthur Schlesinger, Jr.'s, *Age of Jackson* and Hammond's evisceration of it in the *Journal of Economic History*. Unwilling to consign Schlesinger's book—which perfectly matched my preconceptions—to the fiction shelf, I did what all good graduate students are supposed to do, and trotted off to the sources. I have never been the same since. The Jackson that emerged from my research was, if anything, more capricious, arbitrary, and demagogic than even Hammond had suggested. Indeed, I reached the conclusion that the President had killed the Bank of the United States more to satisfy a personal feud with Biddle than to implement any ideological convictions he may have had. It was the code duello, not agrarian principle, that brought down the Bank.

At this point I gave up History for history. I have tried to be courteous about it, since many of my scholarly friends have quite placid common-law marriages with what appear to me to be fictitous spouses. Thus, when various of my friends refer to "historical laws," "the proletariat," "American civilization," "conservatism," "liberalism," or the "New Deal," I react as one does when an archbishop invokes the Trinity—I take off my hat.

Banks and Politics in America—to return to the subject of this essay—is a majestic work of history. Read in conjunction with the studies of state attitudes toward internal improvements (Louis Hartz's on Pennsylvania and Oscar and Mary Handlin's on Massachusetts are the best), and Carter Goodrich's investigations of national, state, and local interaction, Hammond's book should seal the doom of many a hoary dichotomy. For example, it seems perfectly clear (*pace* Louis Hacker) that both Hamilton and Jefferson were neomercantilists, that both accepted the function of the sovereign in economic development. Where they differed was, first, in defining the locus of sovereignty, with Hamilton standing for the prerogatives of the general government, and Jefferson for those of the states; and, second, in their definition of the "national interest" which it was the function of the government to advance. And the first difference should not be pushed too far: given Jefferson's real-estate interpretation of the national interest (which may have had its origins in his physiocratic, land-centered orientation), the Louisiana Purchase was an act of national intervention in the *economic* life of the United States. Halévy to the contrary notwithstanding, the physiocrats were not forerunners of laissez faire, but strong believers in the legitimacy of state action to maintain the agrarian sector of the *political economy*, and Jefferson was a consistent supporter of this agrarian favoritism.

Hammond's greatest contribution, to my mind, is that he has —in Maitland's phrase—thought himself "back into a twilight." His capitalists, who have not read *The Communist Manifesto* and are unaware of their historic mission, split up into factions and cut one another's throats. His bankers, a collection of wild and wonderful characters ranging from peculating rascals to the sober Gallatin, have all the class discipline of Spanish anarchists. His agrarians, as yet unexposed to the vagaries of a complex, industrial economy, react along the staid lines of European peasants ("bury the specie") instead of like wild-eyed Populists ("shoot the bankers").

The core proposition of the work is that there were two main approaches to the economic development of the underdeveloped (!) United States. On the one hand, there was the restrictionist viewpoint which wanted to proceed slowly and rationally with the Bank of the United States as the key agency of control. On the other, there were the dynamic entrepreneurs who wanted to plunge ahead pell-mell as fast and as far as their creditors would permit, and who looked upon the Bank as the unimaginative enemy of easy credit and hence national development. The fight to recharter the Bank in 1832–1836 was a bitter hand-to-hand encounter between these two positions, with the entrepreneurs victorious in large part because they convinced Jackson that the Bank was wicked and its president an aristocratic snob. This defeat for the forces of rational restrictionism, Hammond submits, determined the course of American credit policy for another century. He suggests that the course of events in Canada—where the restrictionists were never overpowered—indicates an alternative and superior route from 1836 to 1933. (It is interesting to raise a question in this regard that Hammond did not touch upon: In Canada banking was virtually a Scottish monopoly, and one may wonder if part of the conservatisim of banking north of the border was not due to the transplanting of rigorously restrictionist Scottish traditions.)

Banks and Politics in America is massive, and this essay can not pretend to a thorough evaluation. Various critics may dissent from some of Hammond's judgments; I, for example, think he lets Nicholas Biddle off too lightly, and suspect he underestimates the role of Albert Gallatin in the crucial period 1801–1814. But whatever differences of judgment do emerge, one fact seems clear: All future analyses of American economic development in the pre–Civil War period will start from Hammond's magisterial volume.

A Review of
The Antifederalists: Critics of the Constitution, 1781-88
by Jackson Turner Main

This is a curious and convoluted book. Professor Main's central thesis is that the anti-Federalists actually were the spokesmen for a majority of the American people in the 1780's, but in some dark fashion they were pushed aside, and a small group of nationalist plotters imposed the Constitution on the helpless masses. In short, the anti-Federalists were robbed; and as I read the book my memory took me back to election night in 1952, and I recalled a distinguished student of American politics explaining the disaster to some mourning Democrats: "The country is Democratic; the people disapprove of the Republican program; Eisenhower isn't even a Republican—it's obvious! The American people are the victims of a conspiracy."

This is the leitmotif of Main's book; over and over again he registers the same complaint in different formulations: "the Anti-federalists did not have a fair chance" (page 198). The Federalists were just plain nasty: they got the state legislatures to pack the Constitutional Convention with their partisans; they rushed ratification through without giving their opponents time properly to organize; their newspapers were positively unfair; and, worse, their candidates for the conventions ignored or misstated the anti-Federalist position. From Main's peculiarly nonpolitical vantage point, the Federalists should have had better manners than to oppose and defeat the (alleged) representatives of the popular will.

But, of course, the Federalists won. And, since he starts with

Reprinted, with permission, from the *Political Science Quarterly*, Volume 77, Number 2, June, 1962, pages 271–273.

the premise that a majority of the people opposed the Constitution, Professor Main has to explain the shambles of anti-Federalism in 1787–1788 as a defeat of the popular will. Moreover, there is no evidence to indicate that the elections to the state conventions were any less democratic than other contemporary elections; thus, the conniving Federalists cannot be indicted for election rigging. The state legislatures which sustained Professor Main's (and his mentor, Professor Merrill Jensen's) beloved Confederation were chosen by roughly the same electorate. What went wrong?

There are two answers: Either the anti-Federalists were political incompetents who lost whatever majority they may have had among the population to a brilliantly organized nationalist opposition, or anti-Federalism was the victim of a conspiracy. While Professor Main does a fine job of documenting the first alternative, he never lets go of the conspiracy theme. He goes a long way, for example, toward suggesting that the anti-Federalist leadership—an upper-class group allegedly motivated by sympathy with their Federalist upper-class opponents—unconsciously sold the pass. Since he never defines "class" except in circular terms (the upper class is the class above the middle class, and so on), and assumes what has to be demonstrated if his terminology is to have analytical value (that, for example, big debtors like Robert Morris and James Wilson had the same "class interest" as wealthy creditors rather than sharing a "class" bed with small debtors), this argument simply leaves me mystified. But however faulty the logic, the conclusion emerges intact: The vibrantly democratic and egalitarian anti-Federalist masses were sacrificed on the altar of their leaders' ambitions.

This story of the ravishing of the democratic innocents by self-interested elites is most touching. Unfortunately, it rests on divination rather than on any empirical base. Main has provided an enormous amount of documentation, but regrettably it is evidence for a different thesis; namely, that the anti-Federalists *thought* they were the spokesmen for the popular will; that they were politically outplayed at every turn by Madison and his colleagues; and that when they were overwhelmed in the state conventions, they took refuge from reality (as many politicians have over the years) in the comforting myth that they had been swindled. To assert that the elected delegates to the ratifying conventions betrayed the will of the people is simply unverifiable. In fact, any assertion about the will of the people is based on the anterior premise that when the electorate chose delegates, it was confronted with a clear ideological choice between pro- and anti-constitutional positions. In certain districts, notably in Virginia and Massachusetts, this seems to have occurred, but Professor Main puts his finger on the key consideration when he notes, almost parenthetically, that "only in New York was there an Antifederal 'party' in the sense connoted by that word—that is, an organization with a central committee of sorts which raised money, distributed propaganda, and corresponded with leaders within the state and in other states" (page 233). In other words, the anti-Federalists failed dismally to present to the voters their view that the Constitution was a dangerous innovation and, in the absence of this ideological polarization, the choice of delegates was generally based on traditional considerations; that is, trusted local figures were sent to the conventions to do what they thought best.

The Federalists, in a superbly organized campaign which I have examined in the *American Political Science Review* (Volume 55, Number 4, 1961), convinced these various assemblages of notables that the "national interest" required a new, more centralized, form of government. The anti-Federalists, spokesmen for parochialism, were beaten in a fair fight, and wandered off into the limbo reserved for the defeated. While their history is worth analysis, they hardly merit the sympathy Professor Main has so generously bestowed upon them.

III. The Socialist Impulse

The Crisis in British Socialism

British Socialism is today in the throes of a profound internal crisis. If we are to believe what we read in the American newspapers, Aneurin Bevan's strength is growing daily among the British trade unions, and no less an authority than *The New York Times* highlighted the recent Labour Party Conference at Morecambe as a Bevan victory. Some "experts" on British Socialism even tell us that Aneurin Bevan will be the next Labour Prime Minister. In short, we are led to believe that the extremists are virtually in command of the Labour Party.

It is the purpose of this analysis to demonstrate that these prophets of gloom are mistaken, that their analyses are based on inadequate knowledge of both the internal organization of the Labour Party and of the political process in general, and finally that the real nature of the Bevanite threat is quite different from that suggested above. In fact, it is here submitted that Aneurin Bevan can never capture the Labour Party as it is now constituted, but he can ruin it. To put the point precisely, the Bevanites may make it impossible for the British Labour Party to win another election, which in political terms is to condemn the party to death by slow strangulation. British Socialism has not been an "ideology" in the Continental sense; it has been a concrete bid for political power. Thus, if the pragmatic and thoroughly nondialectical average British Socialist decides that the Labour Party is destined to be a permanent minority, he may well take his political business elsewhere.

Reprinted, with permission, from *The Antioch Review*, Volume 12, Number 4, December, 1952, pages 387–397.

The leaders of British Socialism are on the horns of a horrible dilemma. On one extreme stand the powerful trade-union bureaucrats who would destroy the party sooner than have it fall into Bevan's hands, while on the other, stand Bevan and his associates who cripple the party's power to win elections. The major bone of contention is the British middle class. The facts are clear: in 1945, and to a lesser extent in 1950, the Labour Party victory was based on middle-class support. In 1951, the party lost precisely because this bourgeois segment of the electorate was alienated. The Labourites did, indeed, win a "moral victory" over the Conservatives by polling a larger percentage of the total vote than did the victors, but this slight overall advantage was more than offset by the fact that Labour piled up unnecessary majorities in safe constituencies. Under the British electoral system, as in the United States, a one-vote majority elects as surely as a majority of ten thousand. Thus, while the Labour Party can gain limited comfort from its popular plurality, it is also acutely aware that, in the words of a great rugby coach, "Moral victories are for the chaps who can't get the other kind."

To win the other kind of victory, Labour must regain the confidence of the middle-class voter. The working class of industrial Britain simply can not, at least under the present election system, go it alone. And, although Mr. Churchill has, in the course of his campaign to seduce the Liberal Party into the Conservative bed, grumbled some favorable comments about proportional representation, it may be assumed that the single-member constituency is a permanent feature of British political life. The implications of this electoral situation are tremendous, and may be summarized in one sentence: If the Labour Party is to win any future elections, Socialism must be given even more of a middle-class veneer. Or, to put it another way, British Socialists, unless they are prepared to become permanent wilderness dwellers, must formulate a program acceptable to the middle class.

To many foreign Socialists, this would appear to be unnecessary. British Socialism has long been considered petty bourgeois reformism by the Continental comrades, and further adjustments in the program of the Labour Party would probably appear unimportant in the Sanhedrin of Socialist orthodoxy—or at worst, as another step in the betrayal of Socialism that began a half-century ago. But at this particular time there happens to be a considerable opposition within the Labour Party to the further *embourgeoisement* of British Socialism, and it may yet appear that the type of schismatic who gives an air of authenticity to a Continental Socialist Party will pop up in British Socialism. Aneurin Bevan, although his chances of dominating either the British Labour Party or the British Trades Union Congress are virtually nonexistent, could serve as the catalyst and spearhead of a movement that would disrupt the Labour Party and weaken the bonds between the party and the Trades Union Congress.

In order to put Bevan in perspective, it is necessary to review briefly the internal history of the Labour Party. Initially formed by a reluctant marriage between the Trades Union Congress and Socialist intellectuals (the majority at the Trades Union Congress Convention which in 1899 authorized independent political action was a scant 5 to 4), the Labour Party soon became the nesting place of every radical reformer in Great Britain. Pacifists, vegetarians, feminists, anti-bloodsporters, republicans, all joined the Independent Labour Party which served as the intellectual organization in the overall federal party structure. (It was not until 1917 that the Labour Party accepted individual memberships except through intermediate constituent organizations.) In addition, a considerable body of Christian Socialist intellectuals— doctors, lawyers, dons, ministers—affiliated with the party on the ground that it was continuing the nonconformist tradition abandoned, in their view, by the Liberals.

The trade unionists, interested primarily in their own objectives, viewed the tremendous accretion of intellectuals with some alarm, but recognized that these "toffs" were helping them in their fight for industrial democracy. Furthermore, the unions had the situation in the party thoroughly under control. When all the shouting at party congresses was over, and the radical speeches at last subsided, the trade unionists with their bloc votes could decisively settle matters in a respectable fashion. In addition, it should be noted that the unionists were themselves in a radical frame of mind, and, if they were not particularly interested in

Socialist metaphysics, they were decidedly in favor of the immediate demands of the metaphysicians. Consequently the unions
supplied the funds for Socialist education and agitation, while
taking little direct leadership in the campaign.

The intellectuals who joined the party and led it throughout
its early years were divided into roughly two camps. One group,
which included a substantial number of Marxists, talked in traditional class-war terms. They looked upon capitalism as a foul
cancer which should be cut from the British body politic at the
earliest possible date and by whatever means were necessary and
expedient. This segment of the party was violently antimilitarist,
as distinguished from pacifist, and frequently expressed its scorn
for the reformist tactics of the trade unions. In the eyes of these
intellectuals, and their few trade-union allies such as young Ernie
Bevin, real democracy could develop only under Socialism, and
the "mere political democracy" that existed in Britain was a snare
and a delusion. Capitalism, they insisted, could not be modified
into Socialism through the democratic process, for the latter was
designed by capitalists for their own protection and would be
abandoned in favor of suppression if any real threat to capitalism
arose. Socialism would come first; democracy would come later.

The second segment of intellectuals took a different view of
the matter. Strongly influenced by the nonconformist Christian
tradition, these Labourites tended to look upon the capitalist as
Christ looked upon the sinner: a man more to be pitied than
hated. A strong pacifist contingent vigorously opposed class-
war doctrines, and an even stronger admixture of Fabians
eschewed radicalism in favor of the "inevitability of gradual-
ness." To the members of this segment, Socialism was a superstructure on democracy, and the way to achieve Socialism was
the democratic route of political victory in peaceful elections.
Indeed, most Fabians were "state Socialists" who unreservedly
advocated the use of the capitalist state apparatus to attain Socialist ends.

The trade-union leaders who were, after all, dedicated to ex-
ploiting capitalism for the benefit of the wage earner rather than
to overthrowing it, aligned themselves firmly with the moderate
intellectuals, and set out on the long, tortuous road to political

power. The extremist intellectuals, with a motley crew of union-ists, mainly syndicalists, worked desperately to move the Labour Party to the "Left," but events both internal and external worked against them. Internally they were confronted by the passionate solidarity of the trade unionist who viewed any attack on his union leaders as both an attack upon his judgment and a bonus for management. Externally, the Russian Revolution and the formation of the British Communist Party as a competitor with the Labour Party created additional difficulties. While the British workers had great sympathy for the Bolsheviks and the Soviet Revolution, they were completely merciless toward scissionists within their movement and party. Thus many of the extremists trickled off into the wilderness where they usually went through successive seizures of Leninist, Trotskyist, Syndicalist, Mosleyite, and other unnamed enthusiasms. The British workers would not even crucify these proletarian messiahs; they simply ignored them.

By about 1935, the pattern was firmly established and had sur-vived several grave crises: The moderate intellectuals ran the Labour Party supported by the great trade unions. Furthermore, two experiences with political power had whetted the appetites of the moderates and the unionists to the point where they would not let any niceties of Socialist dogma interfere with the demo-cratic process of getting votes. Socialism as theory became almost wholly identified with the victory of the Labour Party in a gen-eral election. What content there was to the Labour program consisted almost wholly of projects of public ownership which would alter the conditions of the industrial sector and advance the cause of industrial democracy. But it should again be empha-sized that in the mind of the average Labourite, Socialism was the victory of his party, or, to use the expressive colloquialism, of "our people." Consequently, throughout the twenties and thir-ties the Labour Party began to resemble its own ancestors less and less and its competitors for power more and more.

The genius behind this *embourgeoisement* was Herbert Mor-rison, Labour's apostle to the middle class. He saw the objective of the Labour Party clearly to be the collection of middle-class votes so as to achieve a majority in Parliament, and, as his political talents began to mold the party, less and less was heard about class war and more about common destiny. There was indeed opposition to Morrison's "Socialism without tears," but several factors combined to keep it subdued. First, the desertion of James Ramsay MacDonald and his few followers in 1931 served as a convenient touchstone of Socialism. Morrison could turn to his left-wing critics and say: "If we were not Socialist, would we still be here?" This suggestion that all the untrue Socialists had deserted was difficult to answer, for the immediate rewards for betrayal had been great and the reward for faithfulness had been the devastating Labour defeat in the election of 1931. Second, in spite of the debacle of 1931, or perhaps because of it, the average Labourite devoted even more of his efforts to the achievement of future victory, and was prepared to be ruthless toward potential schismatics who might delay victory. The general feeling seemed to be that the definition of Socialism in specific terms could await the morrow of a Socialist victory. The Labour Party in opposition succeeded in channeling the industry and vigor of all sorts of diversified enthusiasts into one stream directed at overthrowing the Conservatives in the immediate future. The greatly enlarged Labour minority which resulted from the election of 1935 spurred them on to greater hopes. Socialism, real Socialism, was in the offing, and this time the Labour government would not be at the mercy of a capitalist minority, but would have a majority in its own right.

The Labour victory in the general election of 1945 came as a tremendous shock to all concerned. The Labour leadership, while publicly jubilant, were in private quite uneasy about the prospect before them. It is difficult to believe that the electorate voted for Socialism; it would rather seem that several other factors played a more important role: reaction against the war and its restrictions, the feeling that the Tories were unprepared to face the problems of the postwar world, and last, but not least, a not inconsiderable body of sentiment to the effect that while Churchill was ideal to lead a parade, he was not the man to supervise the subsequent streetcleaning. But in any case, and however motivated, the British people installed a Socialist government, and the eager Labourites faced toward the dawn of a new England. The lean years were over, and the enthusiasts swarmed to the building of Jerusalem "in England's green and pleasant land."

This was indeed to be the payoff. The Labour Party had been given such a thumping majority in the House of Commons that there was no possibility of parliamentary sabotage. Nothing now stood in the way of implementing British Socialism except defining it. At first this was easy, for the party had long stood for nationalization of coal, the Bank of England, and transport, and for socialized medicine, and it proceeded to put these promises into legislation. Foreign Secretary Ernest Bevin solemnized the end of the old colonial system by wishing India, Pakistan, Burma, and Ceylon well as they began their ventures as independent nations. The Trades Disputes Act passed as a punitive measure after the General Strike of 1926 was repealed, and the trade-union movement was consulted on matters of industrial policy as it had never been before. The Attlee government could face the British people with the assurance of men who have lived up to their promises; and seldom has a nation been fortunate enough to have a government with such a high level of competence.

But this was not enough. The election of the Socialists, while it had led to the amelioration of the lot of the average Briton, had not transformed the spirit and face of Britain. The coal miners found that the National Coal Board was not greatly different from a private employer. The pacifists discovered that the Labour government had no intention of abolishing the Army. The unions found "their government" coming to them and imploring wage restraint. The enthusiasts began to chafe and mutter that the voice was Attlee's voice but the hands were the hands of capitalism. Some left-wingers began to talk about "state capitalism." Something was wrong, and since it had been accepted that the transformation of Britain would result from a Labour victory, the fact that the world remained largely the same was taken as proof of the inadequacy of British Socialism.

To those in positions of responsibility, it must have seemed as though there were a historical conspiracy against the Labour Party. In the first place, the nation which had been turned over to them in 1945 was on the edge of bankruptcy. The nationalization of coal and transport, far from being noble Socialist experiments, were economic imperatives, for only if the resources of the government were thrown into these fields would reconstruction be possible. Private investors could not have supplied the capital needed, for example, to rebuild the bombed railway system. In the second place, the government was stuck with a world they never made; they had certainly never thought that a large portion of national output would have to be channeled into nonproductive armaments. To take another example, Socialist enthusiasm was of little value in dealing with the dollar shortage. Obviously Socialism was more useful as a slogan of opposition than it was as an operational code for responsible ministers. A new disorder known as "Socialist ulcers" began to trouble the leaders of the Labour Party.

So long as the disillusioned enthusiasts had no leadership, the party leaders did not have to take them too seriously. Indeed, Attlee and his top strategy advisers were remarkably successful in keeping the disgruntled leaderless for so long. The main problem in this respect was obviously Aneurin Bevan, a first-rate demagogue with compulsive proletarian tendencies, but Attlee dampened Bevan's powder by making him Minister of Health, a position with immense responsibilities in the fields of housing, socialized medicine, and public health generally. Bevan was, in effect, told to put up or shut up. He put up, and did a superb job. Nevertheless, Bevan was obviously chafing under the yoke of responsibility, and he did succeed in taking sufficient time off from his ministerial duties to make some speeches which, it is estimated, lost the Labour Party 150,000 votes each among the middle class. It was in one of these that he referred to the Tories as "vermin," with the obvious implication that they should be exterminated. Bevan needed a heavier yoke, so Attlee handed him the heaviest in the Cabinet—the Ministry of Labour and National Service.

This appointment really put Bevan on the spot. The trade unions were becoming more and more restive under the policy of wage restraint, and Bevan was told, in effect, to use his great reputation acquired as Minister of Health to hold them in line. Faced with the acute possibility that he would be required by the imperatives of his position to sacrifice his status as champion of the British worker, Bevan took the first plausible opportunity to resign. At once the leaderless enthusiasts had a leader, and one who could not be called a Communist, and the leaders of the British Labour Party were brought face to face with a showdown that they wanted desperately to avoid.

Before discussing the future of Bevanism, it is important to analyze it. It is almost as difficult to answer the question "What does Bevanism stand for?" as it is to describe precisely the views and program of the party leadership. But this much does seem clear: Bevanism is an amorphous body of complaints about a cruel world. It is, in a real sense, an attempt to recreate the childhood of the Labour Party when the lines between "socialists" and "capitalists" were clearly drawn and enthusiastic crusading was the order of the day. One observer of French politics has noted that the French Socialist Party is the prisoner of its childhood, and it may be suggested that Bevanism represents a similar manifestation in British Socialism.

Practically speaking, Bevanism is characterized by a frenetic repudiation of the middle class, of middle-class virtues, of middle-class Socialism, of gradualism. The defeat of Herbert Morrison for re-election to the Executive Committee of the Labour Party, which occurred at the party conference at Morecambe in October, 1952, was the symbolic vengeance of this group upon the man whom it feels is the incarnation of Socialist Babbittry. The enthusiasts had their revenge on the Grand Inquisitor!

Thus around the standard of Aneurin Bevan have rallied all the social malcontents, the crusading enthusiasts, the crypto-Communists, and others whose common bond is little more than their disillusionment with the democratic process. If there is any one thread that unites the Bevanites, it would seem to be faith in historical shortcuts.

Will Bevan split the party? Probably not, at least, not if he can avoid it. Bevan was on the verge of expulsion in the thirties, at the time of the Socialist League incident, but while Stafford Cripps was then prepared to go into the wilderness with his principles, Bevan capitulated and remained in the party. But his very presence there constitutes a tremendous problem both for him and for the party leaders. Attlee will be very cautious lest he create a martyr; and Bevan will be careful not to give good grounds for expulsion, or to bolt, for he is well aware of the solidarity of the party in the face of schism. At the same time, Bevan makes it very difficult for the moderate leaders to gain the confidence of the middle class, while he cannot himself organize a faction or a new party without being expelled. In short, for the time being, an organizational stalemate exists.

How much support does Bevan have in the Labour Party? At the last party congress at Morecambe, the Bevanites won six seats on the party executive. This was a gain of two, since the Bevan group had four members on the last executive. But the significant aspect of this election was that all six were elected from the Constituency Labour parties. (The twenty-seven-member executive is elected in a peculiar fashion, growing out of the original federal design of the party: two hold ex officio membership, twelve are chosen by the trade unions, six by the whole party membership, and seven by the constituencies. In effect, eighteen are in the pocket of the trade-union section.) Bevanite strength was greatest among the intellectuals, and least among the trade unionists. This last statement should be qualified somewhat, since the trade-union custom of casting each union's vote en bloc may cover up significant minority strength. But at any rate it appears as though Bevan is another proletarian messiah without a proletariat.

Some newspaper accounts tell us of widespread Bevanism in the trade-union movement. However, these analyses fail to distinguish between trade-union agreement with one of Bevan's many complaints, and trade-union support for Bevanism as a political movement. Bevan has voiced so many objections to the present situation that it is virtually impossible for anybody, anywhere, to complain about anything without agreeing with Bevan! But agreement with some of Bevan's views does not make a Bevanite. For example, one of the unions which has complained the loudest about the restraints of British life is the Chemical Workers. Objectively, it would seem to fall into the Bevanite category. But, subjectively, it is dominated by old Independent Labour Party men who consider Bevan to be a dishonest political operator, and would never support him. Consequently, while there is considerable discontent in trade-union circles, it cannot be automatically registered as Bevanism. Moreover, at the Trades Union Congress, held at Margate in September, 1952, the combined oppositions never rallied more than a quarter of the votes.

This does not, however, alleviate the crisis for the leaders of the Labour Party. They are not particularly worried about losing the trade unions to the Bevanites. Their major problem is the middle class, whose fear of undemocratic extremism must be alleviated if another election is to be won for Labour. If the left-wing intellectuals can succeed in alienating the middle class from Socialism over a period of years, the Labour Party may begin to disintegrate. British politics are quite similar to American in this respect: a political party keeps strong by delivering the goods to its supporters. The Labour Party has held the support of the British worker not so much because the latter is committed to "Socialism," as through the worker's conviction that he will be better off with his friends in power. Indeed, it should be noted, the Labour Party's control of the "union vote" is far from complete; it has been estimated in Labour circles that one worker in four votes Conservative. However, if the Labourite workers ever decide that the party has lost its utility, that is, that it can win no more elections, he may very well switch his allegiance.

An additional factor deserves mention. Labor unions in despair take quite different attitudes from unions that are thriving. The Labour Party in the course of its struggle for industrial democracy may, by its very success, have weakened its hold over the workers. It should not be forgotten that the New Deal weakened its farm support largely by creating agricultural prosperity. If the Conservative Party, under the pressure of political imperatives, has really mended its antilabor ways, there is no reason to suspect that the British Trades Union Congress will engage in a quixotic defense of Socialism. As the General Council of the Trades Union Congress recently pointed out to the Churchill government: "On our part we shall continue to examine every question solely in the light of its industrial and economic implications. The trade union movement must always be free to formulate and to advocate its own policies." Gompers himself could not have said it better.

In short, then, the problem the Labourites face is that of

adjusting Socialism to a middle-class, democratic society. To do this, they must face squarely up to the Bevanites, who represent a fundamentally undemocratic tendency. If the Labour Party cannot master this problem in a satisfactory manner, it may well become a permanent and progressively disintegrating minority. There is, however, no reason to suspect that democratic British Socialists cannot overcome this barrier as they have solved the difficulties that faced them in the past. The heart of British Socialism is a mature, humanistic approach to the problems of life and a dedication to the principle that men can, working together in a piecemeal, pragmatic fashion, master their destinies. In all probability, Bevanism will terminate on the scrap heap along with the Independent Labour Party, the Socialist League, and other Labour offshoots that rejected prosaic democratic maturity in favor of conspicuous proletarianism.

The Triumph of Primitivism

If one believes, as I do, that it makes a difference whether the Tories or the Labourites govern Britain, the outcome of the Labour Party's 1960 Conference at Scarborough has implications of historical tragedy. Indeed, I feel that Gaitskell's defeat was a calamity not just for British Socialism, but for democratic Socialists everywhere. By endorsing unilateral nuclear disarmament, and forcing the Parliamentary leadership to challenge this absurd substitute for a defense policy, a motley coalition has in the span of a few short days jeopardized the party's accomplishments over a period of sixty years. The impossibilist compulsion, which is latent in all Socialist movements, has—at least temporarily—triumphed over the integrating forces of solidarity and common sense. The internal consequences are likely to be disintegration and schism; the external consequence is probably a long period of undisturbed Toryism.

In effect, the Labour Party has lost its pragmatic coherence. As the cracked drum of unilateralism beat out the death march, the hard-shell primitives and their odd congeries of allies overpowered the humanistic empiricists who have been attempting to adapt the party to life in the 1960's. If they can consolidate their hold by successfully dominating the Parliamentary Labour Party, the British Labour Party will be destroyed as an effective political instrument. Life in the wilderness may be morally fortifying for the desert fathers of unilateralism, but the political cost of this

Reprinted, with permission, from *Dissent*, Winter, 1960–1961, Volume VIII, pages 16–23.

self-imposed isolation will be permanent conservatism in the society at large.

For the benefit of those readers who may find such a stark focus disconcerting—those who may have dedicated their energies to the quest for Third or Fourth Positions—I should set forth my basic analytical assumption. It is my view that ideological disputes, however esoteric, always in political life come down to a choice between bodies, to a decision to support either X or Y. While metaphysicians and mystics have, of course, the right to evaluate ideologies abstractly, no one in real life has ever found a theory running for office. In fact, if one backs a "new course," he is simultaneously backing a set of "new corsairs," and I insist that the primary concern of the analyst should be the character of the new elite rather than the specific gravity of its ideology. I take my stand with Eduard Bernstein in asserting that the character of the movement is more important than the symmetry or perfection of its goals.

This mode of analysis, by the way, is neither "left wing" nor "right wing" in the traditional sense. Indeed, it bears no relationship whatever to classical programmatic categories. One who utilizes it approaches the whole problem of the nature of a social movement from a different perspective than is customary in Socialist circles. About ten years ago, for example, when Guy Mollet, the "rank-and-file" spokesman from Arras, wrested control of the French Socialist Party from "wishy-washy humanists" (to use the current phrases) of the Blum dispensation, some of us were deeply disturbed. Although Mollet was equipped with a program designed to revitalize the S.F.I.O.'s Marxist tradition and to rescue it from the "revisionist" clutches of men like André Philip and Daniel Mayer, his rise to power in the party was based on ruthless, unprincipled bureaucratic manipulation. Those Socialists, still rigidly attached to Marxist rhetoric, rejoiced that the S.F.I.O. was back on its authentic course—and were later disconcerted to discover Mollet underwriting a savage Algerian policy while Philip, Mayer, and other stuffy old lib-labs followed their principles and founded the Autonomous Socialist Party on a program of unconditional opposition to the shambles in Algeria.

Those who deny that there is a meaningful connection between human character and ideological pretensions have had some problems with Castro's Cuba. A year or so ago when an enthusiastic friend told me we must all rally to Fidelism and bring "real Socialism" to Latin America, I suggested gently that I could not see Social Democrats canonizing a man in love with a tommy gun. The reply: Castro was "utterly unimportant"; it was Fidelism that counted. But Castro was and is important, and I have never known a man who treated a gun as a symbol—instead of an instrument—who was not fundamentally depraved. When such an addict of romantic violence appears in politics mouthing left-wing slogans, are we to deny the insights of experience for the nostalgia of a phrase?

The reader may agree or disagree with this formulation as he chooses, but he should keep it in mind as the foundation of my analysis of the internal situation in the British Labour Party. First I shall briefly discuss the historical background of the Scarborough Conference; second, the events and alignments at the meeting; and finally the current alarms and prospects.

While unilateral nuclear disarmament was the pivotal issue at the Scarborough Conference, Gaitskell's defense policy was not the fundamental cause of dispute. It was merely the fuse which touched off an explosion that has been building up for a decade. The basic problem that has confronted the party since the war, and particularly since 1951, is the withering away of its "natural" constituency, the self-conscious British working class. In objective terms, the "proletariat" still constitutes the overwhelming majority of the British population. But even in Labour's halcyon days roughly a quarter of the objective working class voted Liberal or Tory, and the proportion of the nation's workers and their families which is class-oriented has declined steadily since the war.

The impact of (relative) affluence has been particularly noticeable in the *embourgeoisement* of those who have come of age since 1945. Increasingly the Labour Party has become an ingathering of elderly and middle-aged workers, those whose political attitudes were frozen in the depressed interwar years. This segment is dedicated, in a somewhat ritualized fashion, to Labour, but alone it cannot win a general election. If the party is to win, it must gain the support of the young and of the women, the two categories of the British population which have been most "Americanized."

This "Americanization" of British social values has occurred under Tory auspices in the period since 1951—a fact which has led some Socialist intellectuals to attack television, kitchen appliances, and even social mobility as though they were the work of the Devil. This Luddite manifestation is both perverse and absurd; in fact what has happened is that the destruction of traditional British values has paradoxically worked to the advantage of the *ancien régime* and to the disadvantage of the Jacobins. For half a century the Labour Party fought the class system in the name of equality, and the capitalist system in the name of (we must admit it) affluence. The Labour government of 1945 destroyed the economic foundations of the class system—or those foundations which survived the war—and the Tories reaped the political harvest.

Only this savage paradox can explain the bitterness of the so-called "Labour Left." If one assumes that his political convictions have a cosmic imprimatur, their failure in practice can be explained only by betrayal, by the treason of misleaders. Thus the leaders of the party, who had the bitter historical misfortune of being the receivers in bankruptcy of the United Kingdom and the British Empire, discovered after six years of desperate struggle for survival that their substantial political and economic accomplishments had earned for them a public reputation for austerity and a private indictment for treason. As the supple Conservatives moved in from one side with a program of blatant affluence, the leaders of the party found a guerrilla force of assorted malcontents sniping on the other.

And at this particular moment in time a new set of leaders took over. The old-timers who had nursed the movement from its cradle and supplied great vitality in the 1920's and 1930's began to drop in the 1940's. In private the leadership was something less than a band of brothers: Attlee lived in aloof taciturnity (Morrison noted wistfully in his recent autobiography that he wished he could say that he *knew* Attlee!); Morrison and Ernie Bevin detested each other; Greenwood sulked in his corner; and Cripps and Nye Bevan were always suspect, even when in good standing.

But publicly and collectively they had that enormous zest which arises from constant participation in a living movement, from solidarity and historical assurance. They were, to put it differently, political men who had grown up in the movement, suffered the "treason" of MacDonald and the electoral massacre of 1931, and come back, lived and breathed "Socialism," and known together the unnerving, unexpected, and magnificent moment of triumph in 1945. True, they never really defined "Socialism," but why bother? Their people knew what it meant. (Besides, only troublemakers, ILP-types out to rock the boat, raised divisive questions like that. In operational terms, Socialism: Socialists in power.) Thus, despite their feuds, the old leaders had that sort of confidence in their mission which made it possible for them to work fruitfully in an atmosphere of stabilized distrust. After all, Bevin and Morrison were old enemies, and who is more predictable than an old enemy?

Suddenly, in the early 1950's, the Labour government was out and the old leadership was through: dead, sick, or just played out. And into their shoes stepped those chosen from a new generation to whom the Labour Party was an inheritance, not an achievement. These new men were, and are, tremendously able, but if they have any one characteristic in common, it is political *style*. As public figures they are dispassionate, unemotional, even austere. Could one visualize Hugh Gaitskell screaming bitterly at a party conference, as Bevin did in 1947, that R. H. S. Crossman had stabbed him in the back?

This lack of emotional militance has led to the accusation of insincerity, to the charge that since Gaitskell does not display his convictions in an emotional fashion, he has none. Now, it is true historically that Socialist movements have carried a good deal of demagogic baggage, and I would argue that it is tactically unfortunate that no one of the Gaitskellite group is a good stem-winder, but militancy is no proof of, or substitute for, conviction. Nor are the more militant (in this emotional sense) necessarily of greater virtue than the less ostentatious or extraverted members of society. It is easy for radicals, nostalgic for the good old days when the lines were clear and the trumpet compelling, to exaggerate the virtues of the chiliast; they should apply the same criteria to Marx's Witnesses that they do to Jehovah's.

With a new leadership, particularly one faced with the onerous task of salvaging the party from defeat, came a revival of the so-called "Left" opposition. The first manifestation was "Bevanism," built in fact around the aspirations of that brilliant opportunist rather than around any ideological standard. Bevan marshaled the various battalions of the alienated behind his bid for the leadership, but, once decisively defeated, he dumped his crusaders precipitously to accept a consolation prize worthy of his talents.[1] With Bevan as shadow Foreign Secretary pouring invective on his erstwhile followers for their naïveté, the various oppositions retired to their tents to await a new, authentic leader. Gaitskell's "Left" flank was secure: Bevan, probably the Labour Party's greatest mass orator since the defection of Ramsay MacDonald, could be counted on to prevent any runs around left end.

Two election defeats and the death of Bevan (who *could* possibly have held the line at Scarborough) brought Gaitskell to the 1960 Conference in perilous straits. For this time the disparate oppositions had a common issue, and the party, after three successive defeats each worse than its predecessor, was suffering from bad morale and a natural tendency to make the leader into a scapegoat. Moreover, Gaitskell himself, apparently on the advice of a nonpolitical friend, had tried to seize the initiative on the ideological level by blaming defeat on antiquated economic notions and asking that Clause 4 of the party constitution be amended to eliminate reference to public ownership as the ultimate Labour objective.

This was Gaitskell's worst blunder to date; it is too bad that he never in the course of his education examined carefully the career of Eduard Bernstein. "You don't *say* it, Ede; you *do* it!" the highly political Auer told Bernstein when the latter's penchant for clarification and intellectual honesty had brought him to the brink of expulsion. Gaitskell knows better than anyone else the ceremonial status of nationalization in Socialist thought, and he should have been sagacious enough to let a sleeping dogma lie. No significant segment of the party really wants to nationalize anything in particular (water supply was, I think, the leading candidate when the matter was last debated). At the same time, few people are prepared to amend the Decalogue simply because they commit adultery: indeed, as an analyst of political behavior I would predict that any pro-Decalogue party would be dominated by uneasy lechers.

Gaitskell's (or was it Anthony Crosland's?) proposal to amend the constitution was butchered in the trade unions and eventually withdrawn, but it did serious damage to the leader's prestige: he came to Scarborough with this defeat still fresh and with his enemies for the first time anticipating a possible victory. They had tasted blood, and mustered their forces for a real kill. Moreover, the possibility that Gaitskell might really be brought down stimulated a number of previously inert warriors to shine up their daggers and offer their services—as generals.

In examining what exactly happened at Scarborough, it is essential to analyze the nature of the coalition that handed Gaitskell the first significant defeat any party leader has ever received at a party conference. The decisive votes for unilateralism came from the trade-union side; oddly enough, in view of the reputation of the constituency parties for extremism, it appears that Gaitskell received a majority of the votes in that (small) sector.[2] Two factors explain this trade-union defection from the executive: first, Frank Cousins' unconcealed hatred for Hugh Gaitskell which moved the Transport and General Workers Union into the unilateralist camp; and, second, the general depoliticalization of trade-union membership which has led to situations in which, as a consequence of apathy and "telly," a few activists in a union branch determine *political* policy. These activists—with many Communists and pro-Communists among them—have for the past five years concentrated on "Banning the Bomb," and have succeeded in mobilizing behind this slogan a number of important unions.

Combined with these trade-union forces were, of course, sincere religious pacifists, the mixed Aldermaston bag of principled and expediential unilateralists, R. H. S. Crossman, who sincerely defines truth as what he says at any particular moment, and a platoon of Iagos from the Parliamentary Labour Party who suddenly discovered that their loyalty to their leader was unjustified. This assemblage was, of course, promptly designated the "left wing," and a great ideological battle was joined between the "Left" and the "Right."

The issue of unilateral British nuclear disarmament provided just the right vehicle for this coalition: the pseudo-Left supplied a pseudoprogram. In logical terms, an Englishman could support unilateralism for three reasons: first, because he is a pacifist opposed to *all* weapons; second, because he wants to let the Americans pay the costs of defending Britain; and, third, because he hopes that in the event of war the U.S.S.R. will spare an inoffensive Britain. Each of these is a perfectly legitimate basis for endorsing unilateralism, but not one of them has any relationship to radicalism, to Socialist thought. Nor does unilateralism in concrete terms provide a defense program: the inexorable consequence of all three positions in the world of 1960 is 100 percent reliance on the United States for the defense of Britain. Unilateralism is *not* an answer to the question: What should a Labour government's defense policy visualize? It is an answer to a different question—How can Labour avoid promulgating a defense policy?—and all answers to this category of question are by definition nonpolitical in essence and conservative in practical impact. One has no more right to call the anti-Gaitskell coalition "radical" than he has to apply this designation to hard-shell, Bible-beating fundamentalists or others who turn to ideological primitivism for solace from the shattering dilemmas of modern life.

From the conference at Scarborough the focus has now shifted to Westminster and the Parliamentary Labour Party, the organized body of Labour Members of Parliament. Traditionally autonomous *de facto*, the P.L.P. has always *de jure* been subordinate to the party conference. The terms of subordination are somewhat ambiguous: there is a provision in the party constitution of 1917 which states that for a policy to be incorporated in the party's legislative program a two-thirds vote is necessary—and the unilateralists had only a simple majority. Thus on *constitutional* grounds it is doubtful whether the leader of the opposition and his associates must implement the Scarborough decision.

But the fundamental issue reaches beyond the party constitution to the British Constitution, and involves a key question in democratic theory: Are representatives elected by the people legitimately bound by the decisions of publicly irresponsible bodies? Is a representative, in other words, responsible to any but his official constituents? In unofficial terms, of course, he must be responsive to those who have nominated him and worked for his election, but democratic theory clearly postulates that once elected he is not the servant or the agent of his party but the representative of all those who live in his district—even those who voted against him. (The alternative to this is that form of enlightened brigandage known as the party state.) From this viewpoint, it is immaterial whether the unilateralists got a majority, two-thirds, or nine-tenths of the votes at Scarborough; in no case can a decision of a party conference bind the actions of Parliamentary representatives. And there has been no suggestion that the British electorate is in any mood to endorse unilateralism: all indices of public sentiment indicate the opposite, that nuclear disarmament is an electoral liability.

To demand that the P.L.P. adopt unilateralism is therefore to urge it to commit hari-kari on Macmillan's doorstep. It is highly doubtful whether the millions who voted Labour in the hope of putting their people in power and ending Tory rule would appreciate this act of self-destruction, and they were only marginally and accidentally involved in the decision at Scarborough. I am not for a moment suggesting that the action *at* the conference was undemocratic, but I submit that it would be an act of cowardice for the P.L.P. to accept conference dictation.

Gaitskell made it clear that he would fight the decision, and his enemies have also been clearing for action. As soon as Parliament met, Anthony Greenwood was proposed to run against Gaitskell for the job of leader. Greenwood had the virtue of being an outspoken unilateralist, but the so-called "Left" perhaps felt this was pushing principles a bit hard. At any rate, Greenwood declined in favor of Harold Wilson, who is not a unilateralist but has been around a long time, was a minister in the Labour government, and presumably was thought to have more stature in the P.L.P. than Greenwood. Wilson lost by 2 to 1 (166 to 81); a Gaitskellite, George Brown, was elected deputy leader; and the Gaitskell group won ten of the twelve slots in the Parliamentary Committee (Shadow Cabinet). In short, the Labour Members of Parliament gave Gaitskell a resounding vote of confidence. Institutionally speaking, he is well placed to launch the counterattack.

In pragmatic terms he has two alternative courses of action: first, to refurbish the two-thirds rule in the party constitution and on that basis deny the binding character of the Scarborough vote; second, to proclaim once for all the freedom of the P.L.P. from conference dictation. While the first has a certain tactical attractiveness, particularly in papering over the cracks, it would in the long run weaken Gaitskell's position both in the nation and in the P.L.P. The opposition is not really united by its dedication to unilateralism—its basic bond is a common quest for Gaitskell's head. Wilson's candidacy demonstrates that, and it is probably not unfair to say that Frank Cousins would endorse Zen if he thought it would contribute to Gaitskell's destruction.

Gaitskell then must not be deluded into thinking that these fissures can be verbally bridged. In essence a group within the party is making a (perfectly legitimate) bid for power, and they will be satisfied with nothing less than his elimination and the replacement of his colleagues. He has the power to choose the battleground and establish the framework of dispute: he should strike to the heart of the issue, and strike fast. This imbroglio, after all, is not taking place in a soundproof room and the Tories would like nothing better than to spring an election on Labour at the nadir of its quarrel. The practical consequence is that the P.L.P. has at the outside three years to set its house in order, probably less.

If Gaitskell takes the firm line that the P.L.P. is responsible to the national electorate, certain consequences are predictable. The opposition to Gaitskell is composed of highly fissionable material, and includes several messiahs who will probably split before they accept discipline—their departure from the party should be reluctantly expedited. The damage they can do outside the party is nothing compared with the problems they create within it— and it is at least possible that outside, some of it will hurt the

Tories. If they are prepared to stand the key test of democratic society and run for Parliament, one can predict that they will be defeated in safe Labour seats and possibly put the Tory in where the seat is marginal. A few seats lost in this manner would be a small price to pay for the restoration of unity of purpose in the P.L.P. But the number of bolters would be small: few of Gaitskell's opponents are ideologues; most are men who can be convinced to rise above principle in the interests of unity and their own political futures.

This brings me back to the point from which I began. Obviously I fail to see any division of principle, any "Left"--"Right" split, in the current battle within the Labour Party. In precise terms, I do not consider R. H. S. Crossman, Frank Cousins, Michael Foot, Barbara Castle, Harold Wilson, or Anthony Greenwood as morally or philosophically superior to Hugh Gaitskell, Denis Healey, Anthony Crosland, James Callaghan, George Brown, or Roy Jenkins. On the contrary, the latter group seems to me to be more experimental, more willing to question the received truths of Victorian Socialism, more concerned with the future of democratic Socialism—in a word, more radical—than the *ad hoc* aggregation that confronts them. And finally, when I ask the vital question, or at least the question that must be vital to those who seek the implementation of the Socialist dream in this world we never made, *Who Can Beat the Tories?* there is only one possible answer. Those dominated by the paralysis of perfectionism may say this is an unimportant question, but they can deny its relevance only by *ultimately* opting either for other-worldliness and inner purity or for the dictatorship of an enlightened vanguard.

NOTES

1. An action which was predictable if one concentrated on the analysis of Bevan rather than on "Bevanism": see my "Crisis in British Socialism," *Antioch Review,* Winter, 1952–1953.

2. For an illuminating analysis which injects some factual material into a discussion heretofore conducted on a theological level, see Martin Harrison's recent *Trade Union and the Labour Party Since 1945* (London, 1960).

The Case of Victor Serge:
Introduction to
The Case of Comrade Tulayev,
a Novel by Victor Serge

Victor Lvovich Kibalchich, who as Victor Serge played a notable part in the revolutionary tradition of the twentieth century, was born in Belgium in 1890 of parents who were themselves deeply committed to bringing revolution to czarist Russia, from which they were exiles. It was thus understandable that Kibalchich became at a tender age involved in the anarchist movement. At twenty-three he won his revolutionary spurs by refusing to dissociate himself from an anarchist assassination plot. Although he was in fact quite innocent of complicity, he publicly defended the premises of revolutionary anarchism, and was sentenced to five years' imprisonment.

Released in 1917, Victor Serge became the paradigm of the professional revolutionary. He participated in the Catalonian anarchist rising against the Spanish monarchy in 1917. When it failed, he responded to the bugle sounding from the East, and immediately set out for Russia. The French government delayed his arrival by holding him as a dangerous alien; he did not reach the Soviet Union until January, 1919, when the French exchanged him for a member of the French Military Mission in Russia whom the Bolsheviks had arrested for espionage.[1]

Safely in the "Land of Socialism," Serge shortly became a leading functionary in the Communist International and an editor of the Comintern's monthly organ. In the early years of the Comintern, its ranks contained a fascinating collection of dedi-

Reprinted with permission of Doubleday & Company, Inc., Anchor Books, 1963, pages ix–xxxi.

cated rebels, men and women who had spent much of their lives in revolt, in hiding, in exile, or in jail. Few of them represented any significant Communist movements in their native countries (indeed, the one notable Communist Party outside Russia, the German, had followed the advice of its martyred leader, Rosa Luxemburg, and refused initially to affiliate with the Third International). But now they were designated by Lenin himself as the General Staff of the World Revolution. One can only imagine the sense of mission which pervaded this enterprise: the hounded fugitives had become the hunters, the clarion call to victory in the "workers' revolution" had replaced the despairing cry from the depths.

Stalin later described the Comintern, with his usual brutality of phrase, as a "thieves' kitchen," and Lenin was less than overjoyed by the potentialities of the revolutionary rag, tag, and bobtail that constituted the Comintern striking force. Vladimir Ilich Lenin may have devoted some of his spare time to ideological considerations, but above all he was endowed with an unsurpassed grasp of organizational realities: in institutional terms, he had the instinct for the jugular.

A careful reading, for example, of Lenin's *State and Revolution* (1917) can only lead one to classify it as an anarchist tract. On the basis of views such as these, old anarchist militants such as Serge or the Frenchman Pierre Monatte could easily consider the Bolshevik leader one of their own. But there was another side to Lenin. Presaged in *What Is to Be Done?* (1902) and the "April Theses" (1917) was a ruthless emphasis on organizational imperatives, an emphasis set forth with cold polemical brilliance in *Left-Wing Communism, An Infantile Disorder* (1920). It is no exaggeration to state that these documents convey as the crucial ideological message of "Leninism" the organizational command "Follow me!" This was mitigated by his total lack of *personal* ego—he was a selfless, disembodied agent of History. Like John Calvin, who explained to the great Unitarian Michael Servetus before burning him at the stake that he was only fulfilling God's mandate, Lenin did only what he "had" to do—there was nothing "personal" about his actions and decisions.

Lenin was never so unwise as to turn the Comintern over to

the ebullient foreign comrades. It was set up in Moscow in essence as the foreign department of the Russian Communist Party, and top Soviet Communists provided leadership and guidance. At the outset, this was not resented by the non-Russians (the Germans excepted), who were all too aware of their own impotence and were dazzled pilgrims at the shrine of victorious Socialism. Moreover, Lenin seldom objected to open debate and articulated dissent provided it had no *organizational connotations*. He was prepared to put up with a great deal of nonsense so long as his opponents did not go into business for themselves, that is, establish a faction or some other form of protoparty. With Grigory Zinoviev at the helm and the Russians playing a preponderant role on the Executive Committee (E.C.C.I.), the Comintern would be reliable—and might even be useful.

It is curious how those (including Victor Serge) who later attempted to differentiate between the principles of Leninism and the aberrations of Stalinism, who accused Stalin of destroying "Party democracy" and replacing it by dictatorship, have avoided honest confrontation with *Left-Wing Communism* and other pronouncements of Lenin which make it clear that his attachment to "democracy" was wholly expediential. He was frank enough about it. When in 1920 Bukharin stated in his *Economics of the Transitional Period* that the dominant characteristic of the Soviet regime was "proletarian Bonapartism," Lenin (the proletarian Napoleon) commented, "Correct . . . but not the right word." [2] (Lenin was quite prepared, when "History" required, to violate his own fundamental precepts of organization. When, for example, in 1922, the Party Central Committee appeared to be opposed to his view of the foreign trade monopoly, he told his ally Trotsky to inform the Committee that, if defeated, they would *publicly* attack the decision.) [3] In *Left-Wing Communism*, Lenin took the opportunity to excoriate Communists who engaged in adventuristic, romantic, rebellious activities. In the same year, 1920, Zinoviev dealt with what would now be termed "Right deviationism"; in his famous "Twenty-one Conditions," the Comintern announced its conditions for membership. Let us examine these two policy statements briefly—

they provide vital background material for the events of the next decade.

In *Left-Wing Communism*, Lenin employed an old rhetorical device. Just as Khrushchev denounces the "Albanians" but means the Red Chinese, and the Vatican lambastes the Christian-Democratic Union in Rhineland-Pfalz but directs the lesson at the Italian Demo-Christians, Lenin elaborated at length on the sins of the British and German "Left" Communists for the benefit of the home market. His target was (again to introduce a later designation) "Left-sectarianism"; in historical terms, the Left-Socialist, syndicalist, anarchist groupings who had hailed the Bolshevik Revolution as the dawn of a new era of libertarian freedom, and rushed to stake out claims as the local spokesmen for the forces of liberation. These turbulent characters had for years devoted their vitality to fighting the "radical Establishment"; for example, they were in Britain the militants who had attempted to build a "revolutionary" trade-union movement and had devoted an inordinate amount of revolutionary energy to subverting the "petty bourgeois" leadership of the Labour Party.

When the Bolsheviks seized power in Russia and called for a worldwide movement of sympathy and assistance, the faithful in Britain consisted largely of these enthusiasts, who promptly organized no less than *three* Communist movements.[4] On one thing they were agreed: Now, at last, they could build an organization capable of destroying the Labour Party, that collection of pseudo-radicals and fakirs who had lulled the British proletariat into procapitalist somnolence. Full of fight, but a bit uncertain of the "correct theoretical position" that a British Bolshevik should support, they took their problems to Lenin.

His reply was disconcerting, to say the least. Savagely he ridiculed their Promethean dedication as the antics of childish romantics posing as revolutionaries. In stern paternal tones he called the obstreperous juveniles to order and directed them to swallow their pride—and join the Labour Party! There was no room in this world for revolutionary chastity: the devoted British Communist must eschew the organizational sin of separatism. Instead of building a pure instrument of revolutionary principle, he must master his pride and rancor and infiltrate the corrupt mass organizations of the Social Democrats. The Communist, in short, abandons the rhetoric of rebellion and turns his talents to building a caucus, to capitalizing on the weaknesses of the existing leadership, and to establishing "cadres" who will be completely reliable. And reliability was not evaluated in theoretical terms—there were no weekly quizzes on Marxism—but by acceptance of Party discipline, that is, of the "Party line." "Discipline yourselves," Lenin said to the congeries of Scottish syndicalists, radical suffragettes, anarchists, and militant pacifists who composed the left wing of the Labour movement, "and you may grow up into real soldiers of the Revolution." Their first task, the probationers learned, was to support the Labour Party and earn the confidence of the masses; subsequently, Lenin pointed out reassuringly, they would discover that they had been supporting the Labour leadership "as the rope supports the hanged man." To put it differently, the British and German "Left Communists" were told to suppress their penchant for radical dramatics and obey orders from the General Staff, the Comintern.

While, as I suggested above, these strictures were ostensibly directed at segments of the foreign Communist movement, the real target in Lenin's sights was undoubtedly the embryonic "Left opposition" within the Soviet Party: the collection of quasi-anarchist and libertarian groupings that were instinctively repelled by Lenin's monolithic theory of the Party and his sanguine acceptance of secret-police methods as developed by the Bolshevik reincarnation of the "Grand Inquisitor," Felix Dzerzhinsky, organizer and *deux ex machina* of the Cheka (the forerunner of the O.G.P.U. and N.K.V.D.). Indeed, a number of stormy revolutionaries crossed the Rubicon and broke with the Bolsheviks in March, 1921, when Leon Trotsky brutally extirpated the Kronstadt Revolt, a mutiny of proletarian sailors who, in an uneducated, somewhat confused fashion, denounced the dictatorial character of the regime. (Among the heretics were Emma Goldman and Alexander Berkman, the famous anarchists who had been deported from the United States in 1919.) Serge held his peace.

Zinoviev's "Twenty-one Conditions" [5] (prepared under Lenin's direction) underlined the same requirement of absolute obedience to ordained authority. In every major nation the Socialists had been split into bitter, quarreling factions by the war and the Bolshevik Revolution. (Only in the United States and in Italy did the majority of the Socialist Party support an antiwar position; in Germany a minority broke from the Social Democratic Party in 1917 on the war issue, and this minority, the Independent Social Democratic Party, was in turn split by the Communists.) After the Comintern was organized in 1919, various of these radical organizations applied for membership. It was often very confusing. In the United States, for example, two Communist parties emerged from the Socialist Party in 1919, and each asked Moscow for ordination as *the* American Section of the Communist International. But the Socialist Party, on the basis of a referendum of its membership, *also* decided to request admission. In Italy, the situation was quite similar.

The "Twenty-one Conditions" made it clear that membership in the Comintern was not to be passed out casually. In essence, groups asking to be admitted were told that they would have to repudiate any of their leaders who could not get revolutionary visas from a Bolshevik screening committee and be willing to accept absolute discipline from the "democratically centralist" top, that is, from the "elected" members of the Executive Committee, who were in fact handpicked by the Soviet Politburo. The American Socialists, who had suffered intense governmental persecution and prosecution for their antiwar stand, were, for example, told that they must expel the key spokesmen of their brave position—Morris Hillquit and Victor Berger. (Eugene V. Debs, the tribune of the Socialist Party, presumably escaped excommunication because he was in jail and was rumored to be pro-Bolshevik—Debs actually played a minor role in internal Party matters, and it is not impossible that Lenin's genius led him to appreciate the fact that without Hillquit and Berger, the Socialists would be in organizational terms leaderless).

Lenin hardly made these stringent demands from a passion for ideological purity. He has been quoted as saying that all sorts of "garbage" can be useful in winning a revolution, and Marcel Cachin—who had been a leading pro-war French Socialist, or

"social patriot" to use the polemical term—was warmly welcomed to the French Communist Party and was for many years
the titular editor of *l'Humanité*, the Party paper. His thrust, as
usual, was organizational: men like Hillquit, the Italian Filippo
Turati, the Germans Eduard Bernstein and Karl Kautsky were
international figures in the Socialist movement who, if admitted to
the Comintern, would constitute a perpetual challenge to Soviet
hegemony. With Rosa Luxemburg (who had led the militant left
wing in the prewar Socialist International where the Bolsheviks
were considered a public nuisance rather than a force to be reckoned with) murdered by German reactionaries and other prewar
titans banished from its councils, the Russians could easily dominate the Comintern.

Before we turn to Serge's growing sense of disillusionment, his
spiritual malaise on being cast as a bureaucrat of revolution, one
of Lenin's "organization men," we must examine further the role
of Leon Trotsky in these crucial early years. Later Serge was to
join Trotsky in the latter's break with the other heirs of Lenin,
and was to be expelled from the Communist Party and imprisoned
in 1928 for "Trotskyism." When foreign clamor and agitation
compelled Stalin in 1936 to release him from the "isolator" at
Orenburg, Serge immediately prepared an indictment of the Soviet system, *Russia Twenty Years After*, which was a classic
statement of the Trotskyist indictment of Stalin, second only to
Trotsky's *Revolution Betrayed*. The core of this thesis was that
Stalin introduced into Communist life the monstrous "bureaucratic evil" that destroyed the "democratic customs of the party,"
while Trotsky stood with Lenin as an advocate of "proletarian
democracy." [6] Was this distinction founded on any empirical
basis or was it part of the defensive apparatus of the Trotskyites
designed to conceal the fact that in a rough game they had, un-
willingly, been defeated by superior dirty play?

It should be clear by now that I find no concept of "democracy" underpinning Lenin's political theory. The whole notion of
the "vanguard party," the elite of dedicated, disciplined intellectuals that had as its historical mission the imposition of a proletarian dictatorship on essentially precapitalist Russian society,
eliminated the possibility of democratic restraints on Party de-

cisions. The Party was responsible to the Future, to History, not to any contemporary aggregation of people living in Russia. From the very nature of things, the Future and History cannot vote; they can only be voted by their priests who have been vouchsafed a True Vision. Moreover, as Rosa Luxemburg pointed out in a deductive tour de force, a commentary on the Russian Revolution written from a German prison cell, Lenin's theory of party organization contained inexorable tendencies toward dictatorship of one man *over* the Party.[7] The Russian Mensheviks, the section of the Socialist and labor movement which broke with Lenin in 1903 precisely on the issue of Party rules and advocated what was roughly a democratic position, never ceased to hammer away on this theme. Where was Trotsky?

Ironically, Trotsky abandoned the attack on Leninism as oligarchic and undemocratic at just the point in time when the issue really assumed significance: in the summer and fall of 1917. When in 1903 Lenin split the Russian Social Democratic Labor Party by insisting on his theory of the disciplined, monolithic, "vanguard" organization, Trotsky had penned a savage critique. Characteristically, he refused to join the Menshevik "minority" (in fact, Lenin's majority was ephemeral; it was founded on brilliant shenanigans at the London Congress), but went off to Vienna and organized his own, essentially one-man, faction. Unlike Lenin, Trotsky was well endowed with personal egotism, and in the years that followed he generously offered his position (and himself) to all factions as a basis for unity: where Trotsky sat was the head of the table! In his private organ, the Viennese *Pravda,* Trotsky poured his scorn on all those who would not put the interests of Russian Socialism above their parochial, factional interest; he was particularly harsh on Lenin and his Bolshevik "disruptors" who thrived "only through chaos and confusion." In season and out, Trotsky condemned Lenin's theory of the party as fundamentally anti-Marxist and historically reactionary; in 1907 he observed with startling prescience that "the anti-revolutionary features of Bolshevism strongly threaten to come to light only in the case of a revolutionary victory." [8]

The Bolsheviks saw Trotsky as a formidable enemy, and reciprocated his polemics in kind. But as one of the heroes of the

Revolution of 1905, Trotsky was too important a figure merely to be excommunicated, and it appears that Lenin always hoped that he could be disengaged from his Menshevik ambience and brought into the Bolshevik configuration. In 1916 and early 1917 this seemed to be occurring: Trotsky, who was then living in the Bronx, became closely associated with the Bolshevik group in New York and appeared to be retreating from his militantly anti-Leninist theory of the party. Simultaneously Lenin was in the process of adopting as his own two of Trotsky's major theoretical positions: "revolutionary defeatism" and "permanent revolution."

Lenin had neither the disposition nor the talent to engage in systematic philosophic work. His major contribution to abstract Marxism—*Materialism and Empirio-Criticism* (1908)—has achieved a quiet resting place in the museum of Marxist curiosities. He rarely thought in holistic terms about the issues that confronted him, but relied for his authority on his remarkable tactical ability, his capacity for instantaneous horseback judgment in times of crisis. Harold Draper, in a remarkable feat of scholarly microanalysis, has shown how Lenin's posture toward the war developed by a series of improvisations until eventually he accepted Trotsky's formulation of "revolutionary defeatism" (which asserted that the role of each national proletariat was to fight against its own ruling class and convert the conflict into an international civil war between the proletariat and the bourgeoisie).[9] It was Trotsky's strength—and his crucial flaw—that he looked on the world in systematic fashion; his later defeat by Stalin was in good part occasioned by his inflexibility. (In 1924–1925, Trotsky—the great War Commissar and organizer of Soviet military strength—became a victim of his own ideological rigidity: hypnotized by the Marxist myth of "Thermidor," that the great threat to revolutions came from a Napoleon, a "man on horseback," Trotsky refused to use his great popularity among the Party and the populace against Stalin and his intriguing allies.)

Most important to Lenin in 1917 was a Marxist framework for the revolution which he was tirelessly organizing. Lenin, of course, *knew* intuitively that he was a good Marxist, but it remained for Trotsky to explain the Marxist rationale for the Bolshevik Revolution; this was handled by the theory of "permanent revolution." Without going into the esoteric details of this Marxist epicycle, the dogma of "permanent revolution" was designed to apply traditional Marxist categories to revolutionary goals in what we would today call "underdeveloped nations." Originated in 1905 by a mysterious figure named Alexander Helphand, or "Parvus" (who later became a large-scale munitions magnate), this notion was brought to maturity by Trotsky in the years 1905–1917: it had as its matrix the proposition that in a fundamentally precapitalist society like Russia it was the task of the proletariat to assume responsibility for *both* the bourgeois and the Socialist revolutions.[10]

The high priests of Marxism, notably the Germans Kautsky and Bernstein and the Austrian Rudolf Hilferding, had traditionally assumed that the transition from feudalism to Socialism would have to occur in two stages: first, the bourgeoisie would destroy feudalism and establish capitalism; then, the Socialists, emerging with the industrial working class as an "antithesis" in capitalist society, would take power by "expropriating the expropriators" in a proletarian revolution. The "Parvus"-Trotsky thesis, however, telescoped these two discrete revolutions (the bourgeois revolution *directed by* the bourgeoisie and the proletarian *run by* the Socialist working class) into one "permanent revolution." The proletariat would seize power in its own name in an underdeveloped society and then build capitalism by Socialist methods. There would be capitalism, that is, primitive capital accumulation and industrialization, without capitalists!

This was a neat historical shortcut which in 1917 had for Lenin the great attraction of meshing completely with his specific revolutionary intentions. But the thesis had two major built-in problems: first, it assumed the existence of a proletariat in an advanced state of revolutionary consciousness in an otherwise backward society; and, second, it was premised on the further assumption that the victory of this proletariat would be accompanied by Socialist victories in the advanced industrial societies of Western Europe, notably Germany, and that these nations would provide technical aid, industrial tutelage, and protection from external attack to their Russian comrades. Lenin disposed of the first problem by identifying the Bolsheviks with the Russian working class, a feat which led Shlyapnikov, a leader of the Workers' Opposition, to a sardonic tour de force. In March, 1922, at the end of a losing battle on behalf of the rights of the *actual* Russian workers against the Soviet apparatus, the old revolutionary stated to the Eleventh Party Congress: "Vladimir Ilyich [Lenin] said yesterday that the proletariat as a class, in the Marxian sense, did not exist [in Russia]. Permit me to congratulate you on being the vanguard of a non-existing class." [11]

The second problem was to haunt the Bolsheviks. No Party leader in 1917 or the years immediately following conceived that there could be "Socialism in One Country," that is, that the Russian revolutionaries could go it alone. Later, when the Socialist hothouse on which the success of "permanent revolution" rested failed to materialize, the Communist leadership divided on the strategy to be followed. One wing, with Nicolas Bukharin (the "Nicolai Ivanovich" whom Kondratiev defends to "the Chief" in Serge's novel) as its spokesman, urged a gradualistic reformulation, one which would permit capitalism to develop in the hands of a well-controlled and politically domesticated bourgeoisie; the other, which Stalin—after much tactical maneuvering—dominated, insisted on the forced development of an industrial society at whatever cost in human misery. But this is to get ahead of the story. In 1917 these events were shrouded in the future, and Lenin never worried much about the future until he got to it. For the time being, "permanent revolution" seemed to provide a viable policy, and by the time it became clear that there was to be no Socialist revolution in Germany, Lenin lay crippled and dying.

Trotsky's star rose rapidly after his arrival in Russia in May, 1917; indeed, in no time his great oratorical gifts and organizational talents put him at the center of the October Revolution, and he emerged (to the chagrin of many "Old Bolsheviks" who cherished their ideological seniority) as second only to Lenin in the hierarchy of Soviet power. While Lenin adopted Trotsky's thesis on the goals of the Revolution, Trotsky sealed the marriage by endorsing wholeheartedly Lenin's concept of the role and organization of the Party. Indeed, in 1920, 1921, and 1922, it was Trotsky who became the hammer of the oppositionists, particularly the Workers' Opposition (alluded to above), which maintained thirty-five years before Milovan Djilas that the Communists were subjecting the proletariat and the people to oppression by a "new class," the Party bureaucracy. For the Central Committee of the Party, Trotsky demanded the expulsion of these thorny prophets of militant proletarian democracy. Arguing that no person or group could establish historical standing against the Party, he laid down the main line of suppression which Stalin would later employ so savagely in the Great Purges: the theory of "objective guilt." The Workers' Opposition, and the Social Revolutionaries (peasant radicals) who were tried as criminals during the same period, were "objectively" engaged in counter-revolutionary activity in organizing a political opposition, that is, they were, whether they willed it or not, working for the enemy, for the capitalists who sought to undermine and destroy the Revolution.[12]

Bernard Wolfe has suggested in a fascinating fictionalization of Trotsky's last days, *The Great Prince Died*,[13] that the suppression of the Kronstadt Revolt gave the exiled revolutionary his worst qualms of conscience. It is true, as Wolfe suggests, that the brutal repression of the anarchist sailors lived on to undermine the moral validity of the Trotskyist critique of Stalin. The logic of Kronstadt, and of Trotsky's indictment of the early opposition movements, made it impossible—as John Dewey pointed out in a starkly compelling and unanswerable critique in 1938 [14]—for Trotsky to make more than an expediential complaint about Stalinism: the "wrong" men were holding the guns; the "wrong" people were being shot. When in 1922 Trotsky wrote that "repressive measures . . . in the hands of a historically progressive government . . . may serve as very real means for a rapid cleansing of the arena from forces which have outlived their day," [15] he was unknowingly sealing the commission of the O.G.P.U. agent who in 1940 drove an ice ax into his skull.

Victor Serge lived in the middle of this strange revolutionary universe, a milieu where high theory went hand in hand with low cunning, where idealism and gangsterism often seemed to merge. Like many old syndicalists, Serge was never strong on ideology: he was a "class struggle" radical who knew the enemy, and threw himself joyously into the battle for human liberation. In *The Case of Comrade Tulayev* we have the privilege of meeting one of these fierce old warriors: Deportee Ryzhik before whose assertion of revolutionary proletarian dignity the whole police system was powerless. Ryzhik who had in 1917 requisitioned a printing plant in the name of the Revolution and proclaimed, "Now, comrades, the days of falsehood are done! Mankind will print nothing but the truth!" Ryzhik, whose response to the Chief's command, "Rhyzhik dying? I order him saved!" was to join his old comrades "Dead for the Revolution."

Like Ryzhik ("defended the Workers' Opposition before the Petrograd Committee in '20, but did not vote for it"), Serge initially went along with the suppression of proletarian opposition groups but, as he later noted, with growing unease and uncertainty. Something was clearly wrong inside the system, but Serge and other veteran militants had too precious an emotional stake in the Revolution to disengage immediately. With Lenin's death in 1924, and the subsequent struggle for power among the heirs apparent, they tended to join Trotsky in his ideological critique of the Stalin-Zinoviev-Kamenev "troika" who were, according to Trotsky, planning to reinstitute capitalism in Russia under the guise of "Socialism in one country." Trotsky seemed to represent the revolutionary tradition of the old "Left Socialists" against a growing bureaucratic conservatism. That Trotsky had himself endorsed the principle of bureaucratic domination, that as late as May, 1924, he had stated to the Thirteenth Party Congress, "In the last instance the Party is always right, because it is the only historic instrument which the working class possesses for the solution of its fundamental tasks," [16] did not register on their consciousness. They became "Trotskyites" without realizing that their leader had cooperated in destroying the institutional basis of opposition: the right to dissent from the Party.

To Bukharin, the brilliant young theorist who was later to play clever verbal tricks on Vishinsky, the Public Prosecutor, in one of the greatest of the Moscow Trials and then fall before Stalin's executioner, was attributed the sentiment—which he too was subsequently to regret—that "We might have a two-party system, but one of the two parties would be in office and the other in prison." [17] Such was the fate of Victor Serge and the other members of the Trotskyite opposition when in 1928 Stalin completed his technically superb series of Machiavellian maneuvers and clearly moved to the center of the stage.[18] Although the Trotskyites, now in exile or imprisoned in "isolators," persisted for some time in believing that Stalin was merely a tool of Bukharin and the "Right," they were shortly joined by the right-wingers. (This led to the ironic anecdote of the three prisoners in the "isolator" who were comparing their indictments: the first said, "I was arrested for conspiring with Bukharin"; the second, "I was seized for conspiring against Bukharin"; the third, "I'm Bukharin.")

This has all been set out in some detail because no one can possibly appreciate *The Case of Comrade Tulayev*, or Arthur Koestler's *Darkness at Noon*, or George Orwell's *Animal Farm*, without understanding something of the background of the *Yezhovshchina*, the Great Purge supervised by Stalin and managed by his security chief Yezhov, the spectacular Moscow Trials in which the Old Bolsheviks publicly confessed, one by one, their counterrevolutionary crimes, their longtime affiliation with capitalist espionage agencies, their despicable sins against the "Socialist Fatherland." I have emphasized two contradictory aspects of Bolshevik mentality because each plays an important part in the literature of the purges. Koestler in *Darkness at Noon* turned the trials into a cosmic puppet show: Rubashov, the Old Bolshevik, is led by Gletkin, his implacable interrogator, to an admission of "objective guilt." He confesses to crimes he never committed because of his dedication to the historical proposition that, in Trotsky's phrase, "One can be right only with the Party and through the Party because history has not created any other way for the realization of one's rightness." Rubashov, an ideological caricature *à l'outrance*, makes his final sacrifice to the Revolution. By emphasizing the Bolshevik passion for abstraction, Koestler suggested that the Moscow Trials were essentially exercises in revolutionary psychotherapy in which the rebel ego accepted the mastery of the historical superego.

The theme of Orwell's *Animal Farm* was quite different. The development of Stalinism was portrayed in this savage fable as a function of the Chief's consummate expertise as a nonideological gangster. While Orwell did not devote any significant amount of space to the Great Purge—his book is short and allusive—it is clear that he shared Nazi Foreign Minister Ribbentrop's analysis of Soviet Communism—Ribbentrop reported to Hitler on August 24, 1939, after concluding in Moscow the final arrangements for the Stalin-Hitler Pact, that he had enjoyed himself immensely: he had "felt more or less as if he were among old Party comrades." [19] To Orwell, ideology was strictly instrumental, a technique of manipulation: "All animals are equal, but some animals are more equal than others" was his caustic summary of Soviet egalitarianism. In short, Orwell highlighted the ruthless tradition of "holy opportunism" which, as I have indicated, suffused Leninist political theory and provided an ominous, bizarre backdrop to disputes on theoretical issues. As Anton Ciliga, the Yugolsav Communist who became an involuntary expert on Stalin's jails and emerged in 1934 only because he got the Italian Fascist regime to intervene (he held essentially fictitious Italian citizenship), put it in his neglected classic *Au Pays du Grand Mensonge* (In the Land of the Great Lie, Paris, 1938; abridged and translated into English as *The Russian Enigma*, 1940), "It was sufficient to be present at a few Party meetings to be convinced that discussions of ideology played but a very secondary role in the struggle. The deciding factor [in destroying the opposition] consisted of threats, intimidatory actions and terrorism." [20] The elite—Stalin and his entourage—announced their practical goals, and theory was readjusted to these imperatives. From this viewpoint, the Moscow Trials, far from being disembodied exercises in Marxist logic, were frame-ups, and the confessions were extorted by one means or another. Stalin was not an anointed Agent of History, but a power-crazed, brutal, paranoidal monster.

We now have it on the high authority of Chairman Khrushchev [21] that this explanation cut to the heart of the matter, and Milovan Djilas in his *Conversations with Stalin* has provided new insight into the Stalinist decision-making process—Don't worry about the theoretical aspects, Stalin and Molotov told Djilas, just "swallow" the Communist nation of Albania! [22] (This anecdote was hardly surprising to those who had taken seriously Pierre Laval's account in 1935 of *his* conversation with Stalin. After concluding the Stalin-Laval Pact which allied the two nations in support of collective security, Laval asked Stalin, in essence, to end the bitter opposition to rearmament of the French Communist Party. Stalin told Laval not to worry about it, but Laval persisted in asking what he should do if the French Communists did not revise their stand. "Hang them!" said Stalin genially, and to make the point clear he ran his forefinger across his throat.) [23]

Yet, perhaps because to do so would open a door upon a brutal world which one did not want to confront, few Western intellectuals in the 1930's were willing to admit the cogency of this explanation. Space does not permit an examination of Western reactions to the Moscow Trials—the interested reader is referred to a recent issue of *Survey* devoted to "The Western Image of the Soviet Union, 1917–1962" [24] that contains several splendid studies of this and related problems—but it is safe to say that if a critic in 1937 had characterized Stalin in Khrushchev's terms, he would have been vilified and denounced by the Communists and their fellow travelers. And he would have been treated as slightly deranged—as one suffering from an unfortunate obsession—by many intelligent and decent people who had no use for Stalin or for Communism. These were the people who would go to almost any length to avoid confronting the horrible fact that barbarism was on the march in the rational, modern world (they were equally unwilling to face up to the realities of Nazi policy, to admit to themselves that Hitler *really* planned to murder *all* the Jews).

In the post–World War II period, once the total immorality of Nazi and Stalinist totalitarianism had sunk in, many intellectuals promptly rushed to find a high theory that would account for these aberrations. It was not enough to suggest that modern totalitarianism was merely political gangsterism plus modern technology, nor were these seekers satisfied with Aristotle's recipe for efficient tyranny—"Breed mutual distrust among the people, make them incapable of action, and break their spirit." [25] What they sought was a basis for explaining totalitarianism that would hypothesize a fundamental transformation of human character, one in which victims would cooperate with their executioners because the regime had once for all destroyed human integrity. The ability of the Nazis to murder millions of Jews without significant resistance, and the seemingly complete Stalinist domination of Eastern Europe, triggered the thesis that the modern totalitarian state was *qualitatively distinct* from previous forms of tyranny: it had found the formula for turning human beings into animated conditioned reflexes. (The rise of Chinese Communism led to the similar theory of "brainwashing"—by sinister psychological manipulation the Red Chinese exorcised egotism and left those who had been through the process mere husks, political versions of Pavlov's pups.)

Two influential works in this genre were Hannah Arendt's *Origins of Totalitarianism* and Czeslaw Milosz's *The Captive Mind*. Each in its own fashion presented a somberly pessimistic view of totalitarian accomplishment, indicating that the classic liberal, democratic view of human nature—the notion of an indestructible core of personality which underlies both religious and secular liberalism—was obsolete. Prometheus was replaced by Manipulatable Man. (In a different context, high military figures informed the American people that the enemy in Korea had successfully destroyed the will to resist among prisoners of war; American boys had been turned into puppets by the totalitarian egoectomy.)

The Hungarian Revolt of October–November, 1956, while in the immediate sense a tragedy, blew away the mystique of totalitarianism. Young people, raised first under a Fascist and then a Communist dictatorship—youngsters to whom freedom was a pure abstraction—took arms in behalf of a liberty they had never known. As an eighteen-year-old girl told the United Nations' Investigating Committee, "We wanted freedom, not a good comfortable life. . . . We, the young people, were particularly hampered because we had been brought up amidst lies. We continually had to lie. We could not have a healthy idea because everything was choked in us. We wanted freedom of thought." [26] "The will for freedom," said another witness, a professor of

philosophy, "was the moving force in every action." [27] Another
participant indicated that it was Aristotle, not Arendt or Milosz,
who had supplied the insight into totalitarian power: the Communists had been incapable of maintaining "mutual distrust
among the people." As he put it, "Everyone became convinced
[the 'chains were broken']. No one asked in the street, 'Who are
you? ', everyone used the familiar term of address even in talking
to strangers, everyone was on familiar terms, everyone could be
trusted, everyone had a feeling of complete unity, because the
entire system based on lies collapsed in a moment on the morning
of 23 October." [28] Subsequently the revelations of the Eichmann
Trial and careful analysis of the data on American POW's in
Korea have also suggested that there is no new secret psychological weapon at the disposal of the totalitarians—they specialize
in efficient terror. Khrushchev went to the root of the matter at
the Twentieth Congress; after his famous "Secret Speech" denouncing Stalin, he received a note from a delegate inquiring
why he, Khrushchev, had remained silent in the face of Stalinist
iniquities. The Chairman allegedly replied, "For the same reason
that the comrade who wrote this question did not sign it."

It was, I think, the power of this mystique of totalitarianism
that provided the immense audience for Koestler's *Darkness at
Noon*, while *The Case of Comrade Tulayev*, which appeared in
English in 1950, dropped into a pit, and vanished. Without in
any way deprecating the eerie, Dostoevskian force of *Darkness
at Noon*—it is a powerful book—I suspect that its appeal was
founded in large part on its monolithic theme. In a curious way,
Koestler's book is an inverted "agitprop" novel. (It has some
thematic resemblances to a dreadful "proletarian" morality tract
which appeared under the imprimatur of the League of Proletarian Writers in the late 1920's and was published in this country in 1932: Alexander Tarasov-Rodïonov's *Chocolate*.) Koestler
took the position of those in Russia and elsewhere who justified
the trials on high theoretical grounds and stood it on its head:
the historicism was retained, the logic of confession was sustained, but the *premise* was challenged. In short, Koestler did not
deny the mystique of totalitarianism on pragmatic, humanistic
grounds but in terms of his own metaphysical vision, his "total"

view of the nature of the universe. In a fine critique of *Darkness at Noon*, Irving Howe noted that Koestler's main intent "must surely be to warn against the abstractions of ideology, those abstractions which, if allowed to spawn too freely, tend to dehumanize our lives—yet every line Koestler writes, and one doubts that he can avoid it, is suffused with ideology. He is like a stricken Midas yearning for the bread of life yet, with every touch, turning experience into the useless gold of ideology." [29]

In contrast, *The Case of Comrade Tulayev* is a book that, as Howe also pointed out, "because of its cumbersome, cluttered form is unable to achieve the dramatic concentration of *Darkness at Noon*." [30] Yet in defense of Serge it might be argued that the very art form he employed was admirably designed to fit his purpose. The structural monism of *Darkness at Noon* reflects its author's convictions about the nature of totalitarianism; the diffuseness of Tulayev might be construed as a reflection of Serge's denial of the inexorable monolith and his assertion of the pluralism and contingency that infuse experience even in the totalitarian state.

André Gide once attended a Communist-sponsored writers' conference, listened restlessly to several days' discussion of the "Inevitabilities of History," and then transfixed the delegates with the inquiry, "What does History say of the man killed by a trolley car?" *The Case of Comrade Tulayev* was Victor Serge's demonstration of the absurdity of efforts to answer Gide's question. It also represented Serge's repudiation of the *ideological content* of most of his revolutionary career (as a Leninist-Trotskyite) in the name of the passion for liberation that had always provided his *motivation*. The existential rebel cast off the "essential" dogmas of rebellion, the creedal encrustations of Leninism and Trotskyism alike, in favor of a vitalistic humanism. (Trotsky sensed Serge's disenchantment with Bolshevism, and excommunicated him in 1939.) In a brief essay in *Partisan Review* in 1947, Serge commented: "That philosophies of despair are fashionable in a time like ours does not astonish me. We can well question our own destiny, and from this question draw material for literature. Yet the destiny of the world unfolds with a vitality that outlives individuals and literatures. And for this reason the most justified choice is a resolute confidence in intelligence and the human will." [31]

The Case of Comrade Tulayev introduces us to a widely variegated cast of characters: Kiril Rublev, the ideologue, who fulfills the inexorable imperatives of Leninist logic and agrees to confess because, as he tells Popov, "I have neither thought nor conscience outside of the Party." Ryzhik, the primordial rebel, "weak as an invalid and hard as an old lightning-blasted tree," who by his mortal suicide asserts this spiritual indestructibility. Makeyev, the brutalized peasant, who lusted for power as he did for women and, totally lacking in ideological sensitivity, felt himself "integrated into the dictatorship of the proletariat like a good steel screw set in its proper place in some admirable, supple, and complex machine." He never understood the principles of the machine, and reacted uncomprehendingly when the mechanics scrapped him.

But this is not the place for a summary: the book in all its richness awaits the reader. He will find himself in odd places: in the labyrinthine maze of left-wing politics in the Spanish Civil War (which a reading of George Orwell's *Homage to Catalonia* will help to clarify); in the study of a French fellow traveler, Professor Passereau, who mouths to Xenia Popov a classic Stalinist apologia ("For the justice of your country I have a respect which is absolute. . . . If Rublev is innocent, the Supreme Tribunal will accord him justice. . . ."); and under interrogation of various kinds in the prisons of the O.G.P.U. He will get above all a sense of the random brutality, the eccentric motivation, the absence of any total, dominating theme, which were in fact characteristics of the Great Purge. "The Chief," who has ruthlessly dealt with Erchov—"this cynical traitor"—is capable of decency toward Kondratiev, who has delivered a patently "counterrevolutionary" speech to the military cadets. The "systematic" purge turns out to be a concatenation of unsystematic indictments ("the fact was attested by two agents home from Barcelona, but their testimony might be doubted because they were obviously frightened and had denounced each other"), a witches' brew of denunciations, counterdenunciations, and counter-counterdenunciations stirred by the fears of the security police that failure to attain confession would itself be evidence of complicity. Serge, in sum, rejects the concept of the purge as a massive demonstration of totalitarian planning, and substitutes for this notion of coordinated, total terror one of uncoordinated, Kafkaesque, hit-or-miss "liquidation" that, beginning on a small scale, snowballs into a shambles of improvised charges, arrests, acts of private vengeance, confessions, and executions. While perhaps critics were correct in suggesting that *The Case of Comrade Tulayev* was not outstanding as a novel, I think it is unsurpassed as a portrayal of the inner hopes and tensions, the corruption, the cynicism, the ideological depravity, and *the lack of total vision and purpose* that have characterized the modern "totalitarian" states.

Victor Serge died in Mexico City in 1947. A great revolutionary, he never asked for an armistice, and could always be found with the poor, the oppressed, the despised in their struggle for liberation. A true radical, Serge fought established power in the name of freedom, not of a new "revolutionary" orthodoxy, and never permitted the defeats that marked every stage in his career to dim his humanistic vision of what Man could become. He spent most of his life in the shadow of the gallows, yet never lost his faith in mankind's ability to abolish the gallows state. The world is poorer from the fact that we shall not see his like again.

NOTES

1. I am indebted to Max Shachtman's introduction to Victor Serge, *Russia Twenty Years After* (New York, 1937) for much of this biographical detail.

2. This exchange is cited by Anton Ciliga, "A Talk with Lenin in Stalin's Prison," *Politics*, August, 1946, p. 234.

3. Cited in Isaac Deutscher, *The Prophet Unarmed* (London, 1959), p. 67.

4. See Henry Pelling, *The British Communist Party* (London, 1958), pp. 1-14.

5. Which should be read carefully by any who have ever cherished the notion that the Communist parties at the time of Lenin were encouraged to develop autonomously; see "Conditions of Admissions to the Communist International Approved by the Second Comintern Congress," Aug. 6, 1920, in Jane Degras (ed.), *The Communist International 1919-1943: Documents* (Chatham House, 1956), I, 166-172.

6. Victor Serge, *op. cit.*, p. 144.

7. See Rosa Luxemburg, *The Russian Revolution* (paperback edi-

tion, Ann Arbor, 1961), especially pp. 68–80.

8. For a discussion on this period of Trotsky's life, see Isaac Deutscher, *The Prophet Armed* (London, 1954), Chap. 7. The quotation is cited from Note 4, pp. 178–79.

9. See Harold Draper, "The Myth of Lenin's 'Revolutionary Defeatism,'" *New International*, Vol. XIX (1953), pp. 253–284, 313–351; Vol. XX (1954), pp. 39–59.

10. The best general treatment of this period is Bertrand D. Wolfe, *Three Who Made a Revolution* (New York, 1948).

11. Cited in Isaac Deutscher, *The Prophet Armed*, pp. 14–15.

12. *Ibid.*, pp. 29–30.

13. New York, 1959.

14. John Dewey, "Means and Ends," *New International* (August, 1938).

15. Cited in Isaac Deutscher, *The Prophet Armed*, p. 30.

16. *Ibid.*, p. 139.

17. Cited in Isaac Deutscher, *The Prophet Armed*, p. 518.

18. The best general study of this period is Leonard Bertram Schapiro, *The Communist Party of the Soviet Union* (New York, 1959); for Comintern developments see Hugh Seton-Watson, *From Lenin to Khrushchev: The History of World Communism* (New York, 1961).

19. Cited in Alan Bullock, *Hitler* (paperback edition, New York, 1961), p. 474.

20. Anton Ciliga, *The Russian Enigma* (London, 1940).

21. See any one of the several editions of Khrushchev's Reports to the Twentieth and Twenty-second Party congresses.

22. Milovan Djilas, *Conversations with Stalin* (New York, 1962), p. 143.

23. Reported by Arthur Koestler, *The Invisible Writing* (paperback edition, Boston, 1954), p. 325. Fidel Castro might ponder this!

24. *Survey: The Journal of Soviet and East European Studies*, No. 41 (April, 1962).

25. *Politics of Aristotle*, Barker ed. (New York, 1958), Book V, xii, Sec. 16, p. 246.

26. United Nations, *Report of the Special Committee on the Problem of Hungary* (New York, 1957), p. 68.

27. *Ibid.*

28. *Ibid.*, pp. 79–80. An extremely important book to be published shortly demolishes the mystique of "brainwashing" and "menticide"; see Albert D. Biderman, *March to Calumny: The Story of American POW's in the Korean War* (New York, 1963).

29. Irving Howe, *Politics and the Novel* (New York, 1957), p. 231.

30. From Irving Howe's review of "The Case of Comrade Tulayev," in the *New International*, January–February, 1951.

31. Victor Serge, "The Socialist Imperative," *Partisan Review*, September–October, 1947, p. 517. (I have taken the liberty of retranslating this section from French into respectable English. The present translation is a crude word-for-word affair, and obscures the force of Serge's peroration.)

The Bureaucrat and the Enthusiast: An Exploration of the Leadership of Social Movements [with Stephen Sachs]

The quest for historical uniformities is a dangerous game, and one which generally reveals more about the preconceptions of the observer than about the historical process. The historian, alas, is denied even the camouflage of numbers, which so often permits the social psychologist to portray his hunches as "science"; and he is fair game for countless safaris of cultural anthropologists who are prepared to fire instantly at any suggestion that, say, Zulus have anything in common with Japanese, or Americans with British. Historical speculation, unless cloaked with the rites of numerology, has clearly been consigned to the province of journalists, mystics, and fakirs.

To say this is not to endorse for a moment all that has been done in the name of history. On the contrary, it is patent that historians have brought much of this obloquy upon themselves by their oracular pretenses, by their unfortunate tendency to confuse insight with "fact." Yet, admitting both the uncertain nature of the data and the imperfections of the analyst, the student of politics can learn much from the perusal of history. The specialist in public administration who neglects—to use but one example—Philip Woodruff's superb *The Men Who Ruled India* deprives himself of an invaluable fund of information and insight, and the student of social theory can similarly find in historical and biographical studies an enormous body of significant data.

Reprinted, with permission, from *The Western Political Quarterly*, Volume VIII, Number 2, June, 1955, pages 248–261.

It is in this spirit that we have prepared this brief analysis of leadership types. The technique applied deserves explanation: we have in the text advanced a series of generalizations which are largely, though not exclusively, based on an intensive case study of the history of the British Labour Party. Because we have attempted to keep the generalizations in the text general, the footnotes are unusually elaborate—constituting, in effect, another article. We should like to make it clear that the hypotheses suggested here are not put forth under the imprimatur of science; although we feel that they may have utility in the examination of organizations as different as political parties, churches, and labor unions, we make no claim to universal validity. Furthermore, we assert no copyright on the ideas incorporated herein; other scholars, better equipped than we, have conducted forays of a similar type into the nature of organizational leadership, and we have profited from their explorations. Moreover, the classic exposition of our thesis is Dostoevsky's symbolic tour de force, *The Grand Inquisitor.*

The examination of social movements which seek public support for their political, social, or religious objectives suggests that there is a tendency for two major leadership types to emerge. Their specific characteristics may vary greatly with the cultural context or with the type of goal toward which the organization is oriented, so that precise definition is elusive. Yet, granted this elusiveness, we feel that a meaningful typological distinction can be made, and we have designated the two leadership types the "bureaucrat" and the "enthusiast." [1] To forestall the criticism that we are indulging in psychological monism, we should state at the outset that one individual can, in varying social situations, display the characteristics of both; that is, he can perhaps be a bureaucrat in his union and an enthusiast in his religion. But in any one context, the pattern of behavior tends to remain constant and is thus subject to generalization.

The bureaucrat, as his name implies, is concerned primarily with the organizational facet of the social movement, with its stability, growth, and tactics. To put it another way, he concentrates on the organizational means by which the group implements and consolidates its principles. He will generally be either an officeholder in the organization or interested in holding office. While he may have strong ideological convictions, he will be preoccupied with the reconciliation of diverse elements in order to secure harmony within the organization and to maximize its external appeal. He seeks communication, not excommunications.

In contrast, the enthusiast, seldom an officeholder,[2] and quite unhappy when in office, concerns himself primarily with what he deems to be the fundamental principles of the organization, the ideals and values which nourish the movement. No reconciler, he will concentrate on the advocacy of these principles at the risk of hard feelings or even of schism.[3] While the bureaucrat tends to regard the organization as an end in itself,[4] to the enthusiast it will always remain an imperfect vehicle for a greater purpose. Whereas the bureaucrat is likely to equate "The Cause" with its organizational expression, the enthusiast, with his fondness for abstraction, identifies it with a corpus of principles.[5]

Several other typical characteristics emerge from this fundamental difference in outlook. Outstanding among them is the varying attitude toward compromise in policy matters. The bureaucrat approaches a policy question with a predisposition toward harmony; he is prepared to compromise in order to promote unity and cohesion within the organization and to broaden its external appeal. He considers policy, if not a mere expedient with which to build up organizational strength, no more than a flexible expression of intentions which can be modified as required by "practical" needs.[6] However, to the enthusiast policy is far more than a "political formula," far more than a sonorous exposition of attractive, organization-building slogans; on the contrary, he insists that policy must be the undiluted expression of first principles.[7] The bureaucrat specializes in studied ambiguity; the enthusiast, in credal precision. In short, while the former looks upon policy statements as something less than ex cathedra pronouncements of the whole "Truth," the latter views policy as the living Word, and considers compromise as not only wrong, but also evil.[8]

The same approach to compromise is evident in attitudes toward membership: the bureaucrat is inclusionary, and holds a quantitative emphasis, while the enthusiast is exclusionary, desiring to limit the body of saints only to those full of grace.[9] That this problem of membership has plagued social movements from time immemorial hardly needs elaboration here; suffice it to say that the struggle between the inclusionists and the exclusionists, which inspired St. Augustine's polemics against the Donatists as it does those of the Bevanites against Attlee, is a constant feature in ideologically oriented groups.[10] In particular, it plagues political organizations, for the bureaucrat here is characterized by an acute hypersensitivity toward the marginal voter,[11] while the enthusiast, with full confidence in the truth of his convictions, operates on the principle that if the people refuse to share his vision, so much the worse for them. To the latter, defeat at the polls means nothing; a moral totalitarian, his slogan is "Damn the electorate! Full speed ahead!" [12]

It is perhaps, therefore, valid to suggest that the bureaucrat seeks to extend the area of compromise; the enthusiast, the area of principle.[13] Although we are not asserting that the bureaucrat always flees from principle, nor that the enthusiast is inevitably a moral totalitarian, there is in our view sufficient evidence to justify the establishment of these positions as typical.[14] David Riesman, drawing on the insights of Ortega y Gasset [15] and Erich Fromm,[16] has suggested a similar hypothesis in different language.[17] Following his typology, we might say that the bureaucrat, conditioned and molded by his intense awareness of, and concern for, the opinions of others, both within and without the organization, is "other-directed"; whereas the enthusiast, whose actions and beliefs stem from a set of a priori principles, is "inner-directed." In fact, bureaucratism and enthusiasm are the "other-directed" and "inner-directed" facets of the organizational personality.

However, there is one important qualification to the last generalization which, while it narrows the scope of the thesis, serves also to highlight the fundamental difference in orientation of the bureaucrat and the enthusiast. The bureaucrat, a genial eclectic with respect to policy questions, becomes an uncompromising fighter when he feels that the sovereignty or organizational integrity of the group is menaced. The enthusiast, in his pounding pursuit of principle, is often prepared to compromise organizational integrity, to form "Popular Fronts" or "United Fronts" with those who share his ideological assumptions. Against this form of eclecticism, the bureaucrat will wage ruthless war, as he will against the common tendency of the enthusiast to build a faction, a party within a party. As the history of the Catholic Church's dealings with heresy will indicate, the bureaucrat is prepared to tolerate a wide range of viewpoints within the organization so long as the viewpoints do not become organized factions, but once the enthusiasts raise the standard of organizational autonomy and attempt to institutionalize their ideas, tolerance ends and is replaced by war to the knife.[18]

To say this is not to impugn the motives of the bureaucrat, to assert that he is a self-seeking Machiavellian who consciously manipulates men and ideas in the effort to gain and maintain power. On the contrary, the significance of this typology lies in large part, at least in our view, in the fact that the bureaucrat *does not* deliberately plan his course. In fact, he often plans very badly what little he does plan, permitting enthusiasts to put organizational integrity in great jeopardy before he realizes that a threat exists, and taking counteraction long after an effective Machiavellian would have gone into action. Thus, it is a cast of mind, or psychological pattern of reaction, rather than counsels of greed and guile, that supplies the bureaucrat with his direction.

It is with this difference in fundamental attitudes that we must concern ourselves now. We make no attempt to discuss the factors that influence human behavior in the directions of enthusiasm and bureaucratism except to note a dissent from any monolithic theory, any rigid determinism. What we are concerned with is not the "Why?" but the "What?"—and we shall limit ourselves to an exploration of the objective aspects of the problem, that is, the pattern of action and belief that seems to be associated with our two types. Again we must caution that our remarks and definitions will not be applicable to all situations; rather, we are making probability statements which, although they may not subsume each individual case, have aggregate validity.

"Respectable, conventional, orthodox religion," wrote Emrys Hughes, an outstanding Labourite enthusiast, "is something very different from the living faith. And that is also true of politics." [19] Following this line of demarcation, the bureaucrat is the "respectable, conventional," and "orthodox" churchman. The organizational structure, from which he gets profound satisfaction, and with which he identifies himself, exists concretely—he need only look about him or open his desk drawer to appreciate its reality. His patient, untiring, and probably publicly unrecognized labor has gone into its creation, and the stable security that it offers acts as an antidote to his insecurity. Like the men and women who refused to leave slum hovels during intense wartime bombing because these were "home," the bureaucrat has a psychological commitment to the organization that far outweighs any economic attachments. Thus, it may be predicted that the bureaucrat will be reluctant to depart from habitual and tested practices which have fostered the past growth of the organization; he will assuredly take a dim view of experiments, although he will seldom oppose them frontally. He is the past master of the motion "to table."

In part because he is tradition-oriented, and in part because of the psychological makeup of his opposition, the bureaucrat tends to be anti-intellectual. The proportion of intellectuals among enthusiasts is often quite high, although it must be added that in situations where organization and intellectualism have gone hand in hand, for example, in the Church of England, the enthusiasts may rally around anti-intellectualism and antirationalism of the crudest sort. But even given this qualification, the man who causes trouble in an organization must attempt a respectable intellectual case for his position—indeed, in the twentieth century we have seen the irony of intellectuals building an intellectual foundation for anti-intellectualism! [20]—and so the bureaucrat grows to look with suspicion on people who think too much, who are always popping up with new ideas. He is likewise suspicious of oratory and big meetings, where his hard-built discipline may tumble before the charismatic charm of an enthusiast-demagogue; his natural habitat is the committee room where even if a messiah should reveal himself, he would not recruit more than half-a-dozen disciples. In short, the bureaucrat detests and fears unpredictability and the flamboyance with which the unpredictable often gird themselves; the road to his affection and trust is through hard work, patiently and undramatically executed, and acceptance of hierarchical decision-making.[21]

Unlike the bureaucrat, the enthusiast has no tangible symbols to supply him with satisfaction and security; almost by definition, he must believe in the ultimate value of things unseen, and he is likely to scorn institutions as snares set to draw men from the paths of righteousness.[22] While the bureaucrat is an instinctive collectivist, holding as he does an almost Burkean view of the presumptive validity of tradition, the enthusiast is a militant individualist, prepared like Nietzsche's "Superman" to achieve self-fulfillment at whatever cost to the social fabric. If the bureaucratic personality is dominated by caution and fear of the unorthodox, the enthusiast is a captive of hubris, of cosmic egotism, and of blindness to the fact that "Humanity" is not humanity. He lives in a world peopled by abstractions rather than by human beings, and it is quite possible for him to contemplate, in Koestler's phrase, "sacrificing one generation in the interest of the next."[23]

The ideals the enthusiast seeks to realize, whether a glorious vision of heaven on earth, the resurrection of a romanticized past, or less ambitious versions of both, are hardly capable of attainment in this imperfect world; indeed, such is the nature of ideals. Yet, gripped by his Promethean quest, the enthusiast never ceases in his effort to storm heaven. Against the skeptical patience of the bureaucrat, he pits his passion and his chiliastic dedication; his is indeed a "living faith."[24]

In the light of this analysis of the two polar types, it might be suggested that each makes a major, and vital, contribution to the organization. Enthusiastic cadres supply it with its ideological dynamic, attempting to make it into a "living faith," while the bureaucrat injects organizational stability and a sense of realism. In the same sense that each type contributes its assets to the group, each also donates its liabilities. From the viewpoint of sound organization, let us now examine their respective contributions in the effort to ascertain what relationship between the enthusiast and the bureaucrat provides the firmest foundation for group success and organizational effectiveness.

The faith of the enthusiast may have negative consequences for an organization in two significant regards. First, his firm belief in the basic articles of his credo may lead him to be dogmatic and doctrinaire and into unfortunate excesses. He frequently offends his nonenthusiastic brethren by the rigidity of his viewpoint,[25] as well as by his semblance of sanctimonious piety.[26] The enthusiast specializes in denouncing organizational shortcomings, falls from grace, so to speak, and this role, no matter how reluctantly or humbly it is performed, creates in the minds of listeners the impression that the speaker considers himself pure and uncontaminated, a saint calling upon sinners to renounce the wicked and their ways. Such homilies can arouse great resentment, and sometimes lead to internecine conflict and schism.[27] Externally, the enthusiast's inability to compromise his principles, and the vigor with which he presses them, is likely to alienate potential organization supporters of moderate views, even if the organization does not accept his doctrines.[28]

A second unfortunate consequence of the enthusiast's "living faith" is that it warps his own judgment. With his fervor and sense of righteousness, he can easily become a prisoner of his own presuppositions, with the result that the actual world becomes a handmaiden of his abstractions.[29] Moreover, the more tenaciously the enthusiast embraces his a priori's, the more he loses sight of the pluralism, the diversity, and the complexity of the universe, and the more likely will he be to subscribe to a conspiracy theory which will ascribe his failure in rallying public support to a sinister plot, to a devil.[30] The consequences of such flights from reality can be quite serious, for not only do they hinder the enthusiast from fulfilling his proper calling; they also lead to a weakening of public confidence in the organization.[31]

But, while he creates great problems for an organization, the enthusiast can make an enormously significant positive contribution. In the first place, he supplies a vigor, stemming from his convictions, which is the *sine qua non* of effective organization. Paradoxically, it is this vigor and willingness to work for "The Cause" which forms the foundation of the bureaucratic apparatus. Beyond this, his originality, initiative, and flamboyance, the characteristics which frighten and unsettle the bureaucrat, serve as a stimulant and tonic to the whole movement, and act as an effective and necessary antidote to the traditionalism of the bureaucrat.[32] His idealism and faith contribute an *élan* and a courage, emboldening the movement to expand its horizon and strike out boldly for new worlds to conquer. Indeed, if we believe with Max Weber that only by reaching out for the impossible has man attained the possible, it is the enthusiast who may bring the movement to the fullest realization of its own potentialities.[33] Thus, the enthusiast injects idealism into hard organizational reality, and brings to the movement a priceless leaven.

The second, and equally significant, contribution of the enthusiast is the moral tone which his presence lends to organizational action. His fundamentalism, his very refusal to come to terms with immorality, his frequently prophetic assertion of basic values and aspirations, make him the conscience of the movement, the voice which calls it back to the ways of righteousness.[34] It is this messianic function of the enthusiast which can serve to counteract the ideological myopia of the bureaucrat, and the latter's tendency to compromise his ideals to the point of extinction.[35] Furthermore, the spirit of self-sacrifice which is characteristic of the "true believer," to use Eric Hoffer's phrase, is a wholesome antidote to the opportunism of the bureaucrat.[36]

While anyone who has read widely in the history of enthusiasm tends to sympathize with the bureaucrat in his endless conflict with "wild men," it must be realized that the bureaucrat too has his limitations. Caution and moderation can easily become sluggishness and inaction, and the bureaucrat's dedication to the organizational structure can lead him to an almost paranoidal suspicion of all proposals which involve change.[37] In addition, the collective anonymity of the bureaucracy can encourage an assembly-line approach to the problems of the membership, a depersonalization of the group's function which it is extremely difficult to counteract. "Rank and file" protests he dismisses scornfully as the work of disgruntled, disappointed office seekers because he is incapable of spontaneous action himself, and projects his own personality upon the organization.[38]

But probably the bureaucrat's greatest drawback is his inability to dream the enthusiast's dreams, his fundamental lack of empathy. His concentration on organizational problems may lead him to ignore policy, and particularly to overlook the relationship between policy and principle.[39] Although, as was suggested earlier, this attitude is seldom founded on conscious Machiavellianism, he often comes to the point where he considers a policy question essentially as an organizational gambit: "What do we stand to gain from it?" Similarly, his dislike for policy formulations which may offend potential supporters can lead to wishywashy pronouncements which, far from assuaging discordant elements, only aggravate them further and leave nobody happy.[40] In short, the bureaucrat, preoccupied with organizational politics, may treat policy much too lightly and, in his willingness to compromise both policy and principle for the sake of organizational strength, may destroy the ideals and values which the movement was formed to advance, its very *raison d'être*.[41] If the dangers of enthusiasm stem largely from a rigid maintenance of principle regardless of organizational consequences, the abuses of bureaucratism flow from its hyperconcern for organizational consequences and its callous disregard for the movement's fundamental spiritual values.

Yet, with all his defects, the bureaucrat, too, makes a precious contribution to the success of the movement. First, by his skepticism about the authoritative nature of the enthusiast's revelation, he provides psychological ballast; his assumption, in George Orwell's brilliant phrase, "that Saints must be presumed guilty until proved innocent" [42] helps to keep reason in control and inhibit potential Peter the Hermits from dragging the group into some disastrous charismatic crusade. Against the monism of the enthusiast and the devil theories that so often accompany it, he raises the standard of common sense, asserting that men are men and not abstractions of good and evil. Where the enthusiast is optimistic about man in the abstract, but pessimistic about man in the concrete, the bureaucrat takes the world as he finds it, and judges men as men, rather than as "Man," whom he has never met and probably never worried about.

Second, the bureaucrat's agnosticism and nominalism—his rejection of the enthusiast's true faith and abstract man—combine to make him profoundly suspicious of shortcuts; he is likely to be satisfied with piecemeal progress, scorning as fatuous and unrealistic the "all or nothing" approach which is so characteristic of the enthusiast. "Half a loaf is 50 percent better than no loaf," he submits, "and tomorrow we can go after the other half." [43] To this end, he builds his cadres, convinced that ideals are no stronger than the organization engaged in institutionalizing them, and that organized pressure, not doctrinal purity, is the key to success.

Indeed, it is this dedication to technique, to means, which is the bureaucrat's supreme gift to a movement. It is he who builds the instruments of social action, the structural machinery necessary to channel, concretize, and implement the group's aspirations, and it is he who puts organizational flesh on the bones of theory. Denied the vision of the enthusiast, sneered at by the high-flying intellectual, he spends his life in the quagmire of detail, and in so doing renders a unique and invaluable service to his cause. While the enthusiast is out exploring the nature of the cosmos, the bureaucrat is repairing the mimeograph machine; yet, who will deny that a well-working mimeograph is as essential as correct doctrine to the effective operation of a social movement?

Thus, both the bureaucrat and the enthusiast supply a movement with vital components. Each by himself works badly; left alone, the bureaucrat simply goes in concentric circles around his precious organization, while the enthusiast rushes unbridled from one ideological orgasm to another. Consequently, a healthy vital social movement needs both, and profits from their complementary assets. True, there will always be conflict, for to the bureaucrat, the enthusiast—"impatient," "emotional," "dogmatic," "sanctimonious"—will always *ipso facto* remain a threat to the organization; and to the enthusiast, the bureaucrat—"timid," "opportunistic," "cynical," "manipulative"—will always seem indifferent to, if not subversive of, the very ideals and values from which the enthusiast draws his inspiration. But this conflict, inevitable as it is, is by no means a mere disruptive influence; on the contrary, it is a life-giving dialectical process in which each force counters the weaknesses of the other and from which a movement can emerge with both dynamism and stability.

The history of social movements is the history of this conflict. On the one hand, we find groups, such as the German Social Democratic party of 1900–1914, or the American Federation of Labor of 1900–1937, which have been stricken with bureaucratic paralysis and have lost all power to move. On the other, we see those movements, such as the French Socialist Party of our era, or the Puritan Left of Cromwell's time, which disintegrated, or are in the process of disintegrating from the unchecked centrifugal force of enthusiasm triumphant. These are the extremes, for we can also find organizations which have moved on from generation to generation, expanding their horizons as they go, because they have attained a proper balance between these two forces. How this balance is struck is the subject of another analysis; suffice it here to conclude that the struggle between bureaucratism and enthusiasm is part of a larger canvas on which similar battles, between security and freedom, realism and idealism, means and ends, passion and perspective, are waged, and in which the outcome is likewise determined by the extent to which factors which are logically irreconcilable are reconciled.[44]

NOTES

1. Our "bureaucrat" is a first cousin of Max Weber's bureaucrat, sharing many of the latter's characteristics. Our "enthusiast" is on loan from theological studies where he has had a long and tumultuous career; cf. Msgr. Ronald Knox, *Enthusiasm* (London, 1950).

2. The British Labour Party's bureaucrats generally center in the party executive and the Parliamentary Labour Party, notably in the contingents supplied to each of these bodies by the trade-union movement. The enthusiasts formerly rallied around the standard of the affiliated Independent Labour Party (I.L.P.), and upon its disaffiliation migrated to the Socialist League. Since the latter was disbanded, there has been no nesting place organizationally, but functionally the enthusiasts can al-

ways be located in the Constituency Labour parties and can be spotted ideologically by their vigorous support for Aneurin Bevan. They constitute the readership of the journal *Tribune* and of the *New Statesman and Nation*, and are at present busy learning Chinese.

3. For instance, Stafford Cripps's work for the constitution of a popular front with the Communists and other "anti-Fascist" organizations which led in 1939 to his expulsion from the party. Cripps, of whom Churchill once observed: "There, but for the grace of God, goes God," never faltered for a second in his labors for this cause and, secure in his conviction that it was just, accepted expulsion as the stigma which proved it.

4. The bureaucrat par excellence

of the Labour Party was Arthur Henderson, longtime party secretary and foreign minister in the 1929–1931 government. A good example of the bureaucratic preoccupation with organization and reconciliation was the preparation by Henderson of the 1918 party constitution, a masterpiece of organizational ingenuity; see G. D. H. Cole, *A History of the Labour Party from 1914* (London, 1948), pp. 44 ff. Henderson was severely criticized for not leading opposition to Ramsay MacDonald during the 1929–1931 period, when it appeared to many that the Prime Minister was ignoring party policy, but to do so would have run contrary to Henderson's bureaucratic loyalty. As Cole puts it, Henderson "in that crisis . . . made . . . too many . . . concessions in the hope of holding the Party together." *Ibid.*, p. 305. Henderson, of course, never dreamed that MacDonald would desert the party. Postgate's description of Henderson after that sad event is illuminating in this context: "Henderson seemed shrivelled and bowed, and his usually ruddy face was yellow. Disloyalty was a thing he could not understand. He had given his most unswerving support to the handsome, eloquent leader who had helped him build up the movement; he had never allowed himself to be influenced by the fact that he had not in his heart liked MacDonald and had more than once received discourtesy from him. Now that man had deserted the people in its greatest misery. He could not understand, though he would try to forgive; he looked like a man who had been given a mortal wound." Raymond Postgate, *George Lansbury* (London, 1951), pp. 271–272. Cole elsewhere notes Henderson's identification of the cause and the organization. *Op. cit.*, p. 305.

5. To understand this approach, a reading of the various studies by Archibald Fenner Brockway is invaluable. See his *Socialism over Sixty Years* (London, 1946); *Inside the Left* (London, 1942); and *Bermondsey Story* (London, 1949). Brockway was a paladin of enthusiasm, and his various crusades, and those of the men he chronicles, against the party leadership make exciting reading. One is struck with the resemblance to *Pilgrim's Progress*, for he is transported to a world populated by moral "forms," and the perils of Socialist (the Christian of Brockway's epics) are frightful to behold.

6. For an exhaustive treatment of this theme, see Robert Michels, *Political Parties* (Glencoe, Ill., 1949), and Gaetano Mosca, *The Ruling Class* (New York, 1939). It is also discussed by Max Weber in his essay on "Bureaucracy" in H. H. Gerth and C. W. Mills, eds., *From Max Weber: Essays in Sociology* (New York, 1946).

7. For example, George Lansbury's 1926 motion to "abolish the Navy by discharging 100,000 men," Postgate, *op. cit.*, pp. 236–237, as distinct from the regular Labour motions in favor of disarmament in the abstract. See also the I.L.P. position on "the cruiser issue" in 1924. Brockway, *Inside the Left*, p. 156.

8. The I.L.P. split from the Labour Party on precisely this point. The I.L.P. Members of Parliament demanded the right of private judgment, asserting that an M.P. should vote on the merits of a proposal rather than under party instruction. The Labour Party, operating on the maxim *ex nihilo nihil*, refused to permit this, and the I.L.P. disaffiliated. Brockway, *Inside the Left*, p. 215; Postgate, *op. cit.*, p. 278. The I.L.P. saw the MacDonald defection as the logical conclusion of modera-

tion: "Truly the policy of compromise has brought its reward." Brockway, *Socialism over Sixty Years*, p. 294.

9. This is a function of the perfectionism of the enthusiast, and is a common feature of all enthusiastic political, social, or religious movements. A man can not be saved by "good works," but only by true inspiration, which may or may not lead him to good works. The bureaucrat, essentially Niebuhrian in outlook, is prepared to settle for less on the assumption that while good works may be badly motivated, they are still preferable to bad works, however motivated.

10. For a discussion of this aspect of the Donatist heresy, see Knox, *op. cit.*, Chap. IV. Actually, the Donatists were never officially ruled heretics, but they were treated as such by Augustine and his bureaucratic descendants.

11. According to Cole, MacDonald objected to the I.L.P.'s "Socialism in Our Time" program because "it would only frighten the electorate and ensure a crushing Labour defeat." *Op. cit.*, p. 198. In contrast, the official 1929 program was, according to the same authority, "a moderate social reform programme, in which socialism found neither place nor mention. It was evidently drafted in contemplation of a result to the Election which, at best, might enable Labour to take minority office with a stronger backing than in 1924." *Ibid.*, p. 213. Following the 1931 defeat, Lansbury wrote Cripps that Henderson wanted "to trim our sails so as to catch the wind of disgust which will blow [MacDonald] and his friends out and that he is not anxious for us to be too definite about Socialist measures as our first objectives. Put them in our programme but be sure when we come to power we keep on the

line of least resistance. . . ." Postgate, *op. cit.*, p. 280.

12. For instance, in both 1924 and 1929, in each case when the Labour Party became a minority government, the I.L.P. sought to implement a radical program, knowing that it would bring defeat in Commons. Such a defeat, they urged, would put to the country in stark terms the issue of Socialism versus Capitalism, and would arouse the working class to full militancy in the class struggle. See Cole, *op. cit.*, pp. 157 ff., 210 ff., 218, 246, 281 ff.; Philip Snowden, *An Autobiography* (London, 1934), II, 592 ff.; Brockway, *Socialism over Sixty Years*, pp. 206 ff., 214, 229 ff., 253, 259 ff.

13. As, for instance, when Jowett and Wheatley, ministers in the 1924 government, refused to wear morning dress on a visit to the King. Brockway, *Socialism over Sixty Years*, pp. 208–210; or when Brockway himself, on principled grounds, refused to attend a party given by Lady Astor. *Inside the Left*, p. 201. Surely the high point of this symbolic rejection was achieved by Dr. Salter, a Republican, who kept his hat by his bed so he could quickly put it on when the chimes of a nearby church played "God Save the King" at seven in the morning. Brockway, *Bermondsey Story*, p. 14.

14. That is to say, definable types. Obviously, a man may have a mixed personality, may be enthusiastic with respect to some things and passive about others. But this differentiation is not important for our purposes; we are solely concerned with the relationship of these types to the operation of social movements. How an individual integrates the different facets of his personality is a problem for the psychiatrist and psychoanalyst.

15. The distinction between "mass man" and the "aristocrat" developed

in *The Revolt of the Masses* (New York, 1932).

16. The quest for autonomous personality which is the central theme of *Escape from Freedom* (New York, 1941), and *Man for Himself* (New York, 1947).

17. *The Lonely Crowd* (New Haven, 1950).

18. This may be true even if the bureaucrat is in ideological agreement with the factionalists, a fact which greatly hindered certain C.I.O. unions in their struggle against Communist domination. When an anti-Communist district or local decided that secession was their best program, no one could be more ruthless in fighting them than anti-Communist bureaucrats who put their organizational loyalty above ideological considerations. See Vernon Jensen, *Nonferrous Metals Industry Unionism, 1932-1954* (Ithaca, N.Y., 1954), *passim*, for some classic examples of this manifestation in the Mine, Mill & Smelter Workers. For a similar French experience, see Val R. Lorwin, *The French Labor Movement* (Cambridge, 1955), pp. 125-127.

19. Emrys Hughes, *Keir Hardie* (London, 1950), p. 5.

20. Some of the German and Italian justifications for Fascism, notably those of Schmitt and Gentile, fall into this category, as do certain contemporary French apologies for Communism.

21. The respect for "channels" is very great in bureaucratic circles; indeed, one of the main complaints made against the enthusiast is his disregard for them, his willingness to "appeal to the movement" or to the "people" against unpleasant decisions instead of patiently appealing to the various hierarchical bodies in the apparatus, through "channels," for recourse. Much of Aneurin Bevan's unpopularity in the Labour

Party, notably among the trade-union potentates, is an outgrowth of his lack of respect for decisions collectively made, and his effrontery, as they see it, in appealing these to the wider constituency.

22. This is particularly true of religious enthusiasts, who generally distinguish between true religion and the church much as Jesus contrasted Judaism with the religion of the Pharisees. See Knox, *op. cit.*, *passim*, and for some rather un-Friendly polemics in this vein, *The Journal of George Fox* (Everyman ed.; New York, 1924).

23. Koestler used this figure of speech in an address in New York some years ago. We have not seen it used in any of his works.

24. Eric Hoffer observes: "It is the true believer's ability to 'shut his eyes and stop his ears' to facts that do not deserve to be either seen or heard which is the source of his unequaled fortitude and constancy. He cannot be frightened by danger nor disheartened by obstacles nor baffled by contradictions because he denies their existence. Strength of faith, as Bergson pointed out, manifests itself not in moving mountains but in seeing mountains to move. And it is the certitude of his infallible doctrine that renders the true believer impervious to the uncertainties, surprises and the unpleasant realities of the world around him." *The True Believer* (New York, 1951), pp. 78-79.

25. When MacDonald entered the Dawes Plan negotiations, the I.L.P. demanded that he insist on the total abolition of German reparations, and protested vigorously when all that emerged was a lightening of the German load. Brockway, *Inside the Left*, p. 152. Later, after MacDonald's defection while the regular Labour M.P.'s were seething with hatred toward their former leader, the I.L.P. members aroused much indignation

by their attitude of "good riddance." Brockway records that the others were "indignant [at the I.L.P.] because we remained cool amidst their heated denunciations." *Ibid.*, p. 217. This attitude of "We knew it all along" is calculated to win few friends, particularly since there was good reason to believe that the I.L.P. had been right for the wrong reasons.

26. While Stafford Cripps was probably the leading candidate for canonization, Aneurin Bevan has also been characterized as a "Jeremiah, Cassandra, and guardian of the Holy Socialist tablets." Vincent Brome, *Aneurin Bevan* (London, 1953), p. 202. The I.L.P.'s conspicuous asceticism and its refusal to participate in the gayer side of Parliament irked many Labour M.P.'s, who looked upon these enthusiasts much as a well-fed Benedictine monk probably reacted to a flagellant friar in an earlier epoch. Brockway, *Inside the Left*, Chap. 22.

27. Thus, the I.L.P. attitude towards MacDonald, and their self-congratulatory pose when he "sold out," led to a hardening of relationships between the I.L.P. and the Labour Party. The fact that the enthusiasts had been objectively "right" in their analysis, far from bridging the schism that had been widening throughout the 1929–1931 Labour government, made them absolutely unbearable in the view of the average Labour member. Indeed, the I.L.P. fought the 1931 election as a separate party, although it did not formally disaffiliate until 1932. See Brockway, *Socialism over Sixty Years*, Chaps. 15–17; *Inside the Left*, Chaps. 20–22; Cole, *op. cit.*, pp. 274–275.

28. The Labour Party executive, for instance, went to great lengths in the late 1930's to "disassociate itself" from certain radical positions

taken by the Socialist League which the anti-Labour press had characterized "as revealing the 'real mind' of the Socialists." Cole, *op. cit.*, p. 298.

29. This is particularly true of the enthusiast's approach to war, and to international relations in general. Rejecting concrete alternatives, he may generally be found clinging to a "third position," which, if only implemented, would avoid the dangers of war, oppression, starvation, misery, etc., latent in the other viewpoints. Thus, in recent years, Labour enthusiasts have raised the slogan: "Neither Washington nor Moscow," and have attempted to build "third force" sentiment around Yugoslavia and, more recently, India. See Leon D. Epstein, *Britain: Uneasy Ally* (Chicago, 1954), *passim*.

30. A classic instance of this devil theory in action was the enthusiast's explanation for the failure of the General Strike of 1926. Although it is quite clear that the strike was a failure because the average worker was unprepared to become a revolutionary, and, absent a willingness to start a revolution, the strike had no place to go, the enthusiasts claimed that the "revolutionary will of the Proletariat" had been betrayed by the union leadership. Brockway, *Inside the Left*, pp. 192–193. MacDonald's 1931 defection was, in similar fashion, attributed to Wall Street machinations. Postgate, *op. cit.*, pp. 270–272.

31. See John P. Roche, "The Crisis in British Socialism," *Antioch Review*, Winter, 1952–1953, for a discussion of the consequences of Bevanism on the public view of the Labour Party.

32. The valuable function that the I.L.P. played in creating and stimulating the Labour Party is emphasized by G. D. H. Cole, *British*

Working Class Politics, 1832–1914 (London, 1946), pp. 250 ff. Henry Pelling, in his excellent study *The Origins of the Labour Party, 1880–1900* (London, 1954), credits the energy of the Socialists with much of the success in creating an independent working-class party.

33. Max Weber in "Politics as a Vocation," *op. cit.*

34. This was manifestly the outstanding contribution of George Lansbury to his beloved party, as Postgate's excellent biography makes clear.

35. As, for instance, was the case with the French Socialist deputies who voted *pleins pouvoirs* to Pétain in 1940, or with the German Socialists who became militant chauvinists in 1914 and turned the *Freikorps* on the Spartakusbund after the war. See the bitter critique of the latter by Eduard Bernstein, discussed in Peter Gay, *The Dilemma of Democratic Socialism: Eduard Bernstein's Challenge to Marx* (New York, 1952).

36. For a discussion of this spirit of self-sacrifice and its ramifications, see Hoffer, *op. cit.*, Chap. 13.

37. Robert Michels has given this ample treatment in his *Political Parties*, cited earlier. The German Social Democrats, who have always suffered from an acute case of over-bureaucratization, supply the best examples of this mentality in action. Of course, because he feels that the bureaucracy is not representative of the true feelings of the movement, the enthusiast is perpetually crusading for structural changes that "will increase grass-roots democracy." The French Socialists have been so successful in this that they have fallen off the other side of the bed; see Philip Williams, *Politics in Post-War France* (London, 1954), pp. 60–76.

38. As is usually the case in a trade union under similar circumstances, the bureaucrat, faced with "rank and file" opposition, inquires cynically, "Whose rank and file?" Similarly, the possibility that two or three people could arrive spontaneously at the same viewpoint never enters his head; his immediate reaction is, "They have a caucus." As a projection of the bureaucratic personality, with all its paranoidal trappings, upon a society, the Moscow Trials have never been equaled. Arthur Koestler implicitly makes this point in *Darkness at Noon* (New York, 1941) when Rubashov, a bureaucrat, is hoist by his own bureaucratic petard. See also Victor Serge, *The Case of Comrade Tulayev* (Garden City, N.Y., 1950).

39. Cole suggests that the Labour government was deluded in its notion that it had triumphed in its defeat of the Mosley manifesto in 1930–1931; it might have given this statement far more serious consideration, and profited from some of its suggestions. Cole, *op. cit.*, p. 258. As it was, the party's handling of the unemployment crisis bore no visible relationship to the principles advanced by Socialists; a capitalist government would probably have acted no differently. See Adolf Sturmthal, *The Tragedy of European Labor, 1916–1939* (New York, 1943), for a discussion of the Socialist dilemma of whether to ameliorate or to eliminate capitalism.

40. The history of the Italian Socialist Party supplies superb examples of the failure of this tactic; the centrists, known variously as "integralists" or "unitarians," regularly worked out compromises which aggravated both the Left and the Right wings and, if anything, exacerbated internal tensions. See W. Hilton-Young, *The Italian Left* (London, 1949).

41. See, for instance, the flip-flops,

rationalized in terms of principles, which various Socialist leaders performed on the war issue in 1914; Merle Fainsod, *International Socialism and the World War* (Cambridge, Mass., 1935).

42. In his "Reflections on Gandhi," in *Essays by George Orwell* (Garden City, N.Y., 1954).

43. This conflict between the "possibilists" and the "impossibilists" has been endemic in Socialist movements; see Sturmthal, *op. cit., passim;* as well as in religious organizations; see Knox, *op. cit., passim.*

44. "Passion and perspective" are the criteria submitted as central to political analysis by Max Weber in his "Politics as a Vocation," in Gerth and Mills, *op. cit.*

A Review of
Labour and Politics, 1900-1906
by Frank Bealey and Henry Pelling

Labour and Politics is an extraordinarly irritating book. It is tedious, convoluted, confusing, and scandalously overpriced. Yet it must be read, and read closely, by any serious student of the British Labour Party. The reader should really be supplied with a chart and endowed with a cryptographic bent: The chronology shifts with unnerving abruptness, and even the initiate is likely to be tormented by the constant injection of abbreviations that are obscure to all but a handful of readers. (For instance, couldn't the authors have shortened "the Amalgamated Society of Railway Servants" to "Railway Servants," instead of "ASRS"? This may smack of petulance on my part, but when one is trying to discover whether the ASRS has favored the NDL instead of the LRC because of the intransigence of the SDF and ILP, the flood of initials does get a bit trying. And it gets even worse when coping with the UTFWA.)

I do not want to belabor two authors from whom I have learned a great deal, but I think it is fair to state that *Labour and Politics* is not, properly speaking, a book. It is a collection of discrete scholarly articles dealing with common characters and a common historical period, but there is no unifying theme, no organizational backbone to provide unity to the work. The authors even refuse to generalize on their work—the chapter which winds up the book is seven pages long. Each essay is a model of historical microanalysis, but the package is designed to terrorize any but the expert reader—and even the expert would be well

Reprinted, with permission, from *The New Leader*, August 23, 1958.

advised to refresh himself by reading Pelling's excellent previous study, *The Origins of the Labour Party, 1880–1900*, before he launches himself on this enterprise. One sometimes gets the impression that Bealey and Pelling have gone so deeply into their data that they have lost the urge to communicate effectively with those less versed, and are simply writing for each other.

Yet, despite these reservations, I think that Bealey and Pelling have made an immensely significant contribution to our understanding of the formative years of the Parliamentary Labour Party. They have studiedly, even obstinately, refused to generalize, but my reading of the book leads me to formulate—on their behalf and on their evidence—three important analytical propositions. First, they have dispelled, I hope once for all, the shopworn myth that the Labour Party was conceived by a Socialist paraclete; second, they have demonstrated to my satisfaction that this party was established by the dedicated travail of a few inspired organizers *at the top* rather than by spontaneous ideological combustion at the "grass roots"; and, third, they have implicitly restored Ramsay MacDonald to his proper place as the *deus ex machina* in the creation of the Parliamentary Labour Party. Each of these points deserves some discussion.

With regard to the role of Socialist ideology in the formation of the Labour Party, Bealey and Pelling make it clear that the gradual trade-union accretion to the cause of independent political action was based on motives that Samuel Gompers would have recognized and applauded. Under the combined pressure of a hostile Conservative government and crippling judicial decisions, the trade-union magnates gradually moved toward support for the Labour Representation Committee, realizing that unless they could get special legislation through Parliament, their weapons would be blunted and they would be left at the mercy of the employers. The Labour Representation Committee was, from their viewpoint, an instrument of political pressure, or blackmail, rather than the embryo of a proletarian dictatorship. While Bealey and Pelling do not deal explicitly with the problem, it appears to me from their data that the active, militant Socialists slowed down the growth of support for the Labour Representation Committee—few trade-union magnates have ever had the capacity to understand, let alone trust, the ideological enthusiast with his chiliastic energy and apparently endless supply of uncompromisable, eternal principles.

Moreover, Bealey and Pelling make explicit the eclectic character of the Socialism professed by the early Labour Representation Committee Members of Parliament. In the "great victory" of 1906, which saw twenty-nine of the Committee's candidates victorious and established the Labour Party as a parliamentary force, the Socialist election appeal was anything but ideological: The Labour candidates denounced the Conservatives, endorsed free trade, and in general pushed bread-and-butter issues before their constituents.

After the election, W. T. Stead, editor of the *Review of Reviews*, asked the successful Labour members what books had most influenced their thinking. One mentioned William Morris, one the American economist Richard T. Ely, and two listed Marx. "The great bulk of the answers were taken up with reference to the influence of the Bible and the popular authors of the 19th century such as Carlyle, Ruskin and Dickens. The most striking link between the great majority of the MPs concerned seemed to be their pride in a nonconformist upbringing: Nearly all of them were Methodists of one sort or another, or Congregationalists." In short, the Labour Party first moved into national prominence as a lower-class variant of Liberalism; there were ideological Socialists in the movement, fine dedicated people like Bruce Glasier, but they were the icing on the cake.

As far as the techniques of organization are concerned, Bealey and Pelling have demonstrated conclusively that the Labour Party's initial success was based on the genius of a few untiring men at the center, notably of James Ramsay MacDonald, to whom I shall return later. It was MacDonald, supported by Keir Hardie, who persuaded the Liberal whip, Herbert Gladstone, to commit the Liberal Party to institutional suicide. Apparently a genuine believer in the right of the working class to increased parliamentary representation, and perhaps hoping to attract many Conservative workingmen to the Liberal cause, Gladstone secretly agreed with MacDonald to permit Labour Representation Committee candidates to run without Liberal opposition in certain districts heavily populated by members of the working class.

MacDonald and Hardie—the latter, unhappy about the secret treaty, wrestled a bit with his conscience, but won—agreed in return to prevent Labour candidates from splitting the anti-Conservative vote in other districts. The incredible thing was that MacDonald and Hardie managed to sustain their end of the bargain, but by cajolery mixed with threats they were successful; Gladstone did likewise, and thus deserves a special place in the history of his party, along with Lloyd George, as an architect of ultimate Liberal ruin.

While it is certainly true that there was a great deal of working-class ferment in Britain, it seems equally true that inspired leadership was required to convert this amorphous sense of alienation and resentment into an effective political instrument. This leadership was provided by Ramsay MacDonald in the formative years, and indeed until he faltered in the face of the Depression. Part genius, part manipulator, part idealist, part character actor, MacDonald stood at the center of the Labour Party throughout its adolescent years. Since his defection in 1931, there has been an understandable tendency to play down his earlier role, but as Bealey and Pelling indicate, to do so is to put on *Hamlet* without the Prince.

What has to be remembered is that the Labour Party underwent a notable radicalization in the 1930's. A partial consequence of this, fostered by a certain amount of intellectual dishonesty, was the claim that MacDonald had "betrayed" the principles of Socialism, when, in fact, he had never held the principles he was accused of betraying. Indeed, last year Reginald Bassett, in a careful piece of historical detective work entitled *Nineteen Thirty-one: Political Crisis*, in my judgment cleared MacDonald of the charge of dishonesty over his behavior in the political events of that fateful year.

As *Labour and Politics* documents, MacDonald was always a pragmatist, a politician of the Labour movement, and never an advocate of the class struggle. The man who labored with Stanley Baldwin and Herbert Samuel to form a National Government in 1931 was the same man who negotiated the election pact with Herbert Gladstone in 1903. The wisdom of his techniques is a legitimate subject for debate; but, like it or not, he was a consistent "class collaborationist." Those who have attacked him for his actions in 1931—and I personally think he was mistaken in his tactics—have too often forgotten that had it not been for this policy, there might have been no Labour Party in the first place. And it ill behooved those who silently ate at his table in the fat years to vilify him when the years turned lean.

IV. Liberal Salvos

The McCarthy Issue [with Constance L. Roche]

The pragmatic, rough-and-tumble character of American politics, and the enormous emphasis placed on the immediate as distinct from the long-range, have made efforts to achieve perspective unpopular, unread, and perhaps even un-American. *Homo Americanus* tends to deprecate the long run—"In the long run," he snorts with Keynes, "we are all dead."

In part, this is a healthy tradition, particularly when contrasted with the brooding atmosphere of historical introspection that surrounds European politics; however, it is also in part an unhealthy manifestation of historical rootlessness which contributes to the American political tradition a driving quest for internal security and Internal Security laws. In recent years, the activities of American and Soviet atomic scientists—cosmic security risks all—have exacerbated this historical nominalism, this obsession with the present, to the point where the general public often seems completely uninterested in the relationship between yesterday and today, between today and tomorrow, between this year and ten years hence.

But if American democracy is to survive the era of fission and fusion, it is imperative that Americans gain a sense of perspective, an understanding of the long-range implications of what we do or do not do. Furthermore, it is vital that we get some distance between ourselves and the events in which we are submerged, in order to fit them into context. In keeping with this objective, our purpose in this analysis is twofold: first, to achieve perspective on

Reprinted, with permission, from *Current History*, October, 1954.

the impact of McCarthyism on the elections to Congress this November; and, second, to examine briefly *sub specie aeternitatis* the place of McCarthyism in the American political tradition.

For our purposes, McCarthyism is defined as the employment of the issue of Communist infiltration of American government, and generally of American life, in such fashion as to question the loyalty to the United States of the Democratic administrations of Presidents Roosevelt and Truman, and of the liberal wing of the Democratic Party.

Senator McCarthy has announced on several occasions that the issue of "Communists in government" will be an issue in the elections this fall. Indeed, he went so far as to contradict a statement to the contrary by President Eisenhower. But McCarthy has not been alone in maintaining that the Communist issue would be a live one; some members of the administration have, in what purports to be a maneuver to outflank McCarthy—a sort of McCarthyism without McCarthy—also taken up the cudgels against the Truman administration's alleged coddling of Communists. Thus it is apparent that a considerable segment of the Republican Party hopes to profit from the alleged sins of the Democrats and will do its best to label the Democrats as weak anti-Communists, if not in Senator McCarthy's explicit phrase as the "party of treason."

However, calling an issue an issue does not necessarily make it one. The basic problem therefore is to what extent will McCarthyism *be* an issue in the minds of the electorate. With this question in mind, we turn to the hazardous task of divination. Because of the differing nature of the congressional and senatorial constituencies, the elections to the House and Senate will be treated separately.

The House of Representatives

In analyzing the elections to the House of Representatives, the first step is to note that there is no congressional *election* this fall; there are congressional *elections*. In a presidential year such as 1952, a common ideological denominator may be present in some congressional races—usually in marginal districts where the candidates hope to identify themselves with, and slide in on the coattails of, a victorious President—but in an off year such as 1954, even this slight unifying influence is absent.

Americans do not elect Congress as they elect a President; as Don K. Price has observed, Congress is a collective noun, not a unified reality. Since the only national constituency we have, that which is mobilized every four years to choose a President, is in a state of suspended animation until 1956, it is safe to say that there will be no national issues in November, 1954. To put it another way, McCarthyism, or Indochina, will not be discussed and debated in each constituency as Korea was in November, 1952.

The relatively minor role that issues of a nationwide character play in congressional elections is brought home forcefully by the fact that before this article appears in print, between 75 and 80 percent of the next House of Representatives will be for all practical purposes elected. While we often think of one-partyism in connection with the "solid South," it is not ordinarily appreciated to what extent it is a national phenomenon. In fact, between 75 and 80 percent of the congressional districts in the United States are firmly and effectively in the hands of one party, and once the primary elections are over, these Democrats or Republicans, as the case may be, have smooth sailing. This is not to assert that issues have no place in primary elections—often primaries see bitter fights between liberal and conservative party spokesmen—but rather to note that in this huge block of constituencies, the battle is over long before November.

Thus control of the House of Representatives in the Eighty-fourth Congress hinges on the outcome of congressional races in less than 100 of the 435 districts. In its weekly report for April 16, 1954, the *Congressional Quarterly* examined the 1952 congressional elections and pointed out that only 88 seats were won by less than 10 percent of the vote, that is, by less than a 55 percent to 45 percent margin.

Our own research into House elections from 1944 to date indicates that as a consequence of the five elections that have taken place in that period, only about 25 percent of the seats in the House have changed hands once. This information is admittedly inexact, as the redistricting which followed the 1950 census makes precise analysis of some states, for example, California, Pennsylvania, New York, extremely difficult without extensive geographical data beyond our facilities, but even allowing a margin for error, the extent of one-partyism is apparent.

In three-quarters or more of the congressional races, therefore, the issue of McCarthyism, indeed any issue, will be supererogatory on November 2nd. The voters will simply return their Republican or Democratic standard-bearer with customary numerical finesse. There will, of course, be the usual sprinkling of miraculous upsets: regular Republican districts like New York 1 in 1950, or Kansas 1 in 1952, and normally Democratic constituencies like Maryland 5 in 1952, which suddenly desert the fold. But these will be of little significance in the overall picture.

In general, the voter's rationale for his automatic behavior will be simple: the party nominee will take good care of his interests. The interests he refers to may be cotton, corn, tobacco, peanuts, social security, labor legislation, business, or tariffs; it is highly unlikely that they would be Indochina, the United Nations, or McCarthyism. In short, most congressional elections are a ritualized triumph of parochialism.

Marginal Seats

But what of the remaining 20 to 25 percent, the crucial marginal seats which will determine the overall outcome and the political complexion of the next Congress? Will McCarthyism be an issue in these critical battles? The only valid generalization that can be made in answer to this question seems to be that it is impossible to generalize, at least not with any degree of certainty. However, in this connection, some tentative propositions present themselves as meriting consideration:

First, the bulk of the marginal seats are in urban areas which have been traditional Democratic strongholds. Often, thoughtful Republican-controlled state legislatures, presumably in the interest of maintaining the two-party system, have added suburban appendices onto urban wards so that if there is dissension among the Democrats, or if the G.O.P. can capitalize on a vertical issue, a Republican candidate can squeeze through. In a presidential year such as 1952, vertical issues, that is, those such as Communism, Korea, and corruption, which have strong appeal to all social and economic strata, can be utilized to their fullest effectiveness, particularly if there is a strong candidate at the head of the ticket.

In contrast, vertical issues are difficult to utilize in off-year elections, as the head of the ticket may be occupied by a candidate for state governor who is running on an entirely different set of issues from those useful in congressional races.

Second, given the absence of vertical issues, the elections in these marginal urban constituencies will probably be fought on "pocketbook," or horizontal, issues. The structure of American government, both state and national, is so organized that the urban population has a perpetual grievance. It is immaterial whether a Democrat or a Republican occupies the White House, for in either case, the key positions in the House and Senate, the committee chairmanships, are dominated by "backwoodsmen."

If we take, for example, the House of Representatives won by the Democrats in November, 1944, we find that only three of the chairmen of the twelve key committees (Agriculture, Appropriations, Banking and Currency, Foreign Affairs, Interstate and Foreign Commerce, Judiciary, Labor, Military Affairs, Naval Affairs, Rivers and Harbors, Rules, and Ways and Means) hailed from urban constituencies. In the current, Republican-controlled, Eighty-third Congress, only one chairman of the eleven in comparable positions (Military and Naval Affairs have been consolidated into one Armed Services Committee) is from a district containing a sizable urban vote, in this instance, including Camden, New Jersey.

In short, Congress pays little attention to urban needs, and in off years urban voters often take their vengeance on the party in power for this neglect. Thus it might be anticipated that the battles in these marginal districts will center around such problems as low-cost housing, cost of living, "giveaway" proposals, and unemployment.

Third, assuming for purposes of discussion that McCarthyism has strong roots among urban Catholic voters (a dubious hypothesis which will be discussed in the analysis of the senatorial elections), the Republicans stand to profit little from this purported fact. In areas of Catholic predominance, the Democratic party naturally tends to run candidates of that faith. For instance, of the five Democrats who currently represent Detroit and its industrial environs in the House, four (Thaddeus Machrowicz, Louis Rabaut, George O'Brien, and John Lesinski) are listed as Catholic in the *Congressional Directory*, while the fifth (John Dingell) states no affiliation. Similarly, the two Democratic congressmen from Boston (Thomas O'Neill and John W. McCormack) are both Catholic. The Catholic voter who may be convinced by McCarthy does not demonstrate his conviction by voting Republican in the congressional race in Boston or Detroit; while many Boston and Detroit Catholics apparently did vote for Eisenhower on the issue of "softness toward Communism," they simultaneously returned their Democratic congressmen to the House. In such districts, McCarthyism cannot be an issue, for there is no one to raise it against.

Fourth, the effectiveness of McCarthyism as an issue will in all probability be limited to those congressional contests in which a right-wing Republican confronts a liberal Democrat. California, a state whose capacity for political extremism has gained for it the nickname of the "American Bavaria," will undoubtedly supply a full quota of races in this category. The battle in Contra Costa County (California 6) will probably take first prize, for here the Democratic incumbent, Robert L. Condon, has been accused of being a "security risk."

McCarthyite guns will also sound in several of the Los Angeles contests, notably in California 16, 21, and 24, although the fact that McCarthy's California apostle, Jack B. Tenney, was unsuccessful in this area in his attempt to win the G.O.P. nomination for state senator may serve as a partial muffler. In the course of his campaign, Tenney fired the full barrage at his opponent in an effort to identify her with Communism, and his resounding defeat may indicate that the people of Los Angeles have lost interest in the pitch and have moved on to new enthusiasms.

Elsewhere throughout the nation there will be contests which fall into this last category, but there are factors at work which severely limit the total. It is difficult to believe, for instance, that, given the political climate in New York City, McCarthyism will be a significant issue in the six marginal battles that will take place there in November (New York 5, 6, 7, 12, 24, and 25). Similarly, it would be difficult to inject McCarthyism into those areas where the Democratic candidate is conservative or Catholic or a leader of the local American Legion.

In summary, the elections to the House of Representatives will be won or lost on issues which are fundamentally local in nature —indeed, from three-quarters to four-fifths of the decisions have already been made *de facto*, and await only *de jure* ratification on November 2nd. In the 20 to 25 percent which are competitive in November, McCarthyism will be an issue in the relatively few that meet the requirements suggested above.

However, a word of warning is in order at this point: McCarthy and his allies are masters of the art of publicity, so that whatever activities they undertake will get extensive press and radio coverage. The fact that the newspapers during the campaign may be full of McCarthy should not lead to the easy assumption that McCarthyism is an issue in the minds of the voters.

One must penetrate through the fog of sound and fury which engulfs all national elections to the terra firma of local decision-making before he can make such a judgment, always recalling that while President Eisenhower was receiving an overwhelming mandate for his crusade in November, 1952, Republican candidates for the House of Representatives received 240,000 fewer votes than did their Democratic opponents. Eisenhower won majorities in 297 congressional districts, but Republican congressional candidates won only 221—a telling indication of the degree to which the electorate, even in a presidential year, can ignore the national context in voting for congressmen.

The Senate

Elections to the Senate differ radically from elections to the House. Since it is impossible to gerrymander a senatorial constituency, the urban voter gets a full say in these elections; and many states whose delegations to the House are overwhelmingly Republican, for example, Washington, Illinois, New York, regularly elect a Democrat to the Senate. To put the point another way, the extent of one-partyism is considerably less in the Senate than it is in the House. Relatively few senators outside the South can win the primary and then relax. A direct consequence of this heterogeneity is that senatorial candidates are called upon to stand and declare themselves on a great variety of issues such as immigration policy, foreign affairs, and civil liberties, which seldom invade contests for the House of Representatives. Thus it is apparent that the Senate races this fall supply the natural forums for McCarthyism, but the question again is to what degree will McCarthyism succeed in becoming a matter of vigorous public concern?

Unfortunately, generalizations on Senate campaigns are as risky as those on elections to the lower house, so we are forced to undertake a rather detailed analysis. As of this writing, 37 senators will be elected on November 2nd: 32 for full six-year terms, and 5 for partial terms. The Democrats have 23 of their Senate positions at stake; the Republicans, 14—a ratio which on its face favors the G.O.P. However, of the 23 Democratic seats on the block, 13 (Alabama, North Carolina [2], Georgia, Virginia, South Carolina, Arkansas, Oklahoma, Tennessee, Texas, Rhode Island, Louisiana, and Mississippi) appear to be out of danger. On the other side of the fence, seven of the Republican offerings (New Hampshire [2], Nebraska [2], South Dakota, Kansas, and Maine) are hardly in jeopardy. Thus we are left with 17 active contests in which both sides will concentrate their heavy fire.

But other factors intervene immediately to eliminate seven of these races from serious consideration as potential arenas for a debate over McCarthyism. In Ohio and Massachusetts, the Democratic candidates are leading Catholic laymen, and hence presumably immune from attack as pro-Communist. In Kentucky and New Jersey, the G.O.P. nominees hail from the extreme left wing of the Republican Party and have had no truck with McCarthyism. And in Delaware, Iowa, and New Mexico, the Democrats standing for reelection are from the conservative wing of that party. This leaves a maximum of ten contests (California, Colorado, Idaho, Illinois, Michigan, Minnesota, Montana, Oregon, West Virginia, and Wyoming) meriting serious examination. Two of these (Colorado and Michigan) must be excluded from this analysis, since at the time of writing there is not adequate information available on the Democratic candidates to justify discussion.

In the eight remaining states, we find the ideal condition for a McCarthyite offensive: a liberal Democrat confronting a right-wing Republican. The question thus becomes: To what extent will McCarthyism be an effective issue in these campaigns? Any positive answer to this query would require a temerity and a talent for voter psychoanalysis that are beyond our capacity, but some propositions do present themselves as worthy of tentative consideration:

First, on the basis of statistical analysis it would seem that in the 1952 campaign, when Republicans employed a McCarthyite attack on their opponents, they lost votes by it. Those interested in the statistical detail may find it in Louis H. Bean's *Influences in the 1954 Mid-Term Elections;* suffice it to say here that Democratic candidates for the Senate in the twelve states where McCarthy actively campaigned for the G.O.P. did notably better than Democratic candidates in states where McCarthy did not present his views on behalf of the Republican nominee.

Second, McCarthy's standing with the American people as registered in the admittedly inexact Gallup Polls seems to have decreased considerably since 1952. The senator's safari against the Army, and the resultant hearings, appear to have cut into his strength—he may even have committed the cardinal political sin, that of boring the populace. A Gallup Poll conducted in April, 1954, indicated that while 17 percent of those polled said they would be more likely to vote for a candidate supported by McCarthy, 43 percent stated they would be more likely to vote against a candidate with the senator's endorsement. Furthermore, in the Maine Republican primary in which Robert L. Jones, an outspoken McCarthyite, opposed Senator Margaret Chase Smith, a longtime foe of McCarthy, the outcome was a smashing victory for Senator Smith.

Third, tactics of denunciation are nowhere nearly so useful to a party in office as to a party in the wilderness. A bitter attack on Truman may have had some utility in 1952, but in 1954 it seems a bit irrelevant. Perhaps because the Democrats ran against Herbert Hoover for twenty years, the Republicans believe they can run against Alger Hiss and Harry Dexter White for the next twenty! But while blaming your opponents for your troubles may be effective in a presidential campaign, it would seem to have a limited effectiveness in contests for the Senate and House of Representatives.

Fourth, Senator McCarthy's appeal to the Catholic voter may be nowhere near what it is reputed to be. It should be noted at this point that McCarthyism is in no sense a Catholic political movement; the senator's strongest supporters in Congress seem to be rural Protestants who view him as the avenger of the "socialistic New Deal." However, although McCarthy has been attacked in such Catholic journals as the Jesuit weekly *America* and the liberal *Commonweal,* and by such a distinguished churchman as Bishop Bernard J. Sheil of Chicago, he has received considerable support from some members of the hierarchy, notably Cardinal Spellman of New York, and from Catholic lay groups.

Some analysts have assumed on the basis of this support that McCarthy has great influence on the Catholic segment of the electorate, but Louis H. Bean, in the study cited above, has carefully examined this proposition and come to a quite different conclusion. It is correct, Bean suggests, that McCarthy has *more* appeal to a Catholic voter than to a Protestant or Jew, but the extent of this influence is not sufficient to constitute McCarthyism a decisive factor in Catholic decision-making.

In summary, the McCarthyites will be extremely active in the senatorial elections in such states as Illinois, California, Michigan, and Minnesota, but it remains to be seen whether the electorate will take their issue to heart. Some campaigns may be almost wholly dominated by horizontal issues, for example, public power in Oregon and Idaho, agricultural prices in Minnesota and Iowa, unemployment in Michigan and West Virginia, so that a vertical issue like McCarthyism may never get a hearing. Finally, what indications there are suggest that there has been a significant decline in McCarthy's standing with the public, and the statement by Senator Homer Ferguson of Michigan, a right-wing Republican, that he did not wish the Wisconsin senator to campaign for him may indicate that this decline has been appreciated by G.O.P. candidates.

McCarthyism and the American Political Tradition

Having attempted to get perspective on the effectiveness of McCarthyism as an issue in the elections of November, 1954, it would be useful to conclude this article by a brief appraisal of the place of McCarthyism in the American political tradition.

One of the most striking aspects of American politics, alluded to at the outset of this analysis, is the history-less atmosphere in which they are conducted. Denis W. Brogan, the British historian, recounts that when he visited Alsace after World War II, he asked a peasant how severe the German occupation had been. The peasant replied that the Germans had been nowhere near so brutal as the Swedes—who had last been seen in those parts during the Thirty Years' War! Outside the South, where the Civil War is refought from time to time, there is little such historical brooding in American politics. The average American seems to be born without a political umbilical cord; nor, for that matter, does he feel tradition-bound to any social caste or economic stratum. In terms of the American myth, the individual is not in thrall to the past any more than he is limited by his humble origins or religious affiliation.

The virtues of this political, social, and economic mobility are many and great, and—since they are extolled regularly in all significant organs of mass communication—need no elaboration here. What is important for our perspective on McCarthyism is a disadvantage which is also an outgrowth of this absence of strong tradition: the American tendency to treat each striking event, each political crisis, as though it had no ancestors, as though it were *sui generis*. One might think from reading the papers, particularly the liberal papers, that this was the first time in American history that an extremist had made himself a force in the land, whereas, in fact, political extremism has been a constant component in American politics since the very founding of the Republic. From the Federalist xenophobes of 1798, who maintained that Vice-President Jefferson was a French agent, to Senator McCarthy and his allies, who claim that the Democrats have betrayed the nation to Communism, there has been a long procession of extremists and demagogues who have tried to build political fortunes around the paranoidal tendencies of the American community, tendencies which Americans share with all people, everywhere.

While no one in his political senses could deny the threat that Soviet imperialism constitutes to the free world, it is interesting to note that Senator McCarthy shows little concern for this aspect of the problem. He devotes his efforts to the internal menace of Communism in the United States, and has successfully made a mountain out of a dunghill. Space does not permit an examination of the history of Communism in the United States; suffice it to say that the bumbling, F.B.I.-ridden Communist Party U.S.A. has long been the laughingstock of the international Communist movement.

To say this is not to deny that there are and have been Soviet agents in the United States, but experience indicates that the Soviets are not sufficiently stupid to equip their spies with Communist Party cards and subscriptions to the *Daily Worker*. But the American people, frustrated in their wish to live a peaceful existence in a warless world, have been all too eager to accept a simple explanation for their perpetual crisis-living: that it is the work of traitors within who have sold the pass to the Soviet Union. By the application of retrospective omniscience, the seizure of Eastern Europe by Stalin and the conquest of China by Mao have been credited to treasonous actions by American policy-makers, thus supplying the American people with an almost infinite number of scapegoats.

Senator McCarthy's definition of "treason" thus is broad enough to include the activities of Presidents Roosevelt and Truman, of at least two Secretaries of State, and of an astronomical number of policy-makers of lower rank. Obviously, this is not the approach of a man who is genuinely concerned with uncovering Soviet spies; indeed, by the indiscriminate use of extreme charges, the senator has probably made the task of ferreting out authentic Russian agents considerably more difficult. A really astute Soviet agent today would not carry a copy of *The Democratic Digest* for protective coloration—he would unquestionably be a McCarthyite with three attacks on the "Truman-Acheson policy of treason" to his credit.

Whither McCarthy?

However, the question remains: Where does the senator go from here? Although one must be very cautious in reading lessons from history, the fate of past extremists seems to offer some insight on this matter. Psychologically, the extremist must attack, attack, and then attack again. As Hitler's career demonstrates, the road to power for such a man is unceasing assault. But there are risks in the perpetual attack—it becomes increasingly extreme, shrill and, finally, boring. Unless a demagogue can seize commanding positions of state power in the early stages of his campaign, he is likely to end his days in the political wilderness, a rejected prophet. And it is precisely this fate which American political institutions tend to prepare for the extremist.

In sum, when the Framers of the Constitution divided up the power to govern between Congress and the President, their intention was to create a passion-proof polity that could withstand the initial onslaught of any demagogue or frenzied faction. The delay which is built into every stage of the enactment of public policy, while it frustrates many dedicated to good ends, also thwarts the extremists and forces reflection upon the perhaps unreflecting community. The "sober second thought" of the American community has not always lived up to the expectations of idealists, but it is a rock upon which the projects of extremists have uniformly foundered.

Explaining Away McCarthy:
A Review of *McCarthy and His Enemies*
by William F. Buckley, Jr., and
L. Brent Bozell

McCarthy and His Enemies is an attempt at a rhetorical tour de force, but while the authors give it what might be described as the old college try, they run into the same problem that Mr. Buckley encountered in his earlier *God and Man at Yale:* levitation takes place, but the wires are apparent. Not that Buckley and Bozell are lacking in talent—they are obviously bright young men—but they have gone beyond their depth in attempting the rhetorical version of the Indian rope trick.

To be precise, in *God and Man at Yale* Buckley announced one premise as fundamental to his analysis (that professors should teach what the *alumni* want taught), and then wrote his book on an entirely different premise (that Yale professors did not teach what *Buckley* wanted taught), and in *McCarthy and His Enemies* he has improved his game by adding a second supplementary premise. In effect, *McCarthy and His Enemies* is three books: one concerned with McCarthy, and two with various aspects of American life which the authors contend are relevant to the analysis of McCarthy. The end product, while not lacking in a certain facile charm, simply does not hold up under close logical examination.

Book I: McCarthy and His Intentions. Here, the authors examine McCarthy's various public statements on the subject of Communists in the State Department and decide that, although he exaggerated a bit here and there, his intentions were good. They spend a great deal of time evaluating the argument as to

Reprinted, with permission, from *The New Leader*, May 24, 1954.

whether McCarthy said there were 57 or 205 card-carrying Communists in the State Department, and the reader begins to compliment the authors on their scholarly objectivity until he suddenly recalls that, either way, the statement was a lie. There are also a discussion of the State Department's general disinterest in security in the postwar period and a tiring, conspicuously scholarly evaluation of the Tydings Investigation, directed to the point that, while McCarthy may have lied, he was provoked into doing it by the Democrats—a type of excuse seldom acceptable much beyond the second grade.

However, the breathtaking feature of Book I—and I should make it clear that *my* Book I has no relation to the pagination of Buckley and Bozell; parts of what I call Book I are scattered throughout the text and appendices—is its cold-blooded call for a revision of the democratic ethic and the establishment of what Albert Camus has called the "Kingdom of Ends." True, the authors admit, McCarthy did go too far in his assertions about Jessup, Lattimore, and others, but they suggest that, in the objective view, this extravagance was necessary to destroy the reputations of these men. Whether Lattimore was actually on the Soviet payroll becomes, from this viewpoint, an irrelevant consideration. If he was not getting paid for his good work, he was being cheated of his rightful remuneration. One suddenly has a feeling that he has heard this pitch before, only Vishinsky was proclaiming it to a Moscow jury as proof of Trotsky's role in German intelligence.

Thus, the central proposition of Book I is the infallibility of McCarthy's appraisal of national security and of the measures necessary to secure it. Security, as the current hearings have shown, is not itself an objective concept: McCarthy's spies in the government are not security risks, since presumably, in the long run, they are *promoting* national security by violating security rules. McCarthy's intentions are, say Buckley and Bozell, sound; and if, in the course of saving the country from Democratic incompetence, he is forced to overstate the case, it is regrettable but essential. It was, for example, necessary for the good of the nation that George C. Marshall's reputation be destroyed, and there was no better way of achieving this end than by calling him a Soviet agent. Perhaps lesser means might have been kinder, but the American people unfortunately do not respond to the voice of reason.

Book II: Bureaucratic Responsibility in the United States. Here the authors examine the problem created for a new administration by civil servants with tenure in policy-making jobs. They suggest that a new approach should be employed which would make it possible for an administration to dismiss anyone in such a position without lengthy procedures. In my opinion, their position is sound and is, indeed, supported by many distinguished authorities in the field of public administration. There is a conflict between the principle of civil service tenure and executive responsibility. Each administration attempts to put its own men in policy jobs and then freeze them in with civil service protection: even such an obvious policy job as the Director of the Bureau of Land Management was so frozen by the Truman administration.

But while the authors seem here to be on sound ground in their suggestions, it does not seem to me that what they say is relevant to McCarthy. Presumably, it was this freezing of policy jobs by Truman that made it necessary and just, in their view, for McCarthy to engage in terror tactics, but there is no necessary connection. McCarthy's campaign hardly diminished when Eisenhower replaced top Democrats with Republicans.

Book III: Is This an Age of Conformity? Here Buckley and Bozell examine the oft-repeated charge that McCarthy has imposed an atmosphere of conformity on the American scene, and find it incorrect. Again, I find that I agree with much that they say. There *is* an organized and vociferous opposition to McCarthy; the guillotine has *not* been set up in the shadow of the Washington Monument; and the "liberals" (a term which Buckley and Bozell use as synonymous with the clientele of *The Nation*) have *not* always been men of principle. But, when all this is said and reiterated, it is patent that the atmosphere of conformity (never absent from the American scene) has been intensified and worsened by McCarthy's activities. Perhaps McCarthy has not contributed as much to it as some have claimed, but to assert this is to join the lady who justified her illegitimate child on the ground that it was a *very small* child.

In short, Buckley and Bozell have engaged in rhetorical leger-demain in the effort to draw the reader away from McCarthy by castigating his enemies. But if McCarthy is to be justified or con-demned, it must be done in terms of McCarthy, and not of his opposition or friends. The individualist ethic which supports the democratic faith forbids innocence by opposition equally with guilt by association.

Memoirs of a "Subversive"

Although I enjoy conversation and reminiscence as much as, if not more than, the next man, talking about war experiences has always struck me as a symptom of senility. Not that I don't have a few choice anecdotes to tell, but these are hardly of the blood-and-guts type; on the contrary, they generally point up the basic question which has haunted me for a decade: If our Army was efficient, what did an inefficient Army look like? The war to me was a great stretch of empty time, broken by sporadic fits of activity, in which I lived an essentially vegetable existence. I hated military life, I detested discipline, and above all I was angry with myself for adapting so easily and comfortably to militarism, discipline, and vegetablism. Once discharged, I avoided all attempts to glorify the "good old Army days," and only reluctantly joined the American Veterans Committee, an organization dedicated to the withering away of professional patriotism.

However, recent events have created in me an evergrowing compulsion to pull out my barracks bag of memories and join the minstrels. I do not wish to be misunderstood—I am not joining the Legion or the V.F.W., and I am certainly not going to march in any parades. But the recent burst of headlines about my old alma mater, the Army Information-Education Program, has led me to compromise my principles and set down this chronicle. The Jenner Committee, in the course of its industrious quest for the conspirators who got us into the twentieth century, turned up some wartime Information-Education functionaries as probable

Reprinted, with permission, from *The New Republic*, January 24, 1955.

Communists, and the newspapers screamed *Communists Infiltrated Army Education Program*. The impression that the Committee's findings left with the casual reader was that I.&E. was virtually the American distributor of *Pravda*, if not an arm of the NKVD.

Now I enjoy a good spy story, but too much is too much. I was an Army "subversive": for two years I pushed I.&E. propaganda on the troops; I attended I.&E. School at Washington and Lee University, and I read all the publications of the division. Furthermore, I was, as I still am, a militant anti-Communist liberal who had been through the ideological wars, and could spot the CP pitch a mile away. In view of these qualifications, I should like to advance a quite different interpretation of the effectiveness of Communist activity in I.&E.

There are two separate problems which must be considered: first, What influence did I.&E. have on the views of the average soldier? and, second, How successful were the Communists in infiltrating the I.&E. operation?

From the outset, the I.&E. program, an imaginatively conceived effort to explain to the American soldier why he fought, met with tremendous hostility. Externally, it was attacked regularly by congressmen and newspapers who felt that the program was an effort by the New Dealers to impose their public policy on the GI. Indeed, the educational potential of the program was enormous, for here was a huge captive audience, its individuality broken down by the deliberate and rigorous collectivism of basic training. To the right-wingers it appeared inevitable that Roosevelt would inscribe the dogmas of liberalism on this *tabula rasa*. But, as usual, the President's cunning was overestimated by his enemies.

Internally, I.&E. also met with bitter opposition from old-line Army officers, who maintained that the whole idea was a waste of valuable time, if not dangerous nonsense. In the view of this group, the function of the soldier was not to think. It made no difference to the troops why they were in the war—their job was simply to do what they were told. Some went further, asserting, in effect, that if you let an enlisted man read a book, you might as well shoot him. This variety of anti-intellectualism was endemic in regular Army officers, and consequently, when orders went out from Washington to all commands that one hour per week was to be allocated to Information-Education, many key line officers did everything in their power to sabotage the undertaking.

To cite my own experience, which I learned from other I.&E. men was not atypical, our base commander appointed as I.&E. Officer the most egregious idiot who ever graduated from Army Air Forces Administrative OCS. As one of the three enlisted men on the post who had graduated from college, I was assigned to be I.&E. noncom. My lieutenant, who had about fifteen miscellaneous duties on the station, ranging from Assistant Mess Officer through Assistant Fire Marshal to Assistant Claims & Insurance Officer, gave me roughly an hour's guidance a week. This was plenty, for the advice was always the same: a detailed discussion of the canine ancestry of the base commander and each of his staff officers, coupled with a vigorous demand that I "get on the stick and we'll really buzz this place." While I fully supported his genealogical findings, I found it rather hard to "get on the stick" when there was nobody with any rank and prestige to go to bat for me or the program. I was strictly on my own.

The base commander, a jovial fellow, who was reputed to have observed that it was a lousy war, but better than no war at all, initially ruled that the troops would have to attend the I.&E. session—"that crap from Washington," in his phrase—on their own time in the evening. At this point I was nearly lynched by my barracks mates, and the first sergeant—who ran a black-market business in airplane parts at night—indicated that he would get me busted from S/Sgt to Pvt if the evening schedule went through. I turned to the Regulations and found a requirement that I.&E. be offered on Army time, and fortunately the base inspector took the issue up and forced a rescheduling. The commanding officer complied by assigning me the hour from seven to eight on Thursday morning, and thenceforth every Thursday at seven the troops marched into the base theater to learn why they were fighting. A realist, I usually showed a film for the first forty-five minutes, took five minutes for a news analysis, then woke the boys up and sent them on their way. I can't remember much about the films except that a large number of them showed American fighter-bombers chasing German rail-road trains.

Once, to my grief, I decided to try a bright idea which had been sent down from I.&E. Headquarters, and hold a debate. My standing as an Army subversive probably dates from that un-happy occasion. The subject was innocuous enough—*What Changes Will War Bring to the US?* or some similar topic—and it all began quietly. Three of the four statements went off in a soporific haze, but suddenly, as the fourth soldier, a char-acter from Brooklyn who had strong opinions on almost every-thing, was saying his piece, the atmosphere changed. The Brook-lynite had included in his remarks an endorsement of racial equality, and the southern contingent awoke en masse. No sooner had the speaker finished than a real up-country Georgian jumped to his feet and asked the inevitable question: "Wilson, how would you like it if your sister married a nigra?" Wilson, no man to back away from an ugly situation, snapped back: "Rockingham, my little sister is so ugly she'd be lucky to find anyone who'd marry her." By dint of great effort, I forestalled a riot, but my troubles were just beginning.

An hour later, after the troops had dispersed and Wilson had gone into hiding, I was on the carpet with the base commander and his intelligence officer. Both were from the Deep South, and it was apparent that in their view Wilson, probably at my urging, had that morning raised the Red flag on the station. No sooner had I fulfilled the ritual of saluting and reporting than the intelli-gence officed demanded: "Roche, are you a Communist?" When I said I was not, he pulled out a list of organizations—a wild list which included among various Communist and Fascist groups the America First Committee, the Mennenites [*sic!*] and the Quakers—and asked for my affiliations. I denied any relevant at-tachments, and Intelligence, having reached the end of his string, retired. The colonel picked up the ball: "Roche," he said, in his best court-martial voice, "who authorized you to hold a debate on a controversial subject?" Having come prepared for this gambit, I pulled out my directives from I.&E. Headquarters; he read them over with a look of disgust, and then issued his final mandate: "Roche, if you run any discussions on controversial subjects on this post, I'll court-martial you—and I don't give a damn what those pinkos in Washington tell you to do. Remember, boy, I can put you in the stockade, and they can't get you out." I saluted, withdrew, and put my charges back on a full-time diet of fighter-bombers chasing locomotives.

This may sound like an extreme case, but my conversation with other poor souls who likewise tried to inform and educate the troops leads me to believe that I made out rather well. At least, I didn't land up in the stockade, whereas some persistent I.&E. men did, court-martialed under the elastic 96th Article of War for "conduct unbecoming a soldier." Some commands simply defied Washington and refused to allow any time for the program; others made life so miserable for I.&E. personnel that the latter simply gave up the effort. I.&E. had no real constituency, no powerful brass to go to its defense. Thus the program lived on the periphery of Army life, barely hanging on, and the average soldier went through the war untouched by it. I would therefore conclude that not only did I.&E. not turn American soldiers into Komsomols, but further that it had no impact whatsoever on the thought patterns of the average GI. It was, in brief, an educational flop.

As far as Communist infiltration of the I.&E. operation is concerned, there is no doubt in my mind but that the word went out through Party channels that this was a good spot on which to concentrate. Undoubtedly, a good many Stalinists put in applications for I.&E. work, and probably the proportion of Party-liners among I.&E. personnel was considerably higher than the law of averages would justify. This was certainly the case in my class at Washington and Lee, and I had quite a time, for my anti-Stalinist and anti-Soviet views soon brought me the stern disapprobation of the Party clique among the students. There was no question of persecution involved: if anything, I was the persecutor, as I enjoyed ideological infighting, and was fully prepared to mount the offensive on the drop of a dialectical hat.

In any case, I soon became known in some circles as an "auxiliary of Nazism," and I once had the great pleasure of overhearing one of my roommates, with whom I had just had a bitter argument over the legality of the Japanese-American evacuation and the Espionage Act trial of "Fascists" which was then running in Washington, denounce me to a common acquaintance as an "Irish Christian Fronter." I immediately accused him of racial bigotry, of launching a vicious attack on the Irish minority, and of displaying bourgeois chauvinism. This convinced him that I was a Trotskyite.

But all this was a tempest in a microcosm. Memory plays tricks, but I would estimate that less than 10 percent of the members of my class were Party-liners. On the other hand, not more than two or three of us were outspokenly cynical about the good intentions of the U.S.S.R. The great bulk of the students, probably around 90 percent, simply didn't give a damn. They had volunteered for the school to get "a good deal," and all the hot political arguments passed right over their hedonistic heads. I vividly recall looking in on a poker game in the next room after I had engaged my Stalinist roommate in a dispute over the executions of Ehrlich and Alter, the two leaders of the Polish-Jewish Bund who were shot after they took refuge from the Nazis in Russia, and being asked by one of the cardplayers, "What the hell do you Communists fight about all the time?" To this contingent, anybody who took politics seriously was a Communist, and it was from this apolitical group that the overwhelming proportion of the I.&E. "indoctrinators" hailed.

Thus it would probably be accurate to say that of the *politically conscious* students, the Stalinists were the largest single aggregation, but that the politically conscious members constituted a minute minority of the total body of school-trained personnel. As far as the teaching was concerned, there appeared to be no articulate Communists. The view of the U.S.S.R. that was presented was no less realistic than that of most Americans in the era of Stalingrad. Furthermore, very little instruction centered on politics; most of our time was devoted to first-rate demonstration of techniques of mass education, visual aids, and the like. The closest we came to an overall appraisal of world problems was the graduation address by Hanson W. Baldwin.

However, the publications of the I.&E. division led me to suspect that the Communists had planted some of their people in key editorial positions. The worst offender was the weekly *Army*

Talk, which was given mass distribution throughout the Army and Air Force—at least in theory. This publication showed signs of internal editorial conflicts; that is, there was no overall consistency of outlook—some issues were given straight Party-line presentation, while others were handled with objectivity and balance. (I later learned that my hunch was correct, that there was a constant battle raging among the editors along Stalinist and anti-Stalinist lines.) With regard to the U.S.S.R., to China, and to Far Eastern developments generally, *Army Talk* struck me as extremely biased, even allowing for the contemporary enthusiasm for Communist "democracy" in virtually all sectors of American public opinion. The pamphlets on vital issues distributed by I.&E. were on a much higher level; indeed, most of them were written by leading scholars, and were exceedingly well done.

Even if we assume, for purposes of discussion, that Stalinist colonization of the I.&E. publications branch was more effective than seems to have been true—I was in the field, not in Washington, and thus had no way of knowing what went on except as I sensed it from the publications themselves—there is a basic point that must be taken into consideration: Who read the stuff? I may sound cynical, but I am confident that of the five thousand or more officers and enlisted men on my post, not more than two or three ever bothered to look at the materials that I distributed. Once, when I deliberately suppressed an issue of *Army Talk* which seemed to me to be a particularly noxious dose of Stalinist tripe, one soldier came in to ask me what had happened to the latest release: he had heard it was very good. This was an interesting indication of the effectiveness of Party communications, since he was our one articulate Stalinist! However, in the aggregate, I would suggest that Communist efforts to infiltrate I.&E., and whatever success they had, were just so much wasted time. There may have been a lot of *Army Talk,* but the fact was that nobody was listening.

Yet, despite its drawbacks and failures, the program was, in my opinion, worth undertaking. As Gilbert K. Chesterton once observed, "If a thing is worth doing, it is worth doing badly."

Can Morality Be Legislated?
[with Milton M. Gordon]

The Supreme Court is pondering its decision on how and when to carry out its ruling of a year ago that public school segregation is unconstitutional. It is therefore timely to examine the relationship between law and mores, between the decrees of courts and legislatures and the vast body of community beliefs which shape private action.

While it is not perhaps customary to think of the Supreme Court as a legislative body, the cold fact is that in the *Desegregation* cases the nine Justices have undertaken to rewrite public policy in at least seventeen states and innumerable communities. Indeed, it would be difficult to find a recent congressional enactment that equals in impact and scope this judicial holding. Whether one approves or disapproves of such judicial acts, it is clear that the Court has undertaken a monumental project in the field of social engineering, and one obviously based on the assumption that morality *can* be legislated.

Opponents of the desegregation decision have, with the exception of a fringe of overt white supremacists, largely founded their dissent on the principle that law can not move faster than public opinion, that legal norms which do not reflect community sentiment are unenforceable. They cite the dismal failure of Prohibition as a case in point, urging that basic social change—however desirable—must come from the bottom, from a shift in "grass-roots" convictions.

Reprinted, with permission, from *The New York Times Magazine*, May 22, 1955.

On the other hand, the Court's supporters maintain that virtually every statute and judicial decree is, to some extent, a regulation of morality. Indeed, they suggest, if the moral standards of individuals were not susceptible to state definition and regulation, we would never have emerged from primitive barbarism.

In this article, we shall examine from the viewpoint of the social scientist the evidence on both sides of the question, and see if it is possible to extract any meaningful conclusions.

First of all, we must delve into the relationship that exists in a democratic society between law and community attitudes. While this is a treacherous area, full of pitfalls for the unwary generalizer, it seems clear that, as distinguished from a totalitarian society, law in a democracy is founded on consensus. That is to say that the basic sanctions are applied not by the police, but by the community. The jury system institutionalizes this responsibility in such cases as "mercy killings" or those involving the "unwritten law" by finding citizens who have unquestionably killed, "not guilty."

Conversely, juries applying other sections of the Criminal Code—notably those penalizing subversion—will often bring in verdicts of "guilty" based not so much on technical guilt as upon the proposition that the defendent should be taken out of circulation. In another area of the law, insurance companies, faced with damage suits, have learned to shun juries like the plague. Indeed, they will frequently make unjustified out-of-court settlements in preference to facing a jury that begins its labors with the seeming assumption that no insurance company of any standing would miss $100,000.

From this it should be clear that in the United States law is a great deal more, and simultaneously a great deal less, than a command of the sovereign. Thus one can safely say that no piece of legislation, or judicial decision, which does not have its roots in community beliefs, has a chance of being effectively carried out.

To this extent, it is undeniable that morality cannot be legislated; it would be impossible, for example, to make canasta playing a capital offense *in fact*, even if the bridge-players' lobby were successful in getting such a law on the books. This is a fanciful example, but in our view the Volstead Act and the Eighteenth Amendment were no less unrealistic in objective: like H. L. Mencken's friend, Americans seem willing to vote for Prohibition as long as they can stagger to the polls.

Excluding these extreme efforts to legislate morality, which are obviously unsound, we now come to the heart of the matter: Under what circumstances will an individual accept distasteful regulation of his actions? To put it another way: What are the criteria which lead an individual to adjust his acts to the demands of the state?

Specifically, why do people pay taxes when they disagree strongly with the uses to which the money will be put? A large-scale tax revolt, as the French have recently discovered, is almost impossible to check without recourse to martial law and police-state methods, but here the average taxpayer grouses and pays. While Americans are not, by and large, as law-abiding as their British cousins, it is probably fair to say that most of us obey most laws without even reflecting on their merits.

This problem of the basis of legal norms has proved a fascinating one to sociologists. In the past fifteen years some significant new thinking on the subject has grown out of empirical research, more incisive analysis, and general observation of large-scale experiences with legal desegregation in important areas of American life such as employment, public housing, and the Armed Forces.

The older categorical view, stated in classic fashion by the sociologist William Graham Sumner, was that law could never move ahead of the customs or mores of the people—that legislation which was not firmly rooted in popular folkways was doomed to failure. The implication was that social change must always be glacier-like in its movement and that mass change in attitudes must precede legislative action.

The newer viewpoint is based on a more sophisticated and realistic analysis of social processes. In the first place, it questions the older way of stating the problem in terms of all or nothing. Any large, complex society, with its multiplicity of social backgrounds and individual experiences, contains varying mores and attitudes within itself. On any given piece of legislation there will not just be supporters and enemies; rather there will be many

points of view, ranging from unconditional support, through indifference, to unmitigated opposition.

Thus, the degree of success that will attend such an enactment
is the result of a highly complex series of interactions and adjustments among people with diverse attitudes toward the measure itself and toward the imposition of legal authority. Furthermore, it is predictable that a large segment of the population will
be basically neutral, if not totally indifferent.

To put the matter in an even broader framework, the prediction of behavior must take into consideration not only the attitudes of the individual but also the total social situation in which
his behavior is to be formulated and expressed. For instance,
people with ethnic prejudice are likely to express themselves in
a social clique where, say, anti-Semitic jokes are *au fait*, but will
restrain themselves in a group where such remarks are greeted
with hostility. Once the bigot realizes that he must pay a social
price for his anti-Semitism, he is likely to think twice before
exposing himself to the penalty.

In this connection, Robert K. Merton, Columbia sociologist,
has set up an incisive classification, suggesting that four major
groups can be delineated: (1) the all-weather liberal, who can
be expected to oppose prejudice and race discrimination under
any set of social conditions; (2) the fair-weather liberal, who is
not himself prejudiced but who will stand silent or passively support discrimination if it is easier and more profitable to do so;
(3) the fair-weather illiberal, who has prejudices but is not prepared to pay a significant price for expressing them in behavior,
preferring rather to take the easier course of conformity; and
(4) the all-weather illiberal, who is prepared to fight to the last
ditch for his prejudices at whatever cost in social disapproval.

If we apply this classification to a problem such as desegregation, it immediately becomes apparent that the critical strata, so
far as success or failure is concerned, are groups 2 and 3. Group
1 will support the proposal with vigor, and Group 4 will oppose
it bitterly, but groups 2 and 3 will carry the day.

But because groups 2 and 3 are not crusaders, are not strongly
motivated, they are particularly susceptible to the symbolism of
law. Thus the fact that fair employment practices have been in-

corporated into law, or that the Supreme Court has held school segregation unconstitutional, will itself tend to direct their thinking toward compliance.

The symbols of state power are to the undedicated nonrevolutionary mighty and awesome things, and he will think long and hard before he commits himself to subversive action. Consequently the law tends to become, in another of Merton's phrases, a "self-fulfilling prophecy"; that is, a statute tends to create a climate of opinion favorable to its own enforcement. As John Locke long ago pointed out, the great roadblock to revolution is not the police but the habits of obedience which lead the law-abiding majority to refrain from even legitimate and justified resistance.

American experience over the past decade and a half seems to confirm this hypothesis. By legislative action, executive order, and judicial decision, the race prejudices of Americans have been denied public sanction. Fair employment practices commissions, of national scope during the war and subsequently operative in a number of states and municipalities, integration of the Armed Forces, integration of many segregated schools, elimination of "white primaries," and removal of racial restrictions in many professional associations—all these have provided a living laboratory for the study of the impact of law on the mores.

At virtually every stage in the development, strong voices were raised to plead that morality could not be legislated, that an end to discrimination must await an unprejudiced public. Yet, the results indicate a high degree of compliance, some covert evasion, and only a few instances of violent resistance.

Moreover, it should be kept in mind that the success of de-segregation laws or orders need not be measured against a hypothetical standard of 100 percent, but against the usual standards of law enforcement. Even laws against homicide and rape, which have overwhelming community support, are occasionally violated.

But, while laws may restrain behavior, is there any evidence to indicate that attitudes are affected? Here the evidence seems clear: the law itself plays an important part in the educational process. Again the key to analysis is the social situation.

Legislation and administrative orders which have prohibited discrimination in such areas as employment, the Armed Forces, public housing, and professional associations have brought people of various races together—often with initial reluctance—in normal day-to-day contact on an "equal-status" basis where the emphasis is on doing a job together. Contact of this kind gives people a chance to know one another as individual human beings with similar interests, problems, and capabilities. In this type of interaction racial sterotypes are likely to be weakened and dispelled.

Such a favorable change of attitude as a result of personal contact has been reported in a number of studies. In one carefully designed research project, Morton Deutsch and Mary Evans Collins found that white housewives who had been assigned to public housing projects which were racially integrated tended to develop favorable attitudes toward Negroes, while the vast majority of those who occupied segregated housing tended to remain the same in their racial views. A study of integration in the Army reached a similar conclusion.

Findings such as these support a considerably broader and more complex conception of the relations between legal norms and human acts and attitudes than did the older, simpler Sumner thesis. In this more comprehensive analysis, law itself is seen as a force which, in its impact, does more than prohibit or compel specific behavior. Indeed, in its operation, law actually provides the setting for types of social relationships—relationships which may have a profound effect on the very attitudes which are necessary to adequate enforcement of the statute in question.

We thus come down to the final and crucial problem. It is plain that under some circumstances morality can be legislated, while under other conditions, the laws prove impotent. But what are the specific factors which must be evaluated? What criteria can be offered as a guide to intelligent and effective action in these touchy areas of belief, superstition, and vested prejudice? The following four considerations are suggested as a beginning:

First, the amount of opposition and its geographical spread. If a random group of 15 percent of the population, roughly gauged, oppose some regulation, there will probably be little difficulty in gaining public acceptance and enforcement. However, and this is particularly relevant to the desegregation problem, if the 15 percent all live in one compact geographical area where they constitute a majority, control local government, and supply juries, the magnitude of the problem is much greater.

Second, the intensity of opposition. This is a qualitative matter, for, to paraphrase George Orwell, while all Americans are created equal, some are more equal than others. A proposal which is militantly opposed by "opinion-formers" in the American community—for example, ministers, lawyers, newspaper editors—will have much harder sledding than a nose count of the opponents would seem to justify; and, conversely, a measure which receives the support of this key group, or significant segments of it, can overcome a numerically large resistance.

Much of the success of the Negro in overcoming his legal, social, and economic disabilities has been an outgrowth of the strong stand on his behalf taken by church leaders, journalists, trade unionists, businessmen, and politicians who have created a climate of opinion favorable to Negro claims and who have based their assertions on the values which constitute the American Creed: Equality of treatment under law and human brotherhood under God. With this quality of support, much can be accomplished even against great numbers.

Third, the degree to which sanctions can be administered. Here we turn to the practical problems of enforcement, and it is at this point that Prohibition really should have run aground long before it was incorporated into public policy. Home manufacture of alcoholic beverages has, according to well-informed sources, even survived in the Soviet Union, and if the M.V.D. is incapable of banning private brew, there is little reason to suspect that a democratic society could handle the job.

It can not be emphasized too often that general principles or morality are no stronger than the instruments by which they are implemented; it would thus be legislative folly to try to prohibit people from disliking Jews, Negroes, Catholics, or Protestants. However, making gin in the bathtub, or disliking minorities, is not action equivalent to segregating schoolchildren on the basis of their pigmentation.

Because it is nearly impossible to regulate what goes on in millions of private homes, it does not follow that enforcement of desegregation in public institutions will be equally difficult. In sum, false and misleading analogies must be avoided, and each proposal must be examined on its merits to determine whether or not it is enforceable.

Fourth, the diligence of enforcement. It is extremely important that enforceable regulations be diligently enforced. This is particularly true in the initial period when public attitudes (specifically, the attitudes of Merton's groups 2 and 3) are in the process of formation. Flagrant refusal to obey usually is designed as a symbolic act to rally the undecided, and strong action at such a time will convince many wavering minds that the best course is compliance.

The Milford, Delaware, episode—where parents, stirred up by agitators, refused to send their children to a desegregated school —is a good case study of what should not happen; there vigorous action by the state authorities, such as occurred under similar circumstances in Baltimore, would have dampened the ardor of the fanatics and decimated their fellow travelers. The danger is that successful symbolic defiance plants the dragon seed and brings into the resistance movement those who would otherwise remain interested and sympathetic spectators—at a distance.

In short, to ask, "Can morality be legislated?" is actually to pose the wrong question. What types of morality, under what conditions, and with what techniques for enforcement are qualitative considerations which fragment the question into more answerable units. Our analysis suggests that, although large-scale local considerations may call for special circumstances of implementation, the majesty of the law, when supported by the collective conscience of a people and the healing power of the social situation, in the long run will not only enforce morality but create it.

Security and the Press

Ever since technology and literacy combined to make mass communication possible, free societies have in crisis periods been confronted with problems of press censorship. As early as the War of 1812, General Andrew Jackson had an encounter with a New Orleans editor, Goodwin B. Cotten of the *Gazette*, whom the imperious general felt had violated security requirements by spreading a rumor that the hostilities with Britain were terminated. Later, during the Civil War, the free press created major difficulties for both Abraham Lincoln and Jefferson Davis.

Indeed, throughout the War Between the States the newspapers were a significant source of military intelligence. Union generals would eagerly await the latest issues of the Richmond *Examiner* to ascertain the intentions of the Confederate government, while Lee and his aides avidly perused the Washington *National Republican* for information on Union plans. Often the papers were traded daily by the pickets of the two armies, and a refusal by his pickets to send over the usual journals was one sure sign of impending enemy activity. Even a casual reading of the papers of this era impresses one with the value of the information that could be derived from them, for neither northern nor southern editors felt bound by any but the vaguest security considerations. Northern war correspondents, in particular, seemed to get a peculiar delight from outwitting the clumsy military censorship of telegraphic communications, and it was possible on occasion for the reader of Horace Greeley's *New-York Tribune*

Reprinted, with permission, from *Current History*, October, 1955.

to obtain a fuller picture of military operations than was simultaneously available to the Secretary of War!

The press problem proved less acute in the two world wars. Not only did the military authorities clamp a rigorous censorship on war correspondents, but the newspaper proprietors took a much deeper look at their responsibilities to the nation, and cooperated with the government in a program of self-censorship. This approach worked extremely well, but with the end of World War II a new complication set in. This time the termination of hostilities was not accompanied by an end to the need for security-consciousness. Barely were the Nazis and Japanese defeated when the United States found itself engaged in a "Cold War," which could last for generations, with the Soviet Union. Furthermore, the unveiling of atomic energy and the concomitant possibility that a nation could be destroyed, rather than merely wounded, by an atomic Pearl Harbor have put a new premium on scientific and technical security. Living in a world dominated by the "balance of terror," and competing for survival with a power that has developed the ancient art of espionage into a science, many Americans have perhaps felt that such ideals as freedom of speech and a press free from precensorship are anachronisms which, however well they worked in a leisurely nineteenth century context, must be tempered with a tough realism if we are to maintain our national existence in the twentieth century.

Fundamental, therefore, to this analysis of "Security and the Press" is the question of the function of the press (and, by implication, other instruments of mass communication) in a democratic society. To what extent, we must ask, is a free press a luxury item which can be dispensed with in the interests of security? A second question, hardly less important, is concerned with the proper goals of a security-of-information system and with a realistic examination of the dangers inherent in over-security. Finally, this brief study will be concluded by an attempt to reconcile on a practical level the maintenance of a free press and the operation of an adequate instrument of national security.

The Press and the Democratic Process

Democratic government, to borrow a metaphor from Aristotle, is founded on the premise that the guest is a better judge of the meal than the cook. Restated in somewhat more intellectual fashion, the proposition could read that the citizen who lives in a community is a better judge of the "public interest" than are the experts, the specialists in government, who must of necessity administer the political institutions of the society. Without attempting here to argue the merits of this assumption, the logical consequence of accepting it is a recognition of the citizen's right and power to replace one set of leaders, who have displeased him, with another set, who have promised to fulfill his desires. The democrat may agree with the pessimistic view of Walter Lippmann, most recently advanced in *The Public Philosophy*, that popular judgment is almost always wrong, but he must be prepared to permit "wrong" opinion, which has received popular support, to have its time in power.

It now becomes immediately apparent what a key role freedom of information plays in the operation of a democratic society. Unless the citizen is able to discover what his leaders are doing, and to evaluate alternate programs of action, his power to exercise his choice becomes in effect meaningless. Some commentators, holding what I term the "Hyperthyroid Theory of Democracy," would go so far as to assert that democracy rests upon a "well-informed populace," but this is surely claiming too much. Most people go through life substantially and happily misinformed about a great many things, and society seems none the worse for it. What is important to the operation of a democracy is not that every citizen *is* well informed but that the possibility of obtaining adequate information exists: that *potentially* every citizen can become well informed about matters of concern to him. Usually the intelligent citizen simply accepts the opinion-leadership of someone he trusts; given the complexity of many issues and the limited number of hours in the day, this is the way he must operate.

To put the matter concretely, I know nothing about military strategy, and am therefore unable to propound a formula for dividing up funds and priorities between the Army, Navy, and Air Force. Without even thinking about the question, I simply accepted the views of President Eisenhower as being those of a man who was ideally equipped properly to determine such an issue. Then I read in the *New York Times* the letter which General Matthew B. Ridgway, retiring Army Chief of Staff, sent to Secretary of Defense Charles Wilson. In this document, Ridgway protested vigorously against the existing balance of forces within the Defense Department, and advanced a series of cogent arguments for a changed policy. Ridgway's views impressed me very much; so much, in fact, that I began to study the problem, and shortly reached the conclusion, for whatever it may be worth, that Ridgway's strategic thinking was based on a far more realistic appraisal of Soviet intentions than was that of Eisenhower and Defense Secretary Wilson. However, whether I am correct or incorrect in my judgment is irrelevant to the point at issue; the significant aspect of this autobiographical trivia is that the publication of Ridgway's letter in the *Times* awakened my interest in the subject and eventually led me to reject the President's opinion-leadership in this matter.

In short, the important thing is not that the average citizen is "well informed" in a technical sense on issues of strategy, but that he can, if he chooses, obtain sufficient information on which to base a decision to trust one opinion-leader instead of another. Incidentally, it is from a failure to appreciate this phenomenon of opinion-trusteeship that most deprecatory estimates of the American, and, for that matter, British, French, or German, people arise. Public-opinion pollsters constantly have the League of Women Voters in despair by statistically proving that 45 percent of the people of eastern Pennsylvania do not know the name of the Secretary of State. Though one should certainly not discourage efforts to keep the public up to date on current events, I would submit that this statistic really doesn't prove anything one way or the other about eastern Pennsylvanians. Operating on the ancient principle of the division of labor, the latter vote for a President whom they trust, and assume, perhaps unrealistically, that he will remember the name of the Secretary of State. But always lurking in the background of this opinion-trusteeship is the possibility of revocation: the possibility that the people will withdraw and transfer their allegiance, and the task of protecting their interests, to another trustee. And it is on this level that freedom of information plays such a significant role, for from a free press the citizen can get his first indication that all is not well with his interests, as well as the evidence with which to document his suspicions.

Consequently, a free press is for a democratic society anything but a luxury item—a normative judgment which has time and time again received endorsement in judicial decisions limiting the power of the state to interfere with the publication of even libelous material. Indeed, freedom of the press includes the right to publish, and be sued for, libels; since the Supreme Court's memorable decision in *Near* v. *Minnesota* (1931), it has been an unconstitutional violation of the due-process requirements of the Fourteenth Amendment for a state to engage in censorship of the press. The recent Talbott affair (in which the Secretary of the Air Force was, to put it bluntly, driven from office for a less than conscientious separation of his private from his public functions) demonstrates that the unfettered newspaper serves as the watchdog of public morality.

Although in this instance some irate Republicans recommended the *New York Times* to the Federal Bureau of Investigation as a security risk (and in earlier instances of a similar sort, furious Democrats similarly denounced the newspapers which put them on the spot), both Democrats and Republicans are fundamentally agreed on the value of the free press and on the proposition that any security system which made it possible for politicians and administrators to suppress information on their own activities would be a disaster to the open society. To the timeworn query *Who will guard the guardians?* the democrat replies, *The People,* and the free press is a key instrument in making this abstraction a concrete, politically meaningful process.

Although the section that follows may appear at first sight to be a digression from the topic, it seems to me that before one can discuss intelligently the problems that the free press presents to national security, it is necessary to have in mind a fairly concise definition of the goals of security. Moreover, the presentation of the needs of security is required background material for evaluating the need for restrictions on the press. If one accepts a broad definition of security requirements, he will feel that any information which gives aid and comfort to the enemy, for example, news of a lynching, of labor violence, or of bitter political differences, should be excised from the newspapers. On the other hand, if one accepts a narrow definition of security imperatives, he will assess the need for press censorship in a quite different fashion. In sum, the premises that one holds as to the nature of security determine to a large degree the conclusions he will reach on the adequacy of the present system.

The Goals of Security

Plunged as we have been into the nasty and somehow un-American atmosphere of *Weltpolitik* after a century and a half of complacent security behind our oceans, it is not surprising that Americans have had difficulty in creating a viable security program. The initial reaction of anyone faced suddenly with a security crisis is to yield to the counsels of hypercaution, to slap on rigorous internal security regulations, and, whenever confronted with a choice between potentially risky freedom and safe restriction, to come down on the side of restriction. The latter is, I think, a fair appraisal of what we have done in certain areas, notably government employment and scientific communication.

But it is greatly to the credit of the American people and their leaders that so few demands have been made for full-scale censorship of the press and related organs of mass communication. In part, this restraint may have a foundation in fear (few politicians are willing to risk the unanimous newspaper opposition that would accompany any censorship proposals), but it is also a consequence of the respect and attachment that our political leaders have for the abstraction "freedom of the press."

Some would maintain that this laissez-faire approach to the press is anachronistic, that security demands more. Before we can reply to this criticism, we must determine the proper goals of the security program in the information area. In making this assessment, it is vital that we distinguish between our emotional commitment to survival, which may well lead us to advocate any measure that might conceivably increase our life span, and our rational evaluation of the imperatives of security, which may lead to the conscious acceptance of calculated risks. Moreover, it must be emphasized that the fundamental end of a security system is security, not vengeance. It may be a soul-satisfying diversion to drive alleged subversives from the Fish and Wildlife Service or the Veterans Administration, or other nonsensitive employments, but in a realistic view such a safari contributes little to national security. Soviet intelligence would hardly rejoice over secret data on the Whooping Crane or G.I. insurance returns.

What we must attempt is the difficult task of disengagement from the imbroglios of the moment, trying to assume the cold impartiality of the historian who will, at some point in the future, chronicle our activities. Probably the first thing this historian would note about our security program is its emphasis on subversion and conspiracy. From his vantage point, it may appear that American security was not solely menaced by enemies of the regime. On the contrary, some of the most crucial information leaks were the responsibility of its friends, against whom a vengeance-oriented security system was useless.

To put it another way: in an impartial evaluation of threats to our security, the intent of the participants in the drama is irrelevant. An outstanding episode in support of this contention occurred in June, 1951. A representative of the Defense Department, testifying *in camera* and enjoining his auditors to the strictest secrecy, revealed to the Senate Armed Services Committee the exact number of B-36 intercontinental bombers that the Air Force then had in operation. This was a detail that Soviet intelligence would doubtless have paid a proletarian ransom to obtain, but it cost them only five cents. Some senator, with no reflection on the import of the figure, gave the reporters the full story, which was splashed on Page One of every newspaper in the nation within twenty-four hours. The story subsequently went around Washington that the Russians had fired all their agents in the United States and taken out an airmail subscription to the *New York Times*.

Yet no one questioned the loyalty—as distinct from the discretion and intelligence—of the culpable senator. Similarly, no one could question the loyalty of the Atomic Energy Commission, which published in full the hearings in the *Oppenheimer* case, although some authorities in the field of atomic physics assert that this document supplied any informed reader with information that had, up to that point, been kept under rigid security restrictions. Fortunately, there seems to be some evidence to suggest that the Russians, who can detect a conspiracy in the falling of a sparrow, consider such leaks as these to be a cunning maneuver on the part of American intelligence designed to mislead Soviet strategy. But, however limited the consequences of these revelations may be, it is clear that the protection of national security in the information field consists of far more than apprehending Soviet agents. As important, if not more important, is the plugging of inadvertent leaks by Americans of unimpeachable loyalty.

Another facet of the problem of security of information is the proper scope of restrictions. An inflexible program of rigid secrecy can work to the immense disadvantage of its employer, for it stifles the important process of communications between experts. Scientists working on one aspect of a program are forbidden to talk shop to scientists on related projects, and in recent years there have been authenticated instances of scientists who have been, allegedly on security grounds, barred from their own laboratories and forbidden to work on research they initiated.

The Defense Department in particular tends to go rigidly "by the book," even if the specific application of the rules works a stupid injustice. In part this is an attitude congenital in military professionals, but it is also partly a consequence of the head-hunting activities of congressional committees which have been out searching the country for "Communist-coddlers." If you "go by the book," you may cut the rate of progress in half, but you will never get in trouble for being "soft" on security.

In a different context, war correspondents have long complained about the overzealous application of the security rules by military censors. Often, journalists have been forbidden to publish information that was clearly in the hands of the enemy. For instance, in Korea, Air Force authorities forbade any release on the F-86 Sabre Jet's initial employment against the Chinese MIG's, although the latter were doubtless aware that a new plane was in the air against them. When the *New York Times* succeeded in getting its correspondent's story cleared by the Pentagon, Far East Air Force Headquarters demanded that the *Times* correspondent be banished from Korea for security violations. There can be no rational justification for this sort of censorship; it is founded solely on overcaution and bureaucratic imperialism.

On the basis of this analysis, I would suggest that a rational security program must be quite narrow in scope and purpose. Significant information should be kept from rival intelligence services, but the program should not be designed in such a fashion that a government agency could suppress any information that it considers important, nor should it be employed to suppress information that can not, by its nature, be kept secret. When everything is classified, nothing is secret! Thus the security classification should be reserved for those items that fulfill two prerequisites: (1) they are of vital importance; and (2) the possibility of secrecy exists. A matter may be of great importance, but—like the location of the Hanford plant of the A.E.C. or the bases of the Strategic Air Command—impossible to keep under wraps.

Furthermore, the administrators of the security program must be aware of the dangers of overclassification to the maintenance of a well-informed scientific and technical elite in the United States, and should be prepared to take calculated risks to keep open channels of communication and criticism. If an atomic scientist is forbidden to publish his research findings, another scientist cannot undertake a critique; yet this process of disputation has been the foundation of scientific progress, has been the point of departure for great leaps into the unknown. A society with total security would in all probability be a stagnant pool.

Security and the Press

Having set forth what I conceive to be the functions of a free press in a democratic society, and what I believe to be the proper scope and purpose of a security program, I shall attempt in this concluding section to put the pieces together and suggest the relevance of the security program to the press.

First, it seems to me both unwise and unnecessary to establish any large-scale program of press supervision; the system of self-censorship that worked so well in World War II seems to me to be adequate. American newspapermen and publishers are aware of their responsibilities, and in the unlikely event that some paper consistently refuses to abide by the security ground rules, existing criminal statutes could be invoked. Considered from the broad viewpoint of democratic political theory, a government censorship program would be more dangerous to our national security than a few information leaks could ever be.

Second, a special administrator should be appointed in the Executive Office of the President, whose job it would be to oversee the security-of-information decisions of the line agencies. Line agencies (the State Department, Defense Department, A.E.C., and so on) uniformly tend to exaggerate the importance and secrecy of their activities and to apply higher security standards than an informed outsider would consider justified by the facts. The appointment of such an administrator, who would have the authority to review and revise the decisions below, would provide a central focus and eliminate the confusion and anarchy that now exist. In addition, the line agencies, knowing that their decisions will be subject to review, would exercise considerably more care and discrimination than they now use; on the opposite side of the fence, journalistic playing off of one agency against another would be discouraged.

Third, the administrator, ideally a person with both governmental and journalistic experience, should prepare for the press a Code of Security Practices. This document would be similar in function to the Press Code which Byron Price, Director of the Office of Censorship, prepared in January, 1942, for the wartime guidance of the nation's editors. While purely advisory, this Code would give the journalist a good idea of what information should be handled with circumspection. In cases of doubt, editors could consult with the administrator before publishing, but the final decision on publication would rest with the newspapers.

It may seem naïve to some to advocate so passive an instrument of security protection in the era of fission and fusion. It must be freely admitted that this program is far from disaster-proof, and involves running great risks. But it must be noted that the operation of alternative systems, such as those employed by the Nazis or the Soviet Union, involves great dangers and liabilities. If we chance disaster by emphasizing freedom, they risk stagnation by demanding security. At root, democratic government is a calculated risk, and it is only fitting that, in the effort to survive as a nontotalitarian way of life, a democratic society should assume some calculated risks aimed at preserving precious traditions. A free press is sufficiently meaningful to make its continuation worth the gamble.

Sergeant McKeon and the
Cult of Violence

The court-martial is over, the obscure drill instructor sentenced, and Emile Zola Berman has temporarily vanished to ready the appeals that McKeon's supporters must file. But while peace and quiet have at last overtaken Parris Island, the evidence from the rest of the country suggests that the real issue of the McKeon trial has yet to be faced. The sentence itself is proof of this: obscenely mild if McKeon did kill six men, yet excessive if he were not at fault, if he were merely following the routine established by official policy.

Indeed, McKeon's individual qualities, or failings, long since lost their relevance to the *McKeon* case. The sergeant has lost his personality, has been dehumanized and converted into a symbol, and the real battle that is now going on in the pages of the newspapers, within the ranks of veterans' organizations, and other media, in no real way relates to this discrete atom of humanity named McKeon—the matter at issue is the status in American mythology of the United States Marine Corps.

From a military viewpoint, it has become increasingly difficult in recent years to justify the existence of the Marines. Originally devised by the British to protect H.M. officers from H.M. mutinous crews, and later used by all major naval powers as professional amphibious soldiers, it is hard today to find any military function that the Marines can call their own. Establishing beachheads was once their specialty, but—contrary to public opinion at the time—the great bulk of Pacific invasions were run by the

Reprinted, with permission, from *The New Republic*, August 27, 1956.

Army, which, as the wry joke went, neglected to assign a photographer to each rifle platoon. By the time of Okinawa, Marine divisions were being employed in a fashion in no way different from those of the Army.

The Marine reply to this would probably be that what sets apart the Marine Corps is "not what it does, but the way that it does it." This is undeniably correct, and brings up squarely to the meaning of the *McKeon* case *on the symbolic level.* For what has distinguished the Marine Corps is its emphasis on raw courage and absolute obedience to orders. The real function of its training program is to perform an ego-ectomy on each recruit which will transform him from an individual in uniform to a perfectly meshed gear in a military machine. I doubt if the recruits I took Army basic training with in World War II would simply and without argument or complaint have marched off into the swamps on a Sunday night—certainly not on the verbal orders of a noncom.

This difference in *Weltanschauung* between the Army and the Marines came out in many practical ways during hostilities. To the Marine platoon leader, life, including his own, was expendable, and the quickest way to take an enemy strong point was to storm it. An Army platoon leader, usually a civilian in uniform, tended to take a dim view of compulsive heroism. He was quite prepared to be brave, but faced with the same problem, he would probably relax a bit and send for the mortar. Why get killed to save half an hour? Whenever the Army and the Marines worked together in combined operations, these two ways of military life collided—a famous instance was the shaming of the 27th Division and its General Smith by Marine General "Howling Mad" Smith at Saipan.

I am not depreciating physical courage. What I am suggesting is that stark bravery of this sort is an uncivilian characteristic and functionally out of place in a civilian defense establishment. It would be *politically* impossible for the Army, however much it might desire to do so, to train draftees in the Marine fashion. In fact, given the parents-to-congressmen-to-Pentagon pressure complex, it is sometimes surprising that the Army manages to maintain any discipline at all. The nub of the matter is that the draftee does not give up civilian status when he climbs into his uniform and, more significantly, seldom stops thinking of himself as an individual with an individualized set of aspirations. As experience in two world wars and Korea demonstrates, he can be a peerless soldier, but his performance is always, at least to some extent, delivered on his own terms. British soldiers fighting alongside Americans often expected full-scale mutinies to take place, so bitter was the back talk and so casual the respect for rank. What they failed to realize was that this freewheeling was a symbolic affirmation of American democracy, and was so understood by able officers and noncoms.

The Marine Corps, however, is in a different world. It is not as much a separate service as it is a mystique—a mystique built around the cult of violence. From the day he arrives and takes the oath, the Marine volunteer is violently stripped of his civilian characteristics—including most of his hair. He is absolutely under the authority of noncoms who can employ physical coercion on his person and whose power is as unquestioned as that of Calvin's God. His civilian personality is destroyed.

It will be remembered that one of the charges against McKeon's platoon was that its members were sitting around the barracks on Sunday smoking cigarettes and chatting. For this a fellow drill instructor chided the sergeant—one can almost hear his words: "Well, Mac, when is your platoon joining the Marines?" or some such taunt—and McKeon, angry, went back to have another try at decivilianizing his boots.

Thus the fundamental struggle of the *McKeon* case has been between the military standards of the civilian world and the radical, violent mores of the Marine Corps. By Marine standards, McKeon may have been inefficient, but he was certainly not being too tough. If anything, the fact that he lost six men was proof that he hadn't been tough enough, for if the platoon had been tightly disciplined, the men would have marched in Indian file with each boot keeping track of his neighbors, and the minute one lost position, the alarm would have been sounded. In short, McKeon's sin in the eyes of his superiors was not that he lost six men—men are expendable—but that he did so in a thoroughly unshipshape fashion. This was patently, though covertly, the rationale of the court-marital sentence.

The public reaction to the case has been fascinating to follow. The initial response was almost universally one of horror and anger: Congress swept into action, the commanding general of the Corps emitted guilty pleas for time to clean things up, and the press fulminated. Then, with the staging of the court-martial, the tone began to change—partly because of the superb defense tactics of Berman and partly for the simple reason that the heat was letting up—and the Marines launched their counteroffensive against the civilians. In a sentence, their position is "Hands off the Marines," and today it begins to appear that McKeon may end up scot-free, if not the recipient of a medal.

In short, the Marine Corps has survived the most serious challenge to its existence in many years, a challenge which threatened for a while to end its mystical status and simply make it another branch of the civilian-defense establishment. Why did it survive? The answer is hard to ascertain, if there is one answer, but my hunch is that the best explanation lies on the level of myth in the collective subconscious of the American people. To a nation profoundly civilian in its ideals, violence is a forbidden fruit, with all the ambivalence that this entails. The Marine Corps has over a period of time become a projection of the civilian hero wish, of the secret desire that most men have to exhibit bravery, to purge themselves of selfishness, and live in a world from which bourgeois virtues have been exorcised.

Yet, reason—that supreme civilian virtue—asserts itself, and prevents any substantial institutionalization of violence. But perhaps to assuage the inner call to heroism, a segment of American life is excluded from this ban and permitted to adhere to the code of violence. A typical bourgeois compromise ensures that this sector will not be large and will be peopled by volunteers, but the other side of this same coin ensures that this primordial enclave in American society will be defended. One can rest assured that the Army will never adopt Marine mores, but one can also be confident that the Marines will not be "civilized" or destroyed.

Semper Precocious:
A Review of
The Last Parallel
by Martin Russ

When some months ago I suggested in the pages of this journal that the United States Marine Corps was distinguished from the other branches of the Armed Forces largely by its ideology, its "cult of violence," the wrath of ex-leathernecks cascaded upon my head. However, I now find my analysis richly substantiated by the Korean memoirs of Sergeant Martin Russ, and I trust that the ire of Marine Corps public relations has now shifted to the Book of the Month Club, Rinehart, and Russ.

This is a tough book to tackle, for Russ was clearly an inauthentic Marine and was equally clearly aware of his inauthenticity. "Real" Marines don't keep diaries in which they muse on the cosmos: first of all, it is bad security, and, second, it wastes time that could be put to better use sleeping and oiling the BAR's. Thus there is a disembodied quality about these war memoirs— Russ the bohemian intellectual watches with analytical interest the doings of Russ the expert killer. Obviously Sergeant Russ was a very good and very brave Marine, but Intellectual Russ simply can't settle for *that* old-fashioned view, and has to keep passing blasé wisecracks to prove that he knows that bravery is really just an act.

Thus we get such precocious schmaltz as this, ruining what is otherwise first-rate prose:

The lieutenant pointed out our [patrol] route through the aperture, a very practical way to conduct a briefing. We were allowed to study the terrain through field glasses. When I came in he smiled and said,

Reprinted, with permission, from *The New Republic*, April 8, 1957.

"I wondered if you were going to come along." (Watch that stuff, sir. Throw away that Symposium before it's too late, man.) Later we were . . .

Again discussing his diary, Russ unloads another real cute stream of consciousness:

when I get home, there'll be no hurry; I'll be able to sit down at a warm desk . . . and insert some grace into this jumble of words. (Oh, don't be falsely modest, my boy. You are aware that there is a possibility of your getting killed, and you're writing this the best you know how. Isn't that so?—There is not the slightest possibility of my getting killed. However, I am writing this the best I know how.— Well, we'll have to do a little better than this, won't we?)

These inane parenthetical musings recur throughout the book, and the odd part of it is that I am convinced that Russ was aware of their inanity, but insisted on including them as stigmata of intellectuality, as proof that he didn't take himself seriously. Russ's Main Line of Resistance seems to be an almost existential conviction that the universe is a vast practical joke and that anyone who takes ideals seriously is being taken for a ride. The mark of the wise man consequently becomes his recognition that all the noble sentiments are fake and his nervous embarrassment when he finds them in his own character.

Another aspect of Russ's inauthenticity is his fondness for the *really* titillating four-letter words. This I find shocking, though for aesthetic rather than moral reasons—I have heard the words before. Men at war, like truckdrivers and members of other masculine callings, develop a colloquial patter of incredible obscenity—except that in this context the words are divested of their obscene connotations and become in effect meaningless exclamations. Now, to transcribe these phrases directly for civilian consumption is, I suggest, to do a bad job of translation, for in civilian circles they really are obscene. Indeed, the most realistic transliteration of military language that I recall was in a movie where—for reasons of censorship, and therefore accidentally, I'm sure—one of the soldiers used "rotting" as every second word: "Holy rotting Moses, the lousy rotting Sarge made me take that stinking rotting tent." By aesthetic standards, this was brilliant reproduction of the original meaninglessness of the obscene litany.

However, when these criticism have been registered, *The Last Parallel* still remains as a gripping account of the dirty "little" Korean War. Russ has real talent for graphic description, and if he can divest himself of his self-conscious veneer of cynical precocity, I suspect he will become a fine writer.

The Pasternak Award

SIRS:

It has been some time since I read such a farrago of bad logic and absurd judgments as Massingham's *Communication* on the *Pasternak* case. (*NR*, December 15th). If I may summarize Massingham's arguments, he first accuses the West of making Pasternak a "victim of the Cold War," next equates the Nobel Prize with the Stalin Prize, continues by noting that the award strengthened the hand of the reactionary wing of Soviet literary commissars, and concludes by casually suggesting that *Dr. Zhivago* is not much of a novel and hardly justifies the award.

Let us examine these points in turn:

First, the view that the West, acting through its agents on the Nobel selection committee, victimized Pasternak rests on an assumption about the function of the committee which Massingham never exposes, one which would make these worthy Swedes into combinations of international social workers and combat intelligence officers. Instead of awarding the prize for seeming literary merit, Massingham implies that the committee should investigate the possible political consequences of an award and avoid any benefactions which might get the recipients into trouble. Presumably, after a security clearance, a safe candidate would be named. Perhaps the process could be simplified by obtaining from each nation a list of those writers who would not be persecuted if designated Nobel laureates?

Moreover, to follow up the "perfect" analogy of Walter Lipp-

Reprinted, with permission, from *The New Republic*, December 29, 1958.

mann and the Stalin Prize which Massingham seems to consider a real crusher, is it appropriate for the Nobel committee to get a crystal ball and try to estimate whether the "good" or the "bad" political forces in a nation will be strengthened by an award? Even the most highly trained Marxicologists of my acquaintance have never been notably successful at this game, but the important thing is that the game itself is irrelevant; the award is for literary accomplishment, not for supporting "objectively progressive historical forces." The Russians, not the Nobel committee, have victimized Pasternak.

Second, to equate Nobel and Stalin prizes is to assume precisely the matter that must be demonstrated, namely, that both the West and the Soviets agree that art is a weapon and that the Nobel prizes are stockpiled in the Western Cold War arsenal. The fact that the Soviet scientists accepted their loot without official repercussions makes this view even more complex, for it requires a Talmudic differentiation between the political realm of literature and the nonpolitical realm of science. Or perhaps one can take the more vulgar explanation that Soviet scientists are permitted to roll capitalist drunks, while authors are held to a higher ethical standard?

Yet even on its own terms Massingham's equation does not hold up. Howard Fast and other Americans who have received Stalin Prizes have characteristically welcomed the distinction and accepted it as an honor; we have been exposed to some degrading instances of political persecution in recent American history, but nothing to match the tragedy of poor Pasternak asking mercy from an officially constituted lynch mob. Howard Fast's recantation came from the urgings of conscience, not from the pressure of the FBI or the American Legion.

Third, the suggestion that the award aided Mr. Surkov, "a fanatical Communist and the head of the Soviet Writers Union," and will probably destroy Pasternak's reputation within Russia injects a further refinement in Massingham's position. Now, in addition to worrying about "good" and "bad" political forces, the Nobel committee is supposed to anticipate both internal reactions in the Soviet Writers Union and the future state of Russian public opinion. Plato would not have demanded these qualifications from his guardians. Once again Massingham, who obviously shares the opinion that the award was "political," leads the chase away from the key point: that the award was prima facie for literary merit and that *no evidence has been adduced to the contrary*. He has taken the vigorous Soviet opposition to Pasternak's honor as proof that the prize was given for political purposes— a logical process on all fours with the arrest of a speaker for incitement to violence on the ground that hearers violently objected to his speech.

Finally, perhaps realizing that there is something missing from the logical structure of his argument, Massingham delivers the K.O.: Pasternak is not a first-rate author, so the award was patently not for literary merit. I have not read *Dr. Zhivago* and can enter no opinion whatsoever on the merits, but I can inquire when Massingham became an authority on the contemporary novel. Presumably the Swedish committee was composed of knowledgeable people, and knowledgeable critics in this country have endorsed its judgment with virtual unanimity, but with a wave of his wand Massingham banishes the whole lot of them to literary limbo. This is not to accept the bulk of critical opinion as necessarily infallible, nor do I believe that the Nobel committee speaks with the authority of God, but I am also convinced that some opinions are better than others because their authors have earned the right to be taken seriously.

Can Kennedy Set Them Afire?

If Kennedy is going to win—and he knows this—he must carry New York, California, Pennsylvania, Illinois—the big urban states —and yet to date in these crucial areas one finds a shortage of enthusiasm for the Democratic ticket. True, there are plenty of committees (equipped with exemplary handbooks), but one gets the impression that the members are busy converting one another and working out fine matters of protocol: Whose name goes *first* on the letterhead?

The prizes to be won in these urban commonwealths are obvious: the votes of the minorities and the independent voters of liberal persuasion. The Negroes, for example, have arrived at that level of political consciousness where they are one-issue bargainers. Consequently, the more time Kennedy spends, say, in Texas, the more Negro suspicion develops. Among still unsettled and uncertain Jewish voters, a significant residue of anti-Catholicism can be found: a historical-minded people refuses to forget the medieval ghetto, the savagery of medieval Christendom. This atavistic chord is reinforced by suspicion of Kennedy's reaction to McCarthyism. Obviously, those Jews who are disturbed by the McCarthy theme are not going to vote for Nixon, but on the other hand they are not going to hit the bricks for Kennedy; they are not going to bring out the halt and the lame to vote as they did for F.D.R.

Now, John Kennedy can hardly be blamed for not being F.D.R., but if the senator is going to win an uphill fight against

Reprinted, with permission, from *The New Republic*, September 26, 1960.

the toughest professional of our time (how brilliantly Nixon has adjusted his form to the current Era of Good Manners!), he has got to get up a head of steam in the great urban states. By A.D.A. or *The New Republic* or A.F.L.-C.I.O. standards, Kennedy has a superb voting record. He has every right to raise the standard of liberalism, but so far he has felt compelled to spend most of his time trying to convince people who will probably vote against him anyway that he won't cede the United States to the Holy See.

Although I personally agree with [your commentator] TRB that Stevenson is far more conservative than Kennedy, the senator has clearly suffered in the eyes of some Democrats in these critical urban areas from the contrast with Adlai. Stevenson, that urbane, witty, slightly dilettante figure, was the paradigm of what an intellectual would like a politician to be. One often had the feeling when watching Stevenson speak that one-half of Adlai was clinically observing the other half being a politician; Kennedy, on the other hand, is totally immersed in winning whatever battle is before him. Stevenson strikes one as Greek, with all the *déraciné* charm that this implies; Kennedy is a Roman, and Romans never have been particularly popular with intellectuals, who are always unsettled by people who play for keeps.

Unfortunately, events this summer have strengthened a potentially disastrous public image. The impression a random viewer got of the Democratic Convention on TV was one of gears clicking, wheels whirring, and lights flashing: a triumph of cold, heartless manipulators over sincere, bleeding human beings. This was vastly exaggerated, an image presented largely, I think, by the TV and newspapermen who overplayed and dramatized the strength of the Stevenson forces. But when Goliath floored David, the watching public left with a vague conviction that it had witnessed the Wrong Ending, that ruthless might had crushed righteousness. This sense of injustice was, of course, reinforced by the wild wailing of the Stevenson revivalists in total control of the balconies. Robert Kennedy contributed throughout to this wretched image by acting like a poker player with four aces.

Actually, Senator Kennedy, as he demonstrated in his extemporaneous demolition of Senator Johnson before the Texas delegation, is extremely fast on his feet. His coming TV confrontations with Nixon offer one of his chances, perhaps, to cut loose from the elaborate apparatus he has built and to strike out as a man. Every candidate needs research assistance, speech writers, "idea men," and good line organization, but a candidate who gives the impression that he is tied to a Thinking Machine is unlikely to build up much empathy among the population. No one ever voted for a Thinking Machine (note that Richard Nixon memorized his acceptance speech so he could talk largely without notes, "simply, humbly from the heart"). Moreover, Thinking Machines cost money, and Senator Kennedy cannot afford to overlook the nostalgic anticapitalism of the average man.

In short, Senator Kennedy should unmechanize his campaign and continue the effort he has begun to discuss serious issues informally and frankly. This cannot be done ritualistically, nor can it be handled by the staff. Jewish liberals in New York who are troubled by Kennedy's record of silence on McCarthy cannot be wrapped up and delivered by activating the Liberal Party; Stevenson's following will not be energized by burning a candle at Hyde Park; Negro leaders worried about Lyndon Johnson will not be appeased by an advisory council of eminent Negroes. A human being named John F. Kennedy has got to make clear to them that *he* is the man they can trust, that *he* cares, and shares their dreams.

The Image of Freedom

For the eight years of the Eisenhower administration, the United States abandoned flexibility in foreign policy for "moral" and military rigidity; eschewing our capacities for maneuver, we took refuge behind "massive retaliation." In a sense, we perfected the tactic for dealing with Stalin just as Stalin died. A contest between Secretary of State John Foster Dulles and Stalin would indeed have been a study in rigidity, but instead of Stalin, we suddenly found ourselves dealing with a masterful opportunist, a man cut from true Leninist cloth: Nikita Khrushchev.

While Dulles and the Joint Chiefs of Staff (with the Army Chief a bitter minority of one) repeated the litany of "containment" and invoked the Big Bomb, Khrushchev began an uncontested war of maneuver. The Soviet leader's logic was simple and compelling: with the Big Bombs neutralizing each other, it was safe to play at small conflicts. The Americans, he correctly reasoned, were not prepared to loose hydrogen bombs on Moscow to save Laos—any more than he would be ready to bomb New York to save Castro.

When the Kennedy administration took office, it was confronted by a dismal picture. A set of alliances—NATO, SEATO, the Baghdad Pact (minus Baghdad)—committed the United States to fight under circumstances which Khrushchev would never be stupid enough to fulfill, while our country was ideologically and militarily unprepared to wage the kind of warfare in which Khrushchev specializes. And everywhere in the world that Presi-

Reprinted, with permission, from *Hadassah Magazine*, April, 1961.

dent Kennedy and his advisers looked, they discovered evidences of Khrushchev's disruptive skill, of his brilliant flexibility and opportunism.

My concern here is with one important aspect of American-Soviet competition: the so-called struggle for the allegiance of the uncommitted nations. The new administration is girding itself to launch a "democratic counteroffensive"; we are at last going to take up the Soviet challenge. Before we rush into battle in the "war of ideas," however, it is essential that we examine carefully the tactics of the opposition. In particular, we must avoid exaggerating the ideological aspects of Soviet activity, and of underrating the degree to which the nationalists of Asia, Africa, and Latin America are in fact *committed* to a cause of their own.

To put it differently, we must engage in realistic, long-range "target analysis." There will be no quick victories or easy accomplishments, and to the degree that we expect them or demand them we shall frustrate intelligent foresight. It is probable, in fact, that things will get worse before they get better. One can even doubt the success of the Peace Corps on this ground, for the initial reaction in many places to these dedicated, ebullient young Americans may well be one of annoyance and envy. If, in the great American tradition, we demand a "fast payoff," the Peace Corps will be a disappointment. Yet it is difficult to recall any proposal with greater potentialities for long-run accomplishment on the level of international understanding. With this counsel of caution in mind, let us turn to an examination of contemporary nationalism, Soviet policy toward it, and the fundamentals of an American attitude in this crucial sector of world politics.

The first mistake we often make is implicit in the term "uncommitted nations." While it may be true that a new nation has refused to ally itself with either the United States or the Soviet Union, this in no sense means that it lacks ideals or an ideology. The leaders of the new African states, for example, are not ingenuous primitives shopping around for a political theory. They have one in nationalism—probably the most highly charged ideology the world has known. In other words, these nationalists known exactly *what* they want—power—and approach other nations with a narrowly utilitarian viewpoint: "What can you do for us?"

Last summer I spent five weeks in Israel at the time the American presidential campaign was shaping up. Everywhere, once the political discussion got under way, I was asked the same question: "Is Nixon or Kennedy better for Israel?" The Herutniks seemed to support Nixon, the Mapainiks, Kennedy; but neither group expressed the slightest interest in most American problems. Their total focus was naturally on Israel's national interest. An American friend complained to me about this myopia, and I suggested to him that he take a look at the history of American foreign policy from 1790 to 1815. Throughout this quarter-century our Presidents and Secretaries of State maneuvered against the background of British-French hostilities in the effort to maximize American rewards.

Nationalist movements are always self-centered, myopic, and full of overweening pride. They also have a heavy dose of irrationality about them: every new nation as it emerges from the chrysalis of time believes that it is a "chosen people," that it has a mission and a gift of invincibility. The old rules no longer apply; the law has been transcended.

Moreover, the most recent crop of nationalists always has a complaint against history—a historical inferiority complex, as it were—which leads to infuriating characteristics. Again let me illustrate from my own experience. A year or so ago I was seated next to a Ghanaian intellectual at an international function. He was an extraordinarily bright young man who obviously nursed a massive grudge against the United States. His anti-American tirade was so irrational I could not avoid dispute.

After some lengthy remarks on the evils of American colonialism, the Ghanaian student brought out his bedrock grievance: slavery and the slave trade. I pointed out that the slave trade had been banned by federal law in 1808, and that nearly half a million men had died fighting to extirpate human slavery; but he insisted that we must admit our "historical guilt." I was quite prepared to admit "historical guilt," but I could not resist the temptation to point out that the Ghanaians, as I understand it, share this guilt—they are descended from the dealers who sold the slaves for the middle-passage. Angrily, he accused me of being a white supremacist, and I contained my own annoyance only by realizing that to a nineteenth century British internationalist, the average American intellectual must have seemed just as irrational and chauvinistic as this young man seemed to me. Nationalists are never humble.

We must begin our policy toward these new nationalist regimes with the assumption that they are wholly dedicated to their own interests. During World War I, Prime Minister David Lloyd George once went to Wales to forestall a miners' strike, and concluded a vigorous, patriotic speech with the question, "Do you want to work for the Kaiser?" From the back came a voice—"And how much an hour does the Kaiser pay?" In a different context, this is the key problem: what the nationalists want to know is how much will we, or the Soviets, pay. They still think in terms of old-style manipulation, though the world has changed considerably.

This is no longer the era of James Madison, when distance supplied insulation; and the Communists are not old-fashioned patrons—they play for keeps. Once within the Soviet orbit, there is no return to a neutral bargaining position; the acceptance of Soviet hegemony is a one-way proposition. But nationalists always think they are invincible, and much cleverer than the patrons they are engaged in manipulating.

From our point of view, the Congo or Cuba may be faced with the choice between Democracy and Communism. But this is not the way the "uncommitted" nations see it. Soviet success has to a considerable degree been founded on a deliberate downplaying of ideological issues. Just as Lenin took power on the back of a peasantry aroused by the opportunist slogan of "Peace, Bread, and Land," the Soviets today appeal to the new nations with a potent message of anticolonialism and industrialization. Their emissaries in Africa and Latin America are not pushing copies of *The Communist Manifesto;* they are distributing to eager nationalists studies of economic growth in the U.S.S.R. and other "Socialist countries."

The essence of Khrushchev's statements to the nationalists is, first, that the Soviet Union will protect them from the revenge of the colonial powers. This accounts in my view for the Soviet fury over the murder of Lumumba—he was no Communist, but he was under their "protection." Ironically, the Soviet Union, the world's leading colonial power, has been absolved from the curse of imperialism. Almost by definition Asians and Africans regard imperialism as exploitations of nonwhite populations; as Nehru's rather mild reaction to the suppression of the 1956 Hungarian Revolution indicated, they are not really disturbed when white men exploit other white men—that is a private fight among outsiders.

Second, the Soviets offer to the new nations truly "disinterested" economic assistance (the Czechoslovaks can always be counted on to supply military equipment). The genius of Russian foreign policy in the past five or six years has been based on the Soviets' ability to pose as the protectors of new nations in the struggle against colonialism while simultaneously offering eager nationalists the vision of rapid industrialization under Soviet auspices. When warned about the long-term menace of Soviet infiltration, the nationalists invariably reply that such a threat will not exist in their case—they are too well organized, too dedicated, too shrewd to get mousetrapped. After all, the argument runs, Egypt's Nasser is getting Soviet aid for his Aswan Dam, and he has his Communists in jail.

In sum, the Soviet Union's assault in the underdeveloped nations of the world is not overtly ideological. The U.S.S.R. is not indoctrinating Marxism in any explicit sense, but rather is operating with a brilliant combination of protection and patronage. Of course, on the ground level the Communists are moving in, yet their leverage is not based on "historical materialism," but on Soviet assistance; they are the local agents of the great foreign patron. In the same way that the Communists infiltrated the Spanish Republic after it was deserted by the West in the late 1930's, so are they today moving into positions of power in Cuba.

And where does the United States stand in all this? What is our policy? To a large extent, we have been trapped by our European friends, particularly our NATO allies. They have hung the albatross of colonialism around our neck, and in fact

American equipment buttresses the French army in Algeria and the Portuguese forces in Africa. Algeria has been in revolt for seven years, and it is likely that the next explosion in Africa will occur in the Portuguese colonies. Out of loyalty to an insignificant ally, John Foster Dulles went so far as to justify Portuguese control of Goa, a city in India which has been under Portuguese rule since the fifteenth century and which the Indians want back. The utter folly of supporting the Portuguese against the Indians —the one great hope of a democratic future in South Asia—can be understood only in terms of the European hypnosis which dominated the State Department during the Eisenhower-Dulles years.

Our first task is to escape from this cul de sac and to assert our rightful heritage as spokesmen for freedom and self-determination. As long as the U.S.S.R. preempts world leadership in the "struggle against colonialism," and we meekly defer to the demands of our European allies, we can expect Castros, Lumumbas, and Gizengas. American support of last month's United Nations resolution, sponsored by Liberia, Ceylon, and the United Arab Republic urging reforms in the Portuguese colony of Angola, was a first step toward reestablishing United States leadership in the world struggle for freedom. Under the Eisenhower administration, the United States usually abstained on such motions, thus alienating many of the new nations. But President Kennedy has realistically decided, as he put it in a campaign speech last October, "to ally ourselves with the rising tide of nationalism . . . the most powerful force in the modern world."

The real threat of Communism in Asia, Africa, and Latin America is organizational rather than ideological. If we are to devise a policy which can effectively counter this opportunistic expansion, we must tackle with Russians on their own grounds with great patience and flexibility. This will call for self-restraint, and a certain sense of historical compassion. Many generous American Zionists have, for example, been hurt by the casual Israeli reaction to their beneficence, though under the circumstances it is inevitable. Similarly in Africa, Asia, and Latin America we must anticipate envy and even a certain amount of hatred —nobody but a saint really loves a benefactor.

What we have to make clear is our primary devotion to freedom. We must demonstrate that we are not seeking to establish a world dedicated to capitalism and color television, but rather one in which human beings of all antecedents will have the prerogative of choosing their own futures. In every possible way we must help the new nations to achieve decent living standards. Then, after we have established, as it were, our right to speak for the free society, we can engage in the "war of ideas." And once this has been accomplished, I doubt that "Marxism" will be nearly as formidable an opponent as we, in our uncertainty, often imagine. The ideals of freedom, as history affirms, have a compelling appeal to all men, but we must earn the right to speak on their behalf.

Confessions of an Interventionist

It is distressing to note the way some respected liberal and Socialist figures have reacted to the Cuban debacle. Norman Thomas, for example, circulated an elaborate statement, the gist of which was, first, that the Central Intelligence Agency (CIA) support for Batista elements was immoral; second, that American support for anybody in these circumstances would risk world war; and, third, that we have only ourselves, and our foolish past policies in Latin America, to blame anyhow, since Fidel Castro was virtually our creation.

It is hardly necessary here to note my respect and admiration for Norman Thomas, but in reading this statement I had the curious feeling that I had been here before. And, in fact, I have: the first time I heard Norman Thomas speak was in 1939, and the substance of his speech was that collective security was "collective suicide." I was completely convinced of the correctness of this position, and until Pearl Harbor I was a dogged activist in the "Keep America Out of War Congress" youth movement.

I have never had much truck with confession, and I know that I can no more "repudiate" my past than I can cut off my arm. The years in the "Youth Committee Against War" are part of that past. But I have since become convinced of the fundamentally wrongheaded character of the nonintervention position in 1939–1941, and I deplore the contemporary revival of what can only be called "liberal isolationism." Nuclear devastation terrifies

Reprinted, with permission, from *The New Leader*, May 15, 1961.

me as much as anyone else; yet, in realistic terms, to run away from risks is not to eliminate them. On the contrary, it may well exacerbate the dangers.

Let me make it perfectly clear that in my mind the CIA operation in Cuba was a piece of immoral folly. But it was not immoral because it was intervention, but because it was folly: The character of the intervention was such as seriously to compromise our democratic integrity. The CIA's addiction to right-wing anti-Communism put us in a hopeless position in the eyes of our democratic allies, while providing the Soviet Union with a superb propaganda motif. The operation could not have worked out better for the USSR had it been executed by Soviet agents.

Moreover, the *new* Cuban situation, the result of the CIA's abortive scheme, calls for enormous prudence and self-restraint on the part of the United States. At this point, it seems to me that we have to write off our liabilities, put logic in irons, and realize that if the USSR can afford Yugoslavia, Turkey, and Iran, we can afford a Communist Cuba.

In short, a moratorium on Cuba seems to me in order. But this is a very different thing from asserting that American intervention in general is bad. The liberal, social democratic tradition is one which makes intervention in the internal affairs of all dictatorships obligatory. It postulates the absolute value of certain fundamental principles, and combats every attempt to destroy them.

As Sidney Hook has often pointed out, we cannot employ a double standard. We must be willing to "intervene" in the domestic affairs of all unjust regimes, whether they be dominated by Communists, Fascists, or nonideological gangsters like Rafael Leonidas Trujillo. The liberal must assert the same moral position in all areas of the world; in the same way that he fights white supremacy in the American South, he must combat it in South Africa.

As one who grew up with the slogan "Keep Out of War"—that is, "Hands Off Nazi Germany"—on his lips, I cannot accept a policy of "Hands Off Cuba" except on prudential grounds. We must be prepared to take action of one sort or another to help realize our dream of freedom in this unhappy bipolar world.

To suggest, as Norman Thomas and others have, that Castro is our creation seems to me irrelevant on the level of principle— as irrelevant as the alleged injustices of Versailles were to the evils of Nazi Germany.

The brutal fact is that, however historically occasioned, our allies in vast areas of the world are suffering and dying for our common principles. For us, of all people, to write them off to the enemy because we dare not joggle the balance of terror would be an act of moral cowardice. Such a policy would inexcusably lead to a liberal version of "Fortress America," in which we would stand paralyzed and transfixed because any action we take in the world might lead to devastation. A similar policy of ideological paralysis in the 1930's contributed to the murder of six million Jews and millions of others.

Our moral obligation to help our allies must, of course, be tempered by counsels of prudence. While we should not allow our obsessional fears of annihilation to freeze us in a posture of impotent immobility, we must take every possible step to avoid war. The key to the United States failure in the past eight years was the enshrinement of immobility as our national policy: "Massive retaliation," John Foster Dulles's version of the Maginot Line, served as a substitute for any flexible tactics of a limited character. Actuated by a profound pessimism about the future of the West, we took refuge behind the Big Bomb.

However badly the Cuban expedition may have been botched, it did mark an emergence from this chrysalis of pessimism, an effort to introduce flexibility into our world policy. President Kennedy is not one to make the same mistake twice, nor is he one to panic in a crisis. The Cuban affair was a beginning of the effort to compete with the Soviet Union on the level of ideological operations; it failed because the CIA is an inadequate tool of liberal policy.

The liberal effort thus should be concentrated on devising appropriate and effective means of intervention, not to attacks on the principle of intervention. There should certainly be no moratorium on criticism of the CIA or the President: Kennedy should be encouraged, pressed, and harassed until this *imperium in imperio* is brought to heel. To argue that we should not "rock the boat" is absurd; unless significant changes are made, it could well be the equivalent of "Don't rock the hearse."

To adopt the policy of "liberal isolationism" may provide a tempting escape from the perils of commitment, but it is a betrayal of the deepest values of liberal civilization. There is really no such thing as "nonintervention"; the very existence of a free society is a form of intervention in the internal affairs of dictatorships. In *Arrival and Departure* Arthur Koestler evoked a dream sequence reminiscent of Kafka: A man, brought before a judge and jury in his own likeness, claims that he "never killed a fly," and the remorseless prosecution replies, "Yes, and the flies he didn't kill brought pestilence to a province."

For liberals to stand silent and frozen in the face of injustice is to reject the obligations of their values; it is also a form of intervention in behalf of immobility at a time when we must move. It is our task to help formulate and implement a viable liberal policy which will give the ideals of freedom and justice a chance to win the day without disaster. Our dreams may turn to radioactive ashes, but we must have the "nerve of failure," the dedication to try, even though we have no guarantee of success or survival. To flee from all risk is to elect moral bankruptcy.

Further Thoughts on Intervention

For roughly two weeks, I have been visiting the Instituto de Educación Política on the outskirts of San José, Costa Rica. A unique experiment in democratic political education, the institute is sponsored by sixteen Latin American movements, ranging from powerful government parties such as the Acción Democrática of Venezuela and the Movimiento Nacionalista Revolucionario of Bolivia, to strong opposition groups such as the Partido del Pueblo (APRA) of Peru and the struggling exile movements from the Dominican Republic and Paraguay. Participants from all these groups come to San José for an arduous course in cadre training: intelligent and dedicated, but unsophisticated, party militants are put through a three-month educational wringer which squeezes out ideological water and leaves a firm programmatic foundation for party organization.

Democratic parties in Latin America have traditionally run long on ideological abstractions—"land reform," "economic development," "national integrity"—but short on concrete proposals for implementing these ambiguous goals. At the institute the members of these parties are exposed to a highly qualified faculty (drawn, with only one exception, from Latin America) which forces them to look specifically at the content of their own ideology. For example, Professor Edmundo Flores, the Mexican economist who supervised the technical aspects of Bolivia's land reform roughly a decade ago, lectured on the complexities of

Reprinted, with permission, from *The New Leader*, June 19, 1961.

agrarian political economy. (At one point the students, most of whom know the United States *sub nomine* the United Fruit Company, were rather startled by Flores's praise of General Douglas MacArthur's Japanese land-reform program as an excellent model for certain agricultural nations.)

But this is not the place to discuss the institute in detail. What I want to emphasize here is the attitude of the students, and to some degree of the faculty, toward the United States. In the first place, for most of them, the United States might as well be located in Central Asia—they know virtually nothing about our democratic society and less than nothing about our political institutions. When I explained to them that the United Fruit Company, the bête noire of Central America, could not carry a precinct in its native Boston, they were simply incredulous. Indeed, an American political scientist has the eerie feeling when talking to these fine democrats that they have received their knowledge of the United States from C. Wright Mills. This would be comic under different circumstances, but in this context it has overtones of tragedy.

To a man, the students were militantly anti-Communist and anti-Fidelist; with equal unanimity they despised the dictatorships in Nicaragua, Paraguay, and the Dominican Republic. (A student from the last class at the institute is in Luis Somoza's jail as the "ideological instigator" of an uprising in Nicaragua that occurred when he was in San José. On pragmatic grounds, the charge must be false: no student at the institute has time enough from his studies to instigate anything!) But from their point of view, the United States has to earn the right to speak for freedom. In Latin America, the United States carries the burden of history, and no fine statements from President Kennedy or Secretary of State Dean Rusk can exorcise the shades of imperialism.

Let me give a specific example. When the news came to San José that an anti-Castro invasion was under way, the students began passing the hat to charter an airplane. Volunteers stepped forward to fight in Cuba—*against Castro!* A day later, the project was dead, the student body sullen and frustrated. They had learned that the invasion was launched from Somoza's Nicaragua

—a sufficient indication to them of its restorationist character. (Did anyone in the Central Intelligence Agency even consider this dimension of the problem?)

The point must be made clearly: These are brave and devoted men (many have served their apprenticeship in dictators' prisons) who represent our one hope for the future in Latin America. They are willing to fight and die in the cause of freedom and justice, but they will not lift a hand for the oil companies, United Fruit, or North American investors.

I asked them what they want the United States to do and got a very interesting response, particularly in the light of my earlier remarks about the fictitious character of "nonintervention" ("Confessions of an Interventionist," see page 390). In essence their replies came down to one proposition: The United States should "nonintervene" in favor of democracy in Latin America. They do not want our Marines to oust Somoza, Paraguay's General Alfredo Stroessner, or Trujillo, Jr.—or Castro. Rather, they argue that a vigorous nonmilitary "nonintervention" policy by the United States *against* these dictatorships would spell their doom. To put it another way, they want the United States to eliminate its support for dictatorial governments and militantly endorse, and subsidize, democratic states; they want purposeful, prodemocratic nonintervention.

In cold terms of *Realpolitik* this amounts to a request to pick up the tab and leave them alone; we cannot expect even gratitude. In one sense, this is unfortunate—American congressmen in particular like gratitude. In another sense it is inevitable and even necessary: the strength of Latin America's progressive, popular, or revolutionary democratic movements is precisely their indigenous character. The surge of Fidelism in Latin America, particularly in the universities and among the intelligentsia, is such that it can never be contained by sycophants. Moreover, even the sycophants have never loved us; they have grown fat at our table with the cynical devotion of men sponging off a rich, drunken friend.

We must choose, clearly, between men with democratic integrity, who share our values but not our self-esteem, and others who will cheerfully bleed us dry and depart for Switzerland with their fortunes when the chips are down. It should also be pointed out that the best conceivable United States program of economic support for the people of Latin America will *operationally* be at the mercy of the *Latinos* who administer it. Thus our commitment to freedom, which President Kennedy has so eloquently affirmed, is a meaningless abstraction unless we have ideological allies to implement the program in the spirit of its goals. Our success in Latin America, Asia, and Africa lies in the hands of local democratic cadres—who will not be "our men" but our allies in a common quest. They have suffered a great deal of attrition because of us over the past century; we shall have to get used to some of the same treatment in return.

The choice between "intervention" and "nonintervention," then, is a moral and political fiction. No matter what we do, we are intervening in someone's behalf. To refuse to recognize this fact is in itself a form of intervention on the side of the *status quo*. We must therefore turn to the question which exists in the real world: By what methods and to what ends should United States power be utilized?

It was what seemed to me a stubborn refusal to accept this patent truth that led to my writing "Confessions of an Interventionist." As I read the many petitions which flooded the land after the debacle in the Bay of Pigs, I was deeply disturbed by the sight of fine liberal spokesmen, with whom I have stood on many an occasion, leading a flight to the hills of moral ambiguity.

Roger Baldwin, for example, who has been intervening in everybody's business for half a century, suddenly began to sound like a judge of the International Court of Justice. With an intonation usually reserved for an archbishop reciting the Decalogue, Baldwin went about chanting Article 15 of the Charter of the Organization of American States, that pious absurdity which absolutely forbids direct or indirect intervention "for any reason whatsoever, in the internal or external affairs of any other state." What this injunction would do to the work of the International Commission for the Rights of Man, where Baldwin is a driving spirit, can only be surmised.

Then Norman Thomas, whose letter ("Dear Editor," *The New Leader*, May 29th) I have just read, and to whom I *may* have been unfair. Certainly there was little in his letter, in which he declares that he is "by no means" opposed to "all types of intervention at all times and under all circumstances," that I would take exception to. Yet I still wonder whether this was Thomas's original position. Or is it a defensive trench to which he has moved since the initial turmoil over the Cuban invasion?

I think that I read the statement Thomas asked me to sign, which triggered my article, in the light of his previous public position on Cuba. In the Sunday *New York Times* following the C.I.A. disaster, Thomas subscribed to an elaborate and distinctly pacifist manifesto sponsored by the Fellowship of Reconciliation (F.O.R.). This statement was clearly aimed not at stupid, immoral intervention, but at intervention per se. Denouncing the "deliberate [American] subversion of the Cuban government," the F.O.R. demanded that "the officials of our government vigorously enforce United States laws against the organization of subversion."

Now, I have been under the illusion for some years that in the basic sense of the word Christianity is "subversive." Surely the nonviolent revolutionaries of the F.O.R. are dedicated in their own fashion to undermining the power of the war-making state. But leaving aside as irrelevant the purposes of pacifism, it is certainly the case that most of us who grew up in the progressive, social democratic tradition have devoted much of our time and energy to subverting injustice. In our contemporary support for the valiant efforts of the Congress of Racial Equality and its "freedom riders," we are clearly undermining and subverting the white supremacist *status quo* in Alabama. I am delighted that Attorney General Robert Kennedy used the civil arm to restore order in Alabama, but had the situation degenerated further I would have unhesitatingly endorsed his use of paratroops for this "subversion."

Similarly, I would be pleased to contribute to subverting a Communist or Fascist dictatorship. For historical reasons that are apparent, it would be as disastrous for the United States Marines to install a democratic government in Nicaragua as it has been for us to live with our sponsorship of the Somoza dictatorship. But now we are back again to the argument on methods and techniques, the crucial question which was lost in the moral mists of Thomas's initial pronouncements on Cuba.

What really unsettled me was the first liberal posture, which seemed to me a flinching from action and movement. Partly this can be explained in terms of the Eisenhower years, that dreadful eight-year stretch of national catatonia, when we got used to nothing happening. While on the world stage we are dying the Chinese death of a thousand cuts, at home there is no crisis. The Kennedy administration, trustees in the bankruptcy of "massive retaliation," found the dikes collapsing everywhere. Moving too fast, without time to check the integrity of the techniques, Kennedy introduced the element of movement into our moribund foreign policy. Unfortunately, the consequences were such that those who most vigorously endorsed a dynamic policy suddenly found themselves in bed with the C.I.A., the Joint Chiefs of Staff, and reactionary émigrés. From this dreadful united front many liberal activists took unthinking flight.

My fundamental contention is that we must start, without pessimism or optimism, on a massive program of democratic intervention. I am not going to stop here to argue with Carl Landauer or Moshe Decter ("Dear Editor," *The New Leader*, May 29th)—who are basically shooting over my head at each other—on how much principle must be mixed with how much pragmatism. At either end of the scale lies disaster: Overcaution allows Nikita Khrushchev to make our policies for us and puts us on the escalator to impotence; extreme righteousness leads logically to preventive war and a "first-strike" strategy. (Perhaps I should add that for most of us there is no sense to "Better Red than Dead"—with our political antecedents, there is no conceivable element of choice.)

The Abolitionist Centennial

As the year 1961 opened, it looked as though the Civil War Centennial Commission, ponderously chaired by a grandson of Ulysses S. Grant, was going to have things all its own way. A century ago a large group of leading American politicians and military men, including one former President and most of the top officers of the United States Army, were prepared to commit treason in the interests of human slavery and the social system built upon it. A terrible conflict was fought to end the rebellion, and 600,000 men went to their graves in the first modern approximation of "total war."

Yet under the auspices of the Commission, this sanguinary holocaust became an event worthy of gay celebrations. Throughout the South, early this year, local committees were sponsoring authentic reproductions of events in that baleful spring of 1861: Sumter was again fired upon; Jefferson Davis was inaugurated once more; and the "Bonnie Blue Flag" flapped defiantly in the breeze.

In my wife's family album there is an old photograph that shows two handsome youngsters (her great-great uncles) in Federal uniforms, their arms around an old, weather-beaten Negro. One of the smiling boys inscribed the picture, "He will stay free!"—and they both died to ensure it.

Of course, brave, decent men also left southern hamlets to fight and die. But their courage provides no justification for their cause; they fought for the most despicable ideal Americans have

Reprinted, with permission, from *The New Leader*, August 14–21, 1961.

ever held—the right of a man to own human slaves. If we are to pay tribute to bravery detached from ideals, we must also tip our hats to Kamikaze pilots, S.S. officers, and Communist spies, as well as those who sacrificed themselves for liberty and justice.

The very idea of "celebrating" the Civil War strikes me as a form of sacrilege and desecration—particularly since it is taking place under bipartisan auspices which add retrospective legitimacy to the rebellion. Jefferson Davis, Robert E. Lee, and the other "fathers of the Confederacy" were not playing at some innocuous political game; they were traitors, conspirators in arms against the lawful authority of the United States, and they were fortunate to escape with their heads. In conservative, Burkean Britain, they would have been ceremonially hanged.

I am glad they were not hanged—indeed, I think the compassion of Lincoln, Grant, and Sherman was a compelling demonstration of national virtue—but I insist that they *lost*. If we commemorate the Civil War, we should do so in the spirit of Robert Penn Warren's *Legacy of the Civil War*, a book which emphasizes with poetic brilliance the tragedy and trauma of the War of the Rebellion. To do otherwise is to insult the legion of brave men who sacrificed their lives for the Union.

Visiting the State House in Boston, one is reminded of the forgotten sacrifices. There, in marble, on the Common, Colonel Robert Gould Shaw forever leads his Negro soldiers down the road to freedom—soldiers who were shot on the spot if they fell into Confederate hands. I doubt if historically-minded Negroes are interested in a joint North-South fete in honor of the war; from their point of view it might seem like a joint German-Jewish commemoration of Buchenwald.

This may sound bitter, but I deeply resent the general assumption of southern whites that the "War Between the States" (as they call it) was a legitimate undertaking. And I resent even more the southern success in frustrating the libertarian objectives of the war during the past three-quarters of a century.

Symbolic of this success was the attempted segregation of Negro delegates by Charleston Centennial authorities at the Fort Sumter reenactment. When President Kennedy queried the

Commission about this discrimination, former Governor William
M. Tuck of Virginia blandly replied:

"It is the goal of the National Commission . . . to bring to
the attention of all Americans—and especially our young people
—the lessons we gained from our great war of the Sixties,
acknowledged to have been one of the costliest on record and
yet, from the standpoint of our American unity today, one of
the most rewarding." Tuck, it seems, thought segregation of
Negro and white delegates was a good way of teaching young
Americans the lessons learned from the war.

At this point, however, a group of "new abolitionists" entered
the scene: young men and women began to buy bus tickets to
Jackson, Mississippi. With the same moral courage and dedication
that the fiercely determined abolitionist "agents" of the 1840's
and 1850's displayed, the Freedom Riders set forth to serve as
witnesses to truth. They injected a new element into the battle
against white supremacy, exposing the structure of white domination to a degree that lawsuits cannot accomplish, and added a
new and unexpected note to the Civil War Centennial celebrations.

In a sense, the entire Negro community in the Deep South, and
generally in the rural South, lives in a state of siege. The forms
of coercion in our time are different from those of the antebellum South, where the "slave patrol" rode nightly; now they
are more covert. Whites control the instruments of legal coercion, and Negroes are seldom rash enough to challenge the
white power system head-on.

The average southern Negro is not terrorized; he is simply no
more heroic than the average white in, say, Indonesia. He minds
his own business and hopes that trouble will avoid him. He has
inherited with his culture a built-in survival mechanism and,
whatever he may think as he reads the newspaper, he lies low.
But if a southern Negro rejects these political ground rules, he
is a sitting duck for the white man's brand of justice.

This justice usually involves law enforcement on an "invisible"
level. Conviction is by summary process before a magistrate for
any one of a number of common-law misdemeanors. A good ex-

ample of invisible adjudication in the South was an exceptional case that came before the Supreme Court in 1960.

On Saturday evening, January 24, 1959, Sam Thompson, a Louisville, Kentucky, Negro went into the Liberty End Café and, while waiting for a bus, apparently amused himself by shuffling his feet in rhythm to the jukebox. Two policemen came in, were annoyed by his antics, and arrested him for "loitering." Because, on the way to the police station, Thompson peacefully argued with them, they threw in a charge of "disorderly conduct." He was convicted on both counts in Police Court and fined $20 (he could have been imprisoned).

Normally, Thompson, like others (Negro and white) in the same predicament, would have either paid the fine or worked it off in prison. But somehow he turned up in Police Court with a crack civil liberties lawyer who raised objections at every point in the legal process. The lawyer introduced evidence that Thompson was a reputable citizen, that he had purchased supper in the café, was waiting for the seven-thirty bus, and had merely exercised a citizen's right to declare his innocence of wrongdoing to the police.

The decision was appealed through two Kentucky courts to the United States Supreme Court, which unanimously ruled that Thompson's constitutional right to due process of law had been denied. It was the first time the Supreme Court had ever taken such a conviction under review, and, needless to say, it would never have taken place if the Kentucky chapter of the American Civil Liberties Union (A.C.L.U.) had not carried the burden of the defense.

The average Negro caught in the web of white justice does not usually have an able attorney on hand. The self-validating claims of police officers serve as evidence, and the magistrate acts on the assumption that if the accused were not guilty he wouldn't be in court. In this situation, the Negro pays his fine or serves his time.

The A.C.L.U. or the National Association for the Advancement of Colored People (N.A.A.C.P.) may provide legal protection in special cases. But when a "Nigra gets uppity" in some small rural Mississippi township, the local power system closes in on him, and there are no civil libertarians in town to come to his defense. By the time anyone outside learns of an unjust decision or act, it is usually, in legal terms, too late to do anything about it.

No federal court can take cognizance of facts that were not introduced in the trial record. Indeed, all the record shows is a routine conviction for "disorderly conduct" or "breach of the peace." In an appeal at the appellate level, the lawyer usually cannot introduce new evidence (with rare exceptions, only matters of law are subject to review); he cannot point out with any hope of success that what appears to be a normal conviction for breach of the peace is in fact an enforcement of white-supremacist doctrine. No one, white or Negro, has a constitutional right to engage in disorderly conduct—and that is generally the charge.

Southern abuse of justice has been laid bare by the nonviolent revolutionary techniques of the Freedom Riders. About 150 of them are now serving time in Mississippi jails for "breach of peace." The judges who sentenced them were very careful to announce that racial problems were totally irrelevant; that they were not being convicted for violating Jim Crow laws but only for disturbing the peace. But the Freedom Riders have nevertheless exposed the South's great masquerade of justice and made it a matter of national news and international shame.

Without deprecating the great job of the N.A.A.C.P. in using the courts to undermine the legal standing of Jim Crow, one must also pay tribute to these brave young people for employing the methods of nonlaw to subvert the illegal and invisible foundations of racial discrimination. By rejecting the use of legal defense and going to jail, they, like the abolitionists of old, have laid a concern on the national conscience that transcends legal niceties. I suspect that such warriors for human freedom as James G. Birney, William Lloyd Garrison, and the other original abolitionists, would appreciate this version of commemorating the Civil War Centennial.

The Illusion of Invincibility

The United States is today facing a challenge far more serious than that posed by Nazi Germany or the Japanese in 1941. Then, we could, protected by our oceans, move without disturbance to the massive mobilization of our military power. We could fight the war essentially on our own terms; it was, in that nice archaic phrase, a "foreign war."

Missile technology has destroyed our insulation—and our lead time. Compare the impact of Pearl Harbor—a military defeat—with the consequences of a nuclear strike against our cities and industrial complexes. The classic picture, confirmed by two world wars, of the giant, slow in anger and commitment but invincible once engaged, must be relegated to the museum of political antiquities. We are vulnerable, and to forget it—to relax in the enjoyment of affluence—is to invite disaster.

In fact, ours is the first generation of Americans which has in its hands literally the power to make life-or-death decisions, decisions which may determine whether we as a nation survive. While Lincoln, Wilson, and Franklin Roosevelt could blunder without risking the very existence of the American community, President Kennedy stands on a lonely eminence with no room for second guesses.

And President Kennedy has come to office at an ominous time, in circumstances where the whole structure of American foreign policy is based on outmoded conceptions. Today, for the first time in our history, we confront an opponent on terms of de-

Reprinted, with permission, from *Hadassah Magazine*, September, 1961.

structive parity. We have lost that wonderful freedom of action founded on preponderant power, that freedom which gave President Truman scope for his Greek-Turkish policy and for his Korean intervention. Our whole system of alliances, our policy of containment, were founded on the implicit assumption that no power would ever go to the brink with us, that when the chips were down, the preponderance of American power would inhibit the aggressor. It was this power, and this power alone, which provided the shield of freedom in postwar Europe, which made it possible for the nations of Western Europe to rebuild their broken fabrics in freedom.

This must be reemphasized. There has been so much wishful thinking, so many attempts to soften the hard lines of political reality that we tend to shy away from the stark confrontation of unpleasant truth. It seems to me, much as I may dislike the harsh world of which this is a component, that in the period since Stalin betrayed the Grand Alliance one strong barrier has checked Soviet imperialism. This was not the "force of world opinion" or the fear of the United Nations—it was the knowledge that the United States and its North Atlantic allies would resist aggression, that we would fight. Not only that we would fight, but that we could do far more damage to the Soviet Union than it could do to us in the event of war.

Now all this has changed. It is not that the Soviet Union is now stronger than we are, or that it could defeat us if war did occur. It is rather that the very terms "victory" and "defeat" have become meaningless relics of the preatomic age. Could a victory in a nuclear war be any less destructive to our essential national fabric than a defeat? Or to that of the U.S.S.R.? We have, as a consequence, moved into a Kafkaesque universe in which a distinguished admiral in all seriousness can explain to a congressional committee that the virtue of a big navy is that after the mainland of the United States has been devastated, there will still be a force afloat to win eventual victory.

In short, all our old ways of looking at the world, all the things we have for so long taken for granted about world politics, are out of date. We have lived unknowing through a transformation of international relations as radical as the jump in science from mechanics to relativity. Our old formulas are useless, and we must feel our way into a strange new cosmos where no roads are charted and destruction lurks at our elbow.

This transformation has been under way for almost a decade— it was signaled by the success of the Soviets in combining nuclear and missile technology into intercontinental ballistic missiles. But up to now the American people, and their elected leaders, have stubbornly refused to recognize the agonizing truth. Instead of boldly facing forward and beginning the perilous march, they twice elected an administration whose function was to exorcise the demons and to reassure them that, despite all the evil omens, we did still live in the same old comfortable world.

So, for those eight precious years, while the Soviets moved from the paranoiac rigidity of Stalin to the brilliant, cynical flexibility of Khrushchev, our government fortified our "Maginot Line" of "massive retaliation." The Soviet Union was surrounded by papier-mâché alliances—the Baghdad-less Pact, SEATO—all based on the trip-wire principle, on the proposition that if the Soviets moved out and tripped the line in Iran, Thailand, Pakistan, Germany, they would bring upon themselves the full force of American preponderant power, nuclear war.

A few hardy souls raised the question whether in fact we would invoke nuclear penalties if, say, the Communist Vietnamese invaded Thailand. Others queried whether we would employ the ultimate weapon when we knew that the Soviet Union could equally employ hydrogen bombs on us. They were told gently not to rock the boat; everything was all right; the prophets of doom were misguided fanatics with no national confidence.

Suddenly in 1961—as Major Titov flits overhead—we are, in the face of crises in Cuba, Laos, and Berlin, awakening to the realization that in those gently passing years of the 1950's we were not rising to the responsibilities of world leadership. That while we were progressing toward the domestic triumph of a balanced budget, we were in the international arena dying the death of a thousand cuts. And a brave, able, and lonely man in the White House finds that it is his function to lead the American people, and the free world, into a fearful and uncharted struggle against the twin disasters of destruction and capitulation.

In essence, President Kennedy's task is to overcome the illusion of American invincibility without yielding to the obsession with American vulnerability. The extreme reactions of Americans to our changed power position cluster under these headings. On the one hand we have the "No appeasement," "Don't yield an inch" group—led by certain prominent members of Congress who have simply failed to recognize that we no longer possess preponderant power. "Call Khrushchev's bluff" is their slogan on Berlin, though a cold analysis of the situation suggests that Khrushchev (unlike Stalin in 1948) holds a very strong hand. While it may be that we have a somewhat better hand, it is also the case that humanity can best be served by avoiding a showdown.

This group reacts to—and nourishes—the natural American impatience and unthinking wish that something must be done to end the uncertainty. We are not as a nation accustomed to living with uncertainty, to living out generations in a condition of no war, no peace. We want action, an end to shilly-shallying. Psychiatrists tell us that there are men who commit suicide because they cannot stand worrying about when they will die; I submit that this political configuration is urging a similar escape upon the American people.

At the other end of the spectrum, torn by doubts and genuine fears about the consequences of war to humanity, stand those obsessed with American vulnerability. In essence, although they would not admit it, what they are arguing for is a new isolationism, a liberal variation of "Fortress America." However strongly they may cherish the ideals of freedom and justice, they shrink away from any confrontation with the Soviet Union because any action we might take could lead to devastation. They stand paralyzed and transfixed by the horrors of war and, without meaning to do so, effectively give Khrushchev the power to make our policies for us. If Khrushchev, for example, declares that any American actions against Communism in Southeast Asia may constitute a *casus belli*, and we refrain from action because we dare not joggle the balance of terror, Khrushchev has become the American Secretary of State. In short, we cannot permit their obsessional fears of nuclear annihilation to freeze us in a posture of impotent immobility.

If we should not rush to fight, neither should we flee from our responsibilities. President Kennedy, the trustee in bankruptcy of "massive retaliation," has, I believe, taken the proper course, has set our national mood, and we must as a nation grow up and accept his sober and realistic leadership. What we need is militance and dedication tempered by caution, not fright mitigated by uneasy commitment. Above all, if we are to survive this next quarter-century, and our principles are to survive with us, we must get into motion. Our strategy must be absolute—a total principled quest for liberty and economic justice; our tactics must be flexible, combining a willingness to take risks with a careful assessment of which risks should be taken.

Under no circumstances should we permit others—Nationalist Chinese, Laotian princes, or West Germans—to determine our policies for us or to commit us to their own private causes. If we must, on the one hand, avoid a Munich, we must, on the other, eliminate the possibility of a Sarajevo, and the fearful succession of accidents which brought the Great Powers to the defense of their clients in the bloodbath of World War I.

There is no road map into the future, but with leadership and maturity we shall at least have a compass. And the compass must have as its true North, as the fixed point which guides all our movements, the love of freedom—not affluence, the American Way of Life, or some set of economic clichés. We and our democratic allies are the guardians of the most precious values of Western civilization. We have failed in our trust all too often, but I would argue that the evidence of our failures is itself a witness to the values that we uphold.

Freedom, then, is our central, dominating dream. And we have now the formidable task of sustaining it against an unprecedented assault, of formulating and implementing a viable liberal policy which will give our ideals the chance to win the day without disaster. We cannot flee from risk. In the first place, to do so would be to demonstrate moral bankruptcy; in the second, pragmatically there is no place to hide. Time may well work things out—particularly if we believe in the dynamic force of freedom —and there is much that is negotiable with the Soviet Union, which fortunately is not run by a madman of the Hitler stripe.

But on a fundamental level which you as comrades of the six million martyrs and I as a descendant of butchered Irish patriots need hardly discuss—we cannot betray our identity as free men. While we must in the interests of all humanity temper our dedication with prudence and loose no irresponsible wars of liberation, we are democratic revolutionaries who look (in the same sense that Khrushchev sees his doctrinal ambitions) to the eventual triumph of our aspirations. We must be sensible; we must be prudent; we must take every precaution to avoid war; but we must at the same time make it clear that freedom is not negotiable.

Do-It-Yourself Survival

The history of Western man has chronicled innumerable aberrations, but I doubt if any free society has ever matched the nauseating display of callous individualism we are now observing in discussions of protection against fallout and other possible consequences of a nuclear attack. If our most bitter critics had set out to invent a caricature of American "civilization," they could hardly have approximated the disgraceful mood exemplified starkly and tersely in an October 3rd *New York Times* head: "Fall-Out Shelters Speeded by Hundreds in Suburbs/But Families Tend to Keep Plans Secret to Bar Use by Others in Any Attack." Other stories, for example one in the *Christian Science Monitor* of October 9th, note that an article has appeared in a Jesuit publication justifying such a bar, and that at least one fallout shelter has been surrounded by booby traps to ensure against intruders.

Sauve qui peut!—it seems—is fast becoming the slogan of suburban America. The fallout shelter is assuming the dimensions of the concrete bunker; implicit in the philosophy of do-it-yourself survival is the necessity for defense. The well-equipped suburban householder will not only have his refuge, but will face the imperative of defending it against his neighbors and their families if they have not, from frivolity or lack of foresight, dug their own bunkers.

A major tactical problem is created by the possible rush of urbanites into the countryside. In 1798 the Jersey farmers barricaded the roads from Philadelphia to stop the city folk from

Reprinted, with permission, from *The New Leader*, October 30, 1961.

fleeing the yellow-fever epidemic. It will be rather difficult, however, to enjoy the safety of one's underground refuge and simultaneously guard the Long Island Expressway. Perhaps strategic
bridges can be blown. Or, better still, perhaps there will be insufficient time for city evacuation. (This last consideration poses
a dilemma for the suburban bunkerman who works in the city:
Should he quit work in times of crisis, or run the 5–2 risk that
an attack will occur on a weekday?)

A dentist interviewed by the *Times* reporter "agreed that it
was 'an awful thing' to contemplate barring friends and neighbors
from the shelter," but he explained that "everyone has a chance
now to build his own shelter." One doesn't know whether to
laugh or weep at this Kafkaesque absurdity, this application of
the principle of laissez faire to community survival.

In the first place, the proposition is morally disgraceful. As
Edmond Cahn pointed out so tellingly in *The Moral Decision*,
it is reprehensible to build an ethical code on extreme contin-
gencies. Only in a madhouse could people seriously discuss the
question "Are five people in an open boat justified in eating the
sixth to survive?" When matters of this sort receive serious public
analysis, government action is imperative—but for psychiatric
care, not fallout shelters.

The moral issue aside, the proposition is pragmatically unsound. Not only does it rest on the patently nonsensical assumption that every citizen has the money and the room to build his
bunker; it is also based on a conception of community which
utterly repudiates the one principle which can maximize human
survival in crisis situations: human solidarity. There is an old
story of a shipwrecked sailor who, having killed his mates for
their provisions, was discovered by a relief party in splendid
physical condition, but stark raving mad. Thus if one asserts, as
I do, that a society which rejects fraternity does not deserve to
survive, he can equally urge that it will not—at least not in any
worthwhile form.

Indeed, the postholocaust society that the current philosophy
envisions is nothing less than Thomas Hobbes's State of Nature,
in which individual existence is "nasty, poore, brutish and short,"
a society (to use an inappropriate word) composed of human

atoms at perpetual war with one another. It is a recipe for barbarism pure and simple. Once the suburban bunkerman has asserted his individual sovereignty and his total lack of responsibility for his fellow human beings, he has no ground for complaint if he and his family are cast out into the poisoned atmosphere by superior forces, by more powerful irresponsibles.

If our suburban dentist, quoted above, thinks that desperate men in a world dominated by survival will respect the Law of Trespass, he has misread the auguries. When he by his actions rejects community, he is unknowingly destroying the only substantial basis for that individual safety to which he naïvely clings.

Over two thousand years ago, Aristotle proclaimed that man is a community animal, that outside the bonds of community he must be either a beast or a god. Without endorsing the metaphysics on which he rested his political theory, we can respect its pragmatic validity. We can also profit from his discussion of the weakness of popular government, which he felt was unstable because the rule of many in the interests of the whole so readily degenerated into the rule of many for purely selfish individual goals.

Distressed by the disintegration of Greek communal life that was taking place before his eyes, the Stagirite called for a *politikos*, a statesman, to dramatize, reassert, and symbolize the key ideals of Greek community. But he was pessimistic about the possibilities of reforming democratic communities because the leaders were in fact followers who did not dare to challenge the egocentric demands of their constituents with uncomfortable assertions about the responsibility of the individual citizen to the whole community.

Nothing that has happened recently would refute his pessimism. So far, our leaders have fled from their responsibilities. A few have been whooping it up for fallout shelters; President Kennedy and his specialists in simulated activity have probably fielded the inevitable "task force," and he has indicated that some momentous program is in the works. But no one has proclaimed the essential fact that it is *the community*, not just the suburban dentist with his two children, which is in peril. No one has asserted the obvious: Precautions against danger on this scale must be undertaken by the community—not by those of its component units who have $750 and a quarter of an acre.

The crucial function of leadership in a time like this cannot be underestimated. One type of leader provides the community with a focus, incarnates its values, and in his person exorcises the demons which haunt us all in parlous times. Few would deny the enormous role of Sir Winston Churchill in transforming the Britain of Munich into the Britain of 1940. The other type of leader, weighed down with "realism" like the French parliamentarians of 1940, responds to community stresses by muttering "every man for himself," and abandoning the ship.

This maritime figure of speech can be carried further, for the history of disasters at sea provides a rich source of material on the phenomenon of "survival." In one great tragedy, the men aboard faithfully observed the ancient rule and saved the women and children; in another it was "every man for himself," and all hands perished. It is doubtful whether the men in the first boat were any more heroic than those in the second, but in the first case there were leadership and a collective acceptance of moral priorities; in the second there were disorganization and a repudiation of those values which, as Aristotle noted, make the human animal into a Man.

Our society has undergone only one brutal assault on its foundations. And during the Civil War we were blessed with a President who combined superb political talents with a majestic appreciation of the potentialities and the demonic urges of the community. A dreadful war never became an amoral shambles, which civil wars can so easily become, because Lincoln asserted in his vision and by his enormous authority the ultimate sovereignty of compassion and fraternity: a monumental act of treason was accompanied by no treason trials, and executions for desertion in the face of the enemy were time and again frustrated by the gentle giant in the White House. By that circular process which is the democratic ethic at its best, the representative of the people stood as the incarnation of the highest values of the American community, and led his constituents—while he lived—toward an aspiration which transcended even wartime hate.

The same men who demanded the blood of Confederate traitors

reelected the Lincoln who stood in their path, the Lincoln who would shortly in his Second Inaugural give timeless articulation to the ideals of American community. In the same sense, the men who are today building, equipping, and perhaps fortifying their bunkers are not amoral wretches. Most of them would without hesitation as members of a volunteer fire department risk their lives for their neighbors' children or, for that matter, rush in the path of an oncoming car to rescue an unknown infant. Yet in a different context they can coldly contemplate barring these children from life. The task of our leaders is to change the framework of decision, to enunciate the precious values of community against a philosophy which is appropriate only for a herd of swine.

"Menace" from the Right

Hasn't the time come for a moratorium on exposures of the John Birch Society and the right-wing conspiracy? Hardly a week passes, it seems, without the mailman delivering a monograph or a package of documents portraying in ominous tones the resurgence of the radical Right. Similarly, the liberal journals are studded with articles on the new threat to liberalism. One might think from all this that we have in the United States a powerful right-wing junta, mobilized and waiting for the signal to crush the helpless Kennedy administration and substitute the *National Review* for the *Congressional Record*.

While it is, of course, useful to reveal the activities and the party line of the right-wingers, it is silly to get hysterical about their machinations and give them a lot of free publicity. Anyone who has spent any time in liberal pressure groups knows the extent of our organizational weakness, recognizes the degree to which the liberal monolith is a creation of right-wing fantasies. However, he usually fails to consider the other side of the coin: the extent to which the "menace from the right" is *in effective political terms* an equally mythical bogey, a vapor of the perfervid liberal imagination. We simply lose our perspective. While among ourselves we may on occasion suspect that A.D.A. (known in right-wing circles as the politburo of the liberal machine) could not fight its way out of a wet paper sack, we take the John Birch Society on its own assessment as a tightly knit, single-purposed conspiratorial cadre.

Reprinted, with permission, from *The New Leader*, March 5, 1962.

Ten years ago, in *The New Leader* and elsewhere, I suggested that in this identical sense McCarthyism was a spook. In October, 1954, for example, I noted in *Current History* that politically McCarthyism had no future: I added:

"Where does the Senator go from here? Although one must be very cautious in reading lessons from history, the fate of past extremists seems to offer some insight on this matter. Psychologically, the extremist must attack, attack, and then attack again . . . the road to power for such a man is unceasing assault. But there are risks in the perpetual attack—it becomes increasingly extreme, shrill, and, finally, boring. Unless a demagogue can seize commanding positions of state power in the early stages of his campaign, he is likely to end his days in the political wilderness, a rejected prophet. And it is precisely this fate which American political institutions tend to prepare for the extremist."

In his Senate committee chairmanship McCarthy had an ideal position for conducting guerrilla warfare and campaigns of attrition. Yet the most he could achieve was the status of a nasty, vicious nuisance. In no sense did he pose an organizational threat to the American political system; he built no party and left no inheritance, even in his native state; he was, as Richard Rovere suggested in *Senator Joe McCarthy*, a nihilist with only destructive capabilities.

For saying this I was accused of all sorts of odd heresies. I was "whitewashing McCarthy" said one critic, and a junior Marxman in *Dissent* managed to convince himself that I was objectively anti-civil rights. I know from long experience that nothing can prevent people who do not read articles from writing stupid critiques, but as a perennial optimist let me say right now that I am in no sense arguing for inertia in dealing with the Birchers— or that McCarthy was a nice man.

My attitude toward McCarthy in his day was the same as my current view of the Birchers and their kind: one of contempt rather than fear. And this is no heroic pose; there are a lot of things that scare me to death—nuclear war, automobile accidents, lung cancer, to mention but three—but I have only a limited time to devote to fright. I therefore have a scale of priorities on which the "menace from the Right" ranks twenty-third—between the fear of being eaten by piranha and the fear of college presidents.

Perhaps because I grew up in the bosom of the radical Right (my family ran the full course from Father Coughlin through America First to Joseph R. McCarthy), I have never been able to take these frustrated nihilists seriously as a political force. For a set of wholly nonpolitical reasons, I hold the memory of my father in warm affection, but politically he was a compulsive loser. And if on one scale he made Joseph P. Kennedy look like an editor of the *Catholic Worker*, on another he was totally incapable of action. So for me, at any rate, his opinions were absolved by his inertia. But inert or militant, the fact of the matter is that for the last twenty-five years of his life my father had no political home.

Nor do today's bitter, driven militants have any place to go. They can sponsor raids on school boards, crucify a few hapless teachers here and there, get some hick town to ban UNICEF collection boxes on Halloween, and occasionally even tear hell out of a state legislature or the United States Senate. But they have no institutional base of operations; they don't even control one state government; though, as several corporations can verify, this is not necessarily an impossible attainment.

Put bluntly, much of the liberal frenzy about the resurgent Right seems to rest on the submerged premise that the United States in the 1960's resembles Weimar Germany in the Great Depression. (I actually attended a cocktail party a few years back where the main topic was, "Will Eisenhower be the American Hindenberg?") What this analogy assumes, without demonstrating, is that the United States has a political vehicle for this right-wing extremism, that the Yahoos have a party which presents the American people with a meaningful alternative to the *status quo*. To state this proposition is to reveal its absurdity.

There is no Yahoo Party, and their chances of taking over the existing political machinery except on a sporadic local basis are virtually nonexistent. They simply have nothing to offer; their very nihilism militates against successful organization; they are not political men, and they have no conception of how one conducts a rationally irrational campaign. (This is not intended to be cute or delphic: One of the most interesting aspects of American campaigns is the degree to which irrational elements—demagoguery, charismatic displays, and so on—are treated by politicians and voters as part of the staging. It is considered bad form either to be a "nut"; that is, to act as though you believed your own press releases, or—as Adlai Stevenson discovered—to depreciate the political act.)

Because they are alienated from contemporary American life, right-wing extremists have no real self-confidence. They are wanderers in a hostile land who go into battle with a brooding suspicion that History itself is conspiring against Truth. When you know that *they* have the dice loaded, that *they* have poisoned the wells, that *they* are everywhere, it is hard to have the stomach for a sustained fight. It is usually hit and run. Indeed, at close range a Yahoo crusade is a quite pathetic congeries of the insecure; confronted by intelligent and vigorous opposition, what appears to be a solid phalanx degenerates into paranoidal atoms which scuttle into hiding babbling of Jews, fluorides, and UNESCO.

In this connection, the political future of General Edwin Walker is instructive. Walker's farewell address to Congress identified him as the pure ideologist, the man who lives in a world where words have an autonomous force in history. If Walker were a political man, he would have settled for two punchy paragraphs vividly expressing his dismay with the commander in chief. Instead, he took up a good half-page of the *New York Times* with a manifesto worthy of a thirty-third-degree Trotskyite.

Now Walker has proved useful to Senator Strom Thurmond (Democrat, South Carolina) and others who are willing to use any stick to beat a dog—in this case Senator William Fulbright (Democrat, Arkansas). But this does not mean that they will admit him to the club. Walker, however, is off to the political wars (he has put his name in the Texas Democratic primary for governor), probably under the illusion that the Democratic politicians who were so nice to him in Washington will stand up and be counted for a true-blue conservative. He is in for a shock. What Walker and others have failed to appreciate was tersely put by a former Republican senatorial magnate: "We don't draw any line between conservatives and reactionaries," he said, "but we sure as hell discriminate between the sane and the insane."

There is no reason, then, for the liberals to hit the panic button. These boys aren't so tough. In fact, I would argue that we should take every opportunity to drag them out into the open and have it out. With the exception of William F. Buckley, Jr., and his cadre, who are really in a different class, they are not very effective in ideological warfare, and they much prefer to operate from the shadows.

The extreme Right's chosen weapons are the scurrilous letter (I have a collection that would make a first sergeant blush), the nasty anonymous phone call, the sordid little tract. The last thing one should ever do with Yahoos is display fear or the slightest willingness to compromise—this will bring down the whole pack howling for blood. The best liberal strategy comes from the folk-wisdom of County Mayo: "Stand firm, boys—and when a head comes over the wall, hit it!"

Because a number of liberal intellectuals live in the same universe as General Walker—one in which words substitute for realities—there is generalized *Angst* about coping with the radical Right. The Yahoos are seemingly ferocious, and to take one on does involve a pilgrimage to a Kafkaesque frame of discourse where $2 + 2 = 22$, Alger Hiss $+$ UNESCO $=$ the Berlin Wall, and Katanga $=$ the Ulster of 1961, the Hungary of 1961, or the Spitzbergen of 1961.

I spent an exasperating evening recently disposing of the thesis that UNESCO has corrupted American education and that UNICEF Christmas cards are part of the Communist plot to take Christ out of Christmas and thus destroy the religious foundations of American civilization. (Typical question from Bircher in audience: "Will you comment on the fact that Janie Davis of 347 Woods Street, Suisun, California, read a UNESCO pamphlet on nationalism and then spit on the American flag?") It is a sad, sickening business, but nobody is going to take care of them for us.

This is, I suppose, what disturbs me about many of my liberal friends, and is probably just another formulation of the complaint of the activist. They are distressed about right-wing extremism, exaggerate the power and the efficiency of the right-

wingers, and then await cosmic intervention to avert "Fascism."
If they really feel that freedom is in jeopardy, they may strike
back by subscribing to *The Nation*. No one in his senses prefers
debating with a Bircher to an evening at home, but we have to
make a commitment to slug it out whenever there is a public
audience involved. (There is no point in wasting time in private
combat. Some local Yahoo has been trying to get me to debate
the immorality of the income tax before his Freedom Fighters'
local. I have resisted by offering an alternate topic: "Resolved,
the Kansas-Nebraska Act is a national disaster.")

The most important thing for us to do is cut out the paranoia,
stop looking over our shoulders at Nazi Germany every time a
sick nut pushes an anti-Semitic tract, stop feeling sorry for ourselves for living in a time when—despite our obvious virtue and
dedication to Truth—people say nasty things about us. After
what we have done to the Yahoos in the United States over the
past thirty years, can we really expect them to love us? Let us
leave self-pity to the right-wingers and devote ourselves to giving
them sufficient justification for its exercise.

Finally, we should take our bearings from American history,
and not from German history. If one reads the denunciations of
President Adams by the Jeffersonian press (before he suppressed
most of it), or the Federalist analysis of Jeffersonian democracy
("A great body of domestik traitors," the *Gazette of the United
States* wrote on June 9, 1798), or the Republican Platform of
1876 ("We charge the Democratic party with being the same in
character and spirit as when it sympathized with treason"), he
may be reluctantly led to the conclusion that political manners
have improved over the past century and a half.

The United States has always been a rough country with a
turbulent political tradition at the local level; those who denounce
the Birchers today are surely in no worse shape than Albert Gallatin was in 1794 when he told his neighbors to pay the whiskey
excise and stop behaving "like a mob." The crowd ominously
referred him to a recent local resolution proclaiming "that if anyone called the people a mob, he should be tarred and feathered."

It was inevitable that the election of a liberal Democrat to the
Presidency would unleash the full force of right-wing extremism,
but what we must not overlook is the clear fact that the Yahoos

have been there all the time. Now, at long last, they have a clear sighting on their target: a President who believes in government. (It was difficult to get Eisenhower in the sights: it was obvious that, whatever his *ex officio* role, Ike really did believe in the withering away of the state—though not for the reasons adduced by Robert Welch.)

Furthermore, the politicians of the conservative coalition, while they will not link their destinies with right-wing extremists, are delighted to take box seats at the bullfight. They may even, on occasion, become picadors, stimulating the Yahoo bull against the handsome, self-confident Toreador, secure in the knowledge that no bull has ever replaced a vanquished bullfighter.

My diagnosis, then, is that for at least the next six years, and hopefully for the next twenty, we shall have to pay the price of power and put up with a savage right-wing assault. The extremists will swarm here today, there tomorrow (but always in Los Angeles, the American Munich), and the unsophisticated observer may get the impression that there is a powerful movement surging toward native Fascism. Nothing could be further from the truth. Never have the right-wing stalwarts been so far from power and influence in the United States as they are today.

We have a tough, liberal President who has made it clear, both in his Los Angeles speech and in a recent press conference, that he will take no nonsense from the Right. The death of Senator Styles Bridges removed the last Yahoo magnate from the Upper House—a decade ago we had a good half-dozen. And, most important, the American electorate has probably never been more stable and less susceptible to extremist appeals.

Right-wing extremism, in other words, is an ideology without an institutional base. Its epigones have an almost unbelievable capacity for generating tumult and hate on an *ad hoc* basis, but they have developed no institutional roots, and do not, in my view, constitute a serious threat to our free society. Thus, in our continuing struggle against these twisted prophets we should never underestimate their talent for troublemaking and for hurting the innocent, but at the same time we should keep our perspective and act like men.

The Limits of Kennedy's Liberalism

The other day I ran into an old Socialist friend who spends most of his time these days on the peace circuit. With great gusto he began rubbing my nose in the Kennedy administration; in particular, the defeat of Medicare seemed to have filled him with joyous enthusiasm. After half an hour I began to suspect that the outbreak of nuclear war would really put him into a happy frenzy. He has what might be called a vested interest in catastrophe, though—as I pointed out—resurrection may be a precondition for the proper enjoyment of a final "I told you so."

This is not the time nor place to go into the metaphysics of the peace (or is it the survival?) movement, except perhaps to note that the sentiment "I want to live"—while understandable—is hardly a viable foundation for a radical morality. Frenchmen who collaborated with the Nazis in order to survive are seldom listed among the folk heroes of radicalism.

What concerns me is the performance of the Kennedy administration and the evaluation of its assets and liabilities from a liberal vantage point. There have been literally dozens of "think pieces" in the newspapers and journals attacking the President for his tactical clumsiness with Congress or, in contrast, pointing out that Kennedy is confronting superhuman obstacles, and has really done quite well, given the built-in power of the "conservative coalition." Most of these assessments overlook what is to me the crucial consideration: that the character of the Kennedy administration is at base the determining factor. Character is fate, the

Reprinted, with permission, from *The New Leader*, October 1, 1962.

Greeks said, and both the successes and the failures of the New Frontier appear to me to originate in the operational schizophrenia of modern American liberalism.

There are two distinct threads in the makeup of contemporary liberalism, each running back at least a century, each contributing a vital ingredient to the total outlook. One line, whose immediate if not ultimate source is British utilitarianism, advocates change in the interests of "efficiency."

In England, the Fabian Socialists represented the institutionalization of the utilitarian tradition: Socialism was seen as the most efficient means of attaining the "greatest happiness of the greatest number." Anyone who has read Beatrice Webb's diaries has encountered this manifestation in its purest form; the Webbs' *Soviet Russia: A New Civilization* marked the application of the canons of utilitarian efficiency to Communism. Socialism was the most effective framework for large-scale social engineering, and the Webbs cheered the Bolsheviks because the latter allowed no stupid sentimentalism to interfere with their drive for the efficient order. The bête noire of the Webbs was always the trade-union movement and its political wing: those fools who kept insisting that the workers were better qualified to judge their own best interests than the enlightened prophets of the "New Society."

The gospel of efficiency had its American following, too. It infused much Progressive thought around the turn of the century, perhaps reaching its national zenith in Theodore Roosevelt's Bull Moose Campaign in 1912. On local levels it inspired "sewer Socialism": Municipal ownership of gas and water works was visualized as a bold blow for reform. Like the Fabians, the American Progressives (and many self-styled Socialists were in this category) had little use for the trade unions, whom they saw as modern Luddites attempting to destroy the maximum efficiency of the labor market in the name of self-interest. The inclusion of a sonorific phrase that labor was not a "commodity"—a provision of the Clayton Antitrust Act that soon became a bad joke—was as far as the Progressives would go in recognizing the legitimacy of organized labor.

The efficiency school of liberalism thus developed what was essentially an antipolitical thrust. Politics was by definition "bad" because it was founded on the institutionalization of self-interest. The goal was a government by enlightened administrators who would assert the "national interest" from their blueprints of the good society and ignore the selfish claims of "unenlightened minorities" or "self-seeking pressure groups." The efficiency school is perhaps more aptly described as "technocratic liberalism."

The second component of the modern liberal tradition is radically different. Historically it has condemned the injustices—not the inefficiencies—of the capitalist society. Confronted with a choice between justice and efficiency, it unhesitatingly opts for justice because it asserts the priority of moral values over instrumental fripperies.

Spokesmen of this second group excoriated segregation in the Armed Forces, for instance, on the ground that it degraded our Negro soldiers, not because it was an inefficient utilization of manpower. They fight for better schools as a spiritual birthright of American children, not as a mechanism for beating the Russians to the moon. They have battled for the rights of trade unions because they repudiate the notion that a man is an attachment to a machine, not in order to increase productivity or nourish industrial togetherness ("The Happy Worker Works Harder"). They have no blueprint, but they have a militant sense of injustice. Their reaction to a thalidomide scandal, for example, is to get their pikes and go to war against a system which permits human beings to be played with like guinea pigs. They do not respond administratively—by, say, urging the strengthening of the Federal Food and Drug Administration—but viscerally. In the broad sense, they are political.

It is, I suspect, clear by now where my sympathies lie. I must add, though, that whatever may be my personal reaction to technocratic liberals, they have played and must continue to play a vital role in the development of a vigorous and effective liberal polity. I have known a number of reformers who like People in the abstract but not on the beach; and some who see urban renewal as a good way of "beautifying our cities" by replacing Negroes with trees: They always raise the hair on the back of my neck. Yet the fact is that much of the implementation of liberal ideals over the past thirty years has been in their hands, and they have often performed magnificently. They are necessary, but—and herein lies the weakness of the Kennedy administration—they are not sufficient.

Since the time I first met the then Senator Kennedy in 1957, I have been trying to puzzle him out. He obviously does not fit into the stereotype of the Irish-American politician; characterologically, he is in a different universe from his grandfather "Honey Fitz" or James Michael Curley or Jim Farley. Without getting too involved in imprecise categories, he struck me as the type of Irish-American who would be far more likely to turn up as an archbishop than as a senator. Although he may have changed since, I was convinced, watching him in a Boston crowd, that he did not like to be touched. Curiously, he reminded me strongly of Hugh Gaitskell.

Kennedy impressed me then as a man of great intellectual capacity and as a "liberal" in the context of American politics, and I have not since changed my evaluation on either count. He also unsettled me. He was (like Gaitskell) so clearly a liberal technocrat—there was something disembodied about his political style; his light burned cold. "Kennedy's got the words," an old Boston trade unionist put it, "but he'll never learn the music." Walter Lippmann made the point differently: Kennedy, he suggested, was intellectually a liberal but temperamentally a conservative.

In this world, to paraphrase St. Augustine, one must take his breaks where he can find them. In my judgment Kennedy was the best Democrat candidate, and there was obviously no comparison between him and Nixon. I worked hard for his election. But already during the campaign, the Achilles' heel of technocratic liberalism was noticeable. The Kennedy high command seemed to think that elections, like chess games, went to the man with the best technique. The countryside was full of handbooks, snoops from the Louis Harris pooling operation, countless relatives and public-relations specialists. But where was the candidate? Nobody ever voted for a machine.

Fortunately, the TV debates did bring Kennedy out from

behind the machine. As Nixon committed hari-kari before the cameras, the senator displayed decisiveness and intelligence—and humanity: The side shot which caught him chuckling at Nixon's oleaginous paean to clean language was worth a million votes. Some of his answers were not much, but the crucial function of the debates was not to rack up points on a current-events test. The American people were not interested in who was the better Quiz Kid; they listened to the answers in hopes of determining which of these men would be a *mensch*.

Two years of the New Frontier have now demonstrated both the strengths and the weaknesses of Kennedy's penchant for liberal technocracy. He has appointed to office the finest and most able group of men and women that the government has probably ever seen. New life has been injected into the moribund regulatory agencies, which had suffered first from Truman's appalling appointments and then from the Eisenhower doctrine of the withering away of the state. Administrative techniques for dealing with such problems as civil rights, price fixing, and juvenile delinquency have been increasingly employed. In short, the administrative edge of the government has been honed to a new sharpness. Never, I believe, has so much sheer energy, to say nothing of intelligence, been applied to the problem of government.

But the obsession with technique has led to an unbelieveable shambles in other sections. If Kennedy were a British Prime Minister, with his power resting firmly on an organized party system, he might be able to operate on a technocratic basis; in Washington, however, efforts to take the politics out of politics can only lead to disaster. Kennedy's very success in tightening up the administrative sector has impelled Congress to reassert its ageless prerogative of keeping the Executive in his place. While Robert McNamara's superlative performance as the first *real* Secretary of Defense may bring joy to the hearts of those concerned with civilian control of the military, it brings nothing but despair to those congressional magnates who have for years exercised baronial functions within the Pentagon. Congress has an unarticulated but nonetheless real interest in keeping the Presidency inefficient.

If the President succeeds, as Kennedy has, in bringing unprecedented unity to the sprawling administration, he must pay for his
sins on some other issue.

Kennedy should have anticipated the vengeful assault of Congress on his legislative program. He should have realized, first,
that this was a historically understandable revolt of the barons
against the assertion of royal jurisdiction; and, second, that it
could not be contained, let alone mastered, by intramural techniques, that is, by the hallowed methods of White House pressure,
or by modern techniques of liberal technocrats. The trouble is
that the technocratic manual of "Presidential Leadership" does not
provide guidance in this area. If the right man calls up a congressman and explains why he should support a pending bill, the
legislator may well go along; if seventeen earnest and slightly
menacing young presidential myrmidons hit the phone, he will
probably blow his top. Seventeen times zero is still zero, and nothing arouses a congressman more than being treated as a Thing, as
a piece on the chessboard. Some furious senator recently reported
a call demanding that he support a bill which he had in fact introduced; when he asked why he was thus arraigned, the reply
came, "Because you were on my list!"

After some months of anxiety, the congressmen now sense that
they have the edge on technique. When the earnest young men,
primed with such excellent studies as James MacGregor Burns's
Roosevelt: The Lion and the Fox and Richard Neustadt's *Presidential Power*, go up to the Hill, they are entering the lion's den
and the fox's lair. The minute a President tries to deal with Congress by clandestine finagling, he is trapped: he is playing with
their dice, and in politics all dice are loaded. (This is not intended
as a cynical observation, but rather as an illustration of the theoretical point that political techniques are never neutral. Is there
anything more political than the nonpolitical speeches F.D.R.
kept delivering on the decks of warships in the 1944 campaign?
Or, to take another example from the recent imbroglio in Massachusetts, wasn't Edward Kennedy's call for high-level discussion
avoiding "personalities" a superb rhetorical gambit, designed to
bring Edward McCormack onto the field of battle stripped of his

best weapon, the charge that Kennedy was running on his chromosomes?)

Political efficiency experts have little use for "narrow interests"; their favorite shibboleth is the "common good." But the common good, as technocrats have to learn the hard way, cannot be injected like cold serum, at least, not in a free society. It must grow from shared convictions and shared trust; that is, one must either share the ideals or trust their spokesman *despite* ideological reservations. And on this vital level, cleverness and mastery of technique are secondary to bonds of empathy—a fact few technocrats have ever comprehended. (Those who put their faith in Machiavelli all too often forget that the Florentine died both broke and out of office.) Roosevelt's tremendous authority did not rest at base on his finesse as a manipulator, but on his amazing capacity to inspire trust. To utilize Roosevelt's tactics without F.D.R. is to play *Hamlet* without the Prince.

No one can blame John F. Kennedy for not being F.D.R. The constant calls upon the President to "go to the people" are perhaps based on the illusion that the "Fireside Chat" is a technique of universal validity—with Presidents as interchangeable parts. Yet, the fact remains that the New Frontier, for all its remarkable achievements in many areas, has little political vitality. And the reason for this, I am convinced, is that it has drawn its inspiration almost wholly from the tradition of liberal technocracy.

During the war, I was once dragged out of the barracks at 3:30 A.M. to greet some VIP. The colonel's orders were "BE SPONTANEOUS!" Perhaps to urge the New Frontiersmen to "BE VITAL" is advice in the same self-defeating category. To many it may suggest only that they increase their already unnerving patterns of frenetic activity—hold twice as many conferences, utter twice as many bureaucratic war whoops, run twice as many laps around the Hill.

But the vitality I am talking about is a qualitative, not a quantitative, response. It is a joyous commitment to battle against injustice and inequality which, while it may risk short-run defeats, can provide the foundations for long-run victory. There is a time to throw away the manual on "Efficient Relations with

Congress," to forget about "winning over the business community" (this can be done only by losing to Republicans), to call the roll of your friends and defy your enemies, and run up the old battle flags.

Technocrats, liberal and otherwise, are always leery of the people (who keep intruding *human factors* into the decision-making process). Yet American liberalism took this country from the Yahoos because it blasted away the moral foundations of the "old order" and convinced a majority of the American people that the liberals stood for a new society based on the ideals of political equality and economic justice. And we still have a good distance to go before we can compliment ourselves on the achievements of our time: the Negro and the Puerto Rican still stand outside the door and, despite the claptrap about "trade-union tyranny," there are still great sectors of the work force—agriculture and the service trades, to mention but two—which await transformation from commodities to human beings.

Let us draw the line, and fight. Let us make clear that the Kennedy administration is not in Washington for the sake of the Game, but to attain certain precious goals. We are not playing touch football. From a pragmatic viewpoint, the administration could not have lost its legislative program more ignominiously had it blown the utopian trumpet, and the meticulous etiquette of the administration has only obscured the real issues and provided laughs in Congress: Wilbur Mills, of Arkansas, cannot be cozened by a friendly presidential head-pat on TV; he will merely smile and raise the ante.

The real problem in politics, particularly for those with ideological loyalties, is to sense when *not* to compromise. In a situation where some are arguing that $2 + 2 = 6$, while others assert the sum is 4, there can always be found the "moderates" who want, in the interests of harmony, to split the difference and settle for 5. If one begins with the assumption that all determinations are relative, this is understandable, even commendable: All good pragmatists will rally around $2 + 2 = 5$ as a "focus of consensus," and condemn with equal vigor the "extremists" who maintain that $2 + 2 = 6$ *and* those who stand firm behind 4.

If one proclaims the sovereignty of certain axioms or values, however, this whole process is absurd. If we believe in racial equality, we cannot be prepared to settle for, say, desegregating half the schools. If we believe in freedom, we cannot accept a world *status quo* which legitimizes Communist, or any other, totalitarianism. The principle of "liberation," which has been sullied by its irresponsible associations with the Dulles *frères*, is implicit in the democratic, liberal ethic. Dedication must obviously be tempered by prudence: the long-range assimilation of the Negro will not be forwarded by the use of marital law to desegregate the South, and freedom for those under totalitarian rule can hardly be attained by a nuclear holocaust. But the ideal must be asserted, and expediential considerations—which set tactical limits—cannot be permitted to vitiate the integrity of the premise. We cannot back away from equality because of white resistance, any more than we can backpedal from the goal of freedom because of the risks of war.

The Kennedy administration sadly needs an infusion of liberal enthusiasm (which must be distinguished from activism), of good old-fashioned crusading zeal. I have spent too many years in local politics to depreciate the value of political finesse, but tactical skill can add little to liberal accomplishments unless it is superimposed on substantive commitments. Thus, in a paradoxical sense, my criticism of the Kennedy performance is an outgrowth of my conviction that it is, in the Aristotelian sense, politically inept; that is, it emphasizes technique at the expense of essence.

A liberalism that puts its faith in technocracy can never unleash the creative energies of the American people. The free society of participating equals, which is our collective aspiration, cannot, to borrow some terms from theology, be attained by works alone but only by a dynamic compound of faith and works. Perhaps the real tragedy of the New Frontier arises from its almost neurotic fear of utopian commitments. Can the good society be built by men who are incapable of—or ashamed of—dreaming?

Memo to Today's "Young Radicals"

It is disconcerting to an individual who still thinks of himself as "young" and is proud of his standing as a militant liberal to discover that somehow a new generation of dissenters has slipped in behind him, a generation which views him personally as a decent middle-aged type and ideologically as an ornament of the Establishment. Sometimes this evaluation can be puzzling: my election as National Chairman of Americans for Democratic Action was welcomed in one campus newspaper as proof that one could get ahead in the United States by repudiating the principles of his radical youth! (Perhaps they confused A.D.A. with A.T.&T.?)

Another youngster, more in sorrow than in anger, inquired clinically why I had "betrayed" the "dreams of the thirties." When I told him, first, that I thought he used the verb "betray" rather too casually, and, second, that we were now living in the 1960's, he shook his head in a knowing, patronizing fashion and walked away.

The revolt of one generation against its elders is a timeless phenomenon and perhaps should be accepted in the scientific spirit as predictable "abreaction." Moreover, a case can be made in the best tradition of American pragmatism that youthful radicalism is a harbinger of Success in Life; presumably young people, having sown their wild ideological oats, can then settle in for a life of creative moneymaking, and display considerably

Reprinted, with permission, from *The New York Times Magazine*, October 14, 1962.

more imagination in the process than their staid competitors who have been trapped in the conservative mold. A number of my former radical students are now quite successful lawyers and men of affairs. They always give me an affectionate greeting and inquire how my "crusades" are going, a question asked in the same tone as an inquiry about one's elderly, eccentric maiden aunt.

One can react to this in one of two fashions. On the one hand, he can look on this transformation as an inexorable process, like the ebb and flow of the tides. The classic example of this cast of mind was John Wilkes's response to the stones of a mob: "They are only some of my old pupils," said the elderly agitator, "setting up for themselves." Implicit in this view is the assumption that revolt is merely a generational conditioned reflex and that the ideas and doctrines involved are wholly ancillary to a basic "instinct" of rebellion.

However, if one believes that young men and women become radicals because they believe in something besides spiting their families, he cannot accept this easy out. To do so would be to take refuge in intellectual nihilism, to take a course which must be rejected by anyone who cherishes the vocation of a teacher and the principles which have nourished the American liberal and radical traditions.

These reflections on the current state of radical youth are based on the conviction that a vital current of dissent among young people, on the campus and off, is an essential stimulus, if not a precondition, to the attainment of the free society which is our national and international aspiration. And my reservations about the current generation of young radicals are founded on my suspicion (based on close observation) that it is fundamentally escapist and otherwordly, that its radicalism is that of Fifth Monarchy men or Tibetan lamas rather than that of the abolitionists, Debs, La Follette, or John Dewey. They are not to my mind radical enough.

To be specific, there seems to be a nostalgic regret at not having been young in the thirties. It may seem odd to those who emerged from the Depression into the War to learn that the 1930's were the radical Garden of Eden, that never before or since has there been such a splendid time to be alive and young. The days were full of mass meetings; the police were brutal; the call to the barricades was clear and compelling. And the *theoretical* discussions—they were endless and masterful, with brilliant, devoted leaders polemicizing on Real issues.

So runs the myth—a myth which I regret to say has largely been created and nurtured by a group of professional "Radicals of the Thirties" who seem to be preserved, like flies in amber, in the militant postures of their youth. I have always felt a sense of compassion toward the "student emeritus"—the young man or woman who considers his four undergraduate years the high point of creative experience—and I have the same reaction to these aging Robespierres who clutter up the Left-sectarian journals with their incantations and exhort the young to stand up and be counted on the issues of thirty years ago.

Let me make it clear that I am not "repudiating" my radical youth. To state that the ideas of thirty years ago no longer seem adequate for coping with reality is hardly to do penance for one's sins. Nor does the statement that, viewed with retrospective omniscience, most of these ideas were neither terribly bright nor particularly relevant to the issues of that time. For if our responses were less than prescient, the fact remains that they were *ours*. Nobody gave instructions on how to be a radical; we reacted existentially against our world.

When I became involved with the Young Peoples' Socialist League in the late thirties, I did so as a protest against an economic system which had kept my father unemployed or semiemployed for most of the decade, against a social system which took racial discrimination for granted, and against an international system which seemed to guarantee the triumph of totalitarianism and the menace of war. And if the solutions I expounded were unrealistic, they were hardly less so than those proclaimed by the British Prime Minister, the French Premier, or—be it noted—the American President. (Whatever Roosevelt's inner convictions about Hitler may have been, his public statements of that period hardly indicated any great insight into the true dimensions of the Nazi menace.)

But having stated this, we still must confront the hard fact, which can easily be documented by reference to the radical periodicals of that time, that most of the time and energy of young militants was devoted to windmill tilting and sectarian squabbling. It may well be that many of the ideas of the New Deal were borrowed from old radical platforms, but throughout the 1930's organized radicalism spent much of its efforts disowning its children and invoking the curse of Fascism upon the Roosevelt administration.

With respect to the international scene and the baleful rise of Nazi power, we incessantly and frenetically demanded a positive anti-Fascist policy—one of all steps short of action. We were so mesmerized by the "revelations" about World War I (the outcome of a munitions-industry plot) and burdened by guilt about Versailles (which "created Nazism") that we shied away from any confrontation with the reality of Nazi aggression. If someone pointed out starkly the exact connotations of Hitlerite power, we began hastily to discuss the problem of reparations or the "legitimate demands" of the German people. If he persisted, we called him a "warmonger," and suggested that he was an agent of du Pont or some other "merchant of death."

And the sectarian debates! To make sense out of them at this time would press the talents of a medieval scholastic or Talmudic scholar. Perhaps because we were living in political frustration on the littoral of events, these often assumed the importance of the controversy over the Nicene Creed.

While I cannot give a firsthand account of the early and middle 1930's there are enough accounts that square with my later impressions to indicate that the same generalizations hold for the earlier period. And they add up to one major conclusion: that the myth of the wonderful, creative radical 1930's has been vastly overdrawn for later consumption. This is not to suggest that there were not fresh breezes blowing in the land, but rather to argue that *organized* radicalism was pretty sterile and introverted.

Indeed, as I look back over almost a quarter of a century of involvement in Socialist and liberal movements, I suspect that the greatest contribution that the "Radical Thirties" made was not an ideology (no great ideas emerged) but cadre training!

A steady stream of able and dedicated young people achieved

political maturity in radical activity, and moved into positions in government, trade unions, or the professions. And it is interesting that, while they generally abandoned their sectarian stances and no longer sat up all night debating the consequences of Trotsky's "French turn," these men and women rarely "repudiated" their radicalism or turned ferociously upon their childhood gods. (This became a specialty of ex-Communists.) They retained the ideals of their youth, but abandoned the methods of organized radicalism.

To put the point differently, these concerned people had become radicals because they sought to transform the United States from a nation sunk in poverty and depression, racked by racial and religious discrimination and seemingly on "The Road to War" (to use the title of Walter Millis's savage, best-selling attack on American intervention in World War I), to a society governed by the principles of economic and political justice and human equality, living in a peaceful world.

They did not become radicals for the sake of the title but as a genuine and idealistic response to the world as they saw it. They fought America as it was (seen darkly) in the name of America as it could become; they fought the society because they loved its potentialities, not as a gesture of alienated despair. And by their fighting they helped to accomplish the major transformations which have made the United States today an immeasurably better, freer, more decent society than it was in my childhood, let alone my father's.

In short, the thirties were a time of travail, of absurdity, and of attainment for American radicals. The sad part of the present re-creation and idealization of the radical ambience is its excessive concentration on the absurdities, on the ideological fripperies. (Young postulants seem, for example, far more interested in my encounters with "La Guardia's cossacks"—the mounted police— than they are in the rise of the trade-union movement or the work of the American Civil Liberties Union.)

A second area of historical misinterpretation concerns the role and nature of the Communist Party and its front groups. Many young radicals today see the Communists as a pathetic, persecuted group, respect the *sincerity* of party militants (our time is plagued by what Irving Howe has called the "cult of sincerity"), and accuse liberal spokesmen of "capitulating to McCarthyism" or "joining the Red-baiters." This is part of the mythology of a guilty liberal past which finds left- and right-wingers in a historical united front: we either "Red-baited" or "appeased" the Communists.

Obviously, I cannot here examine this myth in its totality, but I should like to submit two brief historical notes.

First, as Elmer Davis pointed out long ago in an astringent essay, the notion that all or most liberals in the 1930's were fellow travelers is sheer nonsense. On the contrary, the strength of Communist organizations thrived *as a direct coefficient of party endorsement of New Deal liberalism,* that is, in the period from 1936 to August, 1939. Who was fellow-traveling and with whom? And in the period of wartime harmony, liberal and Socialist groups were the source of what few discordant notes emerged about the intentions of Stalin.

Second, it is an interesting historical question whether all American intellectuals put together, had they supported the Soviet Union in disciplined fashion, could have done as much for the "Socialist fatherland" as did William Randolph Hearst (long the most vigorous supporter of recognition of the U.S.S.R. among "the masses" of Americans) and Henry Ford (whose Russian enterprises made an enormous contribution to Soviet technology). Patently, the quest for historical guilt is a dangerous game, one that can best be eliminated from democratic politics.

To return to the narrow concern of this essay—the assumption by many of the "New Left" activists that the Communists are sincere, dedicated idealists—we face a difficult problem in communication. The "young radicals" simply do not know what it is like to deal with an organized party caucus. Yet if this explanation affirms their innocence, it insults their intelligence; it presupposes that each generation of intellectuals must learn everything for itself—a denial of the basic premises of educational theory.

Moreover, these young people have in fact an active appreciation of history; if one criticizes Castro's dictatorial methods, he is liable to receive in return a vehemently detailed exposition of Cuban history since the Platt Amendment. (With the moral—

somehow reminiscent of the Moscow Trials—that the executed, though perhaps "objectively innocent," were "subjectively guilty" of standing in the way of history.)

No, if anything, history is their long suit, and I believe we must seek an explanation elsewhere for their selective historical vision. Though most of them have probably never met a Fascist, they are anything but reluctant to withhold condemnation. I think the real foundation of this moral restraint vis-à-vis Communism is their tremendous—and understandable—concern with peace. With peace as the goal, the logic then runs backward: If the U.S.S.R. is an aggressive totalitarian state like Nazi Germany, there will be war; war means annihilation; therefore, the U.S.S.R. *cannot be* an aggressive totalitarian state.

With this major premise safely anchored, the problem of evidence arises. Here Khrushchev steps into the breach with his speeches to the Twentieth and Twenty-second Party congresses, and the next link is supplied: *The Soviet Union has changed; it is moving toward democracy*. Now the structure of the argument is almost complete. The sins of the "old" Communists, the ones about whom the liberals warn, are all attributed to the wicked Stalin, and a new era of "polycentrism" is dawning. There is then a great rush to the pages of a recent issue of the British New Left Review, which chronicles a fascinating debate in the Italian Communist Party Congress (curiously omitting Togliatti's windup speech) and a joyous conclusion that Communists *now* are almost democratic. Therefore we shall not be annihilated, *unless* we continue our military provocations. Q.E.D.

To challenge this logic is possibly to invite designation as the Chairman of the Committee for an Insane Nuclear Policy, but that risk must be run. Leaving aside the logic, which is patently absurd, this line of argument raises several important issues.

First of all, on the factual level one is justified in questioning the change of heart of the Soviet Party leaders. When a disciplined battalion executes "To the rear—*march*!" the observer does not ordinarily congratulate the commander on the democratic behavior of his troops. I would have been more encouraged by the formation in the U.S.S.R. of a nationwide "Committee to

Secure Justice for Stalin," or by the refusal of the city fathers of Stalingrad to rebaptize their metropolis.

To say this is not to deny for a minute that there are hopeful long-range developments in Soviet society, or to suggest that war is inevitable. The Soviet Union, unlike Nazi Germany, is clearly in the hands of shrewd, cold-blooded leaders who are anything but madmen. Moreover, I lean strongly toward the position of P. M. S. Blackett that the Soviet *nuclear* posture is essentially defensive, with the corollary that the United States is wasting prodigious effort on "overkill" and could move safely toward reallocation of resources to social and economic objectives and a considerable measure of disarmament.

I have therefore vigorous reservations about our current policies, but these are in no way based on the assumption that Khrushchev has "good intentions" toward the West, or that the international Communist movement has done more than switch from Stalinist rigidity to a truly Leninist policy of flexible infiltration.

But my fundamental doubts about the young radical positions on Communism and the nature of the Cold War are not logical or factual, but moral in character. I question the degree to which they are at base devoted to peace. The pacifist occupies a noble place in the radical tradition (though quantitatively speaking a small percentage of pacifists have been radical; the bulk have come from religious bodies with extremely conservative views on matters of social and economic policy); under many circumstances, including in the United States in World War I, the radical pacifist risked his very life in testifying to his convictions.

In other words, to the radical pacifist, here and abroad, peace was a moral good, not a precondition for survival. Men of this caliber stood firm in their beliefs even under Nazi and Communist torture—they had no "favorite wars" and drew an absolute line against the employment of force in human affairs. They defied the ultimate sanction of the state in the name of a perhaps impractical yet luminous ideal.

By contrast with these men and women, whose vital integrity one must venerate even if he can not share their inspiration, today's peace movement—the matrix of young radicalism—seems fundamentally expediential in its approach to war and violence.

Peace is valued as an instrument of survival, and consequently one set of standards is employed with regard to the relations between the U.S.A. and the U.S.S.R. and another to "colonial wars of liberation" (the latter presumably do not threaten radical survival). And while performing these moral acrobatics, the militants keep up a raucous hue and cry against the "Establishment liberals" for being compromisers unwilling to take a "strong stand for peace."

Let me state clearly that there is nothing wrong with survival —I enjoy life immensely and should regret an untimely exit— but it is utterly impossible to build a meaningful ethic, much less a liberal or radical ethic, on the proposition that the core value in life is continued existence. The statement "I want to live" probably reflects the initial response of most of us to any perilous situation, but hopefully our values inject a new dimension of individual and collective aspiration. If they do, we get the heroism of the Warsaw Ghetto or the Hungarian Freedom Fighters. When they do not, we find the supine cravenness of the *Kapo*, the collaborating inmate of the Nazi death camps, or the "progressive" American POW in Korea.

To say this is not to deny any individual's right to choose survival as his key value. What I am suggesting is that those who claim to speak for morality—who on occasion, indeed, indicate that any who question their prophetic insights are little more than immoral warmongers—should look to their premises.

A politics of peace, whatever its operational liabilities, has idealistic integrity; a politics of survival is a form of moral bankruptcy. And perhaps it might be kept in mind that this is not the first generation of young Americans that has lived in peril. The scope of the danger is vastly greater than ever before, but one can die only once.

In essence, I hope that these young activists will not recapitulate the errors in judgment of their elders, that they will make their own mistakes, not imitate ours. What I suppose disturbs me more than anything else is the feeling of *déjà vu* that overwhelms me when I hear the peace slogans or the discussions of Communism. It almost seems as though a conscious spiritual effort were under way to exorcise the hard lessons of the past twenty-five years. But conformity to an archaic heresy can never provide a viable radical ideology; it leads to a form of monasticism built around frozen liturgies and endlessly spinning prayer wheels. A rhetoric replaces a morality.

Each generation of radicals, then, must confront its own demons (not those of its elders); and American life today suffers from the absence of a cogent radical critique, one which attempts to face the new problems that have hit the country and the world since World War II. The young militants have demonstrated some of their potentialities in the brilliantly mounted and disciplined nonviolent campaign against racial segregation, and anyone who knows them recognizes the vast fund of talent they can draw upon.

I hope they will abandon the diversionary pilgrimages to the shrines of the thirties, and their apocalyptic posture toward the crises of our time, and assume the responsibilities, the moral obligations, of radicalism. For radicalism at base is neither a shrill complaint about the tragedy of life nor ancestor worship—it is the elaboration of a moral critique of society which strikes to the existential roots of the human condition.

A Review of *The Ordeal of Power: A Political Memoir of the Eisenhower Years* by Emmet John Hughes

This is a curious book. It is not in fact a *political* memoir of the Eisenhower years, but rather an existential critique of how Ike let Emmet Hughes down. Essentially identifying autobiography with political theory, Hughes has set out what might be described as a semi-*mea culpa*. But still the point remains that Ike, not Hughes, was responsible for the disenchantment—a proposition logically on all fours with blaming the bartender for an alcoholic nightmare.

The Eisenhower myth is a fascinating topic for extended exploration. For some strange reason this extremely decent, unpretentious Kansan became the center of a series of exercises in political witchcraft. Beginning in 1948, when some of my best friends went into a trance and decided that Ike could save American liberalism, ranging through 1952—of which more subsequently— to 1956, when a whole troupe of "Eisenhower Marxists" sprang up dedicated to the thesis that Ike was the "peace candidate," Dwight D. Eisenhower was the repository of the dialectical hopes of all types of essentially nonpolitical Americans. Curiously, no one in these various configurations ever talked much about Eisenhower's capacities as an individual or as a President—he was cherished for his symbolic value, as an incarnation of some "historic force." Indeed, one of the supporting arguments often appeared to be that he lacked personal ambition or ideological dedication, that he would respond to "history" in a fashion that would be impossible in other men, bound by selfish or fanatical loyalties.

Reprinted, with permission, from *The Reporter*, March 28, 1963.

Thus in 1948, he was seen as the instrument for beating the Republicans without intruding into the work of the liberal Establishment, and in 1956 as one who could transcend the petty fanaticisms of the Democratic "cold warriors" and reach a *modus vivendi* with Khrushchev.

Hughes's narrative begins in 1952, and it is to that *annus mirabilis* that we should turn. In that year, with the thunderings of McCarthy filling the air, the notion suddenly got loose in the land that the cure for Republican "irresponsibility" was the election of a Republican President and Congress. It was not a contest between Dwight D. Eisenhower and Adlai Stevenson, but rather a stand at Armageddon for the "two-party system." Although no sane man has ever argued that the cure for bank robbery is to install the robbers as bank presidents, Walter Lippmann and other solemn pundits announced that precisely this principle should govern the electorate's decision in 1952. Those of us who argued (with admitted partisan bias) that the best cure for political irresponsibility was a good beating were disdained as *naïfs*. When I, for example, noted that in Uruguay the Blanco opposition had been out of office for ninety-five years with remarkable therapeutic results, I was informed that democracy in America hung in the balance—that another Democratic victory would drive the Republicans to *real* extremism. When we inquired diffidently if McCarthy defeated in Wisconsin would not be preferable to McCarthy as chairman of the Senate Governmental Operations Committee, we were chastized for insufficient dialectical sophistication.

Now, I am prepared to argue (and have argued at length elsewhere) that the "two-party system" in American politics is a state and local rather than a national phenomenon (and President Kennedy's current travail on the Hill can be adduced in evidence), but what is important here was Emmet Hughes's conviction that a victory for Eisenhower could restore two-partyism to its pristine grandeur. Ike, he believed, would rebuild the Republican Party and bring it into the twentieth century. In harsher moments, a decade ago, I was inclined to think that this two-party hypothesis served many as a convenient rationalization for not supporting Adlai Stevenson, who they admitted was the "better man" but not the better incarnation. However, the human capacity for autohypnosis is almost inconceivable, so let us draw the blinds quietly on this argument, with the parting observation that given the structure of political power in the United States, no President, whatever his genius, can organize his party from the top. What precisely can John F. Kennedy do to Otto Passman? to Harry Byrd? to John Stennis? or, *a fortiori*, to James Eastland?

Eisenhower disappointed Hughes by his lack of leadership in this and other areas of policy. And it is true that Ike did not even put up a fight against his congressional magnates. While a President cannot "build" his party like a child piling up blocks, he can develop an independent constituency of his own and bring great pressure on the legislature. Kennedy certainly believes in this, although his actions to date suggest that he still cherishes the illusion that he can somehow hypnotize the barons on the Hill into jumping through the hoop. (I suspect that 1964 will see a radical shift in this "inside" policy vis-à-vis Congress: the arrival of a year divisible by four has a traumatic effect on Presidents.) Yet, aside from his reading of the speeches he wrote for Candidate Eisenhower, did Hughes have any reason to believe that Ike would turn out to be the leader of his dreams?

In other words, did Eisenhower ever change? If he did, then perhaps Hughes has a case. If not, then it really is unfair to hold the President responsible for the eccentric illusions he created in the minds of the impressionable. To put it differently, Was there anything in his record that would indicate that Dwight D. Eisenhower would confront the crises of the 1950's with imagination and decisiveness? Again making it clear that my political judgment carries with it no slurs on his personal character, I submit that the evidence indicated the opposite. Never a Great Captain —as Douglas MacArthur, for example, unquestionably was— Eisenhower rode George Marshall's coattails to the top of the military pyramid. In essence, he was a military diplomat who could be counted upon (by techniques that became famous, and exasperating to Emmet Hughes in the President) to blur issues and prevent stark confrontations from occurring. His strategy in Europe as it emerged in the disputes with the British was based on a simple West Point maxim: Grant beat Lee. Later, as Chief of Staff, when he was in the slot formerly occupied by the quietly decisive Marshall, he was indecisive, harried, and probably profoundly unhappy. Nasty problems (such as the desegregation of the Armed Forces) which demanded a confrontation with abstractions simply would not go away, no matter how studiously they were ignored or pigeon-holed. Safely reinstalled as SACEUR in the familiar atmosphere of military diplomacy— and with the hard, ruthless mind of Dean Acheson handling the abstractions—he flourished again. To make a long story short, Eisenhower was always allergic to decisions: he was finely equipped to be the adjutant to a decisive chief. Unfortunately, this is more a characterological than an intellectual matter: one cannot take a training course on How to Make Final Decisions.

It may seem unfair to rub salt on Emmet Hughes's already flagellated back, and it would be if these observations were founded on the wisdom of hindsight. But the hard fact is that a number of us said this in 1952—Sam Rayburn probably gave it the classic formulation, "Good man, wrong job"—and while we welcome Hughes to the ranks and cheerfully absolve him, we can hardly be expected to wipe the slate clean. History, after all, did not start the day he took up his pen to write *The Ordeal of Power*.

Index

Index

[A]

Abolitionists, kidnapping of, 50
Abrams case, 218
Acción Democrática of Venezuela, 394
Acheson, Dean, 62, 339, 445
Adams, Henry, 245
Adams, John, 14, 68, 78, 81, 82, 109, 421; on American exceptionalism, 67; and Constitutional Convention, 67, 96; quoted, 16; and Sedition Law, 66
Adams, Sherman, 92
Age of the Democratic Revolution (Palmer), 92
Age of Jackson, The (Schlesinger), 249
Age of Reform (Hofstadter), 65
Age of Roosevelt, The (Schlesinger), 85
Alaskan Cannery Workers case, 200
Algeria, 388
Alien Enemies Act, Gallatin on, 22
Alien and Sedition Acts, 18, 78–84
Allen, John, 79

America, 336
American Civil Liberties Union, 46, 236, 436; Baldwin on, 31–32, 46; Kentucky chapter of, 403; value of, 31–32
American Communism and Soviet Russia (Draper), 87
American Federation of Labor, 313
AFL v. Watson, 181
American Foreign Policy and the Separation of Powers (Cheever and Haviland, Jr.), 146–147
American Legion, 32, 236
American Political Science Review, 254
"American Political Thought and the Study of Politics" (McCloskey), 240
American Revolution, and concepts of liberty, 68–69
American Veterans Committee, 344
Americans Betrayed (Grodzins), 223
Americans for Democratic Action, 416, 432
Anabaptists, 9, 10
Anglicanism, 9–11

Animal Farm (Orwell), 293, 294

Annual Report of ACLU, 67

Antifederalists, The (Main), 252–254

"April Theses," of Lenin, 281

Areopagitica (Milton), 6

Arendt, Hannah, 296, 297; on totalitarianism, 61

Aristotle, 61, 240, 297

Arrival and Departure (Koestler), 393

"Ashwander rules," 196

Associated Press case, 178–179

Aswan Dam, 387

Attlee, Clement, 263, 264, 265–266, 272, 305

Au Pays du Grand Mensonge (Ciliga), 294

Aurora (Bache), 80, 81

Autobiography (T. Roosevelt), 140

Avery, Sewell, 144

[B]

Bache, Benjamin Franklin, 80, 81

Baghdad Pact, 383

Baldwin, Abraham, at Constitutional Convention, 108

Baldwin, Hanson W., 349–350

Baldwin, Luther, 80

Baldwin, Roger, 397; on ACLU, 31–32, 46

Baldwin, Stanley, 323

Banks and Politics in America (Hammond), 247–251

Barnette case, 235

Barnhart, Edward N., 222

Barron v. *Baltimore*, 21

Bassett, Reginald, 323

Batista, Fulgencio, 390

Bay of Pigs Invasion, 397

Bean, Louis H., 335, 336

Beard, Charles, 92

Ben Avon case, 201

Benjamin, Judah P., 42

Bentham, Jeremy, 210

Berger, Victor, 285

Berkman, Alexander, 284

Berman, Emile Zola, 370

Bernstein, Edouard, 270, 274, 286, 289

Bernstein, Irving, 85–87

Bevan, Aneurin, 257–259, 264–268, 273–274, 305

Bevin, Ernest, 260, 263, 272, 273

Biddle, Francis, 31, 222, 224, 249

Biddle, Nicholas, 249

Bill of Rights, 27

Binkley, Wilfred E., 129

Birney, James G., 404

Black, Hugo, 30, 56, 132, 170, 175; and *Carpenters and Joiners Union, Local 213,* v. *Ritters Café,* 181; and *Falbo* v. *United States,* 185; and flag-salute controversy, 236; and *Inland Waterways* case, 181–182; and *Meadowmoor* case, and Murphy, 176; and *United States* v. *Columbia Steel Company,* 182–183; as war hawk, 183

Blackett, P. M. S., and Soviet nuclear posture, 439

Blum, Léon, 270

Bolshevik Revolution, 283, 289

Book-of-the-Month Club, 374

Boorstin, Daniel, 91

Bozell, L. Brent, 340

Brandeis, Louis D., 215, and "Ashwander rules," 196

Brearley, David, at Constitutional Convention, 102, 105, 111

Brewer, David J., quoted, 139–140

Bridges, Styles, 422

British Communist Party, 261

British Labour Party, 269, 283, 303, 320–324; and crisis in British Socialism, 257–268; internal situation in, 271–279; and Scarborough Conference, 269, 271, 275

British Labour Representation Committee, 321–322

British Liberal Party, 322

British Parliamentary Labour Party, 269, 321

British social values, Americanization of, 272

British Trades Disputes Act, 263

British Trades Union Congress, 259, 267

Brogan, Denis W., 337

Brown v. *Board of Education*, 188, 209, 210, 212

Brown, George, 278, 279

Brownists, 9

Buckley, William F., Jr., 340, 420

Bukharin, Nicolai, 282, 290

Bureaucracy, and enthusiasts, 303–319

Burns, James MacGregor, 85, 428; and study of FDR, 245

Burton, Harold H., 153

Butler, David, 212

Butler, Pierce, 169; at Constitutional Convention, 114

Byrd, Harry, 112, 444

[C]

Cabell, Joseph, Jefferson letter to, 11

Cachin, Marcel, 285–286

Cahn, Edmond, 211

Calhoun, John C., 18, 113, 114, 242

Callaghan, James, 279

Callender, James T., 81

Calvin, John, 281

Calvinism, 17

Campbell, Angus, 212

Camus, Albert, 341

Captive Mind, The (Milosz), 61, 296

Cardozo, Benjamin, 27

Carlson v. *California*, 180

Carlyle, Thomas, 322

Carolene Products case, 165

Carpenters and Joiners Union, Local 213, v. *Ritters Café*, 181

Carter v. *Illinois*, 175–176

Case of Comrade Tulayev, The (Serge), 280–301

Case of Victor Serge, 280–301

Castle, Barbara, 279

Castro, Fidel, 271, 390, 392, 396, 437

Catholicism and freedom, 9–10

Censorship, and freedom of information, 359–369

Center for the Study of Democratic Institutions, 76

Chase, Salmon P., 26, 79

Cheever, Daniel S., 146–147

Chein, Isidor, quoted, 211

Chesterton, G. K., quoted, 350

Chocolate (Tarasov-Rodionov), 297

Christian Science Monitor, on fallout shelters, 411

Church of Jesus Christ, Latter-day Saints, persecution of, 70–71

Church and State, separation of, 227, 230, 231, 232–233, 235

Churchill, Winston, 258; and World War II, 414

Ciliga, Anton, 294

Civil liberties, climate in World Wars I and II, 52; current status of, in U.S., 39–64; during World War II, 31–32; state of, in 1900, 73; in U.S., 65–77

Civil Liberties Union of Massachusetts, 233

Civil rights, climate of, in 1930's and 1940's, 30–32, 45–47

Civil War, 400–404, 414; Amendments, 22–23; Centennial Commission, 400–404; and industrialism, 23

Claiborne, William C. C., Jefferson letter to, 244

Clark, Kenneth, and NAACP, 211

Clark, Thomas, 153

Clayton Antitrust Act, 424

Cleveland, Grover, 5; and Railroad Strike of 1894, 138, 139, 153

Clinton, George, 98

Cobbett, William, 81

Code of Instructions for the Government of the Armies in the Field (Lieber), 135

Collins, Harry Evans, 356

Columbia Encyclopedia, 211

Comintern, 280, 281–282, 285

Committee on the Bill of Rights of the American Bar Association, 236

Committee on Public Information, and George Creel, 141

Commonweal, 336

Communism, Chinese, 296; and political freedom, 59–60

Communist International, 280, 285

Communist Manifesto, The, 250, 386

Communist parties, in U.S., 285

Communists, and British Labour Party, 283–284

Comte, Auguste, 210

Condon, Robert L., 332

Confederation, Articles of, 14, 95, 97, 99, 101, 103

Congress of Racial Equality, 398

Congressional Directory, 332

Congressional Quarterly, examines 1952 congressional elections, 329

Conservatism in America (Rossiter), 4

Constitutional Convention, and Electoral College, 111, 112; and Federalists, 252; and motives of Founding Fathers, 91–126

Constitutionalism, theory and practice of American, 91–161

Constitutionalists, and the Constitutional Convention, 91–126 *passim*

Conversations with Stalin (Djilas), 294–295

Cooper, Thomas, 80

Corwin, Edward S., 22, 129, 186; on domestic prerogatives, 138, 142–143; on Roosevelt's "indirect sanctions," 145

Cotten, Goodwin B., and Andrew Jackson, 359

Coughlin, Father Charles, 49, 418

Cousins, Frank, 279

Creel, George, and Committee on Public Information, 141

Cripps, Stafford, 265, 272–273

Crosland, Anthony, 275, 279

Crosskey, William, 118

Crossman, R. H. S., 273–275, 279

Crowell v. Benson, 200

Cuba and the CIA, 390–391, 392

Cudahy Packing Co. v. *Holland,* 177

"Cult of sincerity," Howe on, 437

Cummings, Homer, 31

Curley, James Michael, 426

Current History and McCarthyism, 417

Cushman, Robert E., 22

[D]

Daily Worker, 24, 49, 338

Darkness at Noon (Koestler), 61, 293, 297–298; Howe critique of, 298

Darrow, Clarence, 168

Davis, David, and *Ex parte Milligan,* 186

Davis, Elmer, on liberals, 437

Davis, Jefferson, 43, 400, 401; and the press, 359

Debs, Eugene, 52, 54, 285, 433; on Frank's sentence, 75; and U.S. Supreme Court, 139, 140, 141, 154

Decter, Moshe, 399

Defence of the Constitutions of the Government of the United States of America (Adams), 16, 109

Deists, 17, 18

Dembritz, Nanette, on Nisei, 222–225

Democracy, decline of direct, 52

Democracy in America (Tocqueville), 21, 40

Democratic Digest, The, 339

Dennis v. *United States,* 198, 204

Desegregation cases, and Supreme Court, 351–352, 355

Deutsch, Morton, 356

Dewey, John, 433

De Witt, General, 223–224, 225

Diamond, Martin, critique of McCloskey, 241

Dickens, Charles, 322

Dickinson, John, at Constitutional Convention, 102

Dingell, John, 332

Disquisition on Government (Calhoun), 18, 114

Dissent, 417

Djilas, Milovan, 291, 294

Dominican Republic, 394, 395

Dos Passos, John, 86

Dostoevsky, Feodor, 303

Douglas, William O., 30, 153, 170 177, 180; and *Classic* case, 178; and flag-salute controversy, 236; and *Inland Waterways* case, 181–182; and *Meadowmoor* case, 180–181; and *N.L.R.B.* v. *Highland Park Manufacturing Co.,* 201; and opinion in *Regents' Prayer* case 237; and *U.S.* v. *Columbia Steel Co.,* 182–183; as war hawk, 183

Draper, Harold, on Lenin, 288

Draper, Theodore, 87

Dred Scott case, 22

Duane, William, 21–22

Due process, Field on, 27; and the Constitution, 25–27

Dulles, Allen, 431

Dulles, John Foster, 383, 388, 431; and "massive retaliation," 392

Duncan v. *Kahanamoku,* 186

Dunham, Allison, 165

Dyer, Mary, 229

Dzerzhinsky, Felix, 284

[E]

Eastland, James, 444

Eastman, Max, 86

Economics of the Transitional Period, 282

Eichmann trial, 297

Eighteenth Amendment, 353

Einaudi, Mario, 85

Eisenhower, Dwight D., 252, 333, 342, 362, 399, 418, 422; and Adlai Stevenson, 443; Administration of, 383, 388, 442–445; and Khrushchev, 443

Electoral College, and Constitutional Convention, 111, 112

Elkins, Stanley, 95

Ellsworth, Oliver, at Constitutional Convention, 108

Ely, Richard T., 322

Emancipation Proclamation, Lincoln and, 135

Enthusiasts and bureaucracy, 303–319

Epstein, Leon, 212

Ex parte Merrymen, and Taney, 135

Ex parte Milligan, 136, 137, 186

Ex parte Vallandigham, 135, 204

Exceptionalism, American, 67, 69

Executive, and power of Supreme Court, 127–161

[F]

Fabian Socialists, 424

Fabians, 260

Fairman, Charles, 79

Falbo v. United States, 185

Fallout shelters, 411

Farley, James, 426

FPC v. *Hope Natural Gas Co.*, 201

Federalism, 100; and Alexander Hamilton, 100, 101; and James Madison, 100

Federalist, The, 100, 101, 110, 119–120; quoted, 14–15, 16

Federalists, 18, 78–83, and anti-Federalists, 18; and the Constitutional Convention, 252

Fellowship of Reconciliation, 398

Fenno, John, 80, 81

Ferguson, Homer, 337

Fettered Freedom (Nye), 20, 50, 51

Field, Stephen, 215; on due process, 27

Fifth Amendment, 21

Figgis, John Neville, on political liberty, 11–12; quoted, 244

Fisher v. United States, 168

Fitzgerald, F. Scott, 86

Flag-salute controversy, 227–239 *passim*

Fleming v. Mohawk Wrecking and Lumber Co., 177

Flores, Edmundo, 394–395

Ford, Henry, 437

Founding Fathers, motives of, and Constitutional Convention, 91–126

Fourteenth Amendment, 19

Frank, Leo, case of, 74–75

Frank, John P., on Far East war-crimes procedure, 185; on Murphy, 178–179

Frankfurter, Felix, 30, 153, 163, 170, 216, 219; and *Brown v. Board of Education*, 188; and *Carter v. Illinois*, 175–176; and

Frankfurter, Felix (*Cont.*):
flag-salute controversy, 236; on *Gobitis* case, 165, 234–235; and *N.L.R.B.* v. *Highland Park Manufacturing Co.*, 201

Franklin, Benjamin, 109; at Constitutional Convention, 108, 115

Freedom, Communism and political, 59–60; individual, 8; and religion in U.S., 8–11; in rural America, 8–23; sources of, 75–77; in urban America, 23–33

Freedom Riders, 71, 402, 404

Freedom's Fetters (James Morton Smith), review of, 78–84

French Autonomous Party, 270

French Communist Party, 286

French Socialist Party, 265, 270, 313

Fromm, Erich, 305

Fulbright, William, 419

Fund for the Republic, supports Mary Knowles, 62

[G]

Gaitskell, Hugh, and British Labour and politics, 273, 274, 275, 276, 277, 278, 279, 426

Gallatin, Albert, 250, 421; on Alien Enemies Act, 22

Gallup Polls, 335

Garrison, William Lloyd, 50

Gazette of the United States, 80, 81; on Jeffersonian democracy, 42

Gerhardt case, 165

German Social Democratic Party, 313

Gerry, Elbridge, 115

Gide, André, 298

Gitlow v. *New York*, 27

Gladstone, Herbert, 323

Glasier, Bruce, 322

Gobitis case, 172, 188, 228, 234, 235, 236

God and Man at Yale (Buckley), 340

Goldman, Emma, 284

Goldwater, Barry, 91, 112

Gompers, Samuel, 321

Gooch, George P., quoted, 5

Goodrich, Carter, 250

Gordon, Milton M., on legislation of morality, 351–358

Graham, Howard Jay, 22, 79, 245

Grand Inquisitor, The (Dostoevsky), 303

Grapes of Wrath, The (Steinbeck), 171

Great Depression, 86, 87

Great Prince Died, The (Wolfe), 291

Great Purge, and Stalin, 293

Greeley, Horace, 359

Green, T. H., 219

Greenwood, Anthony, 272, 277, 279

Gregory, Thomas W., 52

Gressman, Eugene, 184

Grier, Robert C., 135, 136

Grodzins, Morton, 223

[H]

Hacker, Louis, 250

Hamilton, Alexander, 12, 13, 66, 91, 92, 93, 129, 133, 250; at Constitutional Convention, 98, 106, 116, 119; and Federalism, 100, 118; and Jefferson, 79–83

Hamilton, Walton, on framers of
    Constitution, 92
Hammond, Bray, 247–251
Handlin, Mary, 250
Handlin, Oscar, 250
Hardie, Keir, 322–323
Harlan, John M., dissent in *Plessy
    v. Ferguson*, 210; on restraint
    by technical rules, 201
Harper, Fowler, on discretionary
    review, 197
Harper, Robert Goodloe, 79
Harrington, James, 109
Harris, Louis, 426
Hart, James K., 129
Hartz, Louis, 91, 243, 250; *The
    Liberal Tradition in America*,
    4, 5
Haviland, H. Field, Jr., 146–
    147
Hayes, Rutherford B., and Rail-
    road Strike of 1877, 138
Healey, Denis, 279
Hearst, William Randolph, 437
Helphand, Alexander, 289
Hemingway, Ernest, 86
Henry, Patrick, 12, 115; at Con-
    stitutional Convention, 116–117;
    quoted, 3
Herberg, Will, 237
Hilferding, Rudolf, 289
Hillquit, Morris, 285
Hirabayashi case, 183, 184, 200,
    224, 225
Hiss, Alger, 62, 336, 420
*Historical and Moral View of
    the Origin and Progress of the
    French Revolution* (Woll-
    stonecraft), 16
*History of Bigotry in the United
    States* (Myers), 19

*History of the United States in
    the Administrations of Thomas
    Jefferson and James Madison*
    (Adams), 245
Hitler, Adolf, 295, 434
Hobbes, Thomas, 17, 68, 412
Hoffer, Eric, on self-sacrifice, 310
Hofstadter, Richard, 65; on aca-
    demic freedom, 51
Holmes, Oliver Wendell, Jr., 27,
    163, 215; on mob rule, 74; Ro-
    dell on, 218
Homage to Catalonia (Orwell),
    299
Hook, Sidney, 391
Howe, Irving, and critique of
    Darkness at Noon, 298; on "cult
    of sincerity," 437
Hughes, Emrys, on politics, 306–
    307
Hughes, John Emmet, 442–445
Hume, David, quoted, 100
Hungarian Revolt of 1956, 296
Hutchins, Robert M., 86

[I]

In re Neagle, and Supreme Court,
    139, 140, 141
Indirect sanctions, Roosevelt and,
    145
Industrial Workers of the World,
    49, 51
Industrialization, and liberty, 29
Inexpertise, doctrine of judicial,
    200–201
*Influence in the 1954 Mid-Term
    Elections* (Bean), 335–336
Information, freedom and censor-
    ship of, 359–369
Inland Waterways case, 181–182

Instituto de Educación Política, San José, Costa Rica, 394
Israel, and United States, 385

[J]

Jackson, Andrew, 249; and G. B. Cotten, 359
Jackson, Robert H., 30, 31, 163, 170, 177, 216; and *Barnette* case, 235; and *Ex parte Quirin*, 183; and flag-salute controversy, 236; and *Gobitis* case, 235–236; and *Jewel Ridge* case, 180; and Murphy, 177; and *N.L.R.B.* v. *Highland Park Manufacturing Co.*, 201; on Rostov, 219; and *Russian Orthodox Church* case, 232; and *Steel Seizure* case, 152; and *The Supreme Court in the American System of Government* reviewed, 215, 219, 221
Jay, John, 95, 119
Jefferson, Thomas, 12, 100, 117, 230, 250, 338; on American exceptionalism, 67; and Constitutional Convention, 96; and Hamilton, 79–83; letter to Cabell, 11; letter to Claiborne, 244; letter to McKean, 42; *Notes on Virginia*, 13, 14; quoted, 10; religious tolerance of, 41–42; Second Inaugural Address quoted, 66–67
Jehovah's Witnesses, 24, 172–173; and flag-salute, 227
Jenkins, Roy, 279
Jenner Committee, 344
Jensen, Merrill, 96, 253
Jessup, Philip, 341
Jewel Ridge case, 180

John Birch Society, and right-wingers, 416–422
Johnson, Andrew, 132
Johnson, Lyndon B., 382
Jones-Laughlin v. *N.L.R.B.*, 132
Jones v. *Opelika*, 172
Journal of Economic History, 249
de Jouvenal, Robert, 95

[K]

Kafka, Franz, 65, 393
Kamenev, Lev, 292
Kansas v. *Colorado*, 140
Kautsky, Karl, 286, 289
Kennedy, Edward, 428
Kennedy, John F., 76, 93, 248, 380–382, 388, 392, 395, 397, 408; administration of, 383–384, 405–410 *passim*, 443, 444; liberalism of, 423–431; and Nixon TV debates, 426–427; and shelter program, 413
Kennedy, Joseph P., 418
Kennedy, Robert, 381, 398
Kent, James, 41, 139
Key, V. O., 212
Keynes, John M., 327
Khrushchev, Nikita, 283, 294, 295, 399, 408, 439; and Eisenhower, 443; foreign policies of, 407–410; "Secret Speech" of, 297; speeches to 20th and 22nd Party congresses, 438; world politics of, 383–384, 386–387
Kibalchick, Victor Lvovich. *See* Serge, Victor
Know-Nothings, 50
Knowles, Mary, case of, 61–62
Knox, Philander C., 140
Koenig, Louis W., 144

Koestler, Arthur, 61, 293, 297–
    298, 393; quoted, 308
Korematsu case, 130–131, 144, 166,
    219, 224–225
Kort, Fred, on "Prediction of
    Supreme Court Decisions Math-
    ematically," 213–214
Kronstadt Revolt, 284, 291
Ku Klux Klan, 86
Kurland, Philip, on Church-State
    issues, 227; on Murphy, 163
Kutcher, James, 53

                        [L]

Labour and Politics, 1900–1906
    (Bealey and Pelling), reviewed,
    320–324
Ladejinsky, Wolf, 60
La Follette, Robert, 433
Landauer, Carl, 399
Lansing, John, at Constitutional
    Convention, 106, 107
Last Parallel, The (Russ), re-
    viewed, 374–376
Lattimore, Owen, 341
Laval, Pierre, 295
Lean Years, The (Bernstein), re-
    viewed, 85–87
Lee, Henry, 115, 117
Lee, Richard Henry, 115
Lee, Robert E., 401
Left-Wing Communism, 281, 282,
    283
Legacy of the Civil War
    (Warren), 401
Legislation of morality, 351–358
Lend-Lease Act, 197
Lenin, V. I., 281–282, 283, 285,
    286, 386; and British Labour,
    283–284; Draper on, 288; politi-

Lenin, V. I. (*Cont.*):
    cal theory of, 286–287, 289–290;
    and Trotsky, 287–288, 289, 290–
    291, 292
Lesinski, John, 332
Letter Concerning Toleration
    (Locke), 230
Lever Act, 138
Liberal Tradition in America
    (Hartz), 4, 5
Liberalism, and radicals, 432–441
Liberty, individual, 7; and indus-
    trialization, 29; pluralism of, 7–
    8; sources of American, 3–87;
    tradition of, in U.S., 1–38; and
    urbanization, 29
Lieber, Francis, 135
Lincoln, Abraham, 401, 405; dur-
    ing Civil War, 414–415; and
    Emancipation Proclamation,
    135; and non-statutory author-
    ity, 134–136; prerogative power
    of, 143; and the press, 359
Lippmann, Walter, 91, 361, 377–
    378, 426, 443
Lloyd George, David, 323, 386
Locke, John, 68, 109, 120, 146,
    230, 240, 355
Long, Huey, 49
Lumumba, Patrice, 387
Lusky, Louis, 165
Luxemburg, Rosa, 281, 286; on
    Lenin, 287
Lynching, of Abolitionists, 50, 51
Lynes, Russell, 54
Lyon, Matthew, 80

                        [M]

MacArthur, Douglas, 146, 395, 444
McCarthy, Joseph R., issue of,
    49, 327–339, 417

McCarthy and His Enemies (Buckley and Bozell), 340–343

McCarthyism, 327–343, 437; and American political tradition, 337; defined, 328; and election to Senate, 333–337

McCloskey, Robert, 240; Diamond critique of, 241

McCloskey v. Diamond, 240–246

McCormack, Edward, 428

McCormack, John W., 332

MacDonald, James Ramsay, 262, 273, 274, 321, 322–323

Machrowicz, Thaddeus, 332

McKean, Thomas, Jefferson letter to, 42

McKeon case, 370–373

McKinley, William, 70

McKitrick, Eric, 95

McReynolds, James Clark, 27, 187–188

McWilliams, Joe, 33

Madison, James, 12, 28, 80, 91, 92, 107, 108, 129, 253, 386; at Constitutional Convention, 102–103, 110, 115–116, 117, 119; and Federalism, 100, 101, 118; on New Jersey Plan, 107; Notes on Constitutional Convention, 99; social theory of, 14–17; and the Three-fifths Compromise, 112–113

Main, Jackson Turner, 252–254

Main Currents in American Thought (Parrington), 66

Maitland, Frederic, 250; on British liberty, 21; on English common law, 6; on Henry Spelman, 4; quoted, 118, 244

Mallory, Stephen, 43

Manwaring, David R., 227–239

Mao Tse-tung, 338

Marbury v. Madison, 137, 204, 217

Marshall, George C., 341, 444

Marshall, Chief Justice John, 21, 41, 80, 139, 166, 215; and *Dennis v. United States*, 204; and *Ex parte Vallandigham*, 204; and *Marbury v. Madison*, 137, 204; and *Mississippi v. Johnson*, 204; Rodell on, 217–218

Martin, Luther, at Constitutional Convention, 99, 100, 106, 109

Marx, Karl, 87, 240, 322

Mason, Alpheus, biography of H. F. Stone quoted, 163–164

Mason, George, 111, 113, 115

Massachusetts Bay Colony, 8; Quakers in, 229

Massachusetts *Body of Liberties* (1641), 62

"Massive retaliation," 392

Materialism and Empirio-Criticism (Lenin), 288

Matson, Floyd W., 222

Mayer, Daniel, 270

Meadowmoor case, 180–181

Men Who Ruled India, The (Woodruff), 302

Mensheviks, 287

Merton, Robert K., 354–355

Metzger, Walter, on academic freedom, 51

Meyer v. Nebraska, 27

Michigan Law Review, memorial issue for Frank Murphy, 162

Miller, Samuel F., 139

Millis, Walter, 13, 436

Mills, Wilbur, 430

Milosz, Czeslaw, 61, 296, 297

Milton, John, 10; and freedom of opinion, 6–7

Mississippi v. Johnson, 153, 204

Mob Rule, and the law, 73–75

Mollet, Guy, 270

Molotov, Vyacheslav, 295

Monatte, Pierre, 281

Montesquieu, Baron de la Brède et de, 109, 120

Montgomery Ward & Co., 144

Moral Decision, The (Cahn), 412

Mormonism, and secular regulation, 232–233

Morris, Gouverneur, 109; at Constitutional Convention, 113, 115

Morris, Robert, 253

Morris, William, 322

Morrison, Herbert, 261, 265, 272, 273

Mosca, Gaetano, on juridical defense, 25

Moscow trials, 293, 294, 295, 438

Movimiento Nacionalista Revolucionario of Bolivia, 394

Moyer v. Peabody, 218

Murphy, Frank, Justice, 31; and *AFL* v. *Watson,* 181; antimilitarism of, 185–186; and *Associated Press* case, 178; biography of, 168; and Black, 176; and *Carlson* v. *California,* 180; and *Carpenters and Joiners Union, Local 213,* v. *Ritters Café,* 181; and *Carter* v. *Illinois,* 175–176; and *Classic* case, 178; criticism of, 163; dissent in *Fisher* v. *United States,* 168; and *Duncan* v. *Kahanamoku,* 186; and Emergency Court of Appeals, 186; and *Falbo* v. *United States,* 185; and Far East war-crimes procedure, 185–186; and FDR, 165, 166, 167, 168–170; and flag-salute controversy,

Murphy, Frank (*Cont.*):
236; and *Fleming* v. *Mohawk Wrecking and Lumber Co.,* 177; and Frankfurter, 176; and H. F. Stone, 183; and *Hirabaya-shi* case, 183; and *Inland Water-ways* case, 181–182; and *Jewel Ridge* case, 180; and *Jones* v. *Opelika,* 172; as judge, 87–188; and the judicial process, 175–178; and *Korematsu* v. *United States,* 166; and *Kovacs* v. *Cooper,* 172; liberalism of, 162–193; and *Meadowmoor* case, 181; and New Deal tradition, 166–172; and Nisei, 184–185; opinions of, 172–186; and Owen Roberts, 177; and *Pennekamp* v. *Florida,* 176; and *Phelps-Dodge* case, 181; and Public Utilities Holding Company Act of 1935, 180; on responsibility of federal government, 179–183; and Robert Jackson, 177; on Sherman Act, 179; and states'-rights, 183; and *Steele* v. *Louisville & N.R.R.,* 173; support of minorities, 174; on *Tennessee Coal, Iron and R.R. Co.* v. *Muscoda Local 123,* 164; and *Thornhill* v. *Alabama,* 180; and *U.S.* v. *Bethlehem Steel Corp.,* 182; and *U.S.* v. *CIO,* 179; and *U.S.* v. *Columbia Steel Co.,* 182–183; and *U.S.* v. *Dotter-weich,* 178; and war powers, 183–186

Muste, A. J., 55

Myers, Gustavus, *A History of Bigotry in the United States,* 19

Myers case, 141
Myrdal, Gunnar, 211

[N]

Namier, Sir Lewis, 244, 247, 248
Nasser, Gamal A., 387
Nation, The, 167, 342, 421
National Association for the Advancement of Colored People, 72, 403, 404
National Review, 416
National War Labor Board, and Wilson, 138, 141
Naturalization Act of 1798, 83
Naylor, James, 10, 229
Near v. *Minnesota*, 363
Nehru, Jawaharlal, 387
Neustadt, Richard, 428
New Deal, 85, 166–172
New Jersey Plan, at Constitutional Convention, 103, 104, 105, 107
New Leader, The, 397, 399; and McCarthy, 417
New Orleans *Gazette*, 359
Newport, R.I., Committee of Inspection, 12
New Republic, The, 87, 167
New York Daily Advertiser, on Constitutional Convention, 100
New York Gazetteer, 12
New York Statute of 1781, quoted, 13
New York Times, 53, 257, 362, 363, 365, 367, 398, 411, 412, 419
New-York Tribune, 359
Nicaragua, 395
Nietzsche, Friedrich, 308
Nine Men (Rodell), reviewed, 215–218

1984 (Orwell), 61
Nineteen Thirty-one: Political Crisis, 323
Nisei, evacuation of, 200, 222–225
Nixon, Richard, 112, 380; and TV debates with Kennedy, 427
N.L.R.B. v. *Highland Park Manufacturing Co.*, 201
Nobel Prize Selection Committee, 377–378, 379
Nock, Albert Jay, 72
Nonconformity, 53–64
Nonpartisan League, 49
North Atlantic Treaty Organization, 383, 387
Notes (Madison) on Constitutional Convention, 107
Notes on Virginia (Jefferson), 14; quoted, 10
Nye, Russell, 20, 50–51

[O]

October Revolution, 290
O'Brien, George, 332
Of the Rise and Progress of the Arts and Sciences, 100
O'Neil, Thomas, 332
Oppenheimer case, 366
Ordeal of Power, The (Hughes), reviewed, 442–445
Organization of American States, 397
Origins of the Labour Party, The (Pelling), 321
Origins of Totalitarianism (Arendt), 296
Ortega y Gasset, José, 305
Orwell, George, 61, 293, 294, 299, 357; quoted, 311
Otis, Harrison Gray, 79

Our Chief Magistrate and His Powers (Taft), 140, 141
Overman Act of 1918, 130, 138
Oyama v. *California*, 174

[P]

Palko v. *Connecticut*, 27
Palmer, A. Mitchell, 31, 52, 86
Palmer, Robert R., 92
Panama Refining Co. v. *Ryan*, 127
Paraguay, 394, 395
Parrington, Vernon, 249; on American liberty, 66
Parsimony, judicial, 199–200
Partido del Pueblo (APRA) of Peru, 394
Partisan Review, 298
Passman, Otto, 444
Pasternak, Boris, 377–379
Paterson, William, at Constitutional Convention, 102, 103, 104, 105, 106, 107–108, 110; and preliminary draft of New Jersey Plan, 105
Pelling, Henry, 320, 321
Pendleton, Edmund, at Constitutional Convention, 117
Penn, William, 9
Pennekamp v. *Florida*, 176
Perkins, Frances, 177
Phelps-Dodge case, 181
Philip, André, 270
Pickering, Timothy, 83
Pinckney, Charles, at Constitutional Convention, 105–106, 113–114
Plato, 95, 240, 241
Plessy v. *Ferguson*, 210
Pluralism, 17; armed, 28
Political Affairs, 49

Populism, 41
Powell, Arthur, 75
Pravda, 345
Prejudice, War, and the Constitution (ten Broek, Barnhart, and Matson), reviewed, 222, 223
Prerogative, quest for, 127–161
President and the Crisis, The (Koenig), 144
Presidential Power (Neustadt), 428
Press, and democratic process, 361–364; security and, 359–369
Price, Byron, 368
Price, Don K., on Congress as collective noun, 329
Prince v. *Massachusetts*, 172
Pritchett, Herman, on civil-rights issues, 198; on Frank Murphy, 163
Prize cases, 135, 136
Public Philosophy, The (Lippmann), 361
Public Utilities Holding Company Act of 1935, 180
Puritanism, 9–11

[Q]

Quakers, 9, 10; in Massachusetts Bay Colony, 227; and military conscription, 231

[R]

Rabaut, Louis, 332
Radicalism, new-fashioned, 48–56
Radicals, and liberalism, 432–441
Railroad Strike of 1877, 138
Railroad Strike of 1894, 138

Randolph, Edmund, 102, 108; at Constitutional Convention, 98, 114, 115

Rathbun v. *United States*, 127

Rayburn, Sam, 445

Reconstruction Acts, 132

Reed, Stanley F., 170; and *Meadowmoor* case, 237

Regents' Prayer case, 237

Regulation, secular, 227, 230, 231, 232–233

Religion, and freedom in U.S., 8–11, 19–20; and intolerance, 227–239

Render unto Caesar: The Flag-Salute Controversy (Manwaring), reviewed, 227–239

Review of Reviews, 322

Revolution Betrayed (Trotsky), 286

Ribbentrop, Joachim von, 294

Richmond *Examiner*, 359

Ridgway, Matthew B., letter to Charles Wilson, 362

Riesman, David, 305; on vested heresies, 8

Right, the, and liberalism, 416–422

Rivington, James, 12

Road to War, The (Millis), 436

Roberts, Owen J., and *Associated Press* case, 179; and Emergency Court of Appeals, 186; and F. Murphy, 177; on *Tennessee Coal, Iron and R.R. Co.* v. *Muscoda Local 123*, 164

Roche, Constance L., on McCarthy issue, 327–329

Rodell, Fred, on Holmes, 218; on Jackson, 218; on Marshall, 217–218; *Nine Men*, 215–218

Roosevelt, Franklin D., 5, 30, 49,

Roosevelt, Franklin D. (*Cont.*): 56, 85, 338, 345, 405; Burns's study of, 245; and evacuation of Nisei, 224; and Hitler, 434; and "indirect sanctions," 145; and Lend-Lease, 197; and McCarthyism, 328; and Murphy, 165, 166, 167, 168–170; and politics, 428–429; prerogative power of, 138, 141–146; and Supreme Court, 127, 128, 131, 132, 137, 215; and War Labor Disputes of 1943, 130

Roosevelt: The Lion and the Fox (Burns), 85, 428

Roosevelt Revolution (Einaudi), 85

Roosevelt, Theodore, 146, 424; *Autobiography* quoted, 140; prerogative power of, 140

Rosenberg case, 62

Rossiter, Clinton, 4, 91, 129, 203; on prerogative power of President, 140; on *Prize* cases, 136; on FDR, 141

Rostow, E. V., on Robert Jackson, 219; on Nisei, 222–225

Rovere, Richard, 417

Runciman, Steven, 241

Rusk, Dean, 395

Ruskin, John, 322

Russ, Martin, 374–376

Russia Twenty Years After (Serge), 286

Russian Orthodox Church case, 232

Rutledge, Wiley B., 30, 163, 172, 175; and Emergency Court of Appeals, 186; and *United States* v. *CIO*, 179; and war powers, 183

[S]

Sacco-Vanzetti case, 86
Sachs, Stephen, on social movement, 302–319
Salvage, The (Thomas), 223
Sam Thompson case, and Supreme Court, 403
Samuel, Herbert, 323
Scarborough Conference of the British Labour Party, 269, 271, 275
Schechter v. United States, and Supreme Court, 127
Schenck case, 218
Schlesinger, Arthur, Jr., 85, 249
Schubert, Glendon, "The Study of Judicial Decision-Making as an Aspect of Political Behavior," 209–214
Schware v. Board of Bar Examiners of the State of New Mexico, 31
Scott v. Sandford, 132
Screws case, and F. Murphy, 174
Second Treatise of Government (Locke), 109
"Secret Speech," of Khrushchev, 297
Security, goals of, 346–347; and the press, 359–369
Sedition Act of 1798, 42, 70, 196
Sedition Acts, 13
Sedition Law, 66
Self-restraint, judicial, 194–208; procedural, 197–198; substantive, 198–201
Senator Joe McCarthy (Rovere), 417
Serge, Victor, essay in Partisan Review, 298; and Trotsky, 286

Serge, The Case of Victor, 280–301 passim
Servetus, Michael, 281
Shaw, Robert Gould, 401
Sheil, Bishop Bernard J., 336
Sherman Act, Murphy on, 179
Shlyapnikov, 290
Simons, A. M., 249
Simple Cobler of Agawam in America (Ward), 9
Slavery, 112
Smith, Adam, 15–16, 17
Smith, General "Howling Mad," 371
Smith, James Morton, Freedom's Fetters reviewed, 78–84
Smith, Joseph, 20
Smith, Margaret Chase, 335
Smith Act, 32, 45, 202
Social movements, leadership of, 302–319
Social Statics (Spencer), 245
Socialism, British, 269; and crisis in British Labour Party, 257–268; in England, 424
Socialist International, 286
Socialist Party, 51
Socialists, and Bolshevik Revolution, 285
Somoza, Luis, 395
Sons of Liberty, 13
Sorenson, Theodore, 92
SEATO, 383, 407
Soviet Russia: A New Civilization (Webb), 424
Soviet Writers Union, 378
Spellman, Francis Cardinal, 336
Spelman, Sir Henry, Maitland on, 4
Spencer, Herbert, 27, 243, 245

Spoilage, The (Thomas and Nishimoto), 223

Stalin, J. V., personality and policies of, 281, 282, 286, 292, 294, 338, 383, 406, 407, 408; and the Purge, 293; and Trotsky, 288

Stalin-Hitler Pact, 294, 295

Stalin Prize, 377, 378

State and Church, separation of, 227

State of Nature, of Hobbes, 412

State and Revolution (Lenin), 281

States'-rights, 183

Stead, W. T., 322

Steel Seizure case, 127–131, 136, 141, 144, 147–155, 219

Steele v. *Louisville & N.R.R.*, 173

Steinbeck, John, 171

Stevens, Thaddeus, 203

Stevenson, Adlai, 381, 419; and Eisenhower, 443

Stone, Harlan F., 163; on *Associated Press* case, 179; and *Cudahy Packing Co.* v. *Holland*, 177; and flag-salute controversy, 236; and *Gobitis* case, 165, 235, 236; and Murphy, 183

Story, Joseph, 41, 139

Stroessner, Alfredo, 396

Structure of Politics at the Accession of George III (Namier), 247–248

"Study of Judicial Decision-Making as an Aspect of Political Behavior" (Schubert), 209–214

Sumner, William Graham, 72, 353

Sunday-closing laws, 231

Sunderland, La Roy, 50

Supreme Court in the American System of Government, The (Jackson), review of, 215, 219–221

Surkov, 378

Survey, 295

Survival, "do-it-yourself," 411–415

Sutherland, George, and *United States* v. *Curtiss-Wright Export Corp.*, 133

Sweet case, 168

[T]

Taft, William H., 140

Taft-Hartley Act, 153

Taney, Roger B., 22, 215; and *Ex parte Merrymen*, 135

Tappan, Arthur, 50

Tarasov-Rodionov, Alexander, 297

Taylor, John C., 242

ten Broek, Jacobus, 222

Tennessee Coal, Iron and R.R. Co. v. *Muscoda Local 123*, 164

Tenney, Jack B., 332

Thomas, Norman, on evacuation of West Coast Nisei, 222–225; views and policies of, 49, 390, 392, 397, 398, 399

Thornhill v. *Alabama*, 180

Three-fifths Compromise, at Constitutional Convention, 112–113

Thurmond, Strom, 419

Titov, G., 407

de Tocqueville, Alexis, 21, 24, 30, 40; on legal profession, 46

Togliatti, Palmiro, 438

Toleration, religious, 11

Totalitarianism, 295

Toynbee, Arnold, 247

Trotsky, Leon, and Lenin, 287–288, 289, 290–291, 292; and Serge, 292; and Stalin, 288; views and policies of, 284, 286, 288, 341, 436

Trujillo, R. F., 391

Trujillo, R. F., Jr., 396

Truman, Harry S. and McCarthyism, 328; and *Steel Seizure* case, 127–131, 147–155; views and policies of, 49, 336, 338, 339, 342, 406

Tuck, William M., 402

Turati, Filippo, 286

"Twenty-one Conditions" (Zinoviev), 282

Tydings Investigation, 341

[U]

Unitarians, 9

Union of Soviet Socialist Republics, relations between U.S.A. and, 383–389, 405–410, 437–440

United Nations, 406; Children's Emergency Fund, 418, 420

United Public Workers case, 200

United States of America

　Army Information-Education program, Communists in, 345–350

　Atomic Energy Commission, and *Oppenheimer* case, 366

　Bill of Rights, 19, 119, and Constitutional Convention, 116; and liberty, 69

　civil liberties in, 57–64, 65–77, 85–87

United States (*Cont.*):

　Central Intelligence Agency, 396, 398, 399; and Batista, 390; and Cuba, 390–391, 392

　Communist parties in, 285

　Constitution of, 22, 119; and the Constitutional Convention, 91–126 *passim;* criminal-procedure Amendments of, 69; and due process, 25–27; First Amendment, 27; Fifth Amendment, 21; Fourteenth Amendment, 23, 27; and liberty, 17–19

　constitutionalism in, 91–161

　current status of civil liberties in, 39–64

　foreign relations and, 405–410

　House of Representatives, McCarthyism and election to, 328–333

　and individual freedom, 70

　and Israel, 385

　Marine Corps, and *McKeon* case, 370–373

　nonconformity in, 53–64

　Office of Censorship, 368

　Peace Corps, 384

　relations between U.S.S.R. and, 383–389, 405–410, 437–440

　Reports, 172, 184

　Senate, McCarthyism and election to, 333–337

　Supreme Court of, and *Alaskan Cannery Workers* case, 200; ban on New York "nonsectarian" formula, 227; and *Brown* v. *Board of Education,* 209, 210, 212; and Debs, 139, 140, 141, 154; and *Dennis* v. *United States,* 198; and de-

United States (*Cont.*):

Supreme Court (*Cont.*):

segregation decision, 63, 76, 351–352, 355; and *Duncan* v. *Kahanamoku*, 198; and Felix Frankfurter, 234; and Franklin Roosevelt, 137, 215; and *Gobitis* case, 228; and *Hirabayashi* case, 224, 225; and *In re Neagle*, 139, 140, 141; and intervention in state affairs, 26–28; and judicial self-restraint, 195–208; and *Kansas* v. *Colorado*, 140; and *Korematsu* case, 130–131, 144, 224–225; and *Milligan* case, 155; and *Near* v. *Minnesota*, 363; and Nisei evacuation, 222–225; and *Panama Refining Co.* v. *Ryan*, 127; and power of Executive, 127–161; and *Prize* cases, 135, 136; and public-school segregation, 351; and *Rathbun* v. *U.S.*, 127; reapportionment decision of, 76; *Rule 38*, 197; and *Sam Thompson* case, 403; and *Schecter* v. *U.S.*, 127; and social psychologists, 209–211; and *Steel Seizure* case, 127–131, 136, 141, 144, 147–155; and Sunday-closing laws, 231; and *United Public Workers* case, 200

tradition of liberty in, 1–38
versus *Bethlehem Steel*, 182
versus *CIO*, 179
versus Curtiss-Wright Export Corp., 133
versus Dotterweich, 178

Upshur, Abel, on executive power, 133
Urbanization, and liberty, 29

[V]

Vested heresies, Riesman on, 41
Vindiciae contra tyrannos, 5
Vinson, Frederick M., on Frank Murphy, 163
Virginia and Kentucky Resolutions, 79, 83, 245
Virginia Plan, 104, 105, 106, 107, 108; at Constitutional Convention, 100–102, 103
Virginia Statute of Religious Freedom (Jefferson), 230
Virginia treason statute, quoted, 13
Vishinsky, Andrei, 292, 341
Volstead Act, 352–353

[W]

Wagner Act, 76
Walker, Major General Edwin, 69, 419–420
War Industries Board, 141
War Labor Disputes Act of 1943, and FDR, 130
War powers, Murphy on, 183
Ward, Nathaniel, 10; quoted, 9
Warren, Charles, 202
Warren, Robert Penn, 401
Washington, George, 93, 106, 111, 117
Washington *National Republican*, 359
Watson, Thomas E., 49
Watson, Tom, 74–75

Webb, Beatrice, 424

Weber, Max, 310

Welch, Robert, 422

Wells, H. G., 213

Wertz, E. S., 52

West Coast Hotel v. *Parrish*, 132

"Western Image of the Soviet Union, The," 295

Whalen, Grover, 63

What Is to Be Done? (Lenin), 281

White, Harry Dexter, 336

Wilkes, John, 433

Williams, Roger, 9, 10, 229

Wilson, Charles, Ridgway letter to, 362

Wilson, Harold, 277, 279

Wilson, James, 253; at Constitutional Convention, 108, 109

Wilson, Woodrow, 52, 130, 222, 405; concept of Presidency, 138; and National War Labor Board, 138; and prerogative power, 141, 143

Winthrop, John, 10

Wolfe, Bernard, 291

Wollstonecraft, Mary, 16

Woodruff, Philip, 302

World War I, 409; civil-liberties climate in, 52; civil liberties in U.S. before, 65–77; and mob rule, 75

World War II, and civil liberties, 31–32, 52

[Y]

Yamashita case, 184

Yates, Robert, at Constitutional Convention, 99, 103

Yezhov, N., 293

Yezhovshchina (Great Purge), 293

Young People's Socialist League, 434

[Z]

Zinoviev, Grigori, 282, 292; "Twenty-one Conditions," of, 284–285